Analytical Decision Making

David Targett

Professor of Information Systems
University of Bath

PITMAN
PUBLISHING

For Chloë and James

PITMAN PUBLISHING
128 Long Acre, London WC2E 9AN

A Division of Pearson Professional Limited

First published in Great Britain in 1996

© David Targett 1996
Copyright © Chapter 9 Peter Stone 1996
Copyright © Chapters 12 and 13 Chris Beaumont 1996
Copyright © Chapter 17 Jerry Raine 1996

ISBN 0 273 60453 8

British Library Cataloguing in Publication Data
A CIP catalogue record for this book can be obtained from the British Library

10 9 8 7 6 5 4

Typeset by Mathematical Composition Setters, Salisbury, Wiltshire.
Printed and bound in Great Britain by Redwood Books, Trowbridge, Wiltshire

The Publishers' policy is to use paper manufactured from sustainable forests.

CONTENTS

PREFACE

Analytical Decision Making has been written with two purposes in mind.

First, the book is a text for business school students – undergraduate, postgraduate and MBA. Most general management programmes in business schools have courses on this topic, with titles such as 'Decision Techniques', 'Managerial Economics', 'Operational Research' and others. The courses may be compulsory or optional. This book is intended to provide a basic text for them all, as a platform from which individual teachers can customise a course to their own requirements.

Secondly, the book is intended as a 'how to . . .' guide for practising managers. Most managers now have a personal computer on their desk and receive quantitative information produced by links with corporate information systems. They often feel frustrated at being unable to capitalise on the potential which this information resource offers. They want to make more analytical use of their data, going beyond tabulating and graphing. This book is intended to help them with this task.

The aim of the book is therefore to show practising managers and future managers, particularly business students, how they can be more systematic and analytical in their use of information for decision making. The background is that managerial culture, particularly in the UK but also elsewhere, designates decision making by talented managers as intuitive rather than analytical. This culture is starting to change because of desk-top computers which bring the vast amounts of readily available corporate and industry information together with the analytical power to analyse it quickly and easily. Information is becoming regarded as a corporate resource which must be properly exploited.

To achieve these aims the book is designed to be essentially pragmatic, showing how analytical decision making can be applied to a range of different areas: marketing, finance, logistics, strategy, etc. It tries to find the right balance between, on the one hand, giving sufficient theory so that decision techniques can be applied properly and, on the other hand, limiting the theory so that the pragmatic approach is not compromised.

A perennial problem with a textbook like this is that while managers think in terms of 'problems', courses operate on the basis of 'techniques'. The book is structured so as to bridge the gap between the two perspectives. The first chapter is problem oriented, categorising the typical decision problems faced by all types of manager and showing what sorts of approaches and techniques can be used in different situations. The remaining chapters are of two types:

1. *Explaining* chapters which cover the techniques one by one. The coverage of the techniques will follow a set pattern:

   - a brief explanation of what the technique does;
   - a series of vignettes demonstrating where it can be applied;
   - a fuller explanation of the technique;
   - a brief illustration of how related software works and how to interpret the output;

- hints for putting the technique into practice;
- recent developments and extensions of the technique;
- cases, of varying size, with worked solutions;
- further questions and cases with brief answers.

2. *Putting into practice* chapters, contributed by practitioners. These chapters show how organisations have applied some of the techniques. They discuss the benefits they have brought and the difficulties of implementation. Questions at the end of these chapters are intended to promote classroom discussion, by relating the techniques to the real world and putting them into their organisational context.

The techniques covered fall into distinct groups and the chapters are classified into four parts which group similar techniques together.

PART ONE

Introduction

Chapter 1   Business Numeracy

Describes typical business problems and analytical techniques and goes on to match one with the other. It reviews the way quantitative techniques are used in practice and provides a matrix showing when different techniques can be effective.

CHAPTER ONE

Business numeracy

The purpose of this chapter is to introduce analytical techniques and discuss their practical relevance. In an increasingly information-intensive environment, many organisations do not capitalise on the potential of these techniques, perhaps because basic skills of business numeracy are lacking. Managers often do not know how to use the information available to them and do not appreciate the practical relevance of quantitative methods. The chapter helps to overcome these problems in two ways. First, some general issues concerned with the use of numerical information – data communication and data analysis – are reviewed. Secondly, a matrix shows where analytical techniques can be effective by matching them with typical business problems.

INTRODUCTION

He didn't shout 'Eureka' nor was he in his bath, but a manager of a major retailing chain certainly felt that he was at a moment of discovery. Although a middle manager rather than a member of the board or close to it, he had just realised that he was in a position to give his company a significant competitive edge. But to do so, he would have to change the way he did his job.

The company had introduced EPOS (Electronic Point of Sale). EPOS is the increasingly familiar system which is replacing the traditional method of keying in details of customer purchases manually. Instead details of purchases are recorded electronically using a scanner to read bar codes on the products (Figure 1.1).

The manager knew that EPOS gave the company benefits such as higher productivity for cashiers, reduced stock levels and more efficient distribution. He had felt confident that experts in the Information Technology Group who had implemented the system were ensuring that it was used to maximum effect. What he hadn't realised and what nobody had told him – because they didn't know – was that EPOS had major implications for his own job as merchandiser of women's fashionwear.

EPOS gave him information on daily sales of fashionwear lines at all the company's stores. He had always received some sales information, but three aspects of EPOS were entirely new. EPOS information was up to date (he received it the next day), detailed (he knew sales by size, colour and region) and highly accurate.

Previously, he had known that a line was not successful or a colour not popular because, towards the end of the season, much of it would be left on the shelves and in warehouses. These lines would be sold off at much reduced prices in end-of-season sales. Now, analysis of EPOS information could tell him what was going to be successful and what was not in the first two weeks of the season, allowing him to negotiate with suppliers to change the colour mix or arrange for a different regional supply schedule.

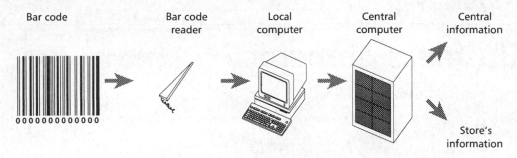

Figure 1.1   IT in retailing

The result? The company could respond immediately to changing customer demand. Popular lines, sizes, colours would always be available; precious shelf space would not be cluttered with unwanted stock; warehouse inventory would be reduced. The personal price to pay? The way he went about his job would have to change. He would have to be more systematic: his job would be driven by electronic information and the quantitative techniques which could analyse it. Merchandising would not be based on supplier push – selling what had been made – but customer pull – making what the customers wanted.

What is the main point of this story? That managers will have to change the way they do their jobs? That EPOS brings a wide range of benefits? No. Both are true of course, but the main point is that many organisations have a valuable resource, information, which is going to waste. In our example it was a middle manager's fortuitous awareness rather than company policy which prevented information being wasted. This is not a problem for the IT department; the deployment of strategic resources is a board-level problem. Unfortunately senior managements do not usually believe in business numeracy – meaning the capability to use quantitative business information profitably – as a key skill. With the possible exception of some accounting knowledge, the idea that numerical and analytical skills might be essential is not often recognised. In fact, the suggestion that quantitative skills might be important is generally greeted with some hilarity.

In this case EPOS and the information it supplied were the triggers which demonstrated that analytical methods could have a substantial and strategic payoff in terms of better customer service, better corporate image, increased revenue and reduced costs. Organisations, and in particular their senior managements, must plan to achieve these business benefits rather than doing so by accident.

WHY HAS BUSINESS NUMERACY BECOME AN ESSENTIAL SKILL?

The fashionwear merchandiser is not an isolated example. Figure 1.2 shows the logical chain reaction which has meant that numeracy is increasing in importance after years of seeming irrelevance.

IT has become cheaper at an astonishing rate – 20–30 per cent per annum for the last 25 years. If jet aeroplanes had reduced in price at a similar rate since their first appearance in the 1950s, an airline would now be able to order a dozen of the latest Boeing jumbos for less than a Concorde pilot's salary.

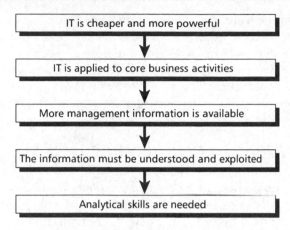

Figure 1.2   Business numeracy

At the same time the capability of computers has improved dramatically. They can handle more data, faster and more reliably. Developments in telecommunications mean that computers in different rooms, buildings, cities and continents can be linked. This, combined with reducing costs, has meant that computers have been applied to a much wider range of tasks. Some industries, financial services and travel for instance, are now inextricably linked with technology. Who could return to the days when automatic banking machines were not available on Sundays? Who would now be prepared to wait several days to hear whether a flight is confirmed or not?

Technology automates tasks and improves efficiency. But in doing so it creates large amounts of management information. This information is a strategic resource. One airline – American Airlines, the first to develop a computerised booking system – is reported as making more money from its information about aircraft seat availability than it does from transporting people in those seats. If information can be such a valuable resource then companies must treat it like any other resource – managing it and ensuring that it is used to its full potential. To do otherwise would be like keeping a large cash reserve under the mattress instead of investing it.

Unfortunately, many organisations are finding themselves unable to capitalise on their large IT investments because they do not know how to use all this information. Business numeracy is the key to unlocking the full potential of the information resource. Correctly used in the right environment, the combination of high-quality information and numeracy skills can bring about competitive advantage, restructure industries and organisations and change the way in which managers do their jobs.

Of course, business numeracy is not only important for dealing with computerised information; it is just that developments in this area have led organisations to see it in a new light. It is helpful to separate out the two broad aspects of business numeracy.

The first is non-technical business numeracy. This means the ability to incorporate numbers in one's thinking processes along with other types of facts, evidence and data. This does not require any specific analytical techniques. It is more to do with having sufficient familiarity with and confidence in numbers that they can be used effectively in the normal course of decision making – just as students of foreign languages reach a stage of fluency when use of the language becomes almost automatic.

The second is technical business numeracy. This means the ability to use quantitative, analytical techniques. This second aspect is the subject of this book.

The next two sections deal with these two aspects of business numeracy. The first suggests some simple ways in which a manager can improve his or her skills of non-technical business numeracy. The second shows which analytical techniques can prove effective in aiding the solution to particular types of business problem.

BUSINESS NUMERACY – NON-TECHNICAL SKILLS

It is important to distinguish between information and data. If this distinction is ignored then the result can be information saturation, or rather data saturation: tidal waves of numbers that nobody has a clue what to do with. Information is data which has been processed so that it is meaningful and useful to decision makers.

Problems with information can happen for a variety of reasons including:

- a belief that more data automatically means better decisions;
- individuals becoming obsessed with the 'technology' of IT rather than the 'information';
- a disproportionate amount of time devoted to hardware and software decisions and not information management.

There are two types of skills which can help. *Data communication* refers to the reduction and presentation of data so that organisations and managers do not suffer from information saturation. *Data analysis* means turning numbers into useful information.

Data communication

There are methods, based on psychological ideas, by which numbers can be put into forms matching the ways the human mind works. The following seven 'guidelines' suggest how numbers can be presented so that they can be more easily assimilated as useful information.[1]

1. *Round* to two effective figures. For example:

Original	Rounded
1287	1300
712	710
37.1	37
3.24	3.2

If there is concern that rounding causes a loss of accuracy, two questions should be asked. First, how accurate are the numbers anyway? What are usually thought to be hard, precise data such as economic and accounting data are surprisingly inaccurate. Secondly, how accurate do the data need to be for the decision being taken? There is no point in insisting pedantically on numbers with four places of decimals when only the first place could conceivably affect the outcome of the decision.

[1] For further details of the techniques of data communication, consult *Data Reduction*, A.S.C. Ehrenberg, John Wiley, 1984.

2. *Order* the rows and columns by size. This gives the whole table a structure which makes it easier to understand and analyse.

3. *Interchange* rows and columns. It is easier to compare numbers when they are arranged in a column than when in a row.

4. *Use summary measures.* These are usually row and column averages. They act as a focus for the eye, helping to pinpoint the trend and variability in a series of numbers.

5. *Minimise the use of grid-lines and white space.* A grid-line or excessive gaps between numbers both hinder the process of assimilation. In general, numbers which are to be compared should be close together and not separated by lines; however, different types of numbers, such as a row average, should be kept apart from the rest by a line or a larger gap.

6. *Label clearly.* This may seem a trivial point, but if drastic abbreviations are used in row and column headings they can cause confusion, waste time and detract from the real information in the table. So often producers of tables assume, falsely, that the readership has the same familiarity with the data that they themselves have.

7. *Use a verbal summary.* This points the analyst in the right direction and overcomes the first hurdle of knowing where to begin. It should be short (maximum two sentences) and factual.

Data analysis

Managers themselves can deal with perhaps 90 per cent of the data analysis problems they face. Only for the other 10 per cent may expert help be required. A do-it-yourself approach has five steps:

1. *Eliminate* irrelevant data. Numbers which are not germane to the purpose of the analysis should be removed so that the relevant facts are more likely to stand out.

2. *Re-present* the numbers in a more digestible form using the seven guidelines. Observation (or 'eyeballing') is important to understanding data, so the numbers must be in a form which maximises the chances of success.

3. *Find a pattern* for the data. This means making a simple, concise summary for the whole table. For example, the pattern might be 'all the rows show an increase of 10 per cent per annum', or 'numbers in the columns representing the north of the country are half as big again as those of the south'.

4. *Mark exceptions to the pattern.* In management it is often the exceptions which are of most interest: does the exception mean that someone has done a particularly good job or have conditions changed?

5. *Compare and validate the results.* It is likely that other data exist, from another region or division, collected at another time or by someone else. These other results should be brought into the analysis. If they are the same then one's own analysis is reinforced; if different, then this prompts some interesting questions concerning the reasons for the differences.

Table 1.1   US Consumption of distilled spirits

Estimated Population	Percent to Total Population	Percent to US Total Consumption		Licence States	Rank in Consumption		Consumption (in Wine Gallons)		Percent Increase/ Decrease	Per Capita Year 2	Per Capita Year 1
		Year 2	Year 1		Year 2	Year 1	Year 2	Year 1			
382 000	0.18	0.33	0.32	*Alaska	46	47	1 391 172	1 359 422	2.3	3.64	3.86
2 270 000	1.06	1.03	0.98	**Arizona	29	30	4 401 883	4 144 521	6.2	1.94	1.86
2 109 000	0.98	0.60	0.56	**Arkansas	38	38	2 534 826	2 366 429	7.1	1.20	1.12
21 520 000	10.03	12.33	12.32	**California	1	1	52 529 142	52 054 429	0.9	2.44	2.46
2 583 000	1.20	1.50	1.49	**Colorado	22	22	6 380 783	6 310 566	1.1	2.47	2.49
3 117 000	1.45	1.69	1.72	**Connecticut	18	18	7 194 684	7 271 320	(−1.1)	2.31	2.35
582 000	0.27	0.35	0.36	**Delaware	45	43	1 491 652	1 531 688	(−2.6)	2.56	2.65
702 000	0.33	1.08	1.14	**Dist. of Columbia	27	27	4 591 448	4 828 422	(−4.9)	6.54	6.74
8 421 000	3.92	5.33	5.28	**Florida	4	4	22 709 209	22 329 555	1.7	2.70	2.67
4 970 000	2.31	2.52	2.35	*Georgia	13	13	10 717 681	9 944 846	7.8	2.16	2.02
887 000	0.41	0.48	0.47	*Hawaii	41	40	2 023 730	1 970 089	2.7	2.28	2.28
11 229 000	5.23	6.13	6.35	**Illinois	3	3	26 111 587	26 825 876	(−2.7)	2.33	2.41
5 302 000	2.47	1.67	1.66	**Indiana	19	20	7 110 382	7 005 511	1.5	1.34	1.32
2 310 000	1.08	0.68	0.70	**Kansas	35	35	2 913 422	2 935 121	(−0.7)	1.26	1.29
3 428 000	1.60	1.14	1.19	**Kentucky	26	26	4 857 094	5 006 481	(−3.0)	1.42	1.47
3 841 000	1.79	1.66	1.59	**Louisiana	21	21	7 073 283	6 699 853	5.6	1.84	1.77
4 144 000	1.93	2.54	2.54	**Maryland	12	12	10 833 966	10 738 731	0.9	2.61	2.62
5 809 000	2.71	3.28	3.38	**Massachusetts	10	10	13 950 268	14 272 695	(−2.3)	2.40	2.45
3 965 000	1.85	2.00	1.99	**Minnesota	15	15	8 528 284	8 425 562	1.2	2.15	2.15
4 778 000	2.23	1.66	1.82	*Missouri	20	17	7 074 614	7 679 871	(−7.9)	1.48	1.61
1 553 000	0.72	0.64	0.64	**Nebraska	36	36	2 733 497	2 717 859	0.6	1.76	1.76
610 000	0.28	1.02	0.97	**Nevada	30	31	4 360 172	4 095 910	6.5	7.15	6.92
7 336 000	3.42	3.73	3.82	**New Jersey	8	8	15 901 587	16 154 975	(−1.6)	2.17	2.21
1 168 000	0.54	0.47	0.46	**New Mexico	42	41	1 980 372	1 954 139	1.3	1.70	1.70
18 084 000	8.42	9.64	9.88	**New York	2	2	41 070 005	41 740 341	(−1.6)	2.27	2.30
643 000	0.30	0.33	0.33	**North Dakota	47	46	1 388 475	1 384 311	0.3	2.16	2.18
2 766 000	1.29	0.92	0.99	**Oklahoma	33	29	3 904 574	4 187 527	(−6.8)	1.41	1.54
927 000	0.43	0.49	0.50	**Rhode Island	39	39	2 073 075	2 131 329	(−2.7)	2.24	2.30
2 848 000	1.33	1.39	1.26	**South Carolina	23	25	5 934 427	5 301 054	11.9	2.08	1.88
686 000	0.32	0.31	0.29	*South Dakota	48	48	1 312 160	1 242 021	5.6	1.91	1.82
4 214 000	1.96	1.32	1.27	**Tennessee	24	24	5 618 774	5 357 160	4.9	1.33	1.28
12 487 000	5.82	4.22	4.06	**Texas	5	6	17 990 532	17 167 560	4.8	1.44	1.40
4 609 000	2.15	2.56	2.54	***Wisconsin	11	11	10 896 455	10 739 261	1.5	2.36	2.33
150 280 000	70.01	75.04	75.22	Total Licence			319 583 215	317 874 435	0.5	2.13	2.13

Example

Table 1.1 shows the consumption of distilled spirits in the 'licence' states of the USA over two years, as presented in an official publication. It is very difficult to understand what the data means or to glean any useful information from it. Suppose an analysis is to be carried out with the objective of measuring the variation in consumption across the states and detecting any areas where there are distinctive differences. How can this be done? The situation can be handled by applying the five stages of data analysis and through them the seven guidelines of data communication. The final result is shown in Table 1.2.

Table 1.2   US consumption of distilled spirits (after analysis)

Licence States (in order of population)	Consumption Wine Gallons (million)		Per Capita
	Year 2	Year 1	Year 2
California	52.0	52.0	2.4
New York	41.0	42.0	2.3
Texas	18.0	17.0	1.4
Illinois	26.0	27.0	2.3
Florida	23.0	22.0	2.7
New Jersey	16.0	16.0	2.2
Massachusetts	14.0	14.0	2.4
Indiana	7.1	7.0	1.3
Georgia	11.0	9.9	2.2
Missouri	7.1	7.7	1.5
Wisconsin	11.0	11.0	2.4
Tennessee	5.6	5.4	1.3
Maryland	11.0	11.0	2.6
Minnesota	8.5	8.4	2.2
Louisiana	7.1	6.7	1.8
Kentucky	4.9	5.0	1.4
Connecticut	7.2	7.3	2.3
S Carolina	5.9	5.3	2.1
Oklahoma	3.9	4.2	1.4
Colorado	6.4	6.3	2.5
Kansas	2.9	2.9	1.3
Arizona	4.4	4.1	1.9
Arkansas	2.5	2.4	1.2
Nebraska	2.7	2.7	1.8
New Mexico	2.0	2.0	1.7
Rhode Island	2.1	2.1	2.2
Hawaii	2.0	2.0	2.3
D Columbia	4.6	4.8	6.5
S Dakota	1.3	1.2	1.9
N Dakota	1.4	1.4	2.2
Nevada	4.4	4.1	7.2
Delaware	1.5	1.5	2.6
Alaska	1.4	1.4	3.6

Stage 1   Reduce data

Much of the data in Table 1.1 is redundant. For example, are population figures really necessary when both consumption and per capita are there? The table can be reduced to a fraction of its original size with minimal loss of real information.

Stage 2   Re-present using the seven guidelines

The numbers can be reduced to two effective figures. Table 1.1 has some data with eight digits, a level of detail which could not possibly have any bearing on the outcome of the analysis. What difference would it make if the eighth digit were a 3 instead of a 7? In any case, if you consider how distilled spirits consumption might be measured then it is difficult to believe that the data can conceivably be accurate to eight digits.

Secondly, the states should be listed in order of decreasing population instead of alphabetical order. The latter is fine for a reference table but does not help analysis. Population order makes it easier to spot states where consumption is out of line with population.

Stage 3   Build a model

A pattern is visible in the amended Table 1.2. Consumption is generally in line with population. The per capita figure for each state is close to the average for all licence states – 2.1 wine gallons – with a 30 per cent variation about this figure. There has been a growth of about 1 per cent between the two years. This basic pattern is not evident from the original presentation in Table 1.1.

Stage 4   Exceptions

The exceptions from the 2.1 +/− 30 per cent pattern are those states whose per capita consumption is outside the range 1.5 to 2.7. Three states stand out clearly from the pattern: Alaska, District of Columbia and Nevada. In the latter two states the explanation is almost certainly that they are small states with large non-resident populations, i.e. there are many people who live there and may drink there but are not included in official population statistics (tourists for Nevada, diplomats for Columbia). The explanation for Alaska is not so clear and a deeper investigation may be needed. Whatever the explanations, the data analysis has been successful – the pattern and its exceptions have been detected.

Stage 5   Comparisons

A comparison between the two years is provided in the table. Further comparisons would be useful:

- 5 and 10 years earlier;
- a breakdown into different types of distilled spirit: gin, whisky etc.;
- other alcoholic beverages

These comparisons should show whether the patterns are long-lasting (and can be relied upon), whether they apply to certain types of spirit and not to others, and whether they are generalised (applying to different products). Comparisons could reinforce the findings or prompt the analyst to question and rethink the conclusions.

Graphs

Graphs are, in general, highly regarded by managers, for mainly good reasons. The human mind has the capability to deal with and memorise pictures as a whole. An entire graph and the pattern represented in it can be absorbed. The same is not true for a table of numbers, only a small part of which can be handled at any one time. Graphs seem therefore to offer greater efficiency for receiving, manipulating and memorising numerical information. They are also an attractive way of communicating numbers. A graph can break up a management report and re-engage the attention of the reader. But there is a definite limit to the effectiveness of a graph. If it is too complicated, nothing will be retained except the impression of confusion.

Graphs are good for:
- attracting attention and making an impact;
- communicating simple patterns and messages quickly.

Graphs are not good for:
- displaying complicated patterns;
- communicating numbers.

Figures 1.3 and 1.4 illustrate these ideas. Figure 1.3 shows US interest rates over a 10-year period. The pattern is clear and memorable: first low, then a rise, then back but not quite to the original low levels. Figure 1.4 shows the interest rates for several Western countries. The data is too complicated and no clear pattern is visible. Nor is it possible to derive any accurate numerical information. What, for example, was the interest rate in Belgium in 1985? If such reference information were needed then a table would have been preferable. The exact dividing line between when graphs are better and when tables are better is, however, a matter of individual taste and the particular circumstance.

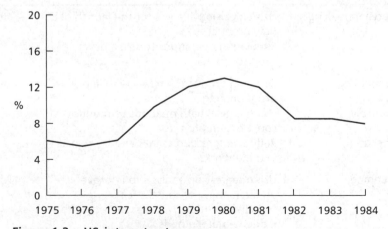

Figure 1.3   US interest rates

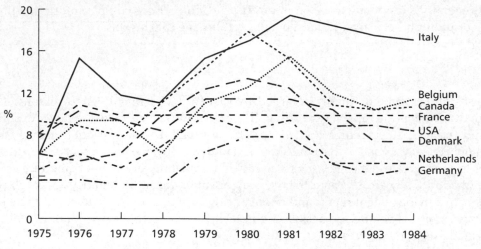

Figure 1.4   Interest rates for several countries

BUSINESS NUMERACY: TECHNIQUES AND THE PROBLEMS THEY CAN SOLVE

The realm of analytical techniques is wide and there is no clear universal categorisation for them. To appreciate their range and where they are useful, we will consider them from three perspectives: management tasks, organisational functions and problem characteristics.

Management tasks

Analytical techniques have the capability to exploit quantitative information in all aspects of the management task: planning, controlling, allocating resources and scheduling. Table 1.3 gives some examples of how they are used to support these activities. The tasks shown

Table 1.3

Task	Application Examples	Section of Book
Decision making	Using decision analysis for the launch of a new product Simulating operations to size a new production plant	II Decision Support
Scheduling	Deciding production mixes with linear programming	III Resource Allocation
Controlling	Using critical path methods to monitor construction projects	
Allocating	Redirecting resources in R and D projects with networks	
Planning	Using regression analysis to improve understanding of cause/effect Forecasting future business activity with judgemental methods	IV Business Forecasting

Table 1.4

Functional Area	Application Examples
Strategy	Economic forecasting
Finance	Managing investment portfolios using linear programming
Human resources	Measuring branch efficiency with data envelopment analysis
Marketing	Using critical path methods to manage a new product launch
Operations	Deciding whether to proceed with an oil exploration using decision analysis

in the table have been categorised into broad classes which reflect the sections into which this book is divided.

Organisational functions

The practical application of analytical techniques can also be viewed from the perspective of the functional areas of management: strategy, finance, human resources, marketing and operations. Different types of technique may have more potential applications within some functions compared to others. Table 1.4 gives some examples of applications in functional areas.

Even in the context of a particular management task within a particular functional area, different problems may have a range of characteristics which can limit the choice of techniques to use. The problems can be categorised according to three main dimensions:

- *timing* – is the problem regular and routine or is it a one-off?
- *data* – does the problem involve a lot of data or a little?
- *complexity* – does the problem involve complex or simple manipulations of numbers?

Figure 1.5 illustrates these dimensions, giving examples.

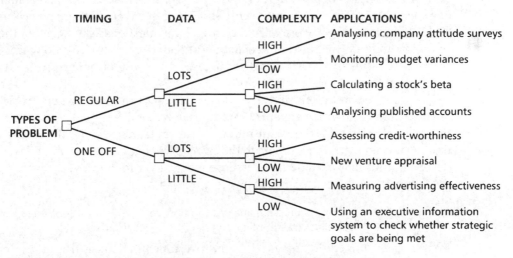

Figure 1.5   Problem characteristics

Example

It may seem that human resources management is one of the least quantitative functions of business, but the following example demonstrates that even there analytical techniques can be used to great effect.

A large high technology manufacturing company with plants in many parts of the UK was finding it difficult to recruit and then keep its skilled employees. With changing demographics the Human Resources Director (HRD) saw no lessening of the problem. Eventually the issue reached board level. The HRD thought that dissatisfaction with working conditions was a major problem and proposed investing in improvements. Some board members agreed with her view but wanted solid evidence on where money should be spent; others were sceptical and thought the question was mainly one of good management.

Eventually a decision was taken to find out more. Specifically the board members wanted to know which aspects of the working environment contributed most to the employees' overall attitudes to the company, and which least. They also wanted to find out where investments could most effectively be made.

The starting point for the project was a company-wide survey of employees' opinions of the company and their working conditions. There were more than 100 questions on the survey form covering everything that could possibly affect attitudes including, for example, overall attitude to the company, remuneration, perks, holidays, quality of supervision, recreation facilities, canteen facilities and so on. For each question an employee had to give a score on a scale between 1 and 7 to reflect his or her opinion.

Survey data like this is essentially straightforward, but making sense of it, especially when it is on such a large scale, is not.

Analysis: an 'ad hoc' approach

The results of the survey were summarised to show the average score for each question. For example, for the question 'how do you rate the external decoration?' each employee had given a score between 1 and 7 and the average score was calculated to be 4.3. Similar averages were calculated for all the questions. Management then knew that canteen food was rated high (5.8) but canteen decor low (2.6). 'So what?' was the response. Graphs and charts were used to display the results, but no one felt they were any further forward.

The problem was that the results could not deal with an essential issue: which factors are important and which are not? Employees may not like the canteen decor but does this matter? Salaries had the same rating (2.6) as canteen decor, but the HRD suspected that the former mattered far more to the employees. The company might invest in new decor but find that it made no difference whatsoever to employees' overall views of the company or the company's ability to attract the right people.

Analysis: a systematic approach

Regression analysis could analyse the survey results much more efficiently. Regression analysis is concerned with relationships between variables. It has two parts: *correlation* is a method for measuring the strength of a relationship; *regression* is a method for determining a formula expressing the relationship. Correlation shows whether a connection exists; regression finds what the connection is.

For example, correlation would indicate to what extent the quarterly sales volume of a product had moved in parallel with advertising expenditure. It would show whether a high level of sales had usually corresponded to a high advertising expenditure in the same quarter (and low with low).

Regression would provide the formula linking sales with advertising. The formula might look like:

$$\text{Sales volume} = 3000 + 3.1 \times \text{Advertising expenditure}$$

This information can be used in three main ways. First, the existence of a strong correlation would tell us that advertising was critically important to the business; likewise a low correlation would bring the value of advertising expenditure into question. Secondly, the regression equation could predict sales in a future quarter for which the advertising level had been decided. Thirdly, the equation would reveal the marginal return on advertising expenditure, i.e. an extra £1000 spent on advertising should produce an extra 3100 sales.

The example involving sales and advertising was one of *simple regression analysis*. Simple means that there was just one independent variable, advertising expenditure. Multiple regression allows for the inclusion of more than one independent variable.

For the company survey, the score for overall attitude was the dependent variable (sales in the above example) and the scores for various aspects of the company are the independent variables (advertising expenditure in the example). At one location the results obtained from the regression analysis (see Chapter 14 for more information on the calculations for regression analysis) were of the form:

$$\begin{aligned}
\text{Overall attitude score} = 0.5 &+ 0.2 \times \text{Working conditions} \\
&+ 0.6 \times \text{Payment levels} \\
&+ 0.1 \times \text{Quality of supervision} \\
&\text{and so on}
\end{aligned}$$

This particular result would indicate that payment levels formed a very important determinant of attitude, quality of supervision much less so. Where there was a high correlation this indicated that the equation included virtually all the factors influencing an employee's overall attitude to the company; a low correlation indicated that there were other factors which had not been included (and they would have to be found) or that there were divergences of views amongst the employees (and that for the regression analysis the employees would have to be grouped, perhaps according to function or rank).

The regression results were used to predict the effect on employees' overall attitude to the company of making changes in the environment. For example, they estimated by how much overall attitude scores would be likely to increase given an expenditure of £100 000 on improved canteen facilities.

The results also showed that attitudes differed from location to location and from department to department. For example, the coefficient relating to quality of supervision (0.1 in the above equation) was much higher at a Scottish plant than elsewhere.

This suggested that supervisory training should be stepped up in Scotland but not in the rest of the UK.

In general, business numeracy in human resources management has to deal with data on a large scale in personnel records, surveys and opinion polls. More and more these systems are computerised. Changing demographics mean that the management role is becoming investigative as well as one of recording and presenting.

CONCLUSION

Business numeracy has always been an important, although sometimes neglected, management skill. The manager who cannot or who chooses not to use numerical information is lacking a vital dimension of competence. This is more true now than ever because the large information systems which exist in almost every organisation of almost every size are storing and circulating quantities of data which would have been unimaginable only a few years ago. These data, if turned into information, are a strategic resource which few organisations are wealthy enough to ignore. Business numeracy is a key skill which can help an organisation realise the potential of this resource.

The aspect of business numeracy with which this book is concerned is the ability to deploy quantitative analytical techniques when appropriate. As a final summary of the relevance of these techniques, Figure 1.6 is a reference matrix giving examples of where they are most often used.

		Spreadsheets	Decision analysis	Simulation	LP	DEA	CPM/PERT	Time series forecasting	Explanatory forecasting	Judgement forecasting
FUNCTIONAL AREAS	Finance	✓		✓	✓		✓	✓		
	Human resources	✓				✓				✓
	Marketing		✓					✓	✓	✓
	Operations		✓		✓	✓				
	Strategy			✓						✓
MANAGEMENT TASKS	Allocation			✓	✓	✓		✓	✓	✓
	Control	✓				✓	✓			
	Planning	✓	✓	✓	✓		✓	✓	✓	✓
	Scheduling				✓		✓			

Figure 1.6   Relevance matrix

QUESTIONS

1. By library research, or from personal experience, discuss reasons why information is a critical resource for:

   (a) an international airline;
   (b) a high street retailer;
   (c) a car manufacturer.

2. From consideration of an organisation you know, either as an employee or a customer, give one example of how it might use an analytical technique in each of the categories of:

   (a) Table 1.3: management tasks;
   (b) Table 1.4 functional areas.

3. A group of 700 motorists, chosen at random, took part in a market research survey to find out about consumers' attitudes to brands of petrol. The ultimate objective was to determine the impact of advertising campaigns. The motorists were presented with a list of petrol brands BP, Esso, Fina, Jet, National, Shell.
   They were also presented with a list of attributes: good mileage, long engine life, for with-it people, value for money, large company.
   The motorists were then asked to tick the petrol brands to which they thought the attributes applied. A motorist was free to tick all or none of the brands for each attribute. The table below contains the results, showing the percentage of the sample which ticked each brand for each attribute.

Attitude	BP	Esso	Brand Fina	Jet	National	Shell
Good mileage	37.1	61.5	7.6	11.9	22.6	85.3
Long engine life	12.2	19.2	3.8	5.0	8.5	19.0
For with-it people	6.9	10.0	1.2	3 1	12.4	10.9
Value for money	24.0	37.8	5.1	39 7	15.3	40.3
Large company	30.4	67.9	5.4	2.3	4.8	59.8

   (a) Analyse this table. What is the main pattern in it?
   (b) What are the exceptions?
   (c) Can you explain the exceptions?
   (d) What further information would be useful to help understand the table better?

   Hint: To analyse the table you will find it useful to re-present it first by rounding, re-ordering, etc.

PART TWO

Decision Support

Chapter 2   Decisions and computer support

Describes the rapid development of information technology in the context of decision making and shows how the role of IT has transformed and extended concepts of decision support.

Chapter 3   Decision analysis

Describes the basics of decision analysis, including the expected value of sample information and the expected value of perfect information, and its application to areas such as new product launches and project planning.

Chapter 4   Advanced decision analysis

Moves on to more complex aspects of the technique, including how it can be used for continuous distributions, how subjective probability estimates can be obtained and how Bayesian revision works.

Chapter 5   Simulation

Describes the different types of simulation, including Monte Carlo methods, and applications such as inventory control and capital expenditure appraisal.

CHAPTER TWO

Decisions and computer support

Analytical decision techniques are now inextricably linked with information technology (IT). In particular, decentralised or 'end-user' computing has made techniques accessible to managers at all levels and greatly added to their day-to-day relevance. This chapter describes the evolution of IT in the context of IT decision making and the benefits it brings, and suggests how it might best be implemented. The role of spreadsheets, the most versatile and popular form of computer support, is discussed. Technical aspects of computer support are not covered.

INTRODUCTION

The term 'decision support system' (DSS) sounds like the usual computer jargon, as irritating and off-putting as all the rest. In fact the term refers to nothing more challenging than a computer system which produces information specially prepared to support particular decisions. Everyday examples are the systems producing bank statements, fuel bills and television (teletext) travel information.

Since, apart from a few eccentrics or masochists, no one would now dream of applying any of the decision techniques described in this book without computer help, the techniques can be rightly viewed as decision support systems. They take raw data and refine it to produce information directly relevant to particular decisions. In some cases, such as linear programming, the refinement goes to the ultimate extent of advising exactly what the decision should be.

There have not always been close links between computers, managers and decision techniques. Until the advent of microcomputers in the early 1980s, the calculations underlying the techniques were carried out either by hand or on a mainframe computer. The former was tedious, time consuming and resulted in errors; the latter interposed an organisation's computer department between the decision maker and the information which the techniques were producing and tended to reduce the effectiveness of that information. Computerisation of the techniques and their role as DSS has revolutionised their relevance to day-to-day management. The techniques and their output are now immediately accessible through microcomputers to managers at all levels.

DSS software, especially that for decision techniques, is readily available off the shelf; it is rarely now necessary to wait in the Data Processing department's priority queue for months or years before finally receiving something which is not quite what was wanted. The off-the-shelf software is generally user friendly and this has increased the accuracy and, more importantly, the usage of the techniques.

The primary purpose of this chapter is to deal with the role of information technology (IT) in applying decision techniques. However, the issues are the same if the much wider, general role of IT and DSS in organisations is investigated. Consequently the chapter, while mainly devoted to IT and management decision making, will go further than just the computerisation of the techniques which are the subject of the following chapters.

To appreciate fully the role of IT, some technical knowledge is required and this is supplied on a 'need-to-know' basis in the first section. The second section describes some applications of IT. The third shows how this role has developed since the 1960s, leading to a section describing the implications of the availability of DSS for the individual manager, emphasising what can be done to promote successful implementation. The fifth section looks at the types of decision support available, particularly spreadsheets. Finally we speculate about possible future developments.

TECHNICAL ISSUES

A manager does not need to become a technical IT expert. Indeed, he or she cannot become a technical expert because the speed of technical developments means that even an IT professional has to specialise and may know little about other technical areas. However, managers do need to know when technology might help solve business problems and how to liaise with experts. They must know enough of the terminology to have confidence to express the user point of view in meetings between users and experts, even in the face of jargon. A dividing line must be drawn between necessary and unnecessary knowledge, in much the same way that a car driver will find a certain amount of technical knowledge helpful in making proper use of the vehicle but prefers not to trespass on the role of the mechanic. This section explains some simple technical terms. People who already have a basic understanding of IT can pass it by.

According to the MIT90s research group,[1] IT has six basic elements:

1. *Computers*: The machines that process the data. They vary from large centralised mainframes to desk-top microcomputers.

2. *Software:* The sets of instructions or programs which tell the computer what to do. Software can be bespoke, specially written for a particular application, or generally available off the shelf such as word-processing and spreadsheet packages.

3. *Telecommunications*: The means for transferring messages and information over distances. This includes the cables which connect one computer to another in the same building, switchboards which link computers in different buildings, and satellites which connect computers in different continents.

4. *Workstations*: The collection of computer-based equipment at which a person works. Typically this includes a microcomputer, a screen, a printer and a means of storing information.

5. *Robotics*: Machinery operated by a computer. For example, the automatic assembly and welding machinery on car production lines is linked to a small-scale computer which

---

[1] Between 1985 and 1991 the MIT90s research group at the Massachussetts Institute of Technology carried out a major project investigating the role of IT in business and management. Their work is described in *The Corporation of the Nineties*, edited by Michael Scott Morton, Oxford University Press, 1991.

tells it what to do and feeds information about the type of car which will arrive next on the assembly line.

6. *Smart products*: Equipment which has built-in computer intelligence. For example, credit cards are being developed which incorporate tiny computers to record and update information such as bank balances and creditworthiness.

A succession of technical breakthroughs has resulted in astonishing reductions in the cost of computing power which is now millions of times cheaper than 50 years ago. If cars had become cheaper at the same rate, a new BMW could now be bought for a few pence. Consequently IT is increasingly important to business organisations as the computerisation of more and more aspects of business becomes feasible and cost effective.

The primary reason for the most recent cost reductions is the silicon chip. This is a small sliver of silicon, the size of a fingernail into which a whole electronic circuit can be etched. The cost reductions have continued as improved technical processes have allowed ever more complex circuits to be included on a single chip. This is known as LSI (large-scale integration) or sometimes VLSI (very large-scale integration).

Reducing costs is one of the reasons for the recent trend to decentralise computer facilities. Instead of one or two large mainframes presided over by a computing department, companies now have, in addition, microcomputers located throughout the organisation and under the control of local users. These computers are often networked together; a manager's workstation may be extensively linked to other managers' workstations, to other company locations, to the company's mainframe computer, to external information sources, to other types of technology-based office equipment. There is a variety of linkages, for example cables, radio waves and satellites.

Networks can give a range of new facilities, particularly electronic mail by which memos, reports etc. are communicated in electronic form by computer, rather than paper. An associated facility is the electronic diary: managers' diaries are held on computer and meetings can be arranged by searches which take a matter of seconds to find the participants' free times. Most importantly, the networks supply management information which is shared by many users. Databases hold locally generated information, corporate information downloaded from mainframe computers and the output of decision techniques.

APPLICATIONS

IT in retailing

Large high street retailing organisations have invested heavily in electronic point of sale (EPOS) technology. When the customer takes purchases to the checkout desk an optical character reader takes information from the bar codes on the products. A bar code is a series of lines which, by being of differing widths, contain coded information about the product: type, brand, size etc.

The optical reader can be hand held or fixed, in which case the product is passed over it. The product information is passed to the local store computer which returns the current price of the product to the checkout. At the end of a customer's transactions the total amount owed can be paid in the usual way by cash, card or cheque but, if the store's

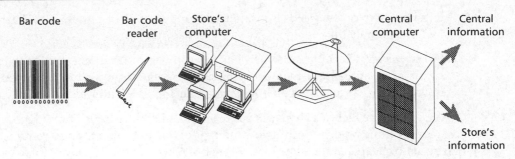

Figure 2.1 Electronic point of sale (EPOS)

computer is linked to banks' computers, funds transfer systems allow the amount to be deducted directly from the customer's bank account.

Meanwhile, information about this sale and all others is stored on the local store's computer and, at the end of the day, forwarded to the company's central computers. Sales information from all stores is assembled and analysed, allowing short-term decisions about purchasing to be taken as well as creating databases of information for longer-term planning. Analysed information, for example in the form of forecasts and schedules, will be passed back to the stores to help with decisions about re-stocking.

There are three main reasons for companies making such huge investments. First, EPOS can speed customer throughput at the checkout. Secondly it provides operational information of a highly detailed kind to improve the effectiveness of distribution systems and inventory control and to allow prices to be changed very quickly. Thirdly, it can provide high-level management information for planning new products and developing strategies. This last benefit is potentially the most valuable but undoubtedly the most difficult to achieve since it requires managers to adopt new information-based ways of working. They must be able to spot potential value in data and to use decision and other techniques to refine it into useful information. The organisation has to see information as a corporate resource and find ways of using it profitably.

IT in manufacturing distribution

Large car manufacturers have multinational operations. Components are taken from international suppliers and brought to assembly plants in different locations. The final products are then shipped to customers all over the world.

Computers control these systems, monitoring the movement of components and completed products between suppliers, assembly plants and customers by air, rail, road and sea. For example, a large multinational car manufacturer claims to be able to find the whereabouts of any part, whether a completed car or a small bolt, at any time within seconds. The system was gradually built up over a number of years. Early versions of the system reportedly provided information which arrived later than the components themselves.

Such systems provide operational advantages, just as EPOS does. Distribution is faster and stock levels can be kept to a minimum. In effect, stock is being substituted with information. The systems provide management information about, for example, the utilisation of vessels, causes for delay and stock costs. They also provide high-level information of strategic importance. For example, a customer looking for a particular model and colour of car with chosen extras can, in theory and increasingly in practice, make an order and have the car built to these specifications and then delivered in a matter of weeks or even days. As in retailing, organisations find it easier to achieve operational benefits than those associated with management information.

THE HISTORICAL PERSPECTIVE

The 1960s

The introduction of large mainframe computers into organisations in the 1960s was successful – success meaning that many, possibly most, projects worked effectively, achieved the anticipated cost savings, were perceived by users as being valuable and were, more or less, on time and within budget. Closer scrutiny, however, revealed that the successes were in particular areas:

- *accounting* – the payrolls and budgeting systems in nearly all large organisations;
- *operations* – inventory control in the car industry, customer accounts in banking;
- *technical* – missile control systems in the defence industry, computer-aided design (CAD) in shipbuilding.

The success was therefore in systems which supported specific functions and operations, and it contrasted with a lack of progress in applying computers to the management of organisations. Specifically there were many failures in developing MIS (management information systems) which were supposed to provide managers with the necessary information for running and developing the organisation. For example, the data in computerised banking systems was potentially available for management decisions to do with marketing, planning and defining strategy, but was not so used. This was the era when large amounts of data from mainframe computers were printed out on vast stacks of paper, circulated to managers monthly and called management information systems. In effect this amounted to the dumping of data rather than the provision of focused information and, as a result, the printouts gathered dust in the corner of offices or were immediately filed in wastepaper baskets. The result was that MIS started to get a bad name.

The 1970s

It took some time for organisations to appreciate what was happening, but by the 1970s the failure of MIS became generally recognised. There was much discussion and analysis[2] of the causes of this failure, a wide range of behavioural and technical reasons being put forward, including the following.

- *Effective user participation was absent*: although users were often involved in the development process, they were rarely able to have a significant influence on events. Not only

---

[2] See for example the references in David Targett, 'An Experience in the Design of a MIS for a Bank', Journal of the Operational Research Society, Vol. 36, no. 11, 1985, pp 999–1007.

were their knowledge, experience and needs not incorporated into the design, but also they became disillusioned and opted out, reacting aversely to what was eventually delivered, feeling that they were not the 'owners' of the systems and information. For example, the implementation of a system to computerise buying in a chain of retail stores was much delayed because the in-store employees who were to use the system were irritated that the IT professionals who had developed it kept them informed of what was happening but did not listen to their views.

- *Many systems did not match the management style of users*: managers had no experience of working systematically with computerised information and the concept of MIS was therefore diametrically opposed to their usual management styles. For example, in a medium-sized plastics manufacturing company, the chemists who had long constituted the senior management group rejected, at the last minute, a computerised costing system when they realised that the system would force on them significant changes in working practices. They had not foreseen these changes.

- *The information was often poorly formatted*: little attempt was made to transform masses of data from the computer into information which might be useful to the decision maker. There was no distinction between data and information. Many early MIS were simply masses of data which confused rather than clarified decisions. For example, a bank's forecasting system was never used because the forecasts were presented in lengthy printouts which were difficult to interpret.

- *Many systems were unrelated to organisational structures*: managers at different levels require information at differing levels of detail and in various formats. There was a tendency for everyone to receive the same dumped data. This problem was also a factor in the non-use of the bank forecasting system described above.

- *Some users had unrealistic expectations of the systems*: many users regarded computers as panaceas and thought that, more or less automatically, they would provide benefits. Strangely, this seemed to be a greater problem than cynical users who would not give the computer a chance. For example, a pharmaceutical company provided a custom-built, sophisticated forecasting package for its marketing group. However, the managers in the group then abdicated their responsibility for forecasting, simply accepting the automated output provided. The resulting forecasts proved to be less good than the previous manual ones. The marketing staff should have used the output in combination with their judgements.

The 1980s

The situation started to change in the 1980s when microcomputers became available. Technically these could do nothing that a terminal linked to a mainframe computer could not do, but their key effect, underlying the massive growth in their application, was that they allowed control of computing to be shared between technical experts and users. A manager no longer had to deal with a centralised data processing department or consultants to obtain computing assistance. There was no question of a project having to wait in a lengthy queue with other projects until the department had the time and resources to be able to tackle it. The manager could use computers with very little outside help: hence the term end-user computing.

The relatively low cost of micros allowed them to be purchased without resorting to formalised capital expenditure procedures and this was another factor contributing to their increasing usage. When cheap easy-to-use software became plentiful, continued growth was assured. These events have run counter to predictions: initially it was thought that micros were going to be successful in homes rather than businesses.

The decentralisation of computing meant that managers were better able to define their own information needs and then to implement the relevant systems. The availability of excellent software meant that micros could be used for the execution of decision techniques, but this was just part of the picture. Other applications, then and now, include the following.

- *Information handling*: corporate data from local sources, from other parts of the organisation and from external sources can be made available on the manager's desk. It can then be manipulated in tables and graphs and used effectively in decision making. This ability is now being extended outside the office as, for example, salespeople are equipped with laptop computers which can be linked to the headquarters' computers.
- *Statistical analysis*: off-the-shelf packages are available for most analytical techniques such as forecasting methods.
- *Financial planning*: spreadsheets are used to compile financial plans and for budgeting.
- *Office automation*: standard office procedures such as typing, filing, mailing and arranging meetings can be carried out electronically. Newer software can track the flow of documents through an office, making sure they are dealt with efficiently and effectively. For example, an insurance company may monitor the flow of customer letters – asking for information on surrender values, loans and so on – so that the enquiries are handled by the right people and do not languish unnoticed on some desk in a 'pending' file.

The present

Organisations are continuing to develop large company-wide computer systems with operating/technical/financial applications. However, the real growth and spread in the use of IT come from local applications, especially those involving management tasks. This growth has centred on the use of micros and is mainly in the following three areas:

- *The analysis of corporate information downloaded from the mainframe*: micros linked to the organisation's mainframe can receive the masses of data, which caused such a problem when printed out in the 1960s and 1970s, and work on them locally to provide information which has been reduced and refined to suit the local decision makers. For example, a chain of retail fashion stores feeds back EPOS information to its store managers so that they can better understand the tastes of the local clientele and therefore be more effective in ordering for the store.
- *Internal linkages*: local area networks, or LANS, link groups of microcomputers. This means that expensive equipment such as high-quality printers can be shared. It also means that information and documents can be passed around and that users can communicate electronically with one another (electronic mail). These linkages are also the basis for enabling better teamworking. Software, known as groupware allows groups of, for example, accountants to work together more effectively on an auditing project.
- *External linkages*: wide area networks, or WANS, link micros or locally networked

micros with the outside world. Information can be transferred across city blocks, countries or continents very rapidly. In particular, company offices in different locations can communicate with one another and this is a major factor permitting the global integration and transformation of the management of multinational organisations. For example, a specialist engineering consultant is able to be part of several teams, working simultaneously on projects in different parts of the world. Without these linkages the specialist would only be able to be part of one team, working in one location.

It probably does not need to be said that the picture is not one of universal success and there are plenty of examples of failure as well as instances where organisations and management have been transformed. Technical education (or the lack of it) can be an initial barrier to progress but it is not a continuing problem, nor is technical breakdown, although both these factors receive undue publicity. The business benefits of computerised management do not accrue automatically and managers have to work to realise them. In particular they have to treat information as an important resource and manage it accordingly.

This will mean controlling information. Information saturation can be a problem: more data does not automatically imply better decisions. It may just cause confusion. It also means keeping information consistent. Having many data sources in different parts of an organisation may result in inconsistent information and therefore inconsistent decisions. Lastly, analytical abilities will have to be encouraged.

IMPLICATIONS FOR THE INDIVIDUAL

What does an individual manager or administrator need to know and do in order to promote the effective use of IT for management decision making? Research[3] into IT projects and their impact on end users gives some answers. Surveys have mainly investigated projects where things have gone wrong. They have shown that technical issues are less important than people issues and that in general people get the systems they deserve. We can associate computer-based analytical decision techniques with IT projects in general, because the first is a subset of the second. Only if a technique were being used by a lone individual in isolation from the rest of the organisation and its decision processes would these issues be unimportant.

To convert the reasons for failure into the characteristics of success, we must turn the findings round. The implications of the research can then be summarised into three dimensions: attitude, approach and the need for specific skills.

What are the right attitudes?

IT project team members, whether users or experts, should demonstrate the following attitudes to the project.

---

[3] These issues are covered in many information systems teaching texts. See, for example, Part 3 of Wendy Robson, *Strategic Management and Information Systems*, Pitman, 1994.

Commitment

The signs of commitment are that personal, departmental and corporate resources (especially management time) have been put into the project. If the project is important, the resources should be allocated; if the resources are not to be allocated, the project cannot be very important and perhaps the decision to go ahead should be reconsidered. A typical sign of a lack of commitment is when attendance at project team meetings is repeatedly cancelled because of various short-term problems and junior staff members are sent, without being briefed, as replacements. Another negative sign is when a low-level clerical member of staff is given the job of system administrator or coordinator – in addition to existing responsibilities.

Senior management must be committed. It is their responsibility to ensure that the project is part of a corporate IT strategy which should in turn be linked to the business objectives and strategy of the organisation. This senior level commitment is frequently lacking, on the old-fashioned grounds that computers are to do with operations and do not concern the board of directors.

Realistic expectations

System users should anticipate substantial benefits but not immediate perfection. Rather they should expect to make adjustments as the project is implemented. And they should appreciate that making changes, just like turning an aircraft carrier, will take time.

Although computing power is enormous there are limits to what can be done. Ambition is commendable but users should not expect too much. A marketing manager of a UK bank, knowing how cheap computing power had become, embarked on a project to build an extensive computerised information database relating to the banking activities of the entire UK population of 57 million. The project never went ahead because the cost of the computing power to manipulate the database was prohibitive.

Motivation

Most senior managers like to obtain information from personal, trusted sources. When they want information they prefer to call an assistant into the office and ask, rather than search on a computer screen. Before making large investments in management information systems, organisations should try to ensure that managers really want it and will use it.

One of the most important positive signs for an IT project is the existence of a champion – a user who sees the benefits and will drive the project forward from the user side of the fence. Research has shown repeatedly that the presence of a champion indicates success and the absence of one will lead to failure.

Persistence

This means a willingness to formulate detailed plans, to follow through the details of the plan and to monitor performance. Many organisations do not attempt to measure benefits. Many more do not monitor whether planned benefits have been achieved or not; there may be strong perceptions of the project's success or failure even though evidence to support these perceptions is entirely lacking.

Fear (or lack of it)

Users should have the right balance between respect for IT and paralysing fear. Surveys have shown cases of managers refusing to have anything to do with IT projects: refusing to use computer output or keyboards. It is never clear whether this means they are showing too little respect or too much fear.

What is the right approach?

Research shows that the way an organisation/project team/individual sets about an IT project should include the following characteristics.

Top-down

The question should not be 'how can IT be used?' but 'what help can IT give so that business objectives are met?' In particular this means that there should be an IT strategy, which is a plan showing what IT investments are to be made and how they are to be used to meet corporate business objectives. An IT strategy should therefore be linked to corporate strategies.

It is surprising how few organisations have meaningful IT strategies. 'Always buy IBM' or 'Never buy IBM' are not IT strategies, although they may be part of one. Surveys have even revealed consultancy companies which advise other organisations on how to develop IT strategies but do not have one themselves.

Bottom-up

The need for a top-down aspect to IT projects does not mean that projects should not also have an element of 'bottom-up' as well. A bottom-up approach, based on users and their requirements, may be an excellent source of ideas and will ensure that the users feel they have ownership of the system which is developed.

Planning based

Planning is of course important for any type of project, but is even more so for IT projects, where the objectives and technologies may not be equally clear to all participants and where there may be large differences in the attitudes and understanding of those taking part in the development process.

Substantial user involvement

No one would seriously question the premise that managers should be involved in the development of the systems they are to use. However, research shows that their involvement must allow them to feel that they are able to influence what is going on. It does not augur well for a project if users attend meetings only to listen to what computer experts have to say and feel inadequate about their limited technical knowledge. It does bode well if users feel they have ownership of the project: they should talk about 'our' project rather than 'their' project.

Flexibility

This means including plenty of contingencies in the plans. In the 1960s and 1970s when banking systems were being computerised, some banks made provision for interest to be paid on current accounts. Others did not, and are now regretting it. Flexibility also means that users should be prepared to change their management practices in order to make more effective use of the system. In a large retailing company re-ordering decisions were always taken on a Tuesday, after the output from the inventory control system had arrived by post following the weekend run on the centralised mainframe. With a new system which was faster and which communicated the output electronically, it made more sense to run the computer on Thursday nights and make re-ordering decisions on Friday morning in time for the weekend which is the busiest time of the week. Such changes implied substantial alterations to the ways managers did their work.

Monitoring

During development and after implementation the system should be monitored to find out whether it is working properly, whether it is achieving the expected benefits and whether its running costs are within budget. Post-implementation project evaluations let the organisation know whether its investment has been worthwhile; they show what adjustments are needed; and they provide valuable lessons for other projects.

Commitment to continuing development

The development and use of a system are part of a continuing process, not a once-for-all event.

What skills and knowledge are needed?

Participants in the development of an IT system should have, between them, the following skills and knowledge of planning processes.

Planning and management of time

Planning is about taking decisions today which affect future events and commitment is the most important ingredient; bad planning is when there is no real plan or no action plan. The benefits of planning, according to management consultants, are summarised by saying that it is the key to success. The other benefits are that it leads to better resource management, improves communications, brings control and influences the future.

Project planning techniques

Critical path methods, as described in Chapter 6, can help to manage system developments.

Table 2.1   Stages of an IT project

(a)	Feasibility study	(e)	Testing
(b)	Requirements	(f)	Parallel
(c)	Specification	(g)	Install
(d)	Programming	(h)	Review

Table 2.2   Rules for managing a transition

1. Set clear objectives for which the organisation can aim. They should be simple, practical, understandable and attainable. They must be known to all concerned.

2. Establish proper plans including defining tasks, estimating the effort involved, cost, duration, priority, sequence etc. and assigning responsibility.

3. Formulate a people policy by analysing the effects of the change on people, assessing the adjustments that may be necessary, deciding how to allow for them and devising a scheme to put them into action. If jobs are to be radically changed or lost this should be dealt with explicitly.

4. Communicate objectives and progress clearly to all involved, giving opportunity for people to voice their own views. Bad news may be better than uncertainty.

5. Ensure an orderly transition by encouraging active involvement in the process, anticipating what can go wrong and being prepared to deal with unexpected developments.

IT project stages

Computer experts will have in mind the standard stages of an IT project. The users should also know what the stages are if they are to play a full part. Table 2.1 lists the usual stages.

Managing a transition

Change is exciting for those carrying it out, but it can be frightening for those on the receiving end. Managing a transition is such a fundamental issue that a full study falls well outside the scope of this book but, as a minimum, the rules shown in Table 2.2 should be adopted.

Research shows that when transitions go wrong, whether they are to do with IT projects or not, they do so because of a lack of funds, communication and understanding, time and education. Few projects fail because of a lack of technical skills.

TYPES OF SUPPORT AVAILABLE

In the early days of personal computing it would not be unusual for a manager, needing help with a particular type of decision he or she regularly faced, to go to the computer department and ask for a program to be written specially. The development process would normally take a long time and the result was not likely to be user friendly. But since no support at all had previously been available, it was welcomed with open arms and the deficiencies overlooked.

As time went by, however, managers got rather tired of the delays, the bugs and the difficulty of using the software. Realising the need, and spotting several gaps in the market, software manufacturers started to produce packages for general use. Now off-the-shelf software is available for most purposes, including for all the techniques described in this book. Moreover, many of the packages are highly flexible and can tackle a range of decision problems. Probably the most flexible of all packages is the spreadsheet, which is a grid on which financial and other plans can be drawn.

Accountants have traditionally drawn up budgets, plans and financial breakdowns on large sheets of squared paper. For example, a corporate plan has financial items vertically down one side and time periods horizontally across the top. Each number occupies one of the cells defined by the rows and columns. Table 2.3 is an excerpt from a plan of an electronic manufacturer's business.

Large spreadsheets present problems since it is easy to make mistakes and difficult to make changes. Electronic spreadsheets, one of the biggest successes in personal computing, provide the solution.

Excel, Lotus 1-2-3, Supercalc and many others are computerised spreadsheets. Data can be entered from the keyboard into each individual cell defined by a row and column. Whenever possible, however, formulae rather than data are entered into the cells. For example, in a financial plan such as Table 2.3, if the sales of, say, watches are projected to grow by 10 per cent per year over the coming years, then a formula is entered into the cells which relate to revenue for watches:

$$1996 \text{ watch revenue} = 1995 \text{ watch revenue} \times 1.1$$

So, the 1996 watch revenue cell contains:

location of 1995 watch revenue cell × location of cell containing 1.1

Table 2.3 Spreadsheet of a financial plan for an electronics manufacturer (values in $m)

	1995	*1996*	*1997*	*1998*
Revenue:				
watches	3.4	3.6	3.9	4.5
calculators	2.1	2.8	3.6	4.9
games	0.3	1.2	2.5	4.4
Total revenue	5.8	7.6	10.0	13.8
Costs:				
materials	0.1	0.1	0.2	0.3
labour	2.2	2.8	3.4	3.4
supplies	0.6	1.4	1.8	2.3
supervision	0.8	0.9	1.0	1.1
R and D	1.1	1.3	1.5	1.7
interest	0.2	0.2	0.2	0.3
Total costs	5.0	6.7	8.1	9.1
Contribution	0.8	0.9	1.9	4.7

Similarly, '1996 total revenue' should be entered not as a number, but as a formula which adds up the 1996 revenue for watches, calculators and games. Formulae make it easier to change data and assumptions, i.e. to carry out sensitivity analysis. For example, sensitivity analysis on the growth rate would involve changing the contents of just one cell – that containing 1.1. By changing it to 1.12 all the product revenue cells will instantaneously reflect the impact of a 12 per cent growth rate.

Overall the advantages of an electronic spreadsheet are:

1.   The spreadsheet is *quicker* to construct, particularly because of copy functions. In Table 2.3 the formula for totalling revenues would be entered for 1995 then copied to other years.

2.   The spreadsheet is *more accurate*. Again, the copy function is important. Once entered accurately for 1995, the formula stays accurate for subsequent years.

3.   Electronic spreadsheets can be much *larger* than manual ones and can extend to thousands of rows and columns.

4.   The most important advantage is the capability to carry out *sensitivity analysis*. The effect of changes in assumptions can be seen at the press of a button. Compare, for example, the difficulty of changing the growth rate in Table 2.3 manually when cells would have to be adjusted individually with risks of errors for each one.

Modern spreadsheets provide a very wide range of facilities and it may seem that learning what a spreadsheet package can do is the prime skill in its use. This is not so. The prime skill is to know how to *model* – for example, how to take a statement of the financial plans of the electronics manufacturer and turn them into a spreadsheet such as the one in Table 2.3 which represents reality accurately and effectively. A few guidelines are particularly useful:

- use formulae rather than numbers whenever possible;
- keep the important output together so that it can be seen in the same window;
- assumptions, for example growth rate in Table 2.3, should be entered separately from the workings so that only one cell needs to be changed in sensitivity analysis.

Modern spreadsheets now produce graphs and have word-processing facilities so that they can produce reports as well as calculations.

THE FUTURE

The rapid evolution of IT over many years means that predictions are difficult and dangerous. However, there is general agreement that the following developments are very probable.

Further technical progress

Computers will become even faster and more powerful. Silicon chips are still being developed and the year-on-year improvements in computing power will continue. A method known as parallel processing speeds up the rate of operation, carrying out instructions in parallel rather than one after another. A processor which does this is known as a transputer.

Software will also change. *Expert systems* are coming into prominence. An expert system is a piece of software which stores knowledge and mimics the role of an expert. For instance, a medical diagnostic expert system helps a doctor diagnose an illness. The details of the symptoms are fed in and then the computer which has been programmed to 'think' like an expert will suggest what the problem could be, usually giving a list of possible illnesses with probabilities attached.

Artificial intelligence (AI) is software that apparently thinks for itself. For example, AI may be added to a statistical package so that the manager can ask questions like 'which type of customer in the Western region has been most profitable in the last three months?' AI takes that 'plain English' question and decides what statistical methods are appropriate. The answer is also given in plain language.

A *neural network* is a method of getting computers to behave like the human brain. The term refers to a type of software whereby the computer acts not as one processor but as if it were a series of networked computer nodes reacting one with another. This approach allows computers to 'learn' from the information they receive.

For example, neural networks have been used on subway transport systems to estimate the number of people on a platform and thereby indicate the point at which the platform should be closed to further passengers for safety reasons. It works in the following way. An exercise is carried out in which the number of passengers on a platform is manually counted second by second over a period of time. The computer is shown video pictures of the platform over this period. By associating the pictures with the true number of passengers, the computer learns how to interpret the pictures. It can then be used in the future to estimate the number of passengers from the video picture at any time and warn station staff when overcrowding is becoming dangerous.

The ease of using equipment will also improve through concepts such as *voice recognition* whereby instructions and data are fed into computers by the spoken word. Such systems are already operational but only in isolated situations where limited vocabulary is used and where there is no problem with different regional accents. For example, production control systems have been implemented which work on a limited and predefined number of words which must be spoken by people with similar accents.

More integration within the organisation

The use of networks will continue to grow, resulting in better communications and reductions in the movements of paper. There is a high initial cost when networks are installed, but once this investment has been made a whole range of other projects become feasible. For example, an office equipment manufacturer installed computer links for all its salesforce: each salesperson could key in an order at the customer's site and receive an immediate response about availability and delivery. Once this investment had been made it was then cost effective to use the network for other purposes, such as communicating price changes and product updates to the salesforce.

More integration with suppliers and customers

An organisation's suppliers and customers will both have IT equipment that links with its own. For example, stock levels will be controlled by linking retailers with their manu-facturing suppliers. Even now it is possible for the stock of a product on a shelf to be moni-tored by sensors and a re-order triggered directly and electronically with the supplier. At the other end of the supply chain, customers will have 'smart cards' to speed up financial transactions.

Information will be used more effectively

After managers have learned how to use the technical equipment, the next logical step will be to learn to make proper use of all the information available because of it. For example, retail stores will learn about the tastes and preferences in their catchment areas allowing products to be targeted at those customers. In general, EPOS data will be turned into information by use of some of the analytical decision techniques to be described in the following chapters.

Companies will cooperate over IT

Companies within the same value chain will link their IT strategies to ensure proper communications; competing companies will form alliances to afford the IT developments which will enable them to protect and expand their market positions. Already airlines have formed global partnerships so that, together with their partners, they cover the world. For example, British Airways is in an alliance with USAir and Qantas and other airlines.

IT will form a major part of corporate strategies

Instead of being a peripheral cost saver, IT will be inherent in organisations' activities. For example, plans to expand into different overseas markets will depend on IT to provide the necessary management information for planning and control. When an organisation's control systems are computerised it does not matter much if a branch office is two blocks away or two continents.

CONCLUSION

IT has had an enormous impact on us all in our everyday lives. The ways we shop, bank, plan, travel, communicate are all unrecognisable from a few years ago. IT is also bringing about a revolution in the business world and in the way both public and private sector organisations compete, are structured and are run. This revolution first had an impact on the operations of organisations as technical and clerical functions such as payroll and inventory systems were taken over by computers. More recently IT has made an impact on management functions at all levels. Decision making in all areas, from strategy formu-lation to day-to-day pricing and purchasing, has started to change. The changes are perva-sive and affect many dimensions of the organisation but some issues are of fundamental importance to anyone in management.

IT *changes businesses*. It is not just a question of being able to do the current job more efficiently, but of doing it differently and more effectively. For example, car manufacturers used to forecast sales and then build cars to stock. Customers wanting a particular variant

– engine size, interior trim, colour, extras etc. – could only have it if it was in stock. Otherwise they had to wait several months for such a variant to be built. Now some manufacturers are using their information systems to build to customer order. The customer chooses what he or she wants and the manufacturer then responds quickly enough for the car to be built and the customer receives it within days. This is a complete transformation of the ordering process – from producer push to customer pull. There is little doubt which arrangement suits the customer best and is likely to result in increased market share.

These changes can go so far as to change the nature of the organisation's business. The main activity of a company in the building industry was installing bathrooms. Then the managing director came across some software for designing bathrooms. It allowed customers to design their new bathroom on screen, being able to see immediately the effect of moving facilities around and to know the cost of different options. The company rapidly became a designer of bathrooms, a much more profitable area of business.

IT *changes work practices*. Not only do companies change their business, people change the way they do their jobs. For example, design engineers used to prepare rough drafts of plans by hand and then send them to a draughtsperson for a full drawing. It would then be returned, amended and so on for several iterations. If the customers changed their minds, the preparation of new plans was a lengthy business. CAD systems (computer-aided design) allows engineers to make their own amendments to plans on screen, speeding up the process, maintaining control and obtaining better results. Some engineers even input their material themselves, cutting out the draughting stage entirely.

In the past computer systems belonged to the computer department and other specialists. The users were kept at arm's length – and generally the computer department liked things this way. Newer systems, based on decentralised resources, *belong* more to the *users* than to the specialists. The users feel responsible for them and feel able to generate new ideas for further developments and new systems.

Although the benefits can be great, so can the problems and IT should be seen as an *iceberg*: 7/8 of an IT project is unseen. IT projects can be so complex and their effects on working practices so great that it is not usually possible to plan every outcome in advance. There will always be surprises. When a retailing organisation first issued its own charge-card, customers who had not used their card were surprised to receive statements telling them they owed 0.00 and should send a cheque for 0.00 by the 15th of the month. Meanwhile, customers who had used their cards a great deal were surprised to receive the two pages of their statement in different envelopes, often at different times. Such experiences point to the inevitability of there being errors and surprises, rather than to negligence.

Perhaps the biggest problem for managers is that IT *changes rapidly*. It is not easy to keep up to date with the latest developments and opportunities for the successful deployment of IT; all the more reason for maintaining a continuing good relationship between user and expert.

Managers must also be aware of the 'information' part of information technology. Information is a corporate resource and should be treated as such. Just as cash would not be left lying around doing nothing and gaining no interest, so information is an asset which should be put to use. Managers should search for useful information not currently available which will support the decisions they have to take. Unfortunately they are too often engrossed in day-to-day problems to think about future information needs.

The above discussion has looked at things from the point of view of 'what can go wrong'. Looking at the situation more positively, the opportunities are immense. The example of an American wholesaler supplying goods to drugstores shows how IT can affect companies and industries at the highest levels with immense benefits for those who use it properly and devastating effects for those who do not.

The company was essentially a warehousing operation, buying goods from manufacturers and holding them in stock until ordered by a drugstore. Understandably the first computer development was inventory control, a typical first functional application. The next step was to computerise sales processing. Again, this was a straightforward choice, but what happened afterwards led to some exciting developments.

The next step was to put terminals in customers' stores at the wholesaler's own expense. There were advantages on both sides. The customer could make an order electronically, know immediately whether the item was available and when it could be delivered. The wholesaler saved on paperwork and staff.

This was quickly followed by a really creative move. Software was installed which showed floor plans of the stores and gave guidance about the most profitable locations for different goods. The customers were given this extra service, helping to manage their stores, at no charge. Once the terminals were in the stores, extra facilities such as the floor plan software could be added at low cost, but bringing the enormous advantage to the wholesaler that it tied in the customer. It would be difficult for a customer to change to a different supplier and revert to the old ways of conducting business.

Success encouraged the wholesaler to offer a further service. The customers reported that one of their major problems was cashflow because part of their business was medical prescriptions – and the government was slow to pay up. The wholesaler offered to pay the prescription fees to the drugstores immediately, charging a fee for doing so. The computer link between wholesaler and retailer made it possible to do this efficiently. Again, there were advantages all round. The drugstores improved their cashflows and, presumably, had fewer excuses for late payments to the wholesaler; the wholesaler expanded its business.

IT had given the wholesaler, and the drugstores, typical benefits such as cost and staff savings, but the later developments had gone much further. The wholesaler had gained competitive advantage by offering a better service and had in fact moved into a new line of business in a different industry: factoring in the financial services industry.

The effect on the drugstore wholesaling industry was dramatic. Naturally other wholesalers could not stand by and had to take action quickly. Some had the expertise to develop their own systems, others had to buy in expertise. Some with expertise were taken over by others without expertise but with money. There were mergers and some companies went bankrupt. The net result was that the number of companies in the industry was reduced to about a tenth of the original. And it all happened very quickly.

The conclusion has to be that IT has the power to affect organisations at all levels as well as the industries of which they are a part. At the centre of what is happening is decision support systems: the use of management information and decision techniques for decision making. Not only are the techniques now more accessible because of the availability of hardware and software, but also the IT revolution is providing the good-quality information which feeds them. The expansion of IT into all areas of management has created an environment in which systematic decision making is becoming essential.

QUESTIONS

1. List the benefits which improved information brings to a retailer using EPOS (electronic point of sale). Try to categorise the different types of benefits in a way that seems sensible to you.

2. List the benefits which improved information brings to a car manufacturer using an integrated information system extending from the component suppliers to the showroom dealers. Try to categorise the different types of benefits.

3. Discuss how the benefits from information have changed and evolved over the last few decades.

4. Choose an information system which you have come across either at work or as a customer of, say, a travel agent or retail store, and analyse the implications for individuals who have to use it.

5. Describe an example of an information system which has brought competitive advantage to an organisation, i.e. has significantly improved the value which the organisation offers to its customers. Describe how the information has evolved to maintain that competitive advantage.

CHAPTER THREE

Decision analysis

Decision analysis is a technique which can help you find the best decision to take in certain types of problems with particular characteristics. This chapter first shows where decision analysis can be applied and how the technique works, with illustrations from a range of practical applications. After examining the underlying concepts, the central sections explain the five stages of decision analysis: structuring the decision tree, inserting payoffs and probabilities, rolling back and drawing the risk profile. Decision analysis produces some valuable management information, especially the EVSI (expected value of sample information) and EVPI (expected value of perfect information), and its uses are described next. The chapter ends with a discussion of the technique's strengths and weaknesses.

To understand the technique you will need to have a basic idea of probability theory. If you have not encountered probability before you should look at the appendix to the chapter which gives a brief, non-mathematical introduction to these ideas.

INTRODUCTION

The term 'decision analysis' sounds as if the technique can be used to resolve any decision problem of any type. Unfortunately this is not the case. Decision analysis can only be applied to a narrow range of decision problems which have particular characteristics. Even for such a problem decision analysis should only be seen as an aid to solution rather than an automatic decision taker in itself. This may not seem very promising, but it turns out that the concepts on which decision analysis is based can equip decision takers with ideas and skills which are invaluable for a much wider range of decisions and which form a platform for decision taking in general.

There are two common elements to every decision problem. First, a choice has to be made. This might be the decision to set some factor (a 'decision variable') at a specific value. For example, the choice might be how much to invest in a newly issued financial bond and the decision variable would therefore be the amount of money allocated to the bond. Or the choice might be of the yes/no variety, such as whether a company should expand or not. Or it might be a qualitative choice, such as selecting the range of colours for a new model of car or choosing a husband.

The second common element is that there must be a criterion by which to evaluate the outcome of the choice – the means by which you distinguish a good decision from a bad one. In business and marriage the criterion is often profit, but it does not have to be. For example, it could be environmental preservation or quality of life (for decisions about motorway routing) or delivery times (for decisions concerned with improving customer service).

Beyond these two common elements the decision problem may have special characteristics which categorise it as being of a particular type, and which enable it to be solved by an appropriate technique. A primary difficulty for a decision maker is to find a technique (if there is one) which matches his or her decision problem. What then are the characteristics of a decision problem which make it amenable to solution by decision analysis?

The two principal characteristics are:

1. The problem comprises a series of sub-decisions spread over time. Interwoven between these sub-decisions are events which provide additional information about the problem, clarifying the range of options before the decision maker. For instance, the problem of launching a new product has several stages:

    - decision: what market research to undertake;
    - information: result of market research;
    - decision: whether first to launch in a test market;
    - information: result of test market;
    - decision: whether to launch or abandon;
    - information: success or failure of product.

    This pattern of decision/information/decision/information . . . is the single most important characteristic of problems which are potentially solvable by the decision analysis technique. The events which provide the additional information are known as chance events since, at the outset, the information they provide is uncertain and to some extent a matter of chance, as with market research results for example.

2. The decisions within the sequence are not quantitatively complex. The decisions in the product launch example are of the type: choose between an option which will result in an estimated present value of X and an option which will result in an estimated present value of Y. The decision is then the easy one of picking the larger of the numbers X and Y. The decision is therefore quantitatively simple, although it may be complex in other senses. For example, the estimation of the present values of the different courses of action may have been very difficult. Compare this with the question of the most efficient way to split a newly arrived batch of crude oil into different types of petroleum products. This is a once-for-all decision based on all the information that is currently available. There is one decision and there is no series of events which will provide additional information. However, the one decision hinges on very complex calculations, requiring a technique such as linear programming (see Chapter 7) to solve. This type of problem cannot be solved by decision analysis.

There are other less important characteristics which will emerge later.

PREREQUISITE IDEAS

Decision analysis hinges on a number of basic concepts and definitions which need to be understood before decision analysis itself can be tackled. We will use a very simple example to illustrate these underlying concepts. The example is that of deciding whether to accept the following gamble. A coin will be tossed. If the coin falls 'heads', you will receive £5; if it falls 'tails', you will lose £4. Will you accept the bet? It is not a difficult problem, but it will help to describe the basic ideas of decision analysis.

Decision trees

The logical sequence of decisions/chance events when represented diagrammatically is called a decision tree:

☐   represents a point at which a decision is taken (called a *decision node*);
○   represents a point at which a chance event occurs (called a *chance node*);
—   represents the logical sequence between nodes.

In the coin example, the decision tree would appear as shown in Figure 3.1.

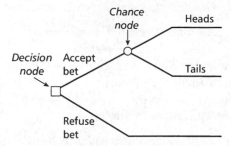

Figure 3.1   Coin example decision tree

Payoffs

At the points at which the decision tree ends (the end of each 'branch' of the tree) there is a *payoff* (usually in monetary terms, but it can be non-monetary) which is the outcome to the decision maker when that particular path through the tree has been followed. Payoffs are only found at the extreme right-hand tips of the tree. In Figure 3.2 the payoffs from the coin example are shown at the ends of the branches.

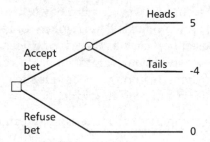

Figure 3.2   Coin example decision tree (with payoffs)

Probabilities

Chance nodes are, as you would expect from the name, subject to chance. In other words you, as the decision maker, cannot decide which branch you will travel down. That will be determined by the toss of the coin, the results of some market research, the outcome

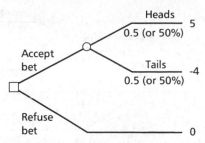

Probabilities are calculated by three methods:
1. *A priori* = reasoning.
2. Repeated trials = toss coin 1000 times and count 'heads'.
3. Subjective = judgemental estimate.

Figure 3.3 Coin example decision tree (with probabilities

of a clinical trial, etc. But it is possible to attach probabilities to the branches. For example, there is a 50 per cent chance that the coin will fall 'heads', or there is a 70 per cent chance that the market research will give positive results, or there is a 30 per cent chance that the clinical trial will demonstrate that the new drug works. Figure 3.3 shows the coin example with probabilities added. Consult the appendix for more information about probabilities.

Expected monetary value (EMV)

Every node, whether decision or chance event, has an EMV associated with it. This is defined as the average outcome which would result if that decision or chance event occurred many, many times. In the coin example you can win or lose each time you accept the bet and the EMV is your average gain (or loss) if you accepted the bet many, many times. If the coin were tossed 100 times, the most likely result (since we suppose the coin is fair and unbiased) is 50 heads and 50 tails. Therefore:

$$\text{Total profit} = (50 \times 5) - (50 \times 4)$$
$$= 250 - 200$$
$$= £50$$

$$\text{Average profit} = £50/100 = £0.5$$
$$= 50p$$
$$\text{EMV} = 50p$$

There is a more convenient method of making this calculation, stemming from the fact that probability can be defined via frequency of occurrence:

$$\text{Probability} = \frac{\text{Number of occurrences}}{\text{Number of trials}}$$
$$= 50/100 \text{ for the coin example}$$
$$= 0.5$$

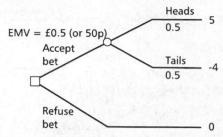

If the coin is tossed 100 times then on average:
50 heads ⟶ +£250
50 tails ⟶ -£200
Net profit = £50
Average profit = £50/100 = 50p
EMV = 50p

Figure 3.4 Coin example decision tree (with EMVs)

EMV can be calculated by multiplying probabilities and payoffs:

$$EMV = (0.5 \times 5) - (0.5 \times 4) = 0.5$$
$$= 50p$$

Figure 3.4 shows the decision tree with the EMVs added. The EMV at the chance node is 0.5, as calculated above. The EMV associated with the 'accept' decision is therefore 0.5. The alternative decision 'refuse' has of course an EMV of 0. Since the 'accept' alternative has the higher EMV, a reasonable strategy would be to accept the bet.

EMV is the usual criterion for decision making in decision analysis. It is also a common criterion in actual decision making. This is quite realistic since the EMV criterion selects options which will 'on average' give the most favourable results. In the coin example, the result of any one toss will be either a gain of £5 or a loss of £4, but over many tosses the result of the bet will be an average gain of 50p. Most organisations take frequent decisions and, although they are not all exactly the same, the risks can still be 'averaged out'. It therefore makes sense to choose options which will on average provide the best outcomes. In the same way professional tennis players play 'percentage tennis' and pension funds are invested in portfolios rather than individual stocks. Decision making based on EMV assumes that there will be a 'swings and roundabouts' effect.

However, EMV is not the only criterion that can be used. There are circumstances in which other criteria are more suitable. We will investigate some others later in the chapter.

APPLICATIONS

You can use decision analysis whenever the main decision comprises sub-decisions interwoven with information resulting from uncertain events. Here are some examples where organisations use decision analysis in practice.

Oil explorations

Some of the earliest applications of decision analysis were in the oil industry – in so-called oil wildcatting. Oil exploration is a speculative business. Oil companies can never be certain that a particular terrain will yield oil until it has actually done so, but they can conduct tests which will help clarify the position. They can carry out geological surveys, take soil tests, drill pilot wells and so on. So, the decision to go all the way and set up a full production well on a site involves a series of sub-decisions spread over a lengthy period of time on whether to stop, proceed or seek extra information. Between these decisions, information on geological structures and results from test wells become available. This is the sub-decision/information/sub-decision . . . structure of a typical decision analysis.

Major technological projects

Major projects such as developing new weapons systems or fulfilling the objectives of a space programme have to rely on a stage-by-stage process. For example, a project to develop a new supersonic airliner such as Concorde's replacement will require a series of new technological breakthroughs for its completion. The exact nature of the developments and how they might be achieved are not known at the outset of the project, which will last many years and involve a great deal of research and development. To achieve a breakthrough in one area, several channels of research must be pursued. As the project progresses, the channels with the most successful outcomes will be the ones incorporated into the overall project. Likewise, the decision to expand a business into Eastern Europe must depend on a variety of market research, political initiatives, etc., the results of which can only be guessed at the outset of the project. A decision tree incorporates decision nodes (deciding which research to start or continue and which to drop) and chance events (the results of the research).

Medical research

Decision analysis has been applied to the screening of pregnant women for defects in the foetus. It was used to determine whether such screening was likely to be beneficial for all women.

Two tests are available for indicating whether a foetus suffers from spina bifida. The first is an easy-to-administer blood test; it gives a reasonable indication but it is not highly accurate. The purpose of screening is to reassure women with healthy foetuses but to offer an abortion to a woman whose foetus is thought to have spina bifida. Therefore an inaccurate test could lead either to the abortion of a healthy foetus or to an unhealthy foetus remaining undetected.

A second test is available which involves drawing fluid from the womb. This test is much more (although not 100 per cent) accurate in detecting spina bifida, but it involves a slight risk that the test itself might trigger a miscarriage. The basic difficulty with this type of procedure is of course that in screening for less than 1 per cent of foetuses with spina bifida, a small percentage of the other 99 per cent would miscarry.

A number of screening plans were drawn up based on the two available tests. For example, one screening plan might be:

- decision: whether to take blood test;
- chance event: result of blood test;
- decision: if blood test positive, whether to take fluid test;
- chance event: result of fluid test;
- decision: if fluid test positive, whether to abort;
- chance event: outcome of pregnancy.

This plan has the sequential structure suitable for the application of decision analysis. The technique was used to compare this plan with other screening plans and the option not to screen at all. The results led to further investigation and the decision to screen only groups of women thought to be vulnerable – older women and those with family histories of spina bifida.

CARRYING OUT DECISION ANALYSIS

A simple example will be used to demonstrate how decision analysis works. The example is intended only to illustrate the technique and does not pretend to be a fully realistic and practical decision problem.

Product launch example

The situation is that a company has developed a new product and is now in a position to launch it onto the market. There are three options:

1. Go ahead with a full launch of the product.

2. Carry out a test market to obtain extra information.

3. Abandon the product and cut the losses.

Financial and probability data relating to the problem are shown in Table 3.1. The question of where this information comes from will be considered later.

If the product is launched fully, market research has shown that the market demand can be categorised as being strong, weak or non-existent and that the probabilities of each level of demand are 50 per cent, 20 per cent and 30 per cent respectively. In practice there are of course many more sophisticated ways in which the level of demand could be categorised.

Table 3.1   New product launch data

Demand	Payoff (£'000s)	No test	Probabilities (%) Favourable	Unfavourable
Strong	1000	50	70	20
Weak	250	20	20	20
Non-existent	−750	30	10	60

Cost of test market = £100 000
Probability (favourable test result) = 60 per cent
Probability (unfavourable test result) = 40 per cent

The company's test marketing group has said that, for a cost of £100 000, it can devise a simple test in a limited market which will give one of two indications – a favourable demand or an unfavourable demand. Extensive knowledge of previous test markets and of the structure of this one enables the group to say that the probability of a 'favourable' indication is 60 per cent; the probability of an 'unfavourable' indication is therefore 40 per cent.

Test market results provide extra information which is likely to change the estimates of the probabilities of different demand levels. A favourable test market result would, for example, make it more likely that the demand for the product is 'strong'. By methods to be described later, the group is able to calculate that if the indication is 'favourable' and the product is launched then the probabilities of strong, weak or non-existent market demands are 70 per cent, 20 per cent and 10 per cent respectively; if 'unfavourable' the same probabilities are 20 per cent, 20 per cent and 60 per cent.

The company's accounting group has calculated the financial implications of different levels of demand. The payoffs for strong, weak and non-existent markets are, respectively £1 000 000, £250 000 and −£750 000. Development costs already incurred have been ignored, since they are sunk as far as this problem is concerned and therefore should have no bearing on the launch decision.

It is easier to carry out a decision analysis if you structure the technique into five stages.

Stage 1: Draw the tree

The first stage can seem the easiest but is often the most difficult: thinking out the logical sequence of decisions and chance events and the interrelationships between them. Usually the tree starts with a single decision node. From this come several branches, at the end of which are chance event nodes. The branches stemming from these chance event nodes lead to more decision nodes, and so on. The final tree consists of decision nodes, chance event nodes and branches linking them. The pattern of decision/chance/decision/ . . . is typical, but should not be followed slavishly. There are circumstances where a series of decision nodes is followed by more decision nodes or chance event nodes by more chance event nodes. It depends on the structure of the problem and what is, for you, the clearest way of representing it.

Figure 3.5 shows the tree for the product launch example. The first decision which the organisation faces is whether to go ahead with a full launch, carry out a test market or abandon the product. This is the decision node at point A. 'Launch' leads to the chance node at B and the three outcomes of strong, weak or non-existent markets. 'Test market' leads to the chance node at C and the two possibilities of a favourable or an unfavourable indication. Given this new data, a more informed decision to proceed or not can be taken. This decision is represented by the nodes at D1 and D2. If the decision is to launch, the next chance events have three possible outcomes, strong, weak or non-existent demands, denoted by the chance nodes at E1 and E2. At any stage a decision to 'abandon' ends that part of the tree.

Stage 2: Insert payoffs

The next stage is to insert the payoffs which are at, and only at, the ends of all branches of the tree. They are usually in monetary terms but not always, as in the medical

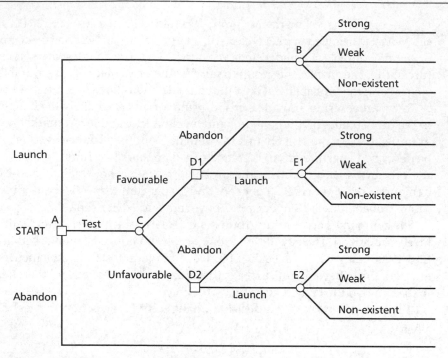

Figure 3.5   Tree for product launch

application, for example. They should be calculated carefully so that irrelevant costs and revenues are excluded, but particularly so that whatever is included or excluded is consistent from branch to branch.

Figure 3.6 shows the tree for the product launch example with the payoffs added. The payoff for 'abandon' is zero since sunk costs have been excluded. It would not make any difference to the result if they were included (as long as they were included on a consistent basis) but the calculations would be more complex and the numbers more unwieldy. The payoffs (£'000s) for strong, weak and non-existent markets are 1000, 250 and −750, as in Table 3.1.

The cost of the test market (£100 000) is represented as a 'gate' at the beginning of the 'test market' branch, indicating that choosing this branch incurs a cost of £100 000. The £100 000 is handled this way purely for simplicity: it makes the calculations easier than the alternative of subtracting £100 000 from the payoffs at the end of each of the branches stemming from the 'test market' decision node. Both methods of dealing with the £100 000 would lead to identical results.

Stage 3: Insert probabilities

The branches leaving chance nodes have a probability attached to them indicating the likelihood of that event occurring. Branches coming from decision nodes do not, of course, have probabilities attached since the decision maker, not chance, determines which branch to follow. The probabilities may have been calculated from market research data, subjective assessment or any of the ways in which probabilities are determined.

The probabilities for the product launch example, taken from Table 3.1, are shown in Figure 3.7. As a quick check that all is in order you should ensure that the probabilities

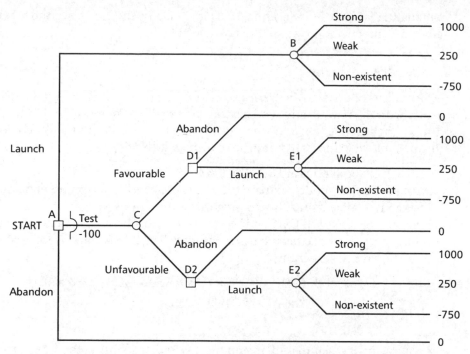

Figure 3.6   Payoffs added to product launch example

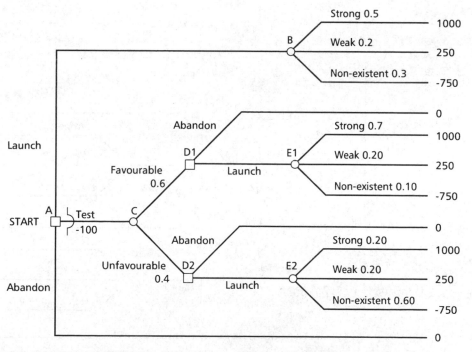

Figure 3.7   Probabilities added to product launch example

emanating from each node sum to 1. This should be the case since the branches at each node are intended to cover all the possible outcomes.

Stage 4: Roll-back procedure

The nucleus of decision analysis is at stage 4. The procedure is called the *roll-back* since it starts with the payoffs and works backwards to the commencement of the tree. Start at the top right of the tree and work leftwards as far as you can go. When you can go no further, return to the right but drop to a lower level.

- at each chance node calculate the EMV;
- at each decision node compare the EMVs of all its branches and eliminate all but the most favourable branch by crossing them through.

Figure 3.8 shows the EMVs added to the tree for the product launch example. Non-optimal decisions have been crossed through. The calculations were carried out in the order shown below, starting top right.

$$\text{At B: EMV} = (1000 \times 0.5) + (250 \times 0.2) - (750 \times 0.3)$$
$$= 500 + 50 - 225$$
$$= 325$$

You may find it easier to understand this calculation by using the frequency, rather than the probability method as with the earlier coin example. Think of repeating the event 1000 times and working out the average return. The same answer, 325, should result.

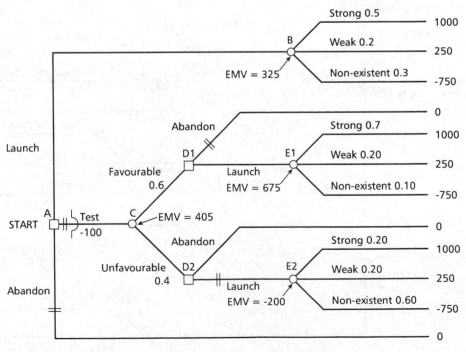

Figure 3.8   Roll-back for product launch example

$$\text{At E1: EMV} = (1000 \times 0.70) + (250 \times 0.20) - (750 \times 0.10)$$
$$= 700 + 50 - 75$$
$$= 675$$

At D1: Eliminate the 'abandon' option, which has a EMV of zero compared with 675 for the 'launch' option. The elimination of a branch is denoted by | |.

$$\text{At E2: EMV} = (1000 \times 0.20) + (250 \times 0.20) - (750 \times 0.60)$$
$$= 200 + 50 - 450$$
$$= -200$$

At D2: Eliminate the 'launch' option, which has an EMV of -200 compared to 0 for 'abandon'.

$$\text{At C: EMV} = (675 \times 0.6) + (0 \times 0.4)$$
$$= 405 + 0$$
$$= 405$$

The 675 and the 0 in the calculation at node C were brought through from nodes D1 and D2 respectively. They were used just as if they had been payoffs.

Continuing to roll back, 100 must be deducted from the 'test market' branch at the 'gate' which represents the cost of the test market. The EMV of the 'test market' branch is therefore:

$$405 - 100 = 305.$$

At A: Eliminate the 'abandon' and 'test market' branches which have EMVs of 0 and 305, compared to 325 for 'launch'.

Stage 5: Summarise the optimal path and draw the risk profile

The final stage is to inspect the results of the roll-back to find the optimal path through the tree. The recommended path should be summarised and the risk profile drawn.

A risk profile is a table summarising all the possible outcomes which could occur when the optimal decision path is followed, along with their probabilities. This is not the same as listing all the payoffs in the tree, since the act of eliminating branches and choosing the optimal path will have greatly reduced the number of payoffs which are achievable. The purpose of the risk profile is to provide summary information about the decision, but more especially to indicate the likelihood of making particular profits or losses. It also acts as a check to reveal whether the EMV, which is an average, is concealing any large (especially large negative) outcomes which have small probabilities. Such outcomes might (because of their small probabilities) have a negligible effect on the EMV but, should they actually occur, the effect on the decision maker could be catastrophic.

For the product launch example, the path is simple: go ahead and launch without a test market.

The risk profile is in Table 3.2. Again, it is simple. There is a 70 per cent chance of making a profit and a 30 per cent chance of losing £750 000. There are no really large negative outcomes hidden away by the EMV in this simple example.

The EMV criterion should not be followed slavishly. On occasions, the decision maker

Table 3.2   Risk profile (optimal)

Outcome	Payoff (£'000s)	Probability (%)
Strong demand	1000	50
Weak demand	250	20
Non-existent demand	−750	30

might prefer an option which, although it has an inferior EMV, has a more attractive risk profile. For instance, there might be an alternative, non-optimal decision with an EMV which is only slightly less than that of the optimal decision. If it also has a much smaller probability of a large loss occurring, then, depending on the decision maker's attitude to risk, this decision might seem more attractive. The possibility is investigated in a later section which considers the validity of the EMV criterion.

To summarise, the task of executing a decision analysis problem can be structured in five stages:

1. Draw the tree.

2. Insert a payoff at the end of each branch.

3. Insert a probability on each branch at a chance node.

4. Roll-back.

5. Summarise the optimal path and draw the risk profile.

THE VALUE OF OBTAINING ADDITIONAL INFORMATION

The basic information provided by decision analysis consists of the optimal path and the risk profile. A typical reaction to this might be, 'Why don't we collect some more information about the problem so that we are a bit more certain that the right decision is being taken?' The extra information could come from many sources: market research, pilot studies, test markets, surveys, etc. Unfortunately they all cost money, so the question arises as to whether the extra information is worth at least as much as it costs.

Fortunately decision analysis is able to give some guidance on the value of extra information. This can be compared with its cost, to make preliminary judgements on whether further market research (or scientific research, or medical trials, etc.) is likely to be worth carrying out. Decision analysis can provide two pieces of information, the *expected value of sample information* (the EVSI) and the *expected value of perfect information* (the EVPI).

Expected value of sample information

The EVSI relates to some *specific* extra information such as a particular piece of market research, or a particular clinical trial. The EVSI is the amount by which the EMV of the decision will increase if this information is available at *zero* cost, i.e. it is the incremental value of the information regardless of what you paid for it. The EVSI is used by comparing it to the *actual* cost of the information to see whether it is worth obtaining. It could also be used in negotiating the price to be paid for the information, for example negotiating with a market research company:

$$\text{EVSI} = \text{EMV with the extra information} - \text{original EMV}$$
$$\text{without the extra information}$$

For instance, in the product launch example:

$$\text{EVSI} = \text{EMV with test market} - \text{EMV without test market}$$

The EMV without the test market is the optimal EMV, 325.

If the test market information had been available at zero cost, the EMV of the test market branch would be 405 (the EMV from the test market branch 305, then adding back the cost of the test market 100, which had previously been subtracted). Therefore:

$$\text{EVSI} = 405 - 325 = 80$$

The average extra payoff which could be expected given the availability of the test market data is thus £80 000, excluding the cost of obtaining the information.

The EVSI gives the *value* of the information. This can then be compared with the *cost* of the information. If some sample (or market or other) information is offered at a price which exceeds its EVSI, it should not be accepted. In the product launch example, the EVSI for the test market is £80 000 compared to its cost of £100 000 and therefore it brings no net benefit.

However, in the product launch example the EVSI is not telling us any more than we already know from the basic decision analysis, since the recommendation was to launch without a test market. As the decision analysis had to be carried through before we could calculate the EVSI, what useful purpose does the EVSI serve? The answer is that the EVSI is a guide to the maximum amount which should be paid for a particular piece of information. If the cost of the test market had not been fixed at £100 000 but could be tailored according to the budget and negotiated with the test market department, then the EVSI would have shown that the information coming from the test market could not possibly be worth more than £80 000 – no more than £80 000 should therefore be paid for it. The EVSI can also be used as financial information in measuring the profitability of market research and other information collection methods.

Expected value of perfect information

Whereas the EVSI measures the worth of a specific piece of information, the EVPI (*the expected value of perfect information*) relates to *any* piece of information. It is the maximum worth of any information in the context of a particular decision. In other words, if all the information you could possibly want in order to take a decision (i.e. perfect information) were available to you, then the EVPI is what it would be worth. It is measured as the amount by which the EMV of the decision would increase if perfect information were available. In the context of decision analysis perfect information means that the decision maker is told the outcome at every chance event node.

$$\text{EVPI} = \text{EMV with perfect information} - \text{original EMV without perfect information}$$

Suppose that in the product launch example, by some magical means, market research was available which could say with certainty what the market for the product would be:

Table 3.3   Response to perfect information

Perfect information says outcome is . . .	Payoff Action	(£'000s)
Strong demand	Launch	1000
Weak demand	Launch	250
Non-existent demand	Abandon	0

this research would be able to say for certain whether the market would be strong, weak or non-existent. The decision maker could then decide to launch or abandon in the light of this perfect information. Table 3.3 shows the action he or she should take in response to perfect information.

By taking the appropriate action suggested by perfect information, the decision maker can increase the EMV.

EMV with perfect information

$$= 1000 \times P(\text{strong}) + 250 \times P(\text{weak}) + 0 \times P(\text{non-existent})$$
$$= 1000 \times 0.5 + 250 \times 0.2 + 0 \times 0.3$$
$$= 550$$

Therefore:

EVPI = EMV with perfect information − EMV without perfect information

$$= 550 - 325$$
$$= 225$$

Perfect information, were it available, would therefore be worth £225 000 in the context of this decision.

A word of caution. When thinking about EVPI it is tempting to believe that 'perfect' guarantees that the best outcome will occur. It does not; it just tells you what will occur, whether good or bad. For the product launch example, perfect information does *not* mean that a strong demand will definitely be the outcome or that a payoff of 1000 will definitely be achieved.

For instance, in the earlier coin example, perfect information would tell you what the outcome of the toss would be, before the coin was tossed. The coin can still land 'heads' or 'tails'. The difference is that the gambler now knows which it is going to be and can take appropriate action. If the perfect information said 'heads', the bet would be accepted and a profit of £5 would result; if the perfect information said 'tails' the bet would be rejected and the profit would be 0. With perfect information there is therefore a 50 per cent chance of making £5 and a 50 per cent chance of making 0, giving an EMV of 2.5 (= 0.5 × 5 + 0.5 × 0) and:

EVPI = EMV with perfect information − EMV without perfect information

$$= 2.5 - 0.5$$
$$= 2.0$$

EVPI is an abstract concept: in practice there is no such thing as truly perfect infor-mation. No market research, or clinical trial, will give 100 per cent correct answers. The value of the concept of EVPI is that it is the *maximum* amount that should be paid for *any* extra information. No survey or market research could possibly give a benefit greater than the EVPI, so if you are offered extra information whose cost exceeds that EVPI, it can be rejected immediately.

In the product launch example, the EVPI is £225 000 and so any market research costing more than this can be rejected immediately. However, since the test market costs £100 000, it cannot be rejected out of hand. Unlike the EVSI, the EVPI cannot be calculated without going through the whole decision analysis process and so, to see whether the test market is worth doing, the decision tree has to be drawn, the EVSI calculated and then compared to the cost.

In the coin example the EVPI was £2. Therefore the maximum it would be worth bribing the 'independent' coin tosser would be £2.

To summarise, the EVPI measures the maximum value of any extra information and can be used to make a preliminary decision to rule out types of information-collecting exercise whose cost exceeds the EVPI. The EVSI measures the value of a specific set of information and can be used to decide what to pay for that information and to provide information on research profitability.

VALIDITY OF THE EMV CRITERION

The criterion used to choose between different decision options has been expected monetary value (EMV). The selection of the 'best' branch at each decision node was made by eliminating all branches except the one with the highest EMV. In very many situations this is the appropriate thing to do. EMV picks the option which, if the situation were repeated many times, would on average be the most favourable. Since most organisations are taking decisions all the time, it makes sense to do as well as possible 'on average', even though there may be losses from time to time. However, there are situations which are not like this and for which EMV is not suitable.

Suppose, in the coin example, that the payoffs were £5 million and £4 million, instead of £5 and £4. And suppose the bet was to be offered to you only once. Is the EMV criterion still appropriate? With the stakes increased a millionfold the EMV of the bet becomes £500 000 instead of 50p. The EMV criterion still recommends that the bet should be accepted: £0.5 million for accepting is preferable to the alternative of zero. In spite of this EMV recommendation, you, as the decision maker, may not want to accept. Whereas you may be able to absorb a loss of £4 quite easily, the 50 per cent chance of losing £4 million on a one-off bet may be too much for you to consider, even alongside the 50 per cent chance of gaining £5 million and in the knowledge that, on average, you would profit from acceptance. When very large payoffs are involved and/or when a decision is to be taken only once, EMV may not be an acceptable criterion to a decision maker.

The existence of payoffs which are large in relation to the bank balance of the person or organisation and which are unique in the context of the normal decisions being taken is the most usual circumstance which may rule out the EMV criterion. EMV's 'averaging out' process can mask sizeable negative payoffs, especially when they have low probabilities. For most individuals and organisations there will always be situations which have outcomes so catastrophic that they cannot be contemplated, however unlikely they may be.

For example, in the new product launch example, there could have been a fourth outcome for the 'launch' decision: a 0.1 per cent chance of losing £10 million (in a lawsuit, perhaps). This only reduces the optimal EMV by £10 000, a negligible amount in the context of the decision and one which does not alter the decision to 'launch'. However, if a loss of £10 million could put the company into receivership then the decision maker might prefer another option, if it exists, with a slightly lower EMV but with no risk of losing £10 million. In short, most decision makers, whether corporate or individual, have ranges of payoffs for which they do not and will not behave as 'EMV decision makers'.

The sizeable payoff with the low probability does not have to be negative – it may be positive. This is what persuades people to gamble on horse racing, football pools and national lotteries. The EMV of a decision to bet £1 on a national lottery is negative, since the total stake money contributes to expenses, overheads, profits and charity contributions. The EMV decision would be to refuse the bet. This, however, is not the gambler's perspective. The gambler argues that while he or she can afford to lose £1 without really noticing it, the bet carries a very small chance of winning an obscenely large amount of money which would radically transform his or her lifestyle, supposedly for the better, in a way that nothing else could possibly do. So bets are placed and national lotteries, football pools and so on are enormously successful.

To deal with this issue, a check should always be made that the optimal EMV decision does not conceal any catastrophies or not-to-be-missed opportunities. This is one of the major reasons for a risk profile always being drawn to accompany the basic results of the decision analysis.

The risk profile also serves a slightly different purpose. Most decisions involve some tradeoff between risk and return, possible losses against payoffs. In decision analysis this balancing act is helped by the the risk profile. Aside from the 'catastrophic loss' situation, there are times when a particular decision maker will prefer an option with a slightly lower EMV if it has a better risk profile. For example, an option with a lower EMV may carry a significantly lower chance of making a loss of any size. Even if the loss is a small one, it may come at a time when it is important for the company or decision maker *not* to be seen to be making a loss, for example when the stock market needs to be shown an especially strong profit and loss account. For example, compare Tables 3.4a (a repeat of Table 3.2) and 3.4b, showing the risk profiles of the 'launch' and 'test market' options in the product launch example.

The cost of the test market, £100 000, has been subtracted from the payoffs in Table 3.4b.

The probabilities of the outcomes in Table 3.4b have been calculated using the multi-

Table 3.4a   Risk profile (optimal)

Outcome	Payoff (£'000s)	Probability (%)
Strong demand	1000	50
Weak demand	250	20
Non-existent demand	−750	30
	Total =	100%

Chance of loss = 30%
Chance of heavy loss = 30%

Table 3.4b   Risk profile (non-optimal)

Outcome	Payoff (£'000s)	Probability (%)
Favourable test:		
Stong demand	900	42 (= 60% × 70%)
Weak demand	150	12 (= 60% × 20%)
Non-existent	−850	6 (= 60% × 10%)
Unfavourable test	−100	40
		Total = 100%

Chance of loss = 46%
Chance of heavy loss = 6%

plication law of probabilities. For two events, A and B:

$$P(A \text{ and } B) = P(A) \times P(B|A)$$

where $P(B|A)$ is the 'conditional' probability of B given the occurrence of A, i.e. the probability of B occurring when it is known that A has already occurred.

Applying the multiplication law to the product launch example, with A being a favourable test market result and B being a strong post-launch market for the product:

P(favourable test and strong market)

$$= P(\text{favourable test}) \times P(\text{strong market/given favourable test})$$

$$= 0.6 \times 0.70$$

$$= 0.42$$

The original decision analysis gave 'launch' an EMV of 325, and 'test market' an EMV of 305. After consideration of the risk profiles, 'launch' may no longer be the preferred option. Although the chance of a loss under 'launch' is lower than for 'test market' (30 per cent vs 46 per cent), the chance of the heavy loss stemming from a non-existent market is much higher (30 per cent vs 6 per cent). There are some risk-averse decision makers who would be willing to exchange the higher EMV in return for this lower risk of a heavy loss. In spite of all the numbers and calculations, there is no 'right' decision because it depends on the preferences of the decision maker.

In general, when the optimal decision has an EMV only slightly higher than alternative options, the risk profiles of some non-optimal decisions should be investigated.

As you might expect, EMV is not the only decision-making criterion which can be used. Another possibility is *maximin*. This criterion is based on choosing the decision option which has the following characteristic: the worst possible outcome which could result from the decision is better than the worst possible outcomes of all other decision options. At each decision node under maximin the branch chosen is the one for which the worst payoff which could result from the decision is best of all the worst payoffs which could result from any of the other branches leaving the node; hence max-i-min.

In the product launch example, maximin means that 'abandon' will be selected. The 'launch' payoff has a worst payoff of −750, 'test market' has a worst payoff of −850, whereas 'abandon' has a worst payoff of 0. 'Abandon' is therefore the maximin selection, having the best, worst payoff. Maximin is a criterion for the totally risk averse decision maker and for situations where caution is the prime requirement.

In other situations opportunity losses may be a crucial element in the decision equation. For example, allocating senior marketing management time to the product launch might mean that, at least in the short term, other profitable activities have to be shelved occasioning opportunity losses. It might then be more appropriate to think of the problem in terms of reductions in overall company profits, and measure payoffs accordingly, rather than in terms of profits from the new product alone. The criterion would then be *expected opportunity loss* (EOL), calculated by multiplying the 'lost profit' payoffs by the corresponding probabilities, just as EMVs are calculated from profit payoffs. At each decision node the option with the lowest EOL would be chosen.

Maximin and EOL are just two of the alternatives to EMV. However, EMV is the criterion which would normally be used, with the reservation that it is important to watch out for extreme outcomes, whether unacceptably disastrous or temptingly attractive.

CONCLUSION

Like other quantitative techniques, decision analysis must be regarded as an aid to decision making, not a substitute for it. All the calculations and numbers to several decimal places can be misleading in the sense of making it seem that the results are more accurate than they are and can be taken at face value. The techniques are simply methods for putting the available information into some sort of order – for making the chaos slightly less chaotic. They cannot capture every nuance of messy real-world decision problems and errors will be made if it is assumed that the techniques are providing perfect models of actual situations.

On the other hand many managers, perhaps feeling unconfident of their quantitative skills, reject their use completely, on the grounds that since they are merely approximations of reality, they cannot be of any use at all. This is 'throwing the baby out with the bathwater'. Properly applied, decision techniques can reflect the most important features of actual situations and can therefore provide a decision maker with valuable help.

As an aid to decision making, decision analysis should be used in conjunction with other decision aids which might be totally non-quantitative – perceptions, opinions, judgements and so on. And it should always be asked to pass common-sense tests and checks. Is the decision tree an accurate model of the decisions faced? Does it represent all the possible options available? How much faith can be put in the probability estimates? Do the reservations about the EMV criterion apply in this case? Only when the assumptions which have permitted the use of decision analysis are realistic can the recommendations be accepted at face value; otherwise the recommendations should be regarded as giving some guidance as to the final decision.

Sensitivity analysis should also be on the common-sense manager's agenda. This means repeating the decision analysis, each time varying those assumptions which appear to be the most doubtful or the most important in terms of the decision recommended. This is best done by computer and many good software packages are available. Decision analysis calculations are generally very simple for computers. The main problem is drawing the diagrams. Even today it is hard to find packages which can display decision trees adequately. Because trees come in varying sizes their on-screen representation is usually cramped.

Sensitivity analysis will demonstrate an important characteristic of the optimal decision: its *robustness*. A robust solution to a decision problem is one for which the optimal decision does not change, at least for small variations in the assumptions and data.

Sensitivity analysis will usually involve the probabilities of the chance events, since they are the part of the technique generally regarded with most suspicion by pragmatists. This is especially true when the probabilities have been measured by subjective assessment. However, subjective probability assessment is not just guesswork and methods of making the estimates as accurate as possible are described in the next chapter. Nevertheless, it is the idea of subjectively assessed probabilities which gives cynics most scope to exercise their cynicism – often with the result that the decision maker reverts to using a few untried hunches and prejudices which have no validity.

In the product launch example the market demands were *discrete*, meaning that they were represented as distinct levels of demand (three of them: strong, weak, non-existent). However, decision analysis can handle continuous distributions. For example, the outcome of the product launch could have been specified by a continuous distribution such as the normal distribution rather than the discrete payoffs. This extension to the technique will also be described in the next chapter.

The most important contribution of decision analysis, however, is not one of the benefits mentioned above. Even when the technique is not carried through to a recommendation of an optimal path and a risk profile, or if the recommendation is ignored by the decision maker, it will still have served a useful purpose. If you are to carry out a decision analysis, you can only do so if you have first acquired a comprehensive understanding of the structure of the decision, of the full range of options and of the true sequence and logical relationships between sub-decisions and chance events. The process of drawing the tree and calculating payoffs and probabilities will therefore have given the decision maker a fuller appreciation of the problem. For example, in many practical situations decision analysis has led to the realisation that there are more options (paths through the tree) than were originally thought, or that the options were available in different sequences than originally supposed. By whatever means the ultimate decision is reached, it should have come about based on a fuller understanding of the nature of the problem.

CASES STUDIES

CASE STUDY 1

An armaments manufacturer is deciding whether to embark on a major project, the development of a new large gun. If the gun is to be a commercial success, it must use computer software linked to radar for targeting and firing. It must also be ready for sale before the product of a rival manufacturer. The R and D Group has estimated that there is a 70 per cent chance that the necessary software can be developed on time. If so, the overall payoff of the project is a profit with a present value of £100 million. A second possibility is that the software's capabilities have to be reduced in order to be ready on time. In this case limited sales would be made and the profit of the project would be

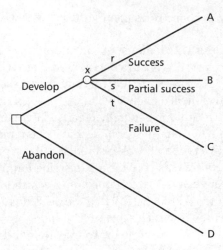

Figure 3.9

reduced to £20 million. The probability of this outcome is 10 per cent. A third possibility is that even a limited version of the software is not ready on time. Then the project would make a loss of £40 million. The decision tree representing the decision to go ahead is shown in Figure 3.9.

1. What are the payoffs at the ends of each branch of the tree, the points A, B, C and D, assuming that sunk costs have been ignored?

2. What are the probabilities on the branches marked r, s and t?

3. What is the expected monetary value at the chance node X?

4. What decision should be taken and what is its expected monetary value?

5. What is the expected value of perfect information?

Solutions

1. *What are the payoffs at the ends of each branch of the tree, the points A, B, C and D, assuming that sunk costs have been ignored?*
The payoffs are: A = 100, B = 20, C = −40, D = 0.
   A represents a fully successful project (£100 million profit), B a partial success (£20 million), C a failure (a loss of £40 million). D is zero because this is the payoff for not attempting the project, ignoring sunk costs.

2. *What are the probabilities on the branches marked r, s and t?*
The probabilities are r = 0.7, s = 0.1, t = 0.2.
   The probability that effective software will be developed on time is given as 70 per cent, hence r = 0.7. Likewise the probability of partially effective software is given as 10 per cent, therefore s = 0.1. The only other possibility is that the project fails and so the remaining probability, t, must be 0.2 (= 1.0 − 0.7 − 0.1).

3. *What is the expected monetary value at the chance node X?*
EMV = 64.

$$\text{EMV at chance node X} = (100 \times 0.7) + (20 \times 0.1) - (40 \times 0.2)$$
$$= 70 + 2 - 8$$
$$= 64$$

4. *What decision should be taken and what is its expected monetary value?*
The correct decision is 'develop' and the EMV = 64.

The decision node at the first point of the tree presents the choice between 'develop' with an EMV of 64 and 'abandon' with an EMV of 0.

5. *What is the expected value of perfect information?*
EVPI = 8.

Perfect information would say whether the outcome was effective software, partially effective software or failure.

Information	Action	Payoff	Probability
Effective	Develop	100	0.7
Partial	Develop	20	0.1
Failure	Abandon	0	0.2

Expected value of project with perfect information

$$= (100 \times 0.7) + (20 \times 0.1) + (0 \times 0.2)$$
$$= 70 + 2 + 0$$
$$= 72$$

To find the expected value of perfect information, the expected value of the project without perfect information must be subtracted from this amount, i.e. EVPI = 72 − 64 = 8

CASE STUDY 2

An electrical company has to decide whether to develop a new type of security device. If it does go ahead, successful completion depends on a research breakthrough. There is thought to be a 60 per cent chance of achieving the breakthrough. If the device is successfully developed, the payoff is a profit of £900 000; if development is attempted but not completed, there will be a loss of £400 000. All overheads and other sunk costs should be ignored. The decision tree is shown in Figure 3.10.

1. What are the payoffs at the end of the three branches (points X, Y and Z)?

2. What is the EMV of the whole decision?

3. Does 'perfect information' mean that the payoff of 900 would certainly be achieved?

4. What is the expected value of perfect information?

Solutions

1. *What are the payoffs at the end of the three branches (points X, Y and Z)?*
The payoffs at X and Y are 900 and −400, in respect of successful and non-successful

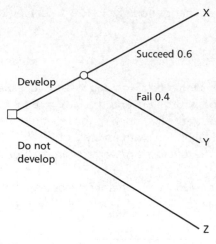

Figure 3.10

development of the device. Since costs are ignored, the payoff for not developing the device, point Z, is 0.

2.   *What is the EMV of the whole decision?*

$$\text{EMV at B} = (0.6 \times 900) + (0.4 \times -400)$$
$$= 540 - 160$$
$$= 380$$

3.   *Does 'perfect information' mean that the payoff of 900 would certainly be achieved?*
No. Perfect information tells what the outcome will be (either successful development or failure). It does not force the best possibility (successful development, a payoff of 900) to occur.

4.   *What is the expected value of perfect information?*
Perfect information will say whether or not the development, if attempted, would be successful. If the development would be successful, then the correct action would be to develop the device and make a profit of 900. There is a 60 per cent probability that perfect information would say this. There would be a 40 per cent chance of the perfect information saying that the development would not be successful. In this case the correct action would be not to attempt the development and the payoff would be zero.

$$\text{EVPI} = \text{EMV with perfect information} - \text{EMV without perfect information}$$
$$= (0.6 \times 900) + (0.4 \times 0) - 380$$
$$= 540 + 0 - 380$$
$$= 160$$

CASE STUDY 3

The main activity of a specialist electrical engineering consulting company is to act as coordinator on large international projects. A client, usually a government, specifies a project

Table 3.5

Project	Value (£ million)
A Aircraft tracking system	25
B Buildings security	80
C Conservation of fuel	200

and then hands it over to the company, which then brings together a team of subcontractors to carry out the project according to the specified standards, price and time schedule. The company itself rarely does any of the work.

The advantage to the client is that it deals in the main with only one company instead of several. Nor does the client have to handle the technical details and complex liaisons that such projects usually involve. In return, the client pays the company a commission which is a percentage of the total value of the project. If the company fails to bring together an appropriate team of subcontractors to meet the client's specifications then it receives no payment.

Recently the company has been trying to expand its overseas business and now has an opportunity to work for an African government which has specified three projects (Table 3.5). The project's 'value' is the total cost of the project, according to the government's budget.

Internal political pressures have made the government in question wary of dealing with Western companies. It is important that there are no slip-ups and it has laid down the following conditions:

> Project A is to be coordinated first. If a satisfactory team cannot be assembled within six months, the company must drop out without having a chance to coordinate projects B and C. On the other hand, if the company is successful with A, it will collect its commission and have the option to stop or to try to coordinate a second project under the same conditions (i.e. assemble a team within six months or no commission and no option to coordinate the remaining project). If it meets with success on the two projects it has the option to try to coordinate the third. The fee for any project successfully coordinated will be 10 per cent of the project's value.

This was an unusual offer and the company's board wondered what it meant. It was the marketing director's job to analyse the proposal. He estimated all the relevant costs of trying to coordinate the projects as well as the chances of being successful (Table 3.6). The projects differed greatly as to the nature of the expertise involved, requiring different subcontractors, and so the view was that successfully coordinating one project would not make the successful coordination of the other two any more or less likely. Of course, the costs incurred

Table 3.6

Project	Cost (£ million)	Probabilities Success	Failure
A	2.0	0.5	0.5
B	1.5	0.7	0.3
C	1.0	0.6	0.4

Table 3.7

Event	Probability	Payoff (£ million)
A successfully coordinated	0.5	0.5
A not coordinated	0.5	−2.0
Expected value = (0.5 × 0.5) − (0.5 × 2.0) = −0.75		

by the consultancy would be the same whether or not teams were successfully assembled. Naturally no costs would be incurred on a project if the company did not attempt to coordinate it.

Project A was the key since it would have to be coordinated successfully before either B or C could be attempted, so the marketing director prepared a table showing profit/loss possibilities for this project alone (Table 3.7).

Thus, based on expected value, project A would be unprofitable, losing on average £750 000. However, success with Project A would return more than just commission. It would provide the opportunity to attempt either B or C next, both of which have lower associated costs and higher commissions.

1. What recommendations should be made to the board?

2. What is the expected value of perfect information to the company?

Solutions

1. *What recommendations should be made to the board?*
Follow the five stages of a decision analysis problem. The stages are illustrated in Figure 3.11.

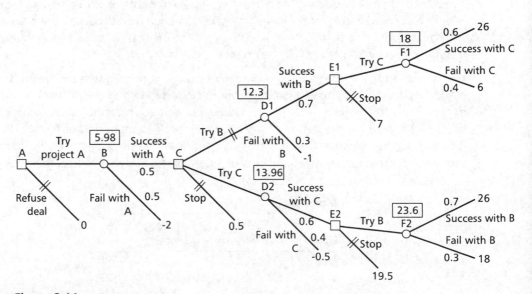

Figure 3.11

Table 3.8

Project	Cost if attempted (£ million)	Commission if successful (£ million)
A	2.0	2.5
B	1.5	8.0
C	1.0	20.0

Stage 1 Draw the tree

The initial decision (node A) is to go ahead with project A or not. If the company is unsuccessful (at node B), everything comes to an end. If successful, there is a decision to be made at node C. Careful reading of the problem reveals what might not have been obvious from a less analytical approach: that either Project B *or* Project C can be attempted next if Project A is successfully accomplished. The company also has the option to stop at this point.

If Project B is attempted after Project A, then chance node D1 represents the outcome. Again, failure brings everything to an end. Success at D1 brings the option (at node E1) to stop or to proceed with Project C. Node F1 represents success or failure with Project C.

If Project C is attempted after A, the tree has the same structure as above but with Projects B and C interchanged. The nodes are at D2, E2 and F2.

Stage 2 Insert probabilities

The probabilities are given in the case information.

Stage 3 Insert payoffs

The calculations of the payoffs are shown in Table 3.8, the commission being calculated as 10 per cent of the value of the project.

The payoffs for the branch ends are calculated as below.

Initial part of tree:
Refuse deal: 0
Attempt A, but fail: -2.0
Succeed with A, then stop: $2.5 - 2.0 = 0.5$

Upper section of tree:

Succeed with A but fail with B: $2.5 - 2.0 - 1.5 = -1.0$
Succeed with A and B, then stop: $2.5 - 2.0 - 1.5 + 8.0 = 7.0$
Succeed A, B, fail with C: $2.5 - 2.0 - 1.5 + 8.0 - 1.0 = 6.0$
Succeed with all three: $2.5 - 2.0 - 1.5 + 8.0 - 1.0 + 20.0 = 26.0$

Lower section of tree:
Succeed with A but fail with C: $2.5 - 2.0 - 1.0 = -0.5$
Succeed with A and C, then stop: $2.5 - 2.0 - 1.0 + 20.0 = 19.5$
Succeed A, C, fail with B: $2.5 - 2.0 - 1.0 + 20.0 - 1.5 = 18.0$
Succeed all three: 26 as before.

Stage 4 The roll-back

The roll-back starts with the chance node F 1 and works back to decision node A.

$$\text{At Fl: EMV} = (0.6 \times 26) + (0.4 \times 6)$$
$$= 15.6 + 2.4$$
$$= 18.0$$

At E1: Eliminate the 'stop' option.

$$\text{At Dl: EMV} = (0.7 \times 18) - (0.3 \times 1)$$
$$= 12.6 - 0.3$$
$$= 12.3$$

No decision can be taken at C unless the roll-back goes forward again to F2 and works back to C through the lower section.

$$\text{At F2: EMV} = (0.7 \times 26) + (0.3 \times 18)$$
$$= 18.2 + 5.4$$
$$= 23.6$$

At E2: Eliminate the 'stop' option.

$$\text{At D2: EMV} = (0.6 \times 23.6) - (0.4 \times 0.5)$$
$$= 14.16 - 0.2$$
$$= 13.96$$

Now the decision at C can be taken and the roll-back can continue to the initial decision node A.

At C: Eliminate the 'stop' and 'try B' options.

$$\text{At B: EMV} = (0.5 \times 13.96) - (0.5 \times 2)$$
$$= 5.98$$

At A: Eliminate the 'refuse' option.

Stage 5 Summarise the optimal path and draw the risk profile

The optimal path is: attempt project A. If successful, attempt Project C. If successful, attempt Project B. Failure at any stage brings matters to a halt. The expected profit is £5.98 million.

The risk profile, in descending order of payoff, is as in Table 3.9.

The probabilities are calculated using the multiplication law. The probability of success or failure of a project is not affected by the success or failure of projects attempted earlier. For example:

$$P(\text{success A, C; failure B})$$
$$= P(\text{success A}) \times P(\text{success C}|\text{success A}) \times P(\text{failure B}|\text{success A,C})$$
$$= P(\text{success A}) \times P(\text{success C}) \times P(\text{failure B})$$

Table 3.9

Outcome	Payoff	Probability
Success: all 3 projects	26.0	$0.21(= 0.5 \times 0.6 \times 0.7)$
Success A, C; failure B	18.0	$0.09(= 0.5 \times 0.6 \times 0.3)$
Success A; failure C	−0.5	$0.20(= 0.5 \times 0.4)$
Fail with A	−2.0	0.50
		1.00

$$= 0.5 \times 0.6 \times 0.3$$
$$= 0.09$$

From these probabilities the chances of finally making a profit or a loss can be calculated. There is a 30 per cent chance of making a profit, a 70 per cent chance of making a loss. However, the size of the losses are very small compared to the profits.

2.   *What is the expected value of perfect information?*
Perfect information would say which projects would be successfully coordinated and which not. There are eight possibilities: (success/fail A) combined with (success/fail B) combined with (success/fail C), i.e. $2 \times 2 \times 2 = 8$ possibilities.

Perfect information does not, of course, recognise the limitations imposed by the tree. For example, perfect information might say: failure with A, success with B and C, not recognising that if project A fails then it is not possible to attempt B and C. The best response of the decision maker to each of these possibilities is shown in Table 3.10.

Table 3.10

Perfect information says:	Action	Payoff	Probability
Success A, B, C	Try all three	26.0	0.21
Success A, C, Fail B	Try A, try C, then stop	19.5	0.09
Success A, B, Fail C	Try A, try B, then stop	7.0	0.14
Success A, Fail B, C	Try A, then stop	0.5	0.06
Fail A with any B,C result	Do not start	0	0.5
		Total	1.00

The probabilities of the outcomes shown in the table are calculated, as before, from the multiplication law.

EMV with perfect information
$$= (0.21 \times 26) + (0.09 \times 19.5) + (0.14 \times 7) + (0.06 \times 0.5) \times (0.5 \times 0)$$
$$= 5.46 + 1.755 + 0.98 + 0.03 + 0$$
$$= 8.225$$

EVPI = EMV with perfect information − EMV without perfect information
$$= 8.225 − 5.98$$
$$= 2.245$$

The maximum that should be paid for any additional information is £2.245 million.

QUESTIONS

1. A manufacturing company is in the process of deciding whether to build a new production plant. If it decides to go ahead then it has to decide whether to build on a greenfield site or to rebuild and extend an existing plant. How should these decisions be represented on a decision tree?

2. A building site is being excavated prior to development. The cost of the development is uncertain because of geological problems but the following estimates have been made: 30 per cent probability of £6 million, 30 per cent probability of £3 million, 40 per cent probability of £1 million. What is the expected value of the cost?

3. What is the EMV at point A in Figure 3.12?

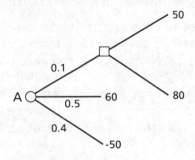

Figure 3.12

4. A bus and coach company is deciding whether to continue its present in-house maintenance function or to contract it to an outside company. A third option is to commission a consultant's report at a cost of £20 000 to provide additional information before making a decision. A decision analysis has resulted in an expected annual cost of maintenance under each option:

Option	Expected cost
1 Continue in-house	£235 000
2 Contract out	£190 000
3 Commission report	£175 000

The expected cost of the third option excludes the cost of the consultant's report.

(a) Which option should be selected?
(b) What is the expected value of sample information?

5. A national driving school renews its fleet of cars every two years. By replacing half of the entire fleet at the same time one year and half at the same time the next it can secure massive discounts on the purchase prices. The size of the present fleet is 1000 cars. The managing director is aware that the number of customers the school has and the frequency with which they take lessons fluctuates according to the economic climate.

Depending on economic factors, therefore, the size of the next fleet might have to be different from the present one.

His planning department has estimated that if he increases the fleet and buys 1200 cars he could earn a profit of £40 million in the next two years given an economic upswing, a profit of £24 million if things stay as they are, and he could lose £16 million if there is a recession. If he buys 1000 cars (keeping the fleet at its present strength), the profit is estimated to be respectively £30 million, £20 million and £12 million. Decreasing the fleet size and buying only 800 cars would earn £20 million, £18 million and £16 million respectively.

He estimates the probability of an economic upswing at 0.5, of staying level at 0.3 and of recession at 0.2.

(a) How many cars should the firm purchase?

(b) The managing director is aware that he can purchase a survey by a well-known economic forecasting team which will give him a clearer picture of economic prospects. What is the maximum he should pay for it?

6. A regional television company has just received details of a new idea for a situation comedy from one of its most successful scriptwriters. The company has now to decide whether to go ahead with a series of eight programmes based on the idea. New comedy series are thought to be risky propositions and the probability of the series being unsuccessful has been estimated to be as high as 75 per cent. Were the series unsuccessful, there would of course be no further series and the company would suffer a net loss of £1 000 000.

On the other hand, if the series were successful the company would go on to make a second series. The probability of this second series failing after a successful first series has been estimated to be 50 per cent. If this were the case no further series would be made and, over the two series, the net profit to the company would be £400 000.

A successful second series would bring the company the option of making a feature film and video for the cinema circuit. This option has the potential for extremely high profits. Three possibilities could arise if a feature film and video were made:

Outcome	Payoff (£ million)	Probability (%)
Major success	50	20
Minor success	5	50
Flop	−15	30

If the feature film option were rejected, the programme could still be continued for several more series, bringing a total net profit, including the first two series, of £6 million.

(a) Should the company go ahead with a series?

(b) If the optimal decision path is followed, what is the probability that the company will make a net loss?

(c) The company has a third initial option. It could make a pilot programme of this situation comedy. The purpose of a pilot programme would be to gain a preliminary indication of whether a series of programmes is likely to be successful. The net cost of a pilot would be £250 000. The probability of its being successful is 40 per cent. This is higher than the probability (25 per cent) of a series being successful, since it is thought that there would be a higher chance of a single programme being favourably received than a full series. If the pilot were unsuccessful, no series would be made and the project would be abandoned. If the pilot were successful, the company has a choice. The idea and the pilot could be sold to another television company to develop. It is thought that a price of £1.5 million could be obtained. Or the company could make a series as before. The options and payoffs (apart from the cost of the pilot) would then be the same as when no pilot is made. However, a successful pilot increases the probability of a successful series to 50 per cent. Should the company go ahead with a pilot?

(d) With respect to the pilot, what is the expected value of sample information?
(e) How do non-optimal alternatives compare with the optimal path in terms of EMV and risk? (i.e. compare the risk profile for the optimal path with those for options which are non-optimal but which have EMVs fairly close to that of the optimal path).

ANSWERS TO QUESTIONS

1. The representations in Figures 3.13 and 3.14 are both correct. The logic of both is the same and either version can be used. It is not necessary for the sequence of sub-decisions and chance events to be strictly decision/chance/decision/chance etc. If it is clearer, two (or more) nodes of the same type can be adjacent.

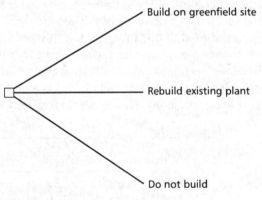

Figure 3.13

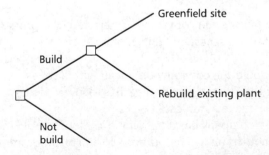

Figure 3.14

2.   The expected value of the cost is £3.1 million.

3.   The EMV is 18.

4.   (a) The best option is to 'contract out'.
     (b) The EVSI is £15 000.

5.   (a) The optimal decision is to buy 1200 cars.
     (b) The maximum that the managing director should pay for extra information is the EVPI, £6.4 million, considerably more than any consultants are likely to charge.

6.   (a) The optimal path is to make a first series of these comedy programmes. If it is successful a second series will always be made. If two series have been successful, the option to make a feature film should be chosen.
     (b) A loss can occur either through a film flop or through an unsuccessful first series. The chances of making a loss are 78.75 per cent.
     (c) The optimal path is to make a pilot; if successful, a series should be made; if two series are successful, the option of a feature film should be taken up.
     (d) The expected value of the pilot is £340 000.
     (e) The option of selling a successful pilot might well be preferred in spite of its lower EMV. For a slightly lower EMV, the option carries a much lower probability of a loss and no chance at all of a high loss. On the other hand, the sell option carries no chance of making a really high profit. Some decision makers might prefer an option just because there is a chance of a high profit.

APPENDIX: PROBABILITY

All future events are uncertain to some degree. That the present Italian government will still be in power in a month's time is likely, but far from certain; that a communist government will be in power in a month's time is highly unlikely, but not impossible. Probability theory enables the difference in the uncertainty of events to be made more precise by measuring their likelihood on a scale. Probability is the means by which we can assess the accuracy of a forecast.

Impossible	Evens	Certain
0	0.5	1
Lifting oneself by one's own bootlaces	A new-born baby being male	There will be at least one car accident in Milan next year

Figure 3.15   Probability scale

The scale is shown in Figure 3.15. At one extreme, impossible events (e.g. that you could swim the Atlantic) have probability zero. At the other extreme, completely certain events (that you will one day die) have probability one. In between are placed all the neither certain nor impossible events according to their likelihood. For instance, the probability of obtaining a head on one spin of an unbiased coin is $\frac{1}{2}$; the probability of one particular ticket winning a lottery in which there are 100 tickets in total is 0.01.

As a shorthand notation, 'the probability of an event A is 0.6' is written in this way:

$$P(A) = 0.6$$

Measurement of probability

There are three methods of calculating a probability. The methods are not alternatives, since for most events only one particular method of measurement will be possible. However, they do provide different conceptual ways of viewing probability. This should become clear as the methods are described.

'A priori' approach

In this method the probability of an event is calculated by a process of logic. No experiment or judgement is required. Probabilities involving coins, dice, playing cards, etc. can fall into this category. For example, the two sides of a coin may be labelled 'heads' and 'tails'. The probability of a coin landing 'heads' can be calculated by noting that the coin has 2 sides, both of which are equally likely to fall upwards (we must assume it will not come to rest on its rim). Since the coin must fall with one side upwards, the two events must share equally the total probability of 1.0. Therefore:

$$P(Heads) = 0.5$$
$$P(Tails) = 0.5$$

'Relative frequency' approach

When the event has been or can be repeated a large number of times, its probability can be measured from the formula:

$$P(\text{event}) = \frac{\text{number of times event occurs}}{\text{number of trials}}$$

For example, to estimate the probability of rain on a given day in April in Paris, look at the last 10 years' records to find that it rained on 57 days. Then:

$$P(\text{rain}) = \frac{\text{number of days rain recorded}}{\text{total number of days } (= 10 \times 30)}$$

$$= \frac{57}{300}$$

$$= 0.19$$

Subjective approach

A certain group of statisticians (Bayesians) would argue that the degree of belief which an individual has about a particular event may be expressed as a probability. Bayesian statisticians argue that in certain circumstances a person's subjective assessment of probability can and should be used. The traditional view, held by classical statisticians, is that only objective probability assessments are permissible. All it is important to know is that probabilities can be assessed subjectively, but that there is discussion among statisticians as to the validity of doing so.

As an example of the subjective approach, let the event be the achievement of political unity in Europe by the year 2010. There is no way that either of the first two approaches could be employed to calculate this probability. However, an individual can express his or her own feelings on the likelihood of this event by comparing it with an event of known probability, e.g. is it more or less likely than obtaining a head on the spin of a coin? After a long process of comparison and checking, the result might be:

$$P(\text{political unity in Europe by the year 2010}) = 0.10$$

The process of assessing a subjective probability accurately is a field of study in its own right and should not be regarded as pure guesswork.

The three methods of determining probabilities have been presented here as an introduction and the approach has not been rigorous. Once probabilities have been calculated by whatever method, they are treated in exactly the same way.

Examples

1. What is the probability of throwing a 6 with one throw of a die?
   A priori approach – there are 6 possible outcomes: 1, 2, 3, 4, 5 or 6 showing.
   All outcomes are equally likely, therefore:

$$P(\text{throwing a 6}) = \frac{1}{6}$$

2. What is the probability of a second channel tunnel for road vehicles being completed by the year 2025?
   The subjective approach is the only one possible, since logical thought alone cannot lead to an answer and there are no past observations. My assessment is a small one, around 0.02.

3. How would you calculate the probability of obtaining a head on one spin of a biased coin?
   The a priori approach may be possible if one had information on the aerodynamical behaviour

of the coin. A more realistic method would be to conduct several trial spins and count the number of times a head appeared:

$$P(\text{obtaining a head}) = \frac{\text{number of observed heads}}{\text{number of trial spins}}$$

4. What is the probability of drawing an ace in one cut of a pack of playing cards?

   Use the a priori method. There are 52 possible outcomes (one for each card in the deck) and the probability of picking any one card, say the ace of diamonds, must therefore be 1/52. There are 4 aces in the deck, hence:

$$P(\text{drawing an ace}) = \frac{4}{52} = \frac{1}{13}$$

CHAPTER FOUR

Advanced decision analysis

This chapter extends the scope of decision analysis. It does so in three ways. First, it explains how continuous probability distributions can be incorporated into the technique. Secondly, it looks in more detail at the question of estimating subjective probabilities, so often the cause of concern to management users. Thirdly, it shows how probabilities can be revised when new information becomes available. The chapter should equip you to handle the majority of decision analysis problems.

INTRODUCTION

The one feature of decision analysis which seems to give managers and new users of the technique a sense of unease is the probabilities of chance events, and in particular the way they are obtained. Strangely, accounting data, which some might think should also be subject to careful scrutiny, is usually accepted without question. Probabilities give rise to two main problems.

The first is that direct and precise statements of probabilities, 10 per cent, 15 per cent and so on, seem uncomfortably explicit. Numbers, when written down in reports, can be challenged and subjective probabilities are easier to challenge than most. It does not matter that, in making instinctive judgements and decisions, managers are likely to use the same probabilities implicitly. For example, the marketing manager who makes plans based on hunches about how big the demand for a particular product could be next year is implicitly assessing the likelihood (or probability) of different market sizes. The point is that, as political animals, most managers would like to keep certain things covered up. Having to justify probabilities in a management meeting could cause embarrassment. This whole issue is a long-term problem, to do with the non-quantitative styles of many Western managers. As more and more managers have personal computers on their desks the problem is receding, albeit slowly.

The second problem is more rational. There will inevitably be some doubt whether a particular event has a probability of, say, 10 per cent or 20 per cent. If the optimal decision is the same whichever probability is used, then it does not matter too much. On the other hand, the decision maker may be aware instinctively, and sensitivity analysis can verify systematically, that the optimal decision will change if the probability is 20 per cent instead of 10 per cent. The fact that the optimal decision is so highly dependent on one probability is valuable information, since it suggests that the decision problem has no clear-cut answer. It also indicates the area where further data gathering would be valuable. Resources in the form of, for example, market research, additional staff or finances may be required in order to reduce the uncertainty. Or such sensitivity may point to the need for delay.

The question remains, however, as to whether there are methods by which probabilities can be estimated or calculated sufficiently accurately to point to 10 per cent rather than 20 per cent. How can we have greater confidence in the probability estimate? This chapter attempts to do this by dealing with three aspects of probability assessment. The first is that of continuous probability distributions. So far in decision analysis the outcomes of chance events have been described in terms of discrete probabilities, for example, 50 per cent chance of a strong demand, 20 per cent of a weak, 30 per cent of non-existent. Chance events which have outcomes with *continuous probabilities* can also be incorporated into the technique. Secondly, *systematic methods* of making a subjective estimate of an event's probability are described, demonstrating that subjective probabilities are a matter of scientific methodology, not merely wild guesses. Finally, the chapter will deal with *Bayesian revision*. When additional information about an event becomes available, the probabilities associated with it are likely to change. For instance, market research information will change the probabilities of success or failure for a new consumer product. The method by which these changes can be calculated is called Bayes theorem. Hence the alteration of probabilities is usually referred to as Bayesian revision.

CONTINUOUS PROBABILITY DISTRIBUTIONS

The decision trees encountered in Chapter 3 had chance event nodes with a limited number of outcomes, usually no more than three. For example, the product launch case used to demonstrate the basics of the technique showed the demand for the product as being 'strong', 'weak' or 'non-existent'. In practice product demand may well be described in this way, but it may also be described in terms of a continuous distribution, represented by a curve showing a continuous range of demand. Figure 4.1 shows what a continuous probability distribution of the estimated weekly demand for a new product might look like.

Figure 4.1 could have been assessed subjectively: the product manager believed that demand would be in the range 200–700 with a peak at 350. Or it may have been the result of data measurement: the weekly demands for similar products over many weeks were collected and formed into a distribution. The next section (on probability assessment) looks in greater detail at how distributions like this can be developed.

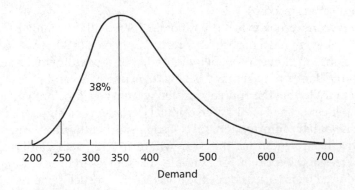

Figure 4.1   Continuous distribution of demand

The next question is how probabilities of different levels of demand can be derived from distributions such as that in Figure 4.1. It is not easy, but the basic approach is to measure the area under the relevant part of the curve. For example, to find the probability that demand will be in the range 250–350 the area under that part of the curve has to be measured, either by counting squares on the graph paper or, if for some reason the mathematical equation of the curve were known, by a technique called integration. The probability is this area as a proportion of the whole area. So if the area between 250 and 350 were 38 per cent of the whole, then the probability of the demand being between 250 and 350 is 38 per cent.

$$P(250 \leqslant \text{demand} \leqslant 350) = 38 \text{ per cent}$$

Measuring areas under curves is a messy business. The task is made easier if the demand distribution is represented differently, by a *cumulative* distribution. This shows the probability of a variable taking a value *less than or equal to* ($\leqslant$) or *more than or equal to* ($\geqslant$) a specified value. In the 'less than or equal to' form the demand distribution of Figure 4.1 would appear as in Figure 4.2. Since demand is in the range 200–700, there is zero probability that demand will be 'less than or equal to' 199 and 100 per cent probability that demand will be 'less than or equal to' 700. Moving from 200 through to 700 the probability increases, at varying rates, depending on the shape of the distribution. The next section shows how we can develop a cumulative distribution.

A 'more than or equal to' curve gives the probability of the variable being more than or equal to a specified value. The curve starts at 100 per cent and decreases through to 0 per cent.

The big advantage of the cumulative form of distribution is that probabilities can be read directly from the vertical scale rather than having to measure areas and count squares. For example, to find the probability that demand will be between 250 and 350, Figure 4.2 shows that the probability that the demand will be less than or equal to 250 is 8 per cent, and less than or equal to 350, 46 per cent.

$$P(x \leqslant 350) = 46 \text{ per cent, and}$$
$$P(x \leqslant 250) = 8 \text{ per cent}$$

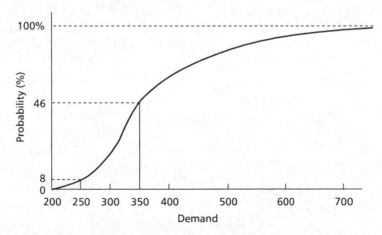

Figure 4.2   Demand distribution in cumulative form

Therefore:

$$P(250 \leqslant x \leqslant 350) = P(x \leqslant 350) - P(x \leqslant 250)$$
$$= 46 \text{ per cent} - 8 \text{ per cent}$$
$$= 38 \text{ per cent}$$

In decision analysis, when the outcome of a chance event node is a continuous distribution, whether or not it is cumulative, it is represented in the tree by a fan, as in Figure 4.3.

Within a decision tree continuous outcomes are dealt with by replacing them by a number of discrete, representative values. Once the fans have been replaced by the representative values then EMVs are calculated simply as if the outcomes were discrete, i.e. just as in the previous chapter. This may sound straightforward, but the difficulty lies in selecting properly representative values. The customary way of doing this is to use *bracket medians*. The procedure is as follows.

1. Decide *how many* representative values you need to cover the range of the distribution. This will depend on:

   - Accuracy. The values will be an approximation of the continuous distribution: how close an approximation is needed in the context of the decision being taken?
   - Continuous distribution. If its assessment has been very approximate, is there any point in being over-precise in choosing representative values?
   - Distribution complexity. If it has many changes in slope and shape then these should be retained by the choice of representative values.
   - Computational load. The representation should not result in unnecessarily heavy computations if speedy sensitivity analysis will be required.

   The usual rule of thumb is that at least five but not more than ten representative values should be chosen. Of course, if you use decision analysis software then a large number of representative values for particularly intricate or sensitive distributions is feasible.

2. Divide the full range of values covered by the distribution into *equi-probable* sub-ranges. There will be as many of these ranges as there are representative values. Equi-probable means that there should be an equal chance of a demand falling in any of the ranges. If, for example, at stage 1 you decided that there should be five representative values for the demand data of Figures 4.1 and 4.2, then from the cumulative form of the distribution, read off the demands relating to 0, 20, 40, 60, 80 and 100 per cent.

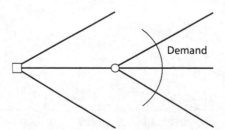

Figure 4.3   Representation of a continuous outcome

There is then an equal chance (20 per cent) that the demand will fall in any of the five ranges marked off by these demands. These are the equi-probable ranges.

3. Find the median of each range. The median of a range is the middle of the range in terms of probabilities. This value is the *bracket median*. For example, for the 0 to 20 per cent range the bracket median is the demand corresponding to the probability 10 per cent. The five bracket medians are therefore the demands relating to the probabilities 10, 30, 50, 70, 90 per cent.

4. The bracket medians now represent the continuous distribution and to each is assigned the probability of the equi-probable ranges. In the example there would then be five branches coming from the chance node, each with a probability of 20 per cent and for which the payoffs are the bracket medians.

The calculations can now proceed as if it were a normal decision tree with discrete outcomes.

Example

What is the EMV for the chance event node shown in Figure 4.4? The payoffs have been estimated as the cumulative distribution of Figure 4.5. Use 10 bracket medians to represent the distribution.

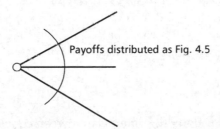

Payoffs distributed as Fig. 4.5

Figure 4.4   Example of bracket medians

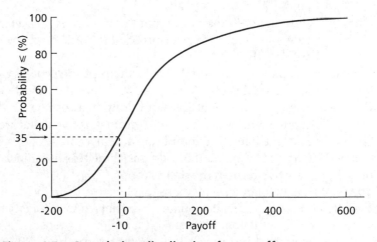

Figure 4.5   Cumulative distribution for payoffs

Table 4.1   Bracket medians for Figure 4.5

Range	Mid-point	Bracket median
0–0.1	0.05	−130
0.1–0.2	0.15	−80
0.2–0.3	0.25	−45
0.3–0.4	0.35	−10
0.4–0.5	0.45	15
0.5–0.6	0.55	40
0.6–0.7	0.65	60
0.7–0.8	0.75	100
0.8–0.9	0.85	180
0.9–1.0	0.95	360

The ten bracket medians will be associated with ten equi-probable ranges, relating to probabilities 0 to 0.1 (i.e. 0 per cent to 10 per cent), 0.1 to 0.2, 0.2 to 0.3 and so on. The bracket medians will therefore correspond to the probabilities 0.05, 0.15, 0.25 etc. and can be read off the cumulative distribution in Figure 4.5. For instance, the bracket median relating to the probability 0.35 is −10. Table 4.1 gives all the bracket medians.

Using the bracket medians the chance event node in Figure 4.4 becomes like an ordinary chance node with ten branches, each of which has a probability of 0.1 and a payoff given by the relevant bracket median.

$$\text{EMV} = (0.1 \times -130) + (0.1 \times -80) + (0.1 \times -45) + (0.1 \times -10) + (0.1 \times 15)$$

$$+ (0.1 \times 40) + (0.1 \times 60) + (0.1 \times 100) + (0.1 \times 180) + (0.1 \times 360)$$

$$= -13 - 8 - 4.5 - 1 + 1.5 + 4 + 6 + 10 + 18 + 36$$

$$= 49$$

The example illustrates the difference between equal ranges and equi-probable ranges. The ranges are not equal, although they have equal probabilities. Each range has the same probability, 0.1, but covers a different span of payoffs. For example, the 0 to 0.1 range covers 100 in terms of payoff (−200 to −100) whereas the 0.1 to 0.2 range covers 40(−100 to −60).

Once you understand the logic underpinning the use of bracket medians, it is of course unnecessary to bother about the equi-probable ranges themselves. You can go to the bracket medians directly.

If the distribution is not in cumulative form, the same process can be applied but it is more complex. The equi-probable ranges are determined by dividing the whole area under the distribution into equal areas, counting squares if necessary. These areas have in turn to be divided into two equal parts (this means two equal areas, not equal ranges) to find the bracket medians. The complexity and inaccuracy of this procedure, compared to that of the cumulative distribution, are the prime reason for insisting on having distributions in cumulative form in the first place.

The requirement for bracket medians to relate to *equi-probable* ranges is convenient but not strictly necessary. A bracket median can be determined for any range, whether or not it is equi-probable with other ranges. For example, the first bracket median may be associated with the probability range 0 to 20 per cent, the next with 20 to 30 per cent, the next

30 to 35 per cent and so on. However, the probabilities assigned to each bracket median will differ: 20 per cent for 0 to 20 per cent, 10 per cent for 20 to 30 per cent, 5 per cent for 30 to 35 per cent, and so on. Circumstances may dictate that bracket medians have to relate to ranges with unequal probabilities. An example of such a situation is given in case study 2 at the end of the chapter.

All the continuous distributions discussed so far have been observed distributions: they were constructed from past data or by subjective assessment. However, the outcome of a chance event node might also be in the form of a standard distribution, such as the normal distribution. In such a case the EMV is simply the mean of the distribution. For example, if the distribution were normal then the EMV is the mean of that normal distribution.

Even so, it will still be useful to represent the distribution by bracket medians, since this will result in a better risk profile at the end of the decision analysis. The standard normal distribution table can be used in doing this. For example, for a normal distribution ten bracket medians can be found from the normal curve table by determining the points which leave an area of 0.05 in the tail, 0.15 in the tail, 0.25 in the tail and so on.

ASSESSMENT OF SUBJECTIVE PROBABILITIES

In the examples encountered so far the probabilities associated with chance nodes have been provided, with little explanation of how they had been derived. Many were subjective probabilities, making explicit opinions, hunches and instincts. It is the assumption that probabilities can be assessed subjectively, which gives some managers cause to doubt the technique. Some may even think that these probabilities are pure guesswork. Why, they say, should we build a complex analysis on the basis of such uncertain data? Garbage in, garbage out! Such wariness does them credit, especially if the same cynicism is also applied to other data they use in, for example, financial and marketing reports.

If the assessment of subjective probabilities were pure guesswork then cynicism would be justified. While it is true that their calculation is to some extent personal and individual, their estimation can be a careful and systematic process. A decision analyst or other facilitator can guide a manager to improving probability estimates. The procedure for doing this and developing a cumulative probability distribution for a variable (for example, new product demand or financial return) has several stages. The analyst/facilitator has to do the following:

1. Set the boundaries for the estimation by discussing with the manager the range of values the variable might take. In doing this he or she will be able to introduce the basics of the procedure gradually, which allows the manager to focus on the technique and what the output of the procedure is to be. This stage is rather like a doctor exchanging pleasantries with a patient before proceeding to an intimate examination.

2. Ask the manager for a number with the following characteristic: it is equally likely that the variable will turn out to be lower or higher. If the variable is demand, he or she is being asked to estimate a level of demand with a 50 per cent chance that the true demand will be higher and 50 per cent that it will be lower. In effect, the manager is being asked to say what the median demand is, in this context called the 50 per cent fractile.

3. Discuss with the manager the ranges on either side of the median, dividing each into two equi-probable halves. In other words, the manager should specify the 25 per cent and 75 per cent fractiles.

4. Check for consistency. The manager should feel comfortable that there is an equal chance of the variable falling between the 25 per cent and 75 per cent fractiles as outside these points (since both have an equal probability, 50 per cent). If he or she does not feel comfortable then there is some inconsistency and they must go over the estimation of 25 per cent, 50 per cent and 75 per cent fractiles once more and try to be consistent.

5. Guide the manager to divide each of the four equi-probable ranges (0 to 25 per cent, 25 per cent to 50 per cent, 50 per cent to 75 per cent and 75 per cent to 100 per cent) into two equi-probable halves, i.e. to estimate the 12.5 per cent, 37.5 per cent, 62.5 per cent and 87.5 per cent fractiles.

6. Check consistency again by asking whether the manager believes it is equally likely that the variable would fall in the range marked by the 25 per cent and 37.5 per cent fractiles or that marked by the 75 per cent and 87.5 per cent fractiles.

7. Continue the process of sub-division until the manager feels no longer able to make any further sub-divisions which are sensible. In practice, a division into 16 equi-probable ranges is usually the maximum that can be attempted.

8. Marking all fractiles on a graph, draw a smooth freehand curve between them. This is the cumulative probability distribution for the variable, similar in concept to the demand distribution of Figure 4.2. It is used in the way described above.

Example

A new product is shortly to be launched and a distribution of the likely demand for it in its first year is to be assessed. The conversation between decision analyst and product manager might be as follows:

Analyst: Before starting to develop your knowledge of the product and your experience of other products into a demand distribution, I'd like to know how you feel about this product in general terms.

Manager: I do have experience of similar products which we marketed in the past and this has helped me form views of this new one. We have known success and failure and learned many lessons. This product is as good as any we have marketed in the past. In fact, if it weren't we wouldn't be proceeding with the launch without further test marketing. It's not perfect but we think we know how to market it to capitalise on its particular strengths. But, as always in recent years we have been under severe cost-cutting pressures and our advertising budget has been restricted by the accountants in central finance. Overall I feel optimistic about the prospects and think we can do pretty well. Forming a distribution of likely demand from all these random thoughts is another matter. I've always just persuaded my boss to trust me and then followed my instincts. My ideas just aren't sufficiently concise to be more scientific. In fact I wouldn't be going along with this at all except that we had that disaster last year. I think it was just one of those things but it means I have to be able to show my boss, and he has to show the Board, that I've considered every angle on this new one.

Analyst: I think you will be surprised how much you do know and how precise those ideas are if only we can be more systematic in drawing them together.

Manager: The fact is, I'm not sure about coming up with a single number as my best guess of the likely demand. I know I had to do it for the budgets but I just stuck my finger in the air and produced a number I thought they would like.

Analyst: If you can, try to forget about playing politics with the accountants. And I wonder what, exactly, you mean by a 'best guess'. But before we get into that I'd like you to give me the broad picture of what might happen after the launch. Do you think it's more likely that the demand is above or below 100 000 units?

Manager: That's not too difficult. It should certainly be above. Advance orders are already not far off that level.

Analyst: Let's go on. What about 800 000. Do you think it is more likely that the demand is above or below 800 000?

Manager: Not too difficult either. Demand for similar products has never reached such a level and with increasing competition it's not likely to in the future. In any case, at full stretch our production capacity could barely produce 800 000 in the first year.

Analyst: Let me try to make it more difficult. Can you give me a single number such that you really wouldn't be able to decide whether the actual demand would be above or below it? Putting it another way, for what value is it equally likely that demand could be above or below it?

Manager: I do indeed find that a harder question. I would have to be somewhere between 400 000 and 500 000. The best I can say is 450 000. But I'm not too happy that I fully appreciate the meaning of the question. What exactly does 'equally likely' mean?

Analyst: 'Equally likely' means that you really cannot decide whether the demand is above or below 450 000. If your life, or a political battle with the accountants, were at stake on the outcome, would you still not be able to say whether demand was going to be above or below 450 000?

Manager: A political battle with the accountants would concentrate my mind wonderfully. I might even be able to be a bit more precise. As we have been talking I've had a gut feeling that 450 000 may be slightly too high. Not much, but the stakes are high and I think I should adjust the number downwards just a bit. I'll go for 440 000.

Analyst: That's good – you do have some pretty clear views about the product. You have now told me that 440 000 divides the demand range into two parts which are, in your judgement, equally likely to happen. Let's push our luck and try to repeat the division process, first concentrating on the range below 440 000. What do you think is more likely – that demand is between 200 000 and 440 000 or below 200 000?

Manager: Definitely between 200 000 and 440 000.

Analyst: Between 400 000 and 440 000 or less than 400 000?

Manager: Definitely less than 400 000.

Analyst: OK, but can you go further? Can you come up with a number X such that you think it equally likely that demand is below X or between X and 440? You have just told me that X = 200 000 is too low and X = 400 000 is too high.

Manager: Now I'm struggling.

Analyst: Let me ask the question in a different way. I'm also making the assumption that you like Caribbean holidays. Suppose I could somehow tell you that demand will definitely be less than 440 000. Can you give me a number X such that you would be indifferent between receiving a prize of a luxurious Caribbean holiday conditional on demand being below X, and receiving the identical prize conditional on demand being between X and 440 000?

Manager: You mean that if I had to choose between receiving the holiday if the demand were below X and receiving the prize if the demand were between X and 440 000, I would find it impossible to make the choice?

Analyst: That's it.

Manager: *(after thinking hard)* Then I would have to say X should be 360 000.

Analyst: You're telling me that it is equally likely that demand is less than 360 000 or between 360 000 and 440 000.

Manager: I didn't think I'd be able to but, yes, that's what I'm saying.

Analyst: Let's now look at the other side of the coin. What about the possibility that the demand exceeds 440 000? Can you divide this range into two equally likely parts, just as for the demand being below 440 000? In other words can you give me a number Y such that it is equally likely that demand is between 440 000 and Y or above Y?

Manager: I'm starting to get the hang of it, although I'm conscious that I'm giving you some highly doubtful numbers. There's no need to offer me another Caribbean holiday – I think Y should be fairly close to 440 000. I'd say 500 000. The chance of the demand turning out to be really high in the present competitive situation is really pretty slim.

Analyst: I'm aware that making such judgements as these makes you lay your cards on the table in a nerve-wracking way. But we're doing well. Let me summarise how far we've got. In your judgement it is just as likely that demand is in any one of the four ranges (less than 360 000), (360 000–440 000), (440 000–500 000) and (above 500 000).

Manager: Agreed.

Analyst: Now for some checking – not to catch you out but just to make sure we are being consistent. Let's consider the situation from a different perspective. What would you rather bet – that demand would be inside or outside the interval 360 000 to 500 000?

Manager: I'd have to say outside. Competition makes me reluctant to predict a high demand, but the future for this market is so uncertain that the demand could well cover quite a wide range. I think this answer makes me guilty of the crime of inconsistency?

Analyst: Yes, but this is not unexpected. Everybody is a little bit inconsistent, especially the first time round, and has to make some adjustments. I would have been suspicious if you had not been. Let's think again about your previous estimates and how the inconsistency crept in.

Manager: I don't have any problems about the 440 000 – I was thinking about those accountants as I made the prediction. The 360 000 is probably the most dubious estimate I've made. I should change it. Perhaps 340 000 would be better. To return to your 'checking' question, I would now want to say that it's a 50–50 bet that demand lies inside or outside the range 340 000 to 500 000.

Analyst: Let's check this new estimate. Do you think it's equally likely that demand is less than 340 000 or between 340 000 and 440 000?

Manager: That's right, but now I'm really worried. If we went for a beer and forgot what we've just done, and then started from scratch again in an hour's time, I might get different numbers. I might easily come up with 325 000, 430 000, 480 000 instead of 340 000, 440 000 and 500 000.

Analyst: It doesn't worry me too much since these numbers are so close to the original ones. But you are right, particularly if the alterations could make a difference to the optimal decision we hope to arrive at. So we should bear in mind your feelings of uncertainty when we come to apply decision analysis and do some sensitivity analysis on the results. On the other hand, I would be very concerned if you told me that on second thoughts you could have easily come up with 200 000, 350 000 and 400 000 which are very far from the original numbers.

Manager: No, it's not that bad – I'm not so uncertain as all that.

Analyst: The next step is to plough on with some further sub-divisions. But before we do let's get the terminology right: the three numbers you've just given me are called the 25 per cent fractile (340 000), the 50 per cent fractile (440 000) and the 75 per cent fractile (500 000). The next sub-dividing will be to come up with the 12.5 per cent, 37.5 per cent, 62.5 per cent and 87.5 per cent fractiles. First, let's deal with the range of less than 340 000. Same question as before: what's the number which would divide this range into two equally likely parts? In other words, what is Z so that a demand less than Z is as likely as a demand between Z and 340 000?

Manager: I would say about 260 000.

Analyst: That means the 12.5 per cent fractile is 260 000. Next, what's the number which divides the range 340 000 to 440 000 into two equally likely parts?

Manager: I would say 400 000.

Analyst: That's the 37.5 per cent fractile. Let's keep going – what about the value which divides the 440 000 to 500 000 range into two parts?

Manager: Roughly 465 000. I'm speeding up!

Analyst: That's the 62.5 per cent fractile. Finally, what about the 87.5 per cent fractile?

Manager: I think 600 000. Can I check that I've got this right? The 600 000 means that I believe it's just as likely that demand will be between 500 000 and 600 000 as that it will be more than 600 000?

Analyst: Exactly. Now we can summarise your judgements in this table I've been building up.

Table 4.2

Fractile %	Fractile value
12.5	260 000
25	340 000
37.5	400 000
50	440 000
62.5	465 000
75	500 000
87.5	600 000

Manager: It looks fine. What next?

Analyst: We use your estimates in the table to draw a cumulative probability distribution of the demand. We should really make some further consistency checks, but I'll sketch the graph to give you an idea of what we're aiming at. The graph will have cumulative probability as the vertical axis and demand as the horizontal axis. Each line of the above table is a point on the graph. The first step is to plot the points and the second is to join them in as smooth a curve as possible.

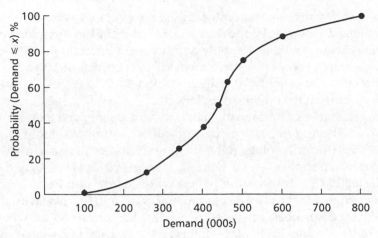

Figure 4.6   Estimation of demand probabilities

Manager: So, this is the distribution from which we get the bracket medians which you were explaining earlier?

Analyst: That's right. As you can see I'm using 100 000 and 800 000 the values we discussed at the very beginning, to be the extreme limits of the distribution – the 0 per cent and 100 per cent fractiles. These were very vague numbers and we will probably have to take a closer look at them before we can finalise the distribution. I have to say that, as I look at even this preliminary and rough version of the distribution, it does seem that you knew more about the distribution of demand than you originally claimed. Now, I'm afraid we have more work to do so let's return to the question of consistency for the last fractiles you gave me . . .

What this conversation illustrates is not the whole story. The process can be tailored to individual circumstances. For example, at each sub-division the ranges do not necessarily have to be halved. The ranges could be split into three (or more) equi-probable parts, depending on what the facilitator and manager feel to be the easiest and most sensible approach. In addition, if the distribution seems to have long, straggly tails (for example, when demand could conceivably have a very wide range but the chances of the extreme values are small) more attention might be given to the tails and more detailed estimates made. For instance, the 6.25 per cent and 93.75 per cent fractiles might be estimated in addition to the 12.5 per cent and 87.5 per cent fractiles. However, it is only necessary to do this when the tails are important because, for example, large profits or losses are involved at these extremes. If the manager feels willing and able to do this, then the extra attention may be valuable.

There are other approaches to the systematic assessment of subjective probabilities, although the one described above is perhaps the most common. For example, an alternative procedure is based on associating values of the variable with events which have known probabilities, such as the result of throwing a die or selecting from a pack of cards.

Sometimes the assessment process has the surprising result that it is welcomed by managers even though they were suspicious of subjective probabilities. They appreciate having an opportunity to discuss and organise their views and opinions. Instead of having to provide single estimates, and then having to adjust them for self-protection and for contingencies, the process allows managers to express their position fully by giving a range of values and associated probabilities. They feel their experience is being put to full use. In other words, the initial barrier to the use of subjective probabilities can be removed and resistance replaced by positive cooperation.

REVISING PROBABILITIES

However systematic the process for assessing probabilities may be, it is still subjective. So it is reassuring to know that some probabilities are calculated in precise ways. Where sample information is involved (or market research, or clinical trials, or any other form of additional information) some probabilities can be calculated by formulae. Chapter 3 described a new product launch problem, involving probability estimates for strong, weak or non-existent demand. There was also an option to carry out a test market. If this option were taken the initial probabilities would, as you would expect, change in the light of the new information provided by the test market: a good test market result would increase the probability of a strong demand, decrease that of a non-existent demand; vice versa for poor test market results.

How these revised probabilities were obtained was not fully discussed. If they had been obtained subjectively, it would have been difficult to ensure that they were consistent with one another and with the earlier probabilities. In fact, they were not obtained subjectively but calculated using a formula called *Bayes theorem*. The process of revising the probabilities in the light of new information is known as *Bayesian revision*. The probabilities given in the product launch example in Chapter 3 were:

$$P(S) = P(\text{strong demand}) = 0.5$$
$$P(W) = P(\text{weak demand}) = 0.2 \tag{1}$$
$$P(N) = P(\text{non-existent demand}) = 0.3$$

$$P(S|F) = P(\text{strong, given a favourable test}) - 0.70$$
$$P(W|F) = P(\text{weak, given a favourable test}) = 0.20$$
$$P(N|F) = P(\text{non-existent, given a favourable test}) = 0.10$$

$$P(S|U) = P(\text{strong, given an unfavourable test}) = 0.20 \tag{2}$$
$$P(W|U) = P(\text{weak, given an unfavourable test}) = 0.20$$
$$P(N|U) = P(\text{non-existent, given an unfavourable test}) = 0.60$$

(1)   These are called *prior probabilities*. They are 'prior' in the sense that they are the probabilities estimated before any sample information is obtained from the test market.

(2)   These are called *posterior probabilities*. They are 'posterior' in the sense that they are the probabilities of the different demand levels estimated after sample information is made available. They are conditional probabilities, the condition being the outcome of the test market. The notation is the usual notation for conditional probabilities, written with a vertical line separating the condition.

$P(\text{strong}|\text{favourable})$ or $P(S|F)$ is the probability of a strong demand given a favourable test market result.

Prior probabilities are usually estimated subjectively, although they could be derived from historical data if available. Posterior probabilities, on the other hand, are usually estimated using Bayes theorem together with:

- prior probabilities;
- information about the known accuracy of the particular sample information which is available.

Information about the known accuracy of new information is generally in the form of using the new product launch example and its test market option – if there really is a strong market demand then the probability that the test will give a favourable result is, say, 84 per cent, and the probability that the test will give an unfavourable result is 16 per cent. Similar probabilities will refer to weak and non-existent levels of demand. In mathematical notation, information about the accuracy of the test market might be:

$$P(F|S) = 0.84$$
$$P(U|S) = 0.16$$

$$P(F|W) = 0.60$$
$$P(U|W) = 0.40$$

$$P(F|N) = 0.20$$
$$P(U|N) = 0.80$$

These data have *not* been calculated. They were given by the devisers of the test market who used their knowledge of the structure of the test and their experience of using it to establish the probabilities and historical data from other test markets. The accuracy of sample or tests (whether in marketing or medicine or wherever) is in this form because this is how the tests are checked, i.e. their performances in known situations are measured. Figure 4.7 is a diagrammatic representation of how Bayes theorem works.

Bayes theorem can be viewed and used from either a mathematical or a graphical perspective. Mathematically, Bayes theorem is a series of formulae for calculating posterior probabilities. Graphically it is represented by a *Venn diagram*, a square which displays the probabilities pictorially. For most people it is easier to start with the graphical method.

Graphical method

There are three steps in using a Venn diagram.

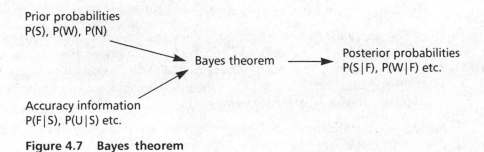

Figure 4.7 Bayes theorem

1. Divide the square vertically to represent the prior probabilities, i.e. draw vertical lines to create rectangles whose areas are proportional to the prior probabilities.

2. Divide these rectangles horizontally to represent the 'sample accuracy' probabilities, i.e. draw horizontal lines to create sub-rectangles whose areas are proportional to the conditional probabilities which are the measures of the accuracy of the information provided by the sample.

3. Combine and divide areas to obtain the conditional probabilities (the posterior probabilities) in the form of ratios between areas.

Example

The procedure is best understood by working through the new product launch example. The relevant probabilities were given above and in Chapter 3.

1. Divide the square vertically according to the prior probabilities. This is shown in Figure 4.8.

2. Divide the diagram horizontally according to the 'sample accuracy' data. This is shown in Figure 4.9. The rectangle relating to a strong market is divided into two parts:
   - a part relating to unfavourable test (the area D) which covers 16 per cent of the 'strong' rectangle because P(unfavourable|strong) = 0.16;
   - a part relating to a favourable test (the area A) which covers 84 per cent of the 'strong' rectangle because P(favourable|strong) = 0.84.

Similarly, the rectangle referring to a weak market is divided into area E (40 per cent of it, because P(U|W) = 0.4) and area B (60 per cent of it, because P(F|W) = 0.6). The rectangle referring to a non-existent market is divided into areas F (80 per cent of it, because P(U|N) = 0.8) and C (20 per cent of it, because P(F|N) = 0.2).

In Figures 4.8 and 4.9 probabilities are proportional to areas which can be measured in the usual way by multiplying length by width. New probabilities, particularly the

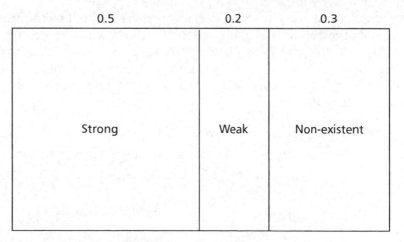

Figure 4.8   Prior probabilities for product launch

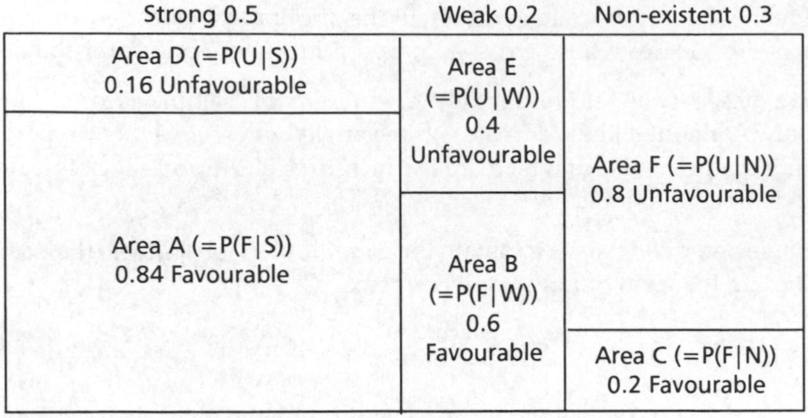

Strong 0.5	Weak 0.2	Non-existent 0.3
Area D (=P(U|S)) 0.16 Unfavourable	Area E (=P(U|W)) 0.4 Unfavourable	Area F (=P(U|N)) 0.8 Unfavourable
Area A (=P(F|S)) 0.84 Favourable	Area B (=P(F|W)) 0.6 Favourable	Area C (=P(F|N)) 0.2 Favourable

Figure 4.9   Venn diagram for product launch

posterior probabilities, can be calculated by referring to the area by which they are represented.

P(favourable test market) = total area associated with favourable test

= Area A + Area B + Area C

= (0.84 × 0.5) + (0.6 × 0.2) + (0.2 × 0.3)

= 0.6

P(unfavourable test market) = total area associated with unfavourable test

= Area D + Area E + Area F

= (0.16 × 0.5) + (0.4 × 0.2) + (0.8 × 0.3)

= 0.4

For conditional probabilities the range of possible outcomes is limited by the condition. In other words, there is a preliminary restriction to a sub-section of the whole square. A conditional probability is given, therefore, not by the area representing the event, but by this area as a proportion of the area which represents the condition. For example, for the probability P(strong demand given a favourable test market), the condition restricts it to the parts of the square relating to a favourable test market (areas A, B and C). $P(S|F)$ is then calculated as the proportion of A + B + C that is associated with a strong demand.

P(strong demand given a favourable test market) = $P(S|F)$

= proportion of area representing 'favourable' which relates to 'strong'

= Area A/(Area A + Area B + Area C)

= (0.84 × 0.5)/0.6

= 0.70

Similar calculations can be made for the other posterior probabilities.

P(weak demand given a favourable test market) = P(W|F)

$$= \text{Area B}/(\text{Area A} + \text{Area B} + \text{Area C})$$
$$= (0.6 \times 0.2)/0.6$$
$$= 0.20$$

P(non-existent demand given a favourable test market) = P(N|F)

$$= \text{Area C}/(\text{Area A} + \text{Area B} + \text{Area C})$$
$$= (0.2 \times 0.3)/0.6$$
$$= 0.10$$

P(strong demand given an unfavourable test market) = P(S|U)

$$= \text{Area D}/(\text{Area D} + \text{Area E} + \text{Area F})$$
$$= (0.16 \times 0.5)/0.4$$
$$= 0.20$$

P(weak demand given an unfavourable test market) = P(W|U)

$$= \text{Area E}/(\text{Area D} + \text{Area E} + \text{Area F})$$
$$= (0.4 \times 0.2)/0.4$$
$$= 0.20$$

P(non-existent demand given an unfavourable test market) = P(N|U)

$$= \text{Area F}/(\text{Area D} + \text{Area E} + \text{Area F})$$
$$= (0.8 \times 0.3)/0.4$$
$$= 0.60$$

All these calculations are summarised in Table 4.3. This is constructed to illustrate the way in which the calculations are built up. It is the conventional form for displaying the results of Bayesian revision.

The posterior probabilities shown in column (6) are the ones obtained when the problem was analysed using the Venn diagram. As always, an intuitive check on the probabilities can be made by working in frequencies.

Table 4.3   Bayesian revision of product launch problem

Test Outcome F or U (1)	Market Demand S, W or N (2)	Prior probabilities P(S) etc (3)	Test Accuracy P(F|S) (4)	Col (3) × Col (4) (5)	Posterior probabilities Col (5)/P(F) or P(U) P(S|F) etc (6)
F	S	0.5	0.84	0.42 (= Area A)	0.70
	W	0.2	0.60	0.12 (= Area B)	0.20
	N	0.3	0.20	0.06 (= Area C)	0.10
				P(F) = 0.60	
U	S	0.5	0.16	0.08 (= Area D)	0.20
	W	0.2	0.40	0.08 (= Area E)	0.20
	N	0.3	0.80	0.24 (= Area F)	0.60
				P(U) = 0.40	

The posterior probabilities in column (6) are also the ones used in the new product launch problem used in Chapter 3, although it was not explained at the time that their derivation was by Bayesian revision.

To summarise: Bayes theorem is used whenever original subjective probability estimates are revised in the light of some new information. In essence Bayes theorem is a method for combining experience with numbers. The posterior probabilities are based on the prior probabilities (experience) combined with sample information (numbers).

Mathematical method

Most people seem to find the Venn diagram approach to Bayes theorem easier to understand than the algebraic approach, at least when they first start to use Bayes. However, the latter is not especially difficult, although the formulae and notation can make it seem tedious to the non-mathematically minded. Bayes theorem stems from the multiplication law of probability. Keeping to the product launch example and the earlier notation:

$$P(S \ and \ F) = P(S).P(F|S)$$

But also

$$P(S \ and \ F) = P(F).P(S|F)$$

Therefore,

$$P(F).P(S|F) = P(S).P(F|S)$$

$$P(S|F) = P(S).P(F|S)/P(F) \tag{1}$$

Equation (1) is nearly in the form needed for Bayes theorem. The posterior probability $(P(S|F))$ is on the left-hand side of the equation. The prior probability $(P(S))$ and the test accuracy measure $(P(F|S))$ are on the right-hand side. The posterior probabilities can be calculated if $P(F)$ is known. $P(F)$ can be calculated from the addition law of probabilities.

A favourable outcome can occur in any one of three ways. It can occur in conjunction with the true demand being strong, weak or non-existent. These three possibilities are mutually exclusive, therefore the addition law applies.

$$P(F) = P(F \ and \ S) + P(F \ and \ W) + P(F \ and \ N)$$

From the multiplication law, this becomes:

$$P(F) = P(S).(F|S) + P(W).P(F|W) + P(N).P(F|N) \tag{2}$$

The right-hand side is a combination of prior probabilities and test accuracy measurements, all of which we know. Therefore $P(F)$ can be calculated. The formula for the posterior probability therefore becomes, from equations (1) and (2):

$$P(S|F) = \frac{P(S).P(F|S)}{P(S).P(F|S) + P(W).P(F|W) + P(N).P(F|N)}$$

Equation (3) can be related to the Venn diagram of Figure 4.9 since this formula is no more than:

$$P(S|F) = \frac{Area \ A}{Area \ A + Area \ B + Area \ C}$$

Bayes theorem merely amounts to a series of formulae corresponding to (3) for calculating all the posterior probabilities. You can check this against the results in Table 4.3.

CONCLUSION

In Chapter 3 the basics of decision analysis were outlined and it was seen as a technique for finding the optimal solution to certain types of decision problems. This optimal solution was to be used in practice as an aid to taking the decision. Even without the optimal solution the technique performed a valuable service in helping decision makers to structure and understand the problem confronting them. The main weakness was perceived to be the nature of probabilities and their estimation. This chapter has tried to overcome this weakness by considering in detail how the probabilities of chance events can be measured and expressed as accurately as possible. This was preceded by an examination of how continuously distributed chance outcomes could be handled. Finally we looked at Bayes theorem, the method by which subjective probability estimates can, in some circumstances, be revised in the light of additional information provided by test markets, market research, clinical trials etc.

Even so, we have considered only the basics of decision analysis. The technique can be extended in many directions. For example, the payoffs can also be handled differently to deal with another of the perceived weaknesses of decision analysis. The problem, that the EMV criterion can mask large payoffs by averaging them out, was described in Chapter 3 and risk profiles suggested as a method for dealing with it. A more sophisticated way of handling the problem is by using a *utility function* which represents monetary payoffs by *utilities* and, in theory, allows EMVs to be applied in a much wider range of problems.

A utility is a measurement which reflects the true value of a monetary amount to the decision maker. For example, in strict accounting and numeric terms a £2 million loss is double a £1 million loss. However, the true consequences of a £2 million loss (bankruptcy?) may be much more than twice as bad as a £1 million loss (a difficult year ahead?). The utility value associated with a £2 million loss would in these circumstances be more than double that associated with a £1 million loss. Similarly, a profit of £2 million might have a utility less than double that of a £1 million profit, because currently the company does not have enough profitable projects in which it could invest the extra £1 million.

To use the concept of utilities the decision maker's utility function is drawn in a similar manner to the assessment of subjective probabilities. The decision maker works with a facilitator to draw a graph which relates utility and money. Utility is a subjective assessment of the true worth of a sum of money to the decision maker, and the graph allows payoffs to be converted from money into utilities. The decision tree and the roll-back deal with expected utility instead of expected monetary value. The end result is an optimal path which does not hide any 'unallowed-for' disastrous outcomes, since they have already been incorporated into the measurement of utilities. A utility function is the decision maker's own and is indicative of what he or she believes to be the real worth of financial amounts. Utility is also found in other areas such as economics. The details of the application of utility functions go beyond the scope of this book.

As with most business techniques, new research is continually being carried out into decision analysis and new experience of applications gained. Where useful, these findings are gradually incorporated into the accepted practice of the technique, which therefore improves as time goes by. Open-minded managers should of course always be ready to put into practice these new developments. The frills and additions, and the availability of user-friendly software, should not, however, obscure the more important task of making proper and full use of what is already known and available. This is especially true for decision analysis which, because of its subjective probabilities and expected values, is probably viewed as one of the more mysterious management techniques. Nevertheless, the concepts it contains can be important attributes of management thinking, extending to totally non-quantitative areas.

CASE STUDIES

CASE STUDY 1

The questions refer to the following 'less than or equal to' cumulative distribution:

Probability	0	10	20	30	40	50	60	70	80	90	100
x variable	100	160	200	240	270	320	380	450	550	750	1000

e.g. $P(x \leqslant 240) = 30$ per cent

The distribution is then split into 5 equi-probable ranges.

1. What x values does the first of these ranges cover?
2. What is the first of the five bracket medians?
3. What is the expected value of x?

Solutions

1. *What x values does the first of these ranges cover?*
The first of five equi-probable ranges would cover x values from 100 to 200 – the first 20 per cent of the distribution, i.e. up to the 20 per cent fractile.

2. *What is the first of the five bracket medians?*
The bracket median for the 0–20 per cent range is the 10 per cent fractile. This is $x = 160$.

3. *What is the expected value of x?*
The 5 bracket medians are 160, 240, 320, 450, 750. These, along with their probabilities of 0.2 (because there are five equi-probable ranges), are used to represent the distribution.

Expected value of x

$$= (0.2 \times 160) + (0.2 \times 240) + (0.2 \times 320) + (0.2 \times 450) + (0.2 \times 750)$$
$$= 32 + 48 + 64 + 90 + 150$$
$$= 384$$

CASE STUDY 2

A manufacturer of household goods is preparing to launch a newly developed, microchip-based dishwasher. In the first year after the launch only one standard model will be offered.

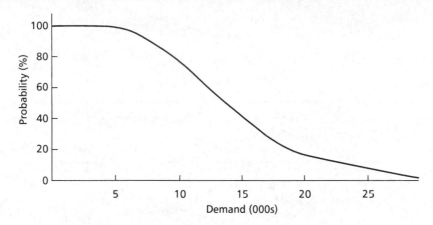

Figure 4.10   Cumulative demand distribution for dishwasher

The price, which is largely dictated by the competitive environment, will be £650. The decision to offer a fuller range of models will be taken towards the end of the first year and will depend on results up to that time. If a fuller range is to be marketed, the number of variants on the standard model will be decided at the same time.

Market research has indicated what the demand for the standard model in the first year might be. This has been expressed as the cumulative probability distribution shown in Figure 4.10. This gives the probability that the demand will be greater than that shown on the vertical axis.

The different decisions which could be taken at the end of the first year will relate to the demand during the first year according to Table 4.4.

1. Express the problem as a decision tree, including probabilities but excluding payoffs (which have not been given in the case).

2. What is the expected demand for the standard dishwasher in the first year?

Solutions

1.   *Express the problem as a decision tree, including probabilities.*
A decision tree is shown in Figure 4.11. There are five demand ranges, each of which leads to two or three decision options as specified in Table 4.4. The probabilities for each demand are taken from Figure 4.10 – they are approximations being read from a rough graph.

Table 4.4   End of first year decisions

Demand	Subsequent decision
0–5000	Re-model standard version or abandon
5000–10 000	Introduce 1 or 2 variants
10 000–15 000	Introduce 2, 3 or 4 variants
15 000–20 000	Introduce 4 or 5 variants
20 000+	Introduce 1 or 2 variants

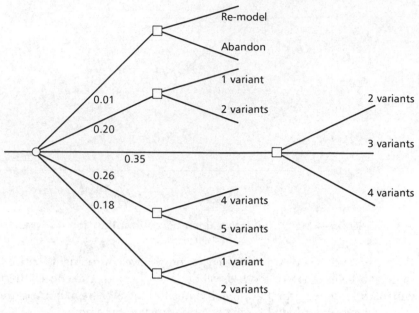

Figure 4.11   Dishwasher decision tree

$$P(\text{demand} \geqslant 0) \qquad = 100$$
$$P(\text{demand} \geqslant 5000) \quad = 99$$
$$P(\text{demand} \geqslant 10\,000) = 79$$
$$P(\text{demand} \geqslant 15\,000) = 44$$
$$P(\text{demand} \geqslant 20\,000) = 18$$

Therefore,

$$P(\text{demand } 0\text{--}5\,000) \qquad = 100 - 99 \ = 1 \text{ per cent}$$
$$P(\text{demand } 5000\text{--}10\,000) \quad = 99 - 79 \ = 20 \text{ per cent}$$
$$P(\text{demand } 10\,000\text{--}15\,000) = 79 - 44 \ = 35 \text{ per cent}$$
$$P(\text{demand } 15\,000\text{--}20\,000) = 44 - 18 \ = 26 \text{ per cent}$$
$$P(\text{demand } 20\,000+) \qquad = 18 \text{ per cent}$$

2.   *What is the expected demand for the standard dishwasher in the first year?*
The expected demand should be calculated by summing over all demand ranges:

Demand for each range × probability for each range

The probabilities of the ranges have already been calculated. The next step is to work out the bracket medians to represent each demand range. This means finding the demand which is at the centre (in terms of probability) of each range. The mid-point in terms of demand (for example 7500 as the mid-point of the range 5000–10000) is an alternative, but this does not reflect the changing slope of the cumulative probability distribution. For example, although 2500 is the mid-point of the 0–5000 range, it is (according to the distribution)

Table 4.5 Bracket medians

Demand	Bracket median
0–5000	4500
5000–10 000	8000
10 000–15 000	12 000
15 000–20 000	17 000
20 000+	22 000

far more likely that the demand will be between 2500 and 5000 than between 0 and 2500. In this sense the mid-point of the range is unrepresentative of demand.

The bracket medians are found by reading off the graph the demand associated with the probability mid-point of each range. For example, the range 0–5000 relates to cumulative probabilities of 100 per cent (for demand = 0) and 99 per cent (for demand = 5000). The bracket median is therefore the demand for probability (100 + 99)/2 = 99.5. From the graph this demand is (very approximately) 4500. All the bracket medians are shown in Table 4.5.

Expected demand = sum of (bracket median x probability)

$$= (4,500 \times 0.01) + (8000 \times 0.20) + (12\,000 \times 0.35) + (17\,000 \times 0.26)$$
$$+ (22\,000 \times 0.18)$$
$$= 45 + 1600 + 4200 + 4420 + 3960$$
$$= 14\,225$$

CASE STUDY 3

Modern electronic musical instruments use computer technology. Technomusic Ltd manufactures the basic micro-electronic components and sells them on to a number of customers who use them in a wide range of instruments, including keyboards and percussion kits.

A particular component, the R210 circuit, used in electronic vibraphones and similar instruments, is currently causing some difficulties. Under the present manufacturing process 20 per cent of the units produced turn out to be defective when assembled in the instruments. The problem is that the defect affects the quality of the sound produced and this is not known until the instrument is finished.

The contribution of this component has been calculated at £80 but, according to the contract with the customer, Technomusic must refund £120 for each component found to be defective, because the customer has to remove the component and replace it with a substitute.

One of Technomusic's engineers has recently developed a simple test to evaluate this component before shipping. For each component the test registers 'positive', 'negative' or, occasionally, 'inconclusive'. While the test is not totally accurate in that it sometimes gives the wrong result, it is consistent for each component, i.e. repeated testing always gives the same result for any one component.

To check the testing device it was tried out on a number of components which were known to be either satisfactory or defective. The results are shown in Table 4.6.

For example, of the components known to be satisfactory, 75 per cent gave the test result 'positive', 15 per cent 'inconclusive and 10 per cent 'negative'. The test costs £5 per component.

Table 4.6

Instrument reading	State of component	
	Satisfactory %	Defection %
Positive	75	20
Inconclusive	15	20
Negative	10	60

Technomusic could rework any components thought to be defective at a cost of £70 per component (regardless of whether it was defective or not). This would guarantee that a component was satisfactory and so it could be sold at the normal price.

1. What is the expected monetary value per component of continuing with the current practice and not using the test?

2. For any given component, what are the probabilities that the test will give a result of 'positive', 'inconclusive' or 'negative'?

3. Should Technomusic use the test and, if so, how should the company use it?

Solutions

1. *What is the Expected Monetary Value per component of continuing with the current practice and not using the test?*
Without the test, Technomusic has two options:

(a) Ship all components without re-working:

$$EMV = 0.8 \times 80 \quad + \quad 0.2 \times (80 - 120)$$
$$\text{(satisfactory)} \qquad \text{(defective)}$$
$$= 64 - 8 = 56$$

(b) Re-work all components before shipping:

$$EMV = \text{contribution for each component}$$
$$= 80 - 70 = 10$$

2. *For any given component, what are the probabilities that the test will give a result of 'positive', 'inconclusive' or 'negative'?*
If the test is used, Bayes theorem is the means of calculating the probabilities of the different test results (see Figure 4.12).

$$Prob('positive') = 0.6 + 0.04 \quad = 64 \text{ per cent}$$
$$Prob('inconclusive') = 0.12 + 0.04 = 16 \text{ per cent}$$
$$Prob('negative') = 0.08 + 0.12 = 20 \text{ per cent}$$

3. *Should Technomusic use the test and, if so, how should the company use it?*
The Venn diagram also gives some other probabilities:

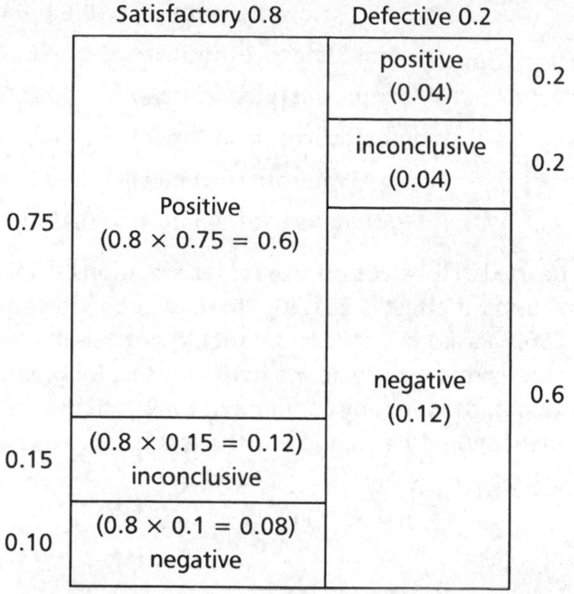

Satisfactory 0.8   Defective 0.2

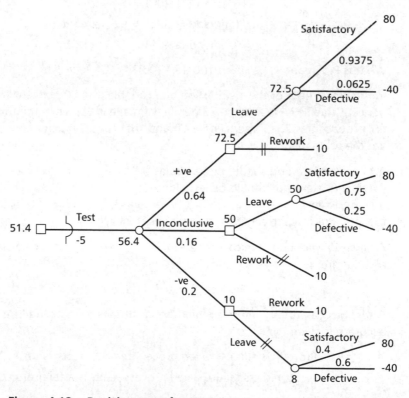

Figure 4.12

Figure 4.13   Decision tree for test

$$\text{Prob(satis | positive)} = 0.6/0.64 \quad = 0.9375$$
$$\text{Prob(defective | positive)} = 0.04/0.64 = 0.0625$$
$$\text{Prob(satis | inconclusive)} = 0.12/0.16 = 0.75$$
$$\text{Prob(defective | inconclusive)} = 0.04/0.16 = 0.25$$
$$\text{Prob(satis | negative)} = 0.08/0.2 \quad = 0.4$$
$$\text{Prob(defective | negative)} = 0.12/0.2 \quad = 0.6$$

These can be used in the decision tree for the situation in which the test is used, Figure 4.13. The EMV of using the test is £51.40. This is slightly worse than the EMV when the test is not used, £56, therefore Technomusic should not use the test.

However, the company may decide to use the test for greater peace of mind and customer service. If it does, then for any component for which the test is 'positive' or 'inconclusive', the component should be shipped. If the test is 'negative' the component should be re-worked.

QUESTIONS

1. A cumulative probability distribution provides the following data:

    $$P(\text{demand} \leqslant 100) = 33 \text{ per cent}$$
    $$P(\text{demand} \leqslant 200) = 74 \text{ per cent}$$
    $$P(\text{demand} \leqslant 300) = 92 \text{ per cent}$$
    $$P(\text{demand} \leqslant 400) = 100 \text{ per cent}$$

    What is P(demand is between 100 and 300)?

2. In the assessment of the distribution of a variable, the 50 per cent fractile is 40, the 25 per cent fractile is 30 and the 75 per cent fractile is 65. Since the range of the variable for probabilities 25–50 per cent is 10 and that for 50–75 per cent probabilities is 25, are the estimates:

    (a) inconsistent and should be revalued?
    (b) inconsistent but should be left alone?
    (c) consistent?
    (d) not indicative of anything about consistency?

3. A newly developed technical process will either work in practice or fail. The prior probabilities are:

    $$P(\text{success}) = 0.7; P(\text{failure}) = 0.3$$

    A test has been designed to predict the eventual success or failure of the process. Its accuracy is given by:

    $$P(\text{predicts success given process really is successful}) = 0.9$$
    $$P(\text{predicts failure given process really is a failure}) = 0.8$$

    (a) What is the probability that the test predicts success?

(b) What is the probability of success given that success has been predicted?

(c) What is the probability of failure given that success has been predicted?

4. A major oil company is to announce its profit for the last year in two weeks' time. A financial analyst has solicited opinions about what the profit is likely to be and uses the information to construct a cumulative 'greater than or equal to' probability distribution:

Probability (%)	100	90	80	70	60	50	40	30	20	10	0
Profit (£billion)	12	16	20	23	26	28	30	33	36	44	52

For example, it is thought that there is an 80 per cent chance that the profit will be £20 billion or greater.

(a) The distribution breaks the total profit range into five equi-probable ranges relating to 0–20 per cent, 20–40 per cent etc. What is the bracket median of the last of these ranges for 80–100 per cent?

(b) What is the expected value of the profit?

5. A team of advisers has just completed an analysis of the prospects next year for five well-known stocks. The prospects depend on the state of the economy. The team has supposed that the economy will be in one of four states:

- further decline (s1);
- holding steady (s2);
- slight improvement (s3);
- major expansion (s4).

The growth per pound sterling for the stocks corresponding to each state of the economy is given by Table 4.7.

Table 4.7

Stock	State of economy			
	s1	s2	s3	s4
A	−.35	−.15	+.15	+.60
B	−.25	−.05	0	+.35
C	−.15	0	+.05	+.20
D	−.05	+.05	+.10	+.20
E	0	+.05	+.05	+.10

(a) Which stock is preferable, stock C or stock D? Why?

(b) The team estimates the probabilities of different states of the economy as:

$$P(s1) = 0.1, P(s2) = 0.3, P(s3) = 0.4, P(s4) = 0.2$$

Using an expected monetary value approach, which stock is preferable?

(c) The team considers commissioning a group of economic consultants to provide an opinion on the likely state of the economy next year. Preliminary discussions reveal that the consultants will be able to give an opinion as to whether, in the context of stock performance, the economy will be (a) good (o1), (b) average (o2), or (c) poor (o3). The reliability of their opinions is given in Table 4.8 derived from their previous performances.

Table 4.8

	State of economy			
Opinion	s1	s2	s3	s4
Good (o1)	0.1	0.2	0.4	0.6
Average (o2)	0.2	0.6	0.4	0.3
Poor (o3)	0.7	0.2	0.2	0.1

What is the EVSI (expected value of sample information) of the consultants' advice?

(d) What is the expected value of perfect information?

6. An African government is trying to determine the best policy for controlling a pest which is damaging the tropical fruits which are one of its major exports. There are three ways of attacking the pest:

- Approach 1: spray with a DDT-type substance;
- Approach 2: spray with a hormone which prevents the pests developing to adulthood;
- Approach 3: use a two-stage programme to upset breeding pattern. First, trap males with the help of a scent. Second, sterilise these males, then release them.

Approach 1 is tried and tested and the outcome is known with near certainty. The DDT-type substances can control but not eradicate, so, although the cost of this approach is not high, neither are the benefits. This approach is the standard against which improvements brought about by the other approaches can be compared. In other words, the net financial benefit of Approach 1 is taken to be zero and the payoffs of Approaches 2 and 3 measured as increments to the benefits which Approach 1 could bring, i.e. the costs and benefits of Approaches 2 and 3 detailed below, are increments to those of Approach 1.

The cost of Approach 2 is £4 million. There is no more than a 0.2 chance that this will work, but if it does the benefit in terms of increased exports is as high as £60 million, because it would eradicate the pest. If it does not work there will be a loss of £5 million, in addition to the cost of the approach, because by the time the failure is known it will be too late to spray with DDT and exports will be lost.

If Approach 3 is followed, the first question is the success or failure of the scent. There is a 0.5 chance that a high number of males will be trapped, a 0.5 chance that a low number will be trapped. Once this is known a decision to spray with DDT or to sterilise and then release the trapped males must be made. The cost of the scent programme is £6 million and the cost of sterilisation is a further £8 million. If the two-stage programme is successful, the benefit in terms of the value of fruit exports, but excluding costs of the approach, is £40 million. If the sterilisation is unsuccessful, this result will not be known in time to spray with DDT this year and the net loss will be £5 million, as for Approach 2. If the first stage traps a lot of the males, there is a 85 per cent chance of success by releasing the sterile males; if the first stage traps few males, there is only a 15 per cent chance of success.

(a) Use decision analysis to decide on the optimal solution.
(b) What is the maximum which should be paid for a series of laboratory trials to research the uncertainties inherent in all three approaches?
(c) A department of a local university offers to carry out some research work on the effectiveness of the hormone. The researchers believe that the accuracy of their work will be 95/80. This means that if the hormone really will work there is a 95 per cent chance that the research will predict it; if it really will not work there is a 80 per cent chance that the research will predict it. What is the maximum which should be paid for this research?
(d) What assumptions and non-quantitative information should be taken into account in coming to a decision?

ANSWERS TO QUESTIONS

1. The probability of demand between 100 and 300 is 59 per cent.

2. (d) is correct.

3. (a) The probability that the test predicts success is 69 per cent.
    (b) The probability of success given that success has been predicted is 0.91.
    (c) The probability of failure given that success has been predicted is 0.09.

4. (a) The range of profits relating to 80–100 per cent is 12–20. The bracket median is the profit relating to 90%, 16.
    (b) The expected profit is 28.8.

5. (a) Stock D is preferable.
    (b) Stock A has the highest EMV, 0.10.
    (c) The EVSI for the consultants' economic opinions is £0.031 per £ invested.
    (d) The EVPI is £0.095 per £ invested. When multiplied by the amount invested this gives the maximum that should be paid for any information.

6   (a) The optimal decision is to adopt Approach 3. If the trapping process is successful, go on to sterilisation; if not, spray with the DDT-type substance. The EMV of this optimal path is £6 625 000.
    (b) The EVPI, the maximum to be paid for any additional sample information, is £13 415 000.
    (c) The most which should be paid for the university research, the EVSI, is £6 884 000.
    (d) Assumptions: (i) the payoffs are discounted cash flows and therefore must be sensitive to the choice of time horizon and the discount rate, neither of which are mentioned in the case; (ii) the payoffs are net benefits/losses based on the incremental effect of the different programmes and these figures must be open to doubt since they are bound to be hard to measure; (iii) the research does not cause delays which effect the payoffs.

    Non-quantitative considerations: (i) Approach 2, and to a lesser extent Approach 3, carry qualitative benefits in that they provide information that may be valuable for future work in this area; (ii) DDT and hormone spraying presumably have environmental disbenefits.

CHAPTER FIVE

Simulation

This chapter describes the concept of simulation from a management point of view: the different categories, the basic structure and mechanics, the output and its interpretation, the key factors in its successful application, and its limitations. The 'management point of view' means that the chapter is about using, rather than constructing, simulations and to this end several typical applications are provided. The chapter does not delve into the computer programming expertise which is the basis for constructing a large simulation.

INTRODUCTION

To simulate means to imitate, mimic or copy. The object of a simulation – the thing that is imitated, mimicked or copied – can be almost anything. It might be the sea, for example when trials of new ship designs take place in wave tanks; it might be the weather, as in the use of wind tunnels to estimate the high-speed performance of a war plane; it might be a piece of equipment, as when flight simulators are used to test the reactions of aircraft pilots. In business a simulation may replicate cashflows in a company to determine the impact of a changing financial environment on profitability; or a simulation may imitate an inventory system to show how different policies may affect costs and the likelihood of being out of stock. In the cases of wave tanks, wind tunnels and flight simulators, the simulation is based on a small-scale physical model. Physical models may also be used in business applications. For example, physical models have been used to plan the layout of a new supermarket. More usually, simulations are mathematical, based on a series of algebraic equations. Large simulations of this second type are of course computerised and software packages are available for constructing simulations.

A typical application of a mathematical simulation might be in the appraisal of capital expenditure plans. For example, suppose the present values of three capital expenditure projects are to be calculated and the results presented to the Finance Committee so that the preferred project can be selected. Suppose the projects are based on the following assumptions which are common to all:

- turnover generated in first year = £10 million;
- operating costs = 40 per cent of turnover;
- overheads = £2.5 million per annum;
- length of projects = 5 years;
- discount rate = 12 per cent.

On the other hand, suppose the three projects have important differences: the initial capital outlay and the rate at which turnover is estimated to increase over the five years

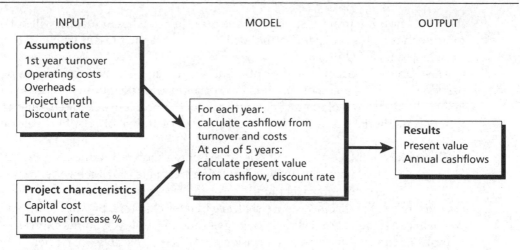

Figure 5.1   Simulation of capital projects

of the project. A present value for each project can be calculated from this data. The calculation process is called a *model*; using the model is a *simulation* (Figure 5.1). Using the common data and the data specific to each project, the model imitates the annual cashflows of the company and produces an overall present value for each project.

The purpose of a simulation is to test the effect of different decisions and different assumptions. In the capital expenditure example the different decisions are the different ways to invest capital – the three projects – the different assumptions are the first year turnover, the relationship between operating costs and turnover, the level of overheads, etc. Initially this simulation would be used to find which project has the best present value and most favourable annual cashflows.

The objective, however, is to go further and see how this decision in favour of one of the projects is affected by changes in the assumptions. Most of the input assumptions are estimates, some accurate, some less so. Do the simulation results point to the same project when interest rates (and therefore the discount rate) fluctuate? What would happen if technological obsolescence meant that the lifetimes of some of the projects were reduced from five years to four? What would be the effect if the forecast of the relationship between turnover and operating costs was different? The answers to these questions might well suggest that another project is preferable and, if the answers gave significant cause for concern, they might point to the need to define some new projects. The real value of a simulation is therefore that it can measure the impact of changing circumstances on decision making. Once a simulation has been constructed, different decisions and assumptions can be tested out quickly and without the expense, risk or (in the case of a flight simulator) the danger of testing out a decision in reality.

Like other quantitative techniques, simulation is an aid to decision making, but the contribution it makes differs from that of optimisation techniques, such as linear programming (LP) and decision analysis, in one important respect. The difference is that the simulation approach, like a large calculator, merely measures the effect of a decision defined by the decision maker. In the capital expenditure appraisal example, the simulation measured the effect of different projects which were pre-defined. The simulation did not suggest, as an optimisation technique might have done, what the optimal level of capital expenditure was. The 'best' decision, or project, meant the best of those which were tested;

there may be other projects superior to the three tested. The simulation will not of course indicate that such a project exists, but will just measure the present values of the projects for which data is fed into it.

This approach differs from the optimisation techniques which themselves define the best decision. LP or decision analysis will come up with the optimal decisions; in simulation, the decision maker must not only model the problem accurately (just as in optimisation methods), but must also propose the whole range of possible decisions to test out.

This makes simulation seem inferior to the optimisation techniques, but simulation also has a great compensating advantage: simulation is capable of a much wider range of applications. The optimisation techniques can only be applied in particular well-defined circumstances. For instance, as we shall see in later chapters, LP applies only when the problem can be structured with an objective function and constraints expressed linearly in terms of continuous variables; decision analysis is applicable only when the problem can be structured as a series of sub-decisions and chance events represented by a decision tree. No such restrictions limit the uses of simulation. Indeed, the widespread use of simulation models stems from the fact that there are so many situations which cannot be contained within the restrictive assumptions of optimisation techniques. Even when the situations are approximated and simplified, as they often are and to an unrealistic extent, the restrictions are still too great. But these situations can usually be tackled using simulation.

APPLICATION: AN INTERNATIONAL DISTRIBUTION SYSTEM

Because it is not restricted to problems with particular characteristics, simulation has a wide range of applications, including financial and corporate planning models, business games, and models of operations in factories, retail stores and logistics. The application described here is the distribution of steel throughout a country and beyond to other countries.

Problem

On a South East Asian Island (see Figure 5.2) a new large steelworks was being built at a west coast location. Before it was in operation all steel was imported, but on completion of the plant all steel required on the island was to be supplied by it. There was a need for steel on all parts of the island – for manufacturing, building construction, transport, etc. Analysis showed that there would be demand at 120 different centres throughout the island. Demand in some neighbouring countries was also predicted. The steelworks was financed by the government and was to be under its overall control.

The construction of the steelworks brought with it another problem, which was what to do with the production. The government had to plan a distribution network for the steel products and this appeared to be an immense task. Three modes of transport were available:

1. *Sea transport* was the only possibility for the international demand. Because of the poor land transport infrastructure, it was also preferable for long-distance distribution on

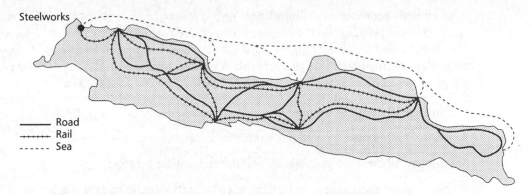

Steelworks

——— Road
+++++ Rail
------ Sea

Figure 5.2   Steel distribution across a South East Asian island

the island. However, suitable harbour facilities were available at only one or two locations.

2. *Rail routes* existed but they were radial as a result of their original purpose, which was (and is) the transport of tea from the growing areas in the mountainous centre to the population and harbours of the coast.

3. *Road routes* covered most of the island, but few of them were suitable for heavy vehicles or even had a tarmac surface.

Simulation

From the start of the planning work it was clear that the problem of planning a distribution network was a very difficult one. The size of the problem was great: there were many different steel products of different shapes and sizes, three modes of transport and 120 demand centres. Some possible solutions were viable but required large and uncertain capital expenditures (in harbour facilities, transit warehouses, road and rail infrastructure). There were many uncertainties (the levels of finance required, almost unpredictable levels of demand, the lack of geographical and geological details).

All these difficulties meant that no optimisation technique would be able to provide a solution. Instead, a simulation was used, one of great size and complexity. The data requirements were enormous. It would be necessary to specify details of all possible links in the transport network and the costs associated with transporting the steel products across the links by each of the transport modes. In essence, the simulation would have to work as follows. Given the quantities of each steel product which were to be transported by each mode of transport along each of its routes, it would have to calculate the total tonnage moving along each route, check that this did not exceed capacity and then calculate the total cost of supplying demand.

A set of routes by which the centres of demand were to be supplied, together with the associated capital investments, was called a *distribution policy*. By combining different modes of transport for the different demand centres, a great many distribution policies could be defined. The policies were then tested with the simulation to calculate the total cost of supplying the demand centres with the steel products, with the objective of finding a policy which met the logistics requirements at low cost.

Even with a computerised simulation, only a few policies could be tested. Because there were so many possibilities it was essential to adopt a structured approach to selecting the few to be tested, in order that the 'best' policy finally chosen was as close to optimal as possible. The approach was to start with very broad policies and then narrow down the range of possibilities stage by stage. The policies tried out first were:

1. Supply all demand by road.

2. Supply all demand possible by rail, the remainder by road.

3. Supply all demand possible by sea, the remainder by road.

4. Supply all centres more than 1000 miles from the steelworks by sea; between 500 and 1000 miles by rail; less than 500 miles by road.

The results from these four policies, together with the costs associated with individual links, indicated the types of policy worthy of further investigation. The process of narrowing down continued. At each stage some policies were rejected, others amended and refined until, finally, a satisfactory policy was evolved.

The purpose of a simulation is to evaluate decisions and assumptions. In this case the decisions are the different distribution policies, the assumptions are the levels of demand in the 120 centres, the capital costs, the transportation costs and capacities of the individual links. By varying the assumptions, the ability of the chosen policy to stand up to changing circumstances is investigated. A 'best' policy which remains 'best' for a wide range of circumstances is called *robust*.

TYPES OF SIMULATION

The steel distribution application is an example of the simulation of a *physical system*. Although the end result is financial, the simulation is based on volume flows down the various links. Similarly when planning a supermarket, a simulation of different layouts is the simulation of a physical system with outputs measured in terms of finance and customer service. On the other hand, the earlier capital expenditure example is a simulation of a *financial system*, based purely on cashflows.

As well as having a physical or financial application, simulations are also classified as *deterministic* or *stochastic* (see Figure 5.3). Deterministic means that the inputs and assump-

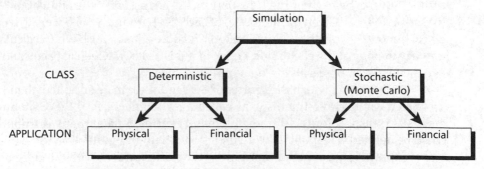

Figure 5.3   Classifying types of simulation

tions are treated as if they are fixed and known: none is subject to probability distributions. The capital expenditure example was like this. The role of a deterministic simulation is that of a large calculating mechanism. It is useful because of the number and complexity of the relationships involved and the need for sensitivity analysis. Corporate planning models are often examples of this type. The impact on profit of different assumptions concerning, say, the growth of sales are calculated by the simulation model. Associated decisions relating to, for example, production capacity or advertising can also be investigated, eventually allowing future plans for the whole organisation to be formulated.

Stochastic means that some of the inputs, assumptions or variables are not fixed but subject to probability distributions, and treated accordingly. For example, the capital cost of building a new harbour facility is not likely to be known *exactly* at the outset. The true cost will emerge as excavation gets under way. Instead it may be specified at the outset as a distribution, centred at, say, £20 million but covering a range from £16 million to £30 million with varying probabilities over this range. When a simulation involves variables such as this, it is used in a different way.

The simulation is run many times (hence the need for a computer) with the probabilistic variable, the capital cost in the above example, taking on different values for each run. But it is done in such a way that, over all the runs, the different values used have the same distribution as the variable's probability distribution. This technique is known as *Monte Carlo simulation*. Stochastic financial simulations are often known as *risk analyses*. An application will be described later.

Monte Carlo technique

The Monte Carlo technique is best explained in the context of a simple problem.

A local education authority has a warehouse which stores the day-to-day items used in its schools. It stores pencils, paper, acetates, cleaning materials and so on. Each day the administrators of the different schools in the area requisition items from the warehouse and naturally the demand for each item varies from day to day. If the warehouse can supply the items, it sends them out on the daily delivery round. Because educational requirements have a high priority, if there is an item which is out of stock the foreman of the warehouse has to obtain it from another source, usually a local retail store. This can be expensive both in terms of the time and labour costs of obtaining the item and of the item's higher price at a retail store. On the other hand, it also costs the education authority money to hold inventory and so it is not the authority's policy to avoid stockouts by holding vast stocks. Instead, when the stock of an item is low and it reaches its 're-order point', that item is re-ordered from suppliers. The time taken for the replenishment to arrive varies from item to item and from order to order.

The authority is now trying to define the best inventory policy. It is starting by looking at one item, a large pack of blank videotapes, data about which is available from store records and from the accounting department.

Table 5.1 shows that the demand for the videotapes varies from 1 to 6 packs per day, with an average of 3.5 per day. Table 5.2 shows that when packs are re-ordered they take from 4 to 7 days to arrive at the warehouse. Table 5.3 shows that the cost of holding a pack for a day is 50p. The cost of not being able to supply a pack when requisitioned is £10.

The authority is trying to find the best inventory policy for this item. The inventory

Table 5.1   Demand distribution

Demand	Probability
1	0.10
2	0.15
3	0.25
4	0.25
5	0.15
6	0.10

Total 1.00

Average $= (1 \times 0.1) + (2 \times 0.15) + (3 \times 0.25) + (4 \times 0.25) + (5 \times 0.15) + (6 \times 0.1)$
= 3.5 per day

Table 5.2   Order lead time

Lead time (days)	Probability
4	0.1
5	0.4
6	0.4
7	0.1

Total 1.0

Table 5.3   Costs

Stockholding cost per item per day = 50p
Stockout cost per item per day = £10

policy is the *re-order quantity* (the number of packs ordered when re-ordering takes place) and the *re-order level* (the level of stock which triggers a replenishment order). A simulation is to be used which will model the operation of the warehouse over 40 days and calculate the cost of running a particular inventory policy over that time. Although the amounts of money involved are small, it is intended to apply the lessons learned from this one item to all items stocked in the warehouse, so the savings resulting from an improved policy are potentially very high.

The daily demand is a crucial input to the simulation. However, because it varies and this variation is represented by a probability distribution, it is not immediately obvious how it should be treated. Clearly, the average value of demand (3.5 units per day) cannot be used because this will obscure the peak and trough effects which are the source of the difficulty. The method for treating demand in the simulation must have the following two essential characteristics.

1. Demand must vary from day to day in such a way that at the end of the 40-day period the distribution of daily demand is like that in Table 5.1. This characteristic ensures that the *level* of demand used in the simulation accords with what occurs in practice.

2. The different daily demands must occur in random order. For example, if the simulation covered 100 days and had a demand of 1 per day for the first 10 days, a demand of 2 per day for the next 15 days, a demand of 3 per day for the next 25 days and so on, then the distribution used in the simulation would be the same as that in Table 5.1; but this would not mimic what happens in practice where daily demand varies but in no set sequence. This characteristic of randomness helps ensure that the *pattern* of demand used in the simulation accords with what occurs in practice.

The two characteristics are required if the simulation is to be an adequate test of different inventory policies. The Monte Carlo technique is a method of providing inputs to the simulation which satisfy both of these. The first requirement is a set of random numbers (see Table 5.4). Random numbers are just what they appear: a series of numbers in random order. They may come from a computer-based generating program (in the same way that winning numbers in a national lottery are selected), or from a table found at the back of most statistical textbooks.

The random numbers are then associated with the different levels of demand, as in Table 5.5. The random numbers in Table 5.4 all have two digits. The 10 numbers (00–09) are associated with a demand of 1 unit per day, 15 numbers (10–24) with a demand of 2 units per day, 25 numbers (25–49) with a demand of 3 units per day, etc. Whenever a demand level is required in the simulation a random number is selected and the associated demand level used in the simulation. Going through the random number table, each demand level has the same chance of occurring as in the original distribution, e.g. there is a 10 per cent chance of using a demand of 1 unit per day in the simulation – because 10 random numbers out of 100 are associated with that demand level. Moreover, the demands used will be selected in random order.

Table 5.4 Random numbers

97	51	88	70	96	77	96	76	18	54
80	94	76	58	70	12	58	63	05	13
14	02	38	66	86	96	91	42	60	63
22	52	78	18	24	77	87	24	08	06
96	44	82	84	70	10	08	86	90	76
49	15	57	51	92	14	67	83	42	07

Table 5.5 Demand distribution

Demand	Probability	Associated random numbers
1	0.10	00–09
2	0.15	10–24
3	0.25	25–49
4	0.25	50–74
5	0.15	75–89
6	0.10	90–99
Total	1.00	

The first random number is 97, so the demand for Day 1 of the simulation will be 6 since 97 is in the range 90–99 which is associated with a demand for 6. The second random number is 51, so the second day's demand will be 4. In this way a stream of daily demands is provided for the simulation which, over the long run, will closely match what happens in practice. Since the numbers are random we can use them in sequence, starting wherever we like in the table.

FLOWCHARTS

Simulating the local education authority's inventory control was a fairly simple process. In practice, situations such as the steel distribution problem are likely to be highly complex. A flowchart is an intermediate stage which helps formulate a verbal description of a problem into the type of logical sequence that can be simulated. It is a diagrammatic representation of the steps which have to be followed in the simulation. It includes the decisions and actions carried out in operating the actual inventory system, as well as the extra steps of recording information during the simulation. In a flowchart, these symbols are used:

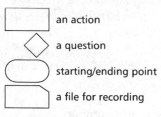

Figure 5.4   (a)

Solid lines show the flow of events through time; dotted lines represent movements of information. Figure 5.4 shows the flowchart for the inventory problem.

The first step each day is to see whether new supplies will arrive that day. This requires information from the replenishment file which stores details of orders which are in the system but have yet to arrive. If new supplies are to arrive then the replenishment file and the inventory file (showing the current level of stock) must be updated; if not the simulation moves on to the next step, which is to generate the day's demand by the Monte Carlo method.

The question is then asked: is the demand greater than current inventory? This requires information from the inventory file. If demand can be supplied, parts are moved from the store and the inventory file is updated; if not, as much of the demand as possible is shipped and the rest is recorded as lost demand in the lost demand file.

The next step is to calculate costs. In this illustrative example there are just two kinds of cost, the cost of holding inventory and the cost of losing demand. Both are calculated from the appropriate file information.

Next the end-of-day inventory level is inspected to see if it has reached the point at

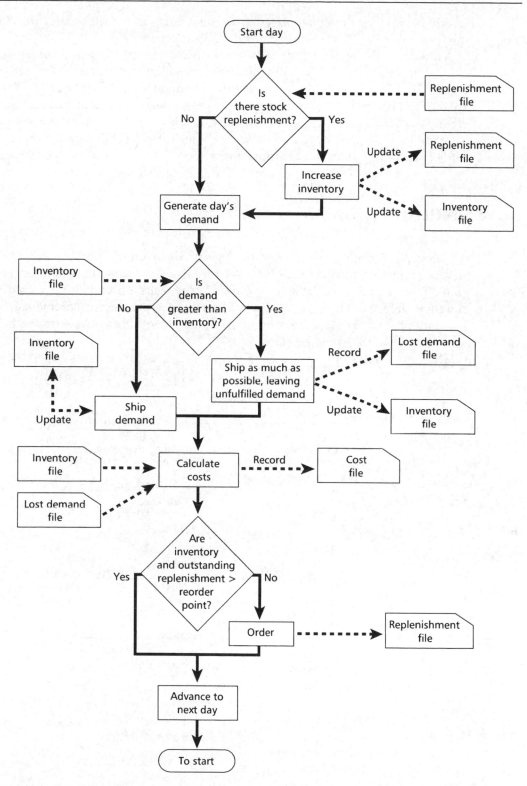

Figure 5.4   Flowchart

which a new order should be placed. If so, the replenishment file records the placing of the new order. Finally, the simulation advances to a new day.

A flowchart, therefore, describes the problem in the strictly logical fashion required by simulation, reflecting the way in which the simulation will attempt to imitate the real system. There are other ways of representing simulations diagrammatically, but flowcharts are the most common. The symbols used in the flowchart are not standard and other flowcharts may use different symbols. Whatever the style of representation, all these diagrams have the same purpose, which is to describe the logical steps of the simulation as a preliminary to carrying out an actual simulation.

HOW SIMULATION WORKS

The flowchart should have clarified the logic of the inventory problem and the simulation can now be constructed. Table 5.6 is a repeat of the demand distribution with associated random numbers. Table 5.7 is the lead time distribution with associated random numbers. Table 5.8 shows the manual simulations of the inventory problem. In practice it would probably be done by computer, but the aim of this manual version is to show what is happening inside the black box.

The simulation is run for 40 days. There is nothing mandatory about the choice of 40,

Table 5.6   Demand

Demand	Probability	Associated random numbers
1	0.10	00–99
2	0.15	10–24
3	0.25	25–49
4	0.25	50–74
5	0.15	75–89
6	0.10	90–99
Total	1.00	

Table 5.7   Lead time

Demand	Probability	Associated random numbers
4	0.1	00–09
5	0.4	10–49
6	0.4	50–89
7	0.1	90–99
Total	1.0	

Table 5.8   Details of the simulation

Inventory at start of day 1 = 30
Re-order quantity = 40
Re-order point = 20
Stockholding cost = 50p/item/day
Lost demand cost = £10/item

| | (A) | | | (B) | (C) | | (D) | | | |
| | Inventory file | | | | | Cost file | | Replenishment file | | | |
Day	Start inventory	Receipts	Demands	End inventory	Stock cost	Lost demand	LD cost	Order placed	Lead time	Due in	On order
1	30		6	24	12						
2	24		4	20	10			40	7	9	40
3	20		5	15	7.5						40
4	15		4	11	5.5						40
5	11		6	5	2.5						40
6	5		5	0	0						40
7	0		6	0	0	6	60				40
8	0		5	0	0	5	50				40
9	0	40	2	38	19						
10	38		4	34	17						
11	34		5	29	14.5						
12	29		6	23	11.5						
13	23		5	18	9			40	5	18	40
14	18		4	14	7						40
15	14		4	10	5						40
16	10		2	8	4						40
17	8		4	4	2						40
18	4	40	4	40	20						
19	40		1	39	19.5						
20	39		2	37	18.5						
21	37		2	35	17.5						
22	35		1	34	17						
23	34		3	31	15.5						
24	31		4	27	13.5						
25	27		5	22	11						
26	22		6	16	8			40	6	32	40
27	16		6	10	5						40
28	10		3	7	3.5						40
29	7		4	3	1.5						40
30	3		4	0	0	1	10				40
31	0		2	0	0	2	20				40
32	0	40	4	36	18						
33	36		5	31	15.5						
34	31		2	29	14.5						
35	29		2	27	13.5						
36	27		5	22	11						
37	22		5	17	8.5			40	6	43	40
38	17		2	15	7.5						40
39	15		1	14	7						40
40	14		1	13	6.5						40
				Total = 379		Total = 140					

or any other number, but whatever simulation length is chosen should adequately reflect a cycle of the firm's business. For example, if there are quarterly seasonal variations in demand the period covered by the simulation should be at least 250 working days to cover a whole year (and, of course, the generation of daily demand should also reflect this seasonality).

On the first day the starting inventory is 30, chosen as a typical inventory level. In a short simulation this choice might significantly affect the results and, consequently, in some cases simulations are repeated using different starting conditions.

In a simulation the operator must define the policies to be tested. For this inventory problem the policies are defined as specifying the re-order quantity (the number of parts ordered when an order is placed) and the re-order point (the level of inventory which triggers off a new order). The first policy to be tested has been selected, based on experience, with these values at 40 and 20 respectively.

For the purposes of the example, two types of cost are specified: that of holding stock and that of unfulfilled demand. The stocking cost is 50p per item per day, and the cost of not being able to meet demand is estimated as £ 10 per item. In a practical application many more costs would have to be taken into account.

For each day the simulation follows the sequence specified in the flowchart (Figure 5.4). Column (A) shows the inventory at the start of that day. If the replenishment file shows that a new order is to arrive that day, the order is added to the inventory. Demand for the day is generated using the Monte Carlo method (see Table 5.9) and subtracted from the inventory to leave an end-of-day inventory in column (B). The cost of holding this inventory overnight is calculated in column (C). If inventory on hand is insufficient to meet demand, as much demand as possible is met (and inventory reduced to zero) and the remainder is recorded as lost demand. The cost of lost demand is calculated in column (D). Finally, the end-of-day inventory is compared with the re-order point to see if a new order should be placed. If so, the quantity order, the lead time before delivery (generated via Monte Carlo, see Table 5.10), the date of arrival and the amount currently on order are recorded in the replenishment file. The simulation then passes on to the next day.

Table 5.9   Simulated demand

Day	Demand	Random numbers	Day	Demand	Random numbers	Day	Demand	Random numbers	Day	Demand	Random numbers
1	6	97	11	5	80	21	2	14	31	2	22
2	4	51	12	6	94	22	1	02	32	4	52
3	5	88	13	5	76	23	3	38	33	5	78
4	4	70	14	4	58	24	4	66	34	2	18
5	6	96	15	4	70	25	5	86	35	2	24
6	5	77	16	2	12	26	6	96	36	5	77
7	6	96	17	4	58	27	6	91	37	5	87
8	5	76	18	4	63	28	3	42	38	2	24
9	2	18	19	1	05	29	4	60	39	1	08
10	4	54	20	2	13	30	4	63	40	1	06

Note: The random numbers used in this table are taken from the first four rows of Table 5.4.

Table 5.10   **Simulated lead times**

Re-order	Random numbers	Lead time	Re-order	Random numbers	Lead time
1	96	7	6	10	5
2	44	5	7	08	4
3	82	6	8	68	6
4	84	6	9	90	7
5	70	6	10	76	6

Note: The random numbers used in this table are taken from the fifth row of Table 5.4.

INTERPRETING THE OUTPUT

At the end of the 40 days the costs have to be calculated and recorded. Table 5.11 shows that for this policy (re-order level 40, re-order quantity 20), the stockholding cost is £379 and the cost of the lost demand is £140, making a total of £519. There was a stock-out, i.e. demand was not fully met, on 10 per cent of days. This can be checked from Table 5.8.

Table 5.11 shows the results of running the simulation for a selection of other inventory policies. The best appears to be a re-order quantity (ROQ) of 30 and a re-order point (ROP) of 20. It would be expected that a policy with a low re-order quantity would work out favourably. Such a policy would involve making a lot of re-orders, each for a small quantity. Since the administration cost of re-ordering has not been included in the simulation, frequent re-ordering is not penalised. A more sophisticated simulation would include this cost.

The simulation has only tested the policies defined for it. It may be that policies such as (ROQ 30, ROP 17), (ROQ 30, ROP 22) etc. work better. There are very many possible combinations. The time and cost of finding a true optimum may not be worthwhile and an approximately optimal solution may be the most realistic outcome.

The results in Table 5.11 are based on a particular set of random numbers, which

Table 5.11   **Simulation summary**

Policy	COSTS			% days out of stock
	Stock holding	Lost demand	Total	
1. ROQ40 ROP 20	379	140	519	10
2. ROQ 50 ROP 20	534	110	644	5
3. ROQ30 ROP 20	314	110	424	5
4. ROQ 40 ROP 15	339	180	519	12.5
5. ROQ 40 ROP 25	433	80	513	5

Table 5.12   Policy 1 with different random numbers

| | | COSTS | | |
Trial	Stock holding	Lost demand	Total	% days out of stock
1	379	140	519	10
2	408	60	468	7.5
3	398	70	468	7.5
4	394	0	394	0

generated the demand and lead time variables. While the numbers were certainly random, purely by chance they may have been in some way unusual. If they were the demands and lead times would then not be representative of their distributions. For example, if the random numbers tended to be high, the demands would be high and the lead times long. There are two ways to deal with this problem. The first is to check the simulated distributions with the originals, but this is time consuming. It is more practicable to repeat the simulation for the (ROQ 40, ROP 20) policy several times, each time generating new sets of random numbers (and therefore of demands and lead times). This allows the policy to be evaluated across different data patterns. The results for four repetitions (= four random number streams) are shown in Table 5.12. The policy gives total costs ranging between 394 and 519.

With such variations as shown in Table 5.12, it would be dangerous to base a decision on a simulation covering just one 40-day period. The simulation should be run many times, with different random number streams, and the average costs for each policy compared.

Table 5.13 shows the results of testing the same policies as were tested in Table 5.11. However, instead of just being from one 40-day simulation, the results are the averages of fifty 40-day simulations. Table 5.13 confirms the earlier results, and backs the intuitive reasoning that a low re-order quantity policy will give the lowest costs.

While several different random number streams should be used to evaluate a policy, it is important that the same streams are used to evaluate other policies. The reason is that the results from two policies should differ because the policies are different, not because

Table 5.13   Averages of fifty 40-day simulations

| | | | COSTS | | |
Policy		Stock holding	Lost demand	Total	% days out of stock
1.	ROQ 40 ROP 20	425	23	448	0.9
2.	ROQ 50 ROP 20	508	29	537	1.1
3.	ROQ 30 ROP 20	324	47	371	1.8
4.	ROQ 40 ROP 15	359	103	462	3.7
5.	ROQ 40 ROP 25	509	1	510	0.1

they have been tested on different demand patterns. For example, in Table 5.13 each policy was evaluated over 50 runs. The same 50 streams were used for each policy, so that like was compared with like. Most computer programs cater for this by asking the user to specify the starting random number. If the starts are the same, the streams will be the same. Each of the 50 runs had a different starting number, but the same 50 starting numbers were used for each policy.

As well as measuring the average costs of different policies, the simulation will also compare their risks. Risk is measured by calculating how often very high costs are recorded. Two policies, A and B, may have the same average costs over many runs, say 500, but if policy A had a range of 300–650 for individual runs, it would be regarded as more risky than policy B with a range of 460–560.

Risk is also measured by the percentage of days on which demand is lost. Lost demand, besides its financial implications, may also have important non-quantifiable disadvantages. The 'best' policy may then be decided by making a tradeoff between average cost and percentage of days lost.

The number of simulation runs required in order to be reasonably satisfied with the final decision almost certainly means that even a simple simulation such as that for the inventory problem needs to be put on the computer. A relatively small computer program (about 100 lines) is sufficient to perform a similar simulation. The key factors involved in using a simulation such as this are summarised in the concluding section of this chapter.

RISK ANALYSIS

The local education authority warehouse example was of a physical simulation. Another example of a physical simulation is of arrivals and departures of ships at a port where help is required to plan the provision of loading and unloading facilities. A further example is of supermarket operations to determine how many checkout desks are needed. The steel distribution example was also a physical simulation.

When a stochastic simulation uses the Monte Carlo technique to model cashflows it is usually known as a *risk analysis*. For example, risk analysis could be used to compare the possible ways of providing production facilities when an organisation has developed a new product. One of the stochastic variables might be the rate of growth of sales of the new product. In this case the simulation is run many times as if the capital decision were being taken many times over (compare the previous example where the warehouse simulation was run over many days). For each run a different growth rate is used (as selected via Monte Carlo) and a different present value (or internal rate of return) is calculated. Over many runs a distribution of present values is obtained. Not only is the average present value calculated, but also the risk (hence the name of the technique) of obtaining an unacceptably low profit from the project. A risk analysis does not differ from other stochastic simulations because any new technique is involved. It differs only in terms of its application (to financial problems).

Problem

A small town in Scotland took its gas supply from a coal gas plant located in the town. The plant, which manufactured the gas from coal and stored it in large gasholders, supplied gas only for the town and its immediate environment. The plant, however, was about a hundred years old and had reached the point where it was beyond repair. Deteriorating rapidly, it was likely to cease functioning within two years. The local Gas Board had three options:

1. Close the plant down, sell off the site and cease supplying gas to the town. This would mean that existing customers would have to be compensated for the expenses they would incur if the supply were cut off and they had to purchase new equipment, for example a new electric cooker.

2. Close the plant down and then build a liquid natural gas (LNG) plant on the site. This would be virtually a pumping station. LNG would be brought to the town by tanker, converted to gas and pumped to customers just like the old coal-based gas. Such plants are cheap but the LNG and transport are expensive.

3. Close the plant down and sell off the site, but extend a nearby (60 miles away) North Sea gas main and supply the town with North Sea gas. At the time of this decision most of the United Kingdom had just been covered with a network of North Sea gas mains which supplied most of the country, but it had proved uneconomic to extend it to smaller places in rural areas. It had not originally been intended to supply the small town with North Sea gas. Extending the main would be very expensive but only a small, low-cost pumping station would have to be built in the town.

The Gas Board wanted to take the decision on economic grounds, evaluating the three options by measuring their present values. However, a straightforward calculation of present value would not, it was thought, fully reflect the great uncertainties involved. The costs of extending the main, compensating cut-off customers and the rate of growth of demand if, for example, North Sea gas should be available, were all variables which were not known with any certainty. It was decided to use risk analysis.

Simulation

The cashflows resulting from each of the three options were simulated over a 25-year period, the expected lifetime of the new equipment included in the options. For each option 100 runs were made using different values for the 'uncertain' variables, the values being generated by the Monte Carlo technique. The distributions of the 'uncertain' variables which were the basis of the Monte Carlo technique had to be obtained in a different way from those in the inventory problem. In that problem the demand and lead time distributions were obtained from past records. The same was true (with the additions of some forecasting) for the demand distributions of steel products example. In the Gas Board case there were no past records and the distributions had to be assessed subjectively. For example, using the standard assessment techniques described in Chapter 4 in the context of decision analysis, engineers had to estimate, in the form of a distribution, the capital cost of extending the North Sea gas main. Eventually distributions of all the stochastic variables – capital building costs, demand growths, operating costs, etc. – were developed. Although this process was time consuming, the engineers and managers accepted it well since the final result, in their eyes, made better use of their expertise and more accurately represented what was likely to happen than the single-point estimates which would otherwise have been used.

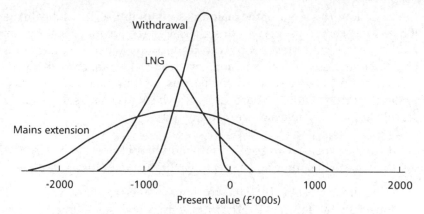

Figure 5.5   Graphical results of gas simulation (£'000)

Table 5.14   Present   values   from   gas
simulations (£'000s)

Option	Average present value	Range of present values
Withdrawal	−193	−910 to −50
LNG	−692	−1400 to +250
Extension	−471	−2200 to I 1200

For each option the simulation was run 100 times and thus 100 calculations of present value were made. A different starting random number was used for each of the 100 runs, but the same 100 starting numbers were used for each option. The results are shown in Table 5.14 and presented as a graphical distribution in Figure 5.5.

The information in Table 5.14 was the basis for choosing between the options. The Board considered the likely spread of financial results and the downside risk (the chance of a big loss) just as much as the average. The 'withdrawal' option is the best in terms of both average present value and the spread of results (the narrower the better because there is less uncertainty). 'Extension' has the best chance of making a profit, but this is offset by the likelihood of a really big loss. Economically, the Board thought that 'withdrawal' was preferable but, politically, decided it was unacceptable – the publicity surrounding the withdrawal of services would be bad. So the Board chose the next best option according to average present value, 'extension'. Since this option gave the best chance of making a profit (of up to £1.2 million), they used this information to argue that 'extension' was in fact the best option overall.

CONCLUSION

Simulation is a much less restrictive aid to decision making than are optimisation techniques such as mathematical programming and decision analysis. The preconditions for being able to use the optimisers (e.g. algebraic formulation, linearity in LP) do not apply to simulation. This is one of the major reasons for its use. It has the further advantage that it does not seem so mysterious to sceptical general managers as do some of the mathematical techniques. Most people can understand what a simulation is by reference to analogies such as wind tunnels and, as a result, they are more likely to have confidence in simulation and consequently to make use of it in their decision making.

On the other hand, there are some drawbacks in using simulation which may not be readily apparent. The major shortcomings are:

1. It can be expensive to apply. Simulation models tend to be large, which means that they take a long time and a great deal of resources to develop.

2. It requires a great deal of data which may not be readily available. Collecting the data, especially the subjective distributions, may take some time.

3. It is not an optimiser and relies on the creativity of the operator. The technique can only indicate the best policy of those tried – if only poor policies are tried, a poor decision will result.

4. Establishing the validity of the model is time consuming. A rigorous series of tests may be required to determine the accuracy of the calculations and to throw up any logical errors in the methodology, especially when it is computer based. The simulation must be a reasonably close model of reality.

5. Since the nature of simulation (non-optimising) requires many different policies to be tried out, it is inevitable that it will take time to obtain a reasonable answer from it.

It would be unusual for managers to develop a simulation themselves. Their interest will primarily be in its application to decision making, although they may have a role in the management of the development process as with, for example, the construction of a corporate model. In this case they will need to be aware, in general, of what a simulation can do and of its drawbacks.

However, once the simulation is ready its use must not be left to the programmers: the managers should take control. Managers must ensure that the simulation is focused on its prime purpose – aiding decision making. Managers/decision makers will also be the only people who know the correct 'what if?' questions to ask and in general how to handle the sensitivity analyses which are at the heart of simulation.

The key factors in using a simulation are:

● using a structured approach in deciding what options to test;
● assessing a suitable time period for the simulation to cover;
● deciding how many times to run the simulation;
● knowing when to use the same random number streams and when different ones;
● judging the influence of starting conditions.

The key factors were discussed earlier in the context of the inventory example. Perhaps the most important of these is the need to adopt a structured approach to the simulation. If many policies are feasible and the simulation is computerised, it is easy to try out policies almost at random. A better approach is to plan a series of trial policies which are so structured that the range of options can be gradually narrowed down until one is obtained which is sufficiently near to being optimal. Initially policies covering the whole spectrum of possibilities should be tried. This should indicate obviously unreasonable options, and suggest sections of the spectrum which need further investigation. These sections will be explored so that a further narrowing down is possible and so on. It is especially important to structure an approach in situations such as the inventory problem and the steel distribution problem where the range of possibilities is extremely wide. In other cases, for example the gas industry problem, the options are pre-defined and structuring becomes less vital.

CASE STUDIES

CASE STUDY 1

This case is concerned with a cross-channel car ferry operator which is assessing new staffing levels for the check-in kiosks at one of its ports. A Monte Carlo simulation is being carried out based on the arrival pattern of cars. Random numbers between 00 and 99 have been allocated to the distribution in Table 5.15, which is the number of cars arriving per minute during the afternoon in the busy summer period.

1. Which random numbers relate to six arrivals?

2. What is the arrival rate associated with the random number 84?

Table 5.15

Demand	Probability
4	0.01
5	0.02
6	0.04
7	0.09
8	0.16
9	0.24
10	0.28
11	0.12
12	0.04
Total	1.00

3. For each possible staffing arrangement, the Monte Carlo simulation is run many times and the average queue length, waiting time etc. calculated. These averages, along with other information such as costs, are used to decide on the preferred staffing level. Why must the simulation be run many times?

Solutions

1. *Which random numbers relate to six arrivals?*
The numbers 3–6 relate to six arrivals. The numbers should be allocated as in Table 5.16.

Table 5.16

Demand	Probability	Random numbers
4	0.01	0
5	0.02	1–2
6	0.04	3–6
7	0.09	7–15
8	0.16	16–31
9	0.24	32–55
10	0.28	56–83
11	0.12	84–95
12	0.04	96–99

2.   *What is the arrival rate associated with the random number 84?*
The random number 84 is in the range 84–95 which refers to a demand of 11.
3.   *For each possible staffing arrangement, the Monte Carlo simulation is run many times and the average queue length, waiting time etc., calculated. These averages, along with other information such as costs, are used to decide on the preferred staffing level. Why must the simulation be run many times?*
Since the numbers are chosen at random they could, by chance, present an arrival pattern not representative of what happens in practice. Several simulation runs using different random number streams help to average out any resulting bias.

CASE STUDY 2

For several years a pharmaceutical company has been developing a new drug for the treatment of asthma. The development and testing process is now complete and government approval in the form of a licence has just been obtained. The product will be introduced onto the market next year. The marketing and production managers have been trying to estimate demand in the first year in order that sales and marketing plans can be finalised and production facilities made ready. Between them they have prepared Table 5.17 showing their estimates of the likely spread of demand, measured in thousands of packs. How would this distribution be used in a simulation of the likely profitability of the product?

Table 5.17   Demand

Cases (000s)	Probability (%)
100– 200	5
200– 400	20
400– 600	35
600– 800	25
800–1000	10
1000–1500	5

Solution

First, associate two-digit numbers with the different demand levels in proportion to the probabilities. Secondly, let the mid-point of each category represent the whole category, e.g. the 200–400 class is represented by 300. This is an approximation, but since the original distribution was subjectively estimated, the approximation should not be too unreasonable in the context (Table 5.18). Numbers in the range 00–04 are associated with a demand of 150 000 cases, 05–24 with 300 000 cases, and so on.

The simulation would be run many times, each time choosing a different random number and thereby using a different level of demand sampled from the distribution.

Table 5.18

Mid-point (000s)	Cases (000s)	Probability (%)	Numbers
150	100–200	5	00–04
300	200–400	20	05–24
500	400–600	35	25–59
700	600–800	25	60–84
900	800–1000	10	85–94
1250	1000–1500	5	95–99

CASE STUDY 3

A large national chain of food supermarkets has 200 out-of-town stores. The number of checkout desks at each store varies between 20 and 50, depending on the size of the store. At any store not all of the checkouts are staffed at any one time: the supermarket manager uses her judgement to decide how many staff are needed at any particular time of the day.

In the last year the chain has focused its attention on customer service and as part of this initiative is looking more closely at checkout staffing, trying to balance customer service against staff costs. To help with this investigation the chain's management services group is developing a computer-based simulation of checkout operations to determine what staffing levels are appropriate at different times of the day.

The first task for the management services group is to draw a flowchart of checkout operations, in consultation with store managers. To start the consultation process the group has decided to draw a flowchart for the busy early evening period of 18.00 to 20.00. During these hours the distributions of (a) the number of customer arrivals per minute at the checkouts and (b) the service time (the time a customer is actually dealing with a cashier) are both known, having been derived from a recent survey. The assumption is made that a customer will always join the shortest queue, although this may not be strictly true since customers make allowances for the number of purchases which other customers in the queue have made. The output of the simulation will consist of information on the percentage of time cashiers are busy, average queue length, and average time a customer spends waiting.

Draw a flowchart for the simulation.

Solution

The simulation will proceed minute by minute between the hours of 18.00 and 20.00. See Figure 5.6.

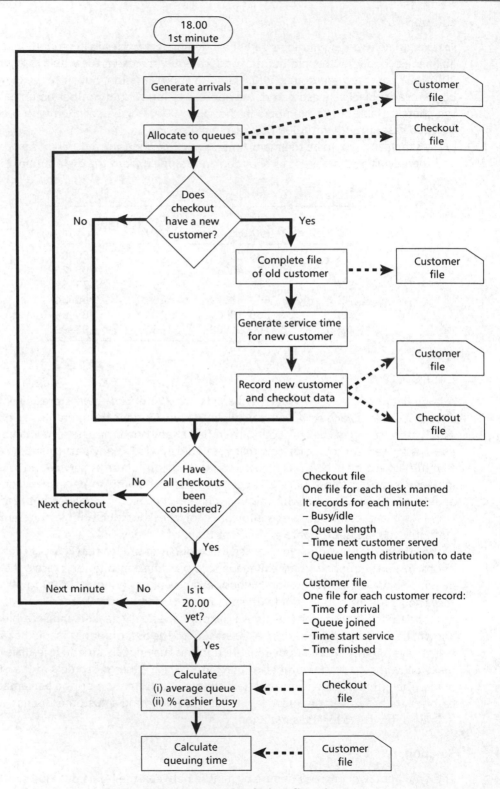

Figure 5.6   Supermarket checkout simulation flowchart

CASE STUDY 4

A logistics company is the subsidiary of a large chain of high street retailers and is responsible for the transportation of goods from manufacturers and wholesale warehouses to the high street stores. To accomplish this task it owns a fleet of trucks which are serviced at its workshop. Legal requirements and the company's own strict safety procedures have resulted in a policy of inspecting every truck each week. The inspection takes 30 minutes, after which, if the truck has no faults, it is returned to duty. If minor faults are found, they are repaired there and then. If the truck has a major fault it is taken to a specialist garage for repairs.

The time a truck spends at the inspection facilities can be as little as 30 minutes – if it has no faults or has major faults. However, should minor repairs be required the truck can spend up to four hours in the workshop. The distribution of time spent at the facilities has been constructed from historical records and is shown in Table 5.19. The time shown is to the nearest 30 minutes because this is how it has been recorded.

Trucks are taken to the inspection centre when schedules allow. The arrival rate distribution has been derived from past records and is shown in Table 5.20. The inspection facilities comprise three identical and adjacent units, each of which deals with one truck at a time.

Because of fierce competition in the retail sector the retail chain is looking carefully at its cost structure and the truck workshops have recently come under close scrutiny. A

Table 5.19

Time spent (minutes)	Probability (%)
30	65
60	5
90	3
120	4
150	6
180	9
210	5
240	3
Total	100

Table 5.20

Number of buses arriving in 30-minute period	Probability (%)
0	25
1	35
2	20
3	10
4	8
5	2
	100

recommendation to close one of the three units has been made, because, it is felt, the units can be left unused for large parts of the day. This has resulted in a great many complaints from managers, drivers and trade unions who take the view that such a closure would lower safety standards. It is also argued that a two-unit workshop would in fact be uneconomic because of the greater time buses would spend waiting for an inspection.

The Director of Traffic Operations has decided to make further investigations by simulating the operation of the inspection facilities. He intends to produce the facts and figures which will enable him to make a proper decision.

1. How should the distributions be handled in the simulation?

2. Produce a flowchart for the simulation.

3. Which factors are relevant to the argument taking place, i.e. what should the output of the simulation be?

Solutions

1. *How should the distributions be handled in the simulation?*
A Monte Carlo simulation should be carried out with arrival rate and service time as the stochastic variables. The distributions would be sampled with random numbers and the values so obtained used to make cost calculations.

2. *Produce a flowchart for the simulation*
See Figure 5.7.

3. *Which factors are relevant to the argument taking place, i.e. what should the output of the simulation be?*
Economically the argument involves a tradeoff between the time trucks/drivers are kept waiting for inspection against the time the inspection units may be idle waiting for trucks to arrive. Safety might be affected if the queues of waiting trucks were so long that the inspection mechanics hurried their work and made mistakes. Overall the relevant factors would seem to be:

Operational: Average time/week units are used
Average time a truck is queuing for an inspection
Average number of trucks in a queue
Maximum queue length

Financial: Cost of drivers having to wait
Cost of trucks having to wait
Cost of units being idle
Saving in running costs from having two units only

QUESTIONS

1. Which of the following statements concerning the use of simulation are true?

   (a) Physical models are never used in business-related simulation.
   (b) Using simulation is only worthwhile where the variables have probability distributions.

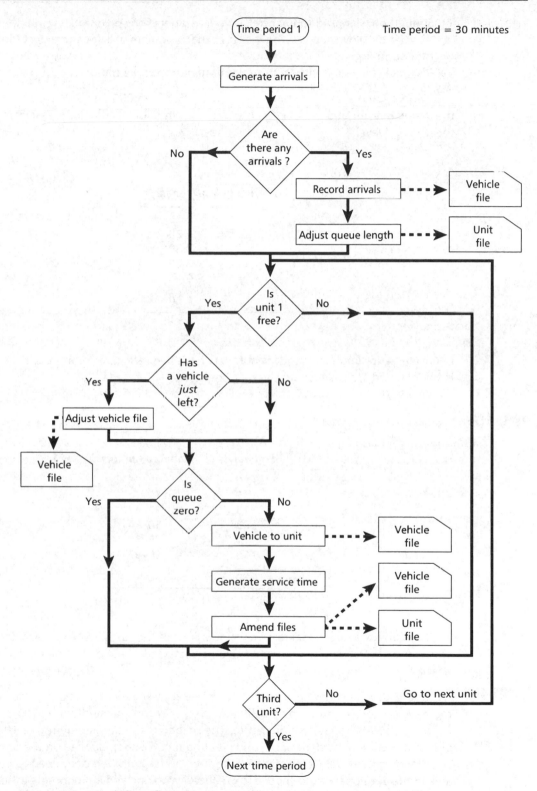

Figure 5.7 Workshop flowchart

(c) Simulation is applied to financial as well as operations problems.

(d) Simulation allows the decision maker both to compare policies and to test the effect of assumptions.

(e) Risk analysis and Monte Carlo simulation are the same thing.

2. In a Monte Carlo simulation random numbers between 000 and 999 are allocated to the demand distribution in Table 5.21. What random numbers should be associated with the demand level 5?

Table 5.21

Demand	Probability
3	0.15
4	0.20
5	0.30
6	0.25
7	0.10
Total	1.00

3. In Monte Carlo simulation random numbers have been allocated as in Table 5.22. What is the demand associated with the random number 25?

Table 5.22

Demand	Probability	Associated random numbers
6	0.10	00–09
7	0.15	10–24
8	0.25	25–49
9	0.25	50–74
10	0.15	75–89
11	0.10	90–99
	1.00	

4. The two profiles in Figure 5.8 relate to simulations of the cashflows from projects A and B. If you had to choose between the two projects and select one to be implemented, which one would you choose?

5. A property developer has been working on plans for two new investments. One involves the development of an old football stadium, renewing the stadium and in addition building a sports and recreation centre. The second is the development of a 100-year-old railway station, modernising it and creating a new shopping mall on the same site. The planning has reached the stage where substantial sums of money need to be spent and so the developer has to choose to go ahead with one and abandon the other. Both developments require the same initial investment. A risk analysis of the cash flows over

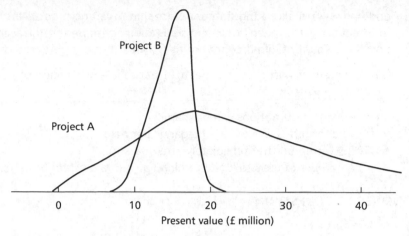

Figure 5.8   Simulation of project cash flows from Projects A and B

Table 5.23   Results from 100 iterations

	Average present value (£ million)	Standard deviation
Product A	144	48
Product B	180	180

a 25-year period produces the results shown in Table 5.23 – a distribution of the present values of each development. Plotted on a graph both distributions have the shape of a normal distribution.

(a) For each development, what is the probability of:
   - a loss (a negative present value)?
   - a substantial profit (a present value greater than £360 million)?
(b) Which product should be launched?

Note: To answer these questions it is necessary to know that, for a normal distribution:
   - 68 per cent of distribution lies within +/−1 standard deviation of the mean
   - 95 per cent of distribution lies within +/−2 standard deviation of the mean
   - 99 per cent + of distribution lies within +/−3 standard deviation of the mean

6. A small general cargo port has just two berths where ships of various sizes arrive for unloading and reloading. The amount of cargo to be unloaded and loaded depends mainly on the size of the ship, as does the maximum number of gangs needed for unloading and loading. Naturally, the rate of unloading and loading depends on the number of gangs used. The total number of gangs available each day varies and is allocated to the ships by given allocation rules.

The port authority is aware that there is an opportunity to expand port operations, attracting ships and cargoes from developing European Union trade. A plan to increase the number of berths has been put forward. In order to assess this proposal, a computerised simulation is to be carried out in order to investigate the amount of congestion and find ways of allocating staff to reduce ships' waiting time at least cost. Appropriate information on the mean number of ships queuing for berths, the average queuing time and the amount of idle time for berths is available from port records.

(a) Draw a flowchart showing the main stages in a simulation of port operations.
(b) State any assumptions made.

The following assumptions can be made:
- Only one shift is worked by the gangs per day.
- Ships vacate berths immediately after loading.
- The number of days to load or unload a ship takes integer values only.

ANSWERS TO QUESTIONS

1. (c) and (d) are true.
2. The numbers are 350–649. The numbers should be allocated as follows:

Demand	Probability	Numbers
3	0.15	0–149
4	0.20	150–349
5	0.30	350–649
6	0.25	650–899
7	0.10	900–999

3. The random number 25 is in the range 25–49 which refers to a demand of 8.
4. The average present value of project A looks slightly better but project B is less risky, having a narrower spread. Deciding which is preferable depends therefore on the decision maker's view of risk: how he or she trades off risk against return. Without this knowledge it is not possible to say which project is superior.
5. **(a)** For A: $P(loss) = 0$; $P(profit > 360) = 0$
   For B: $P(loss) = 16$ per cent; $P(profit > 360) = 16$ per cent
   (b) The choice between high average PV/high risk and low average PV/low risk depends on the developer's finances and attitude to risk.
6. Assumptions: once started a gang will complete work on a ship; work is carried out seven days a week; all days are the same working length; there is no seasonal variation in port operations.

PART THREE

Resource Allocation

Chapter 6   Project planning techniques

Describes established techniques such as PERT and CPM and their application to decision making and resource control in areas such as construction projects and technological developments.

Chapter 7   Linear programming (LP)

Describes the basic technique of LP – formulation, graphical solution and basic computer solutions – and typical application areas such as distribution, financial investments and oil refining.

Chapter 8   Extensions to linear programming (LP)

Goes beyond basic LP to deal with sensitivity analysis, dual values, related decision problems such as transportation and non-linear programming.

Chapter 9   DEA (data envelopment analysis) in a major bank

Author: PD Stone.

A case study of the application of Data Envelopment Analysis (a form of LP) to monitor the efficiency of the bank's branches. Discusses implementations problems and critical success factors.

CHAPTER SIX

Project planning techniques

This chapter describes a network technique for planning and controlling large projects involving multiple activities. The technique is usually known as PERT (programme evaluation and review technique) or CPM (critical path method). The chapter will cover basic tasks such as calculating project completion times, scheduling activities and defining key actions. The latter constitute the critical path, which is the sequence of activities which cannot be delayed without delaying the whole project. The chapter goes on to deal with extensions of the basic technique such as re-allocating resources in order to reduce the project completion time, measuring the potential effects of uncertainties in the durations of activities, and making tradeoffs between time and cost.

INTRODUCTION

Major construction enterprises, new product planning and the development of new military hardware are all examples of extremely large projects which take a long time and massive resources to complete. If they are not completed on time and within budget, the effect on the organisation concerned is likely to be unfortunate; there are many examples, particularly in computing, where large projects have gone over time and budget with catastrophic consequences.[1]

These large projects usually consist of very many smaller activities which have to be completed by a variety of individuals and groups. Each activity has a logical place in the project: it may be done at the same time as some activities and strictly before or after others. It is the vast number of different tasks, together with their intricate sequencing and the diversity of people and resources needed to carry them out, which result in delays and additional costs. A project with twice as many activities as another is generally much more than twice as difficult to manage. The coordination of all these tasks and the individuals and groups performing them is inevitably a complex task. If it is done to anything less than the highest standards then the project will be completed behind schedule and over budget. Network planning techniques are aids to help project managers in this task, enabling them to do their job more effectively.

Critical path method (CPM) and programme evaluation and review technique (PERT) are two of the best-known examples of network planning techniques. Broadly similar, they help to plan and control large projects by scheduling activities, estimating completion dates and highlighting likely causes of delay. They show by how much extra resources could shorten the project completion time and fewer resources lengthen it.

---

[1] The London Stock Exchange's TAURUS project was cancelled in March 1993 with great financial loss and, worse, it left London at a competitive disadvantage. According to some commentators the sheer size and complexity of the project were at the root of its problems.

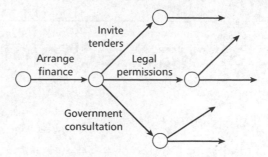

Figure 6.1   Network

A wide range of industries use these techniques. For example, they have been applied to building new schools, developing opencast coal mines and manufacturing missile systems. In summary, network planning methods work in the following way.

First, the project is broken down into a series of small individual activities and their logical sequence specified. The task of building a new school would be split up into hundreds or thousands of activities including arranging finance, seeking tenders from architects, obtaining legal permissions, laying foundations, ordering sports equipment and recruiting staff. Since some activities have to be completed before others can start and some activities can take place at the same time as others, the activities and their sequence are usually represented as a network such as Figure 6.1. The lines are the activities, the circles (called *nodes*) mark the start and completion of activities.

Secondly the duration of each activity is estimated. A crucial task for the technique is then to find those activities which are *critical*. Critical activities are defined as those for which the smallest delay in starting or completing them will delay completion of the whole project. The critical activities define a *critical path* through the network. Other activities are *slack*. They can be delayed to some extent without delaying the whole project. For example, it might be shown that arranging finance was critical since nothing can start until that is done. Ordering apparatus would probably be a slack activity since it can be done at any time while the building is being constructed.

Thirdly, attention is concentrated on the critical activities. A rearrangement of resources might speed them up (and hence the project). For example the temporary reallocation of senior staff or the use of an external consultant might quicken the process of arranging finance.

Network planning techniques are of particular value for large projects which involve the coordination of many different skills, functions and contractors. Project planners often have to deal with enormous networks, but their task has been eased by the development of computer programs which can rapidly re-analyse the network.

APPLICATIONS

Building a health centre

Local authorities encourage and oversee the development of health centres to house local medical facilities including doctors' practices, specialist nursing units and administrative sections. From start to finish the development is likely to take several years and will involve architects, town planners, builders, medical representatives, interior designers and many other groups. The local authority has the responsibility for controlling the project so that it does what is required, is finished on time and does not exceed budget. Network planning is used to do this. Essentially the task is one of *coordination*, linking together all participants and ensuring they appear in the plan at the right time.

Developing the Polaris submarine

The design, prototyping, testing and construction of Polaris submarines in the USA were controlled by network planning. The objective was of course to coordinate all the groups involved and to keep costs down, but the essential problem was the *management of time*. At the outset many of the technological breakthroughs necessary for the project to be completed had not taken place. The duration of such activities was therefore particularly uncertain, but on the other hand extra money could be spent on pieces of research which were proving especially difficult.

The network planners had to keep a close watch on the critical path since it was likely to change as some breakthroughs were achieved ahead of time while others lagged behind. Resources were switched between activities so that overall completion was not delayed while at the same time minimising cost overruns. PERT and CPM are usually given credit for the fact that Polaris was operational two years ahead of schedule.

Office relocation

A large insurance company used network techniques to plan its move from a city centre location to a cheaper site about 100 miles away. Functions and staff had to be moved in an order which minimised the disruption of business and family life. Activities ranged from the purchase, transfer and sale of equipment and furniture to devising schemes for assisting staff in buying new homes and for temporary travel arrangements. Here network planning performed its usual role in coordination and time and cost control, but more than this it played a vital part in clarifying senior management's thoughts about a *new one-off procedure*. The very act of drawing up a network and estimating durations pinpointed issues which otherwise might have remained hidden until too late.

Housing development

In property developments the building process is often controlled through network techniques. Much of the building work will be carried out by a series of individual subcontractors rather than the main contractor. The activities in the network are broken down in sufficient detail to reflect this. In situations such as this network planning is essentially being used for *cost control*.

For example, the subcontractors will be booked to appear along with their equipment at particular times. Were they to arrive and find that, because of delays to previous activities, they were not yet required, they would nevertheless have to be paid. The network can help avoid this. With a slack activity the subcontractor need not arrive at the earliest possible time. He can arrive later and the overall completion time will not be affected. He should therefore be booked to arrive later than his earliest start time. The risk of his arriving before he is able to start work will then be reduced without interfering with the overall completion time of the project.

DRAWING THE NETWORK

The first step in applying a network planning technique is to draw the network showing all the activities and the sequence in which they must be done. This is often more difficult than it might seem. This is the stage when the verbal statement of a situation is converted into a strictly logical structure, akin to the drawing of the decision tree in decision analysis. A picture of the network, rather than a written description, makes it much easier to understand the nature and scale of the whole project. Drawing the network has three stages.

List all activities

The project should be broken down into individual activities. The extent of the breakdown depends on the project planner and the scope of his or her management role. For example, the local government officer in charge of health centre developments would probably not need to have internal plastering and internal painting as separate activities, since they are the responsibility of the same building contractor. On the other hand, the project planner working for the building contractor would probably want them kept separate because they are carried out by different subcontractors.

Identify the predecessors of each activity

For each activity, those other activities which must be completed before it can start are listed. This is usually not too difficult although it must be done carefully: the wrongful inclusion or omission of a predecessor can have a bigger impact on the plan than virtually anything else.

A common mistake is failing to distinguish between the sequence in which activities *customarily* take place and the sequence in which they *logically* must take place. For example, taking a trivial situation, the usual method for sending out invoices may be to the following:

1. Check invoice.

2. Put invoice in envelope.

3. Seal envelope.

4. Address envelope.

Logically there is no reason why the envelope cannot be addressed before the invoice is inserted. A network should reflect all possibilities, not just traditional practices.

In listing the sequence only the immediate predecessors of each activity need be included. In the invoice example, the immediate predecessor of 'sealing the envelope' is 'inserting the invoice'. It is not necessary also to list 'checking the invoice' since this should already have been included as a predecessor of 'inserting the invoice'.

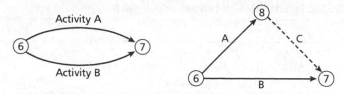

Figure 6.2   Dummy activities

Draw the network

A network comprises a series of lines and nodes. The lines represent the activities and the nodes are 'milestones' in the completion of the project. Each activity must have a node at its start and one at its end. The whole network is usually directed from left to right and is constructed to reflect the logical sequence in which activities are carried out. If there is any doubt about the 'flow of the network' the activities can be arrowed. The node at the *beginning* of an activity line should be the end node of all activities which are immediate predecessors of the activity; the node at the *end* of an activity should be the beginning of all activities for which the activity is an immediate predecessor. Figure 6.1 is an example of how a network might appear.

Networks sometimes include 'dummy' activities. Represented by dotted lines, they are not real activities and are used for two reasons. First, they avoid the situation in which two activities have the same start and end nodes. This is possible since there is no reason why two activities cannot have the same predecessors and the same successors. But it is undesirable because activities, particularly with computerised networks, are denoted by the numbers of their start and end nodes. For example, the activity represented as the line between nodes 6 and 7 is denoted as activity 6,7. If two activities share exactly the same nodes they would then be indistinguishable. Figures 6.2a and 6.2b show how a dummy activity overcomes this problem.

Secondly, some logical dependencies can only be represented if dummies are used. Without them 'false dependency', where the network shows, wrongly, that one activity is the immediate predecessor of another, may arise. This is illustrated in the example below.

Example

A local government officer is in charge of the development and construction of a health centre (see the first application above). She is going to coordinate and control the project through a network technique.

List the activities

The left-hand column of Table 6.1 is a much shortened and simplified list of the activities involved.

Identify the predecessors of each activity

Table 6.1 shows the activities and their predecessors. In identifying predecessors every effort must be made to put in the minimum required by logic, overcoming the tempta-

Table 6.1   Health centre: activity list

Activity	Predecessors
A Design	–
B Obtain outline planning permission	–
C Obtain full planning permission	A,B
D Put out to tender/select contractor	C
E Excavate	D
F Build structure	E
G External decor	F
H Consult medical authorities	C
I Sign contracts with occupants	H
J Partition accommodation	I,F
K Internal decor	J
L Commission building	K,G

tion to be restricted to the sequence for previous health centres. For example, consultations with medical authorities had usually been started only when building was under way. In fact, the consultations can take place much sooner, before any site work has been done. Usually this option might be unimportant, but in some circumstances it could be valuable and so should be included.

Draw the network

Figure 6.3 shows the network starting with a node, numbered 1. Two activities, A and B, have no predecessors and they are therefore the two branches emerging from node 1. Activity C has both A and B as predecessors. This situation can only be represented on a network by using a dummy activity. Without a dummy activities A and B would stretch between the same nodes, as shown in Figure 6.4, and this is not good practice for the reasons described above.

Activity D has C as its predecessor as does H, so there are two branches leaving node 4. The network now embarks on two parallel courses. D is followed by E, F and G; H is followed by I, J and K. J also has F as a predecessor and this is represented through another dummy variable. The use of a dummy variable here is to prevent false dependency. Without the dummy the network would be as in Figure 6.5, which seems to imply, falsely, that I as well as F is a predecessor of G. The two parts of the network finally come together for activity L which has both K and G as predecessors.

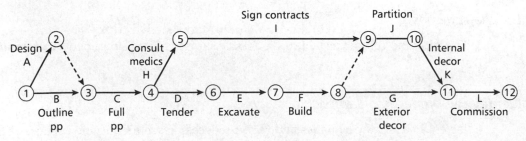

Figure 6.3   Health centre network

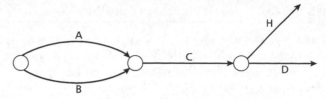

Figure 6.4   Start of network, without dummy

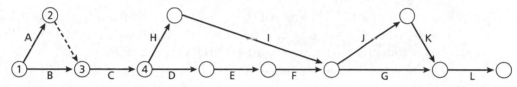

Figure 6.5   False dependency

ANALYSING THE NETWORK

By drawing the network planners have already gained significant benefits because their understanding of the project has increased. They may also have spotted previously unseen opportunities to run activities in parallel. They can now make further progress by analysing the network to determine timings and schedules. The analysis has five stages.

Estimate activity durations

The expected or average time for the completion of each activity has to be estimated. For some activities there may be a historical record of the times taken to complete them and the average is a matter of simple calculation. In the health centre example, records will be available showing how long it has taken to gain planning permission for scores of similar projects. The average can be calculated from the records. For other activities the duration is a matter of subjective estimation. For example, the design of the health centre will be dependent on the nature of the site and the particular requirements of the staff who are to occupy it. The architect will have to make a special one-off estimate.

Forward pass

A forward pass means going through the network activity by activity to calculate for each an '*earliest start*' time and an '*earliest finish*' time, using the following formulae.

$$\text{Earliest finish} = \text{Earliest start} + \text{activity duration}$$

$$\text{Earliest start} = \text{Earliest finish (of previous activity)}$$

If there are several previous activities, the latest of their earliest finish times is used since this is the soonest that the activity can start. This may seem complex at first sight, but in a practical situation it is a matter of common sense. The example below should make it clear.

The earliest finish time for the final activity in the network is of course the shortest completion time for the whole project.

Backward pass

A backward pass means moving through the network activity by activity starting with the final activity and ending with the first. For each activity a '*latest finish*' and a '*latest start*' time are calculated from the following formulae. In this context 'latest' means 'latest without delaying completion of the whole project'.

Latest finish = Latest start (of following activity)

Latest start = Latest finish − activity duration

If there are several following activities, the earliest of their latest start times is used since this is the latest that the activity can finish without delaying completion of the whole project. Again, this may appear complex but it is only common sense and the example below should clarify what is meant.

Calculating float

An activity's *float* is the amount of time for which it can be delayed without delaying completion of the entire project. In other words, it is the difference between its earliest and latest start times (or between the earliest and latest finish times – which is the same thing).

Float = Latest start − earliest start

Determining the critical path

For some activities the float will be zero. The earliest and latest start times are the same and there is no room for delay. Such activities are *critical*: any delay to them will delay completion of the whole project. All critical activities form a *critical path* through the network. If the total completion time for the project has to be shortened, then one or more activities on the critical path have to be shortened.

Continuation of health centre example

The network for the health centre example has already been drawn (Figure 6.3). The analysis of the network proceeds as follows.

Estimate activity durations

Table 6.2 shows the expected durations of the activities. This was not the first health centre built in the local authority area and consequently the duration estimates could be based on the past records. However, since each health centre is not exactly the same it was not a matter of just calculating the average: adjustments had to be made for ways in which this health centre was different. For example, the site was sloping and so the expected building time was adjusted upwards (based on subjective judgement) to allow for the effect of this.

Table 6.2   Activity durations for health centre

Activity	Predecessors	Duration (weeks)
A Design	–	20
B Obtain outline pp	–	10
C Obtain full pp	A,B	10
D Tender/select	C	8
E Excavate	D	4
F Build structure	E	20
G External decor	F	8
H Consult medics	C	14
I Contract occupants	H	10
J Accommodation	I,F	6
K Internal decor	J	12
L Commission	K,G	6

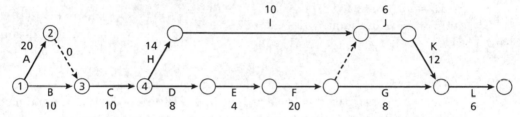

Figure 6.6   Health centre network

Forward pass

The forward pass starts with the network showing the durations of the activities, as in Figure 6.6. The analysis then goes through the network activity by activity calculating earliest start and finish times. These are put onto the network on either side of the duration. For example:

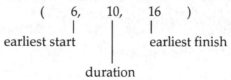

The outcome for the health centre is shown in Figure 6.7. Activity by activity:

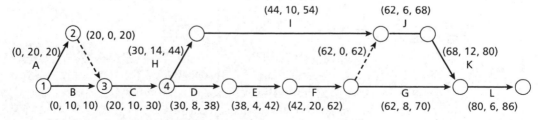

Figure 6.7   Forward pass for health centre

(ES = earliest start, EF = earliest finish)

A: Since this is the first activity, ES = 0.
EF = ES + duration = 0 + 20 = 20

Dummy: ES = 20 (the EF for A)
EF = ES + duration = 20 + 0 = 20

B: As with activity A, ES = 0.
EF = ES + duration = 0 + 10 = 10

C: ES = 20 (the later of the EFs for the two preceding activities, the dummy and B)
EF = ES + duration = 20 + 10 = 30

D: ES = 30 (the EF for C)
EF = ES + duration = 30 + 8 = 38

E: ES = 38 (the EF for D)
EF = ES + duration = 38 + 4 = 42

F: ES = 42 (the EF for E)
EF = ES + duration = 42 + 20 = 62

Dummy: ES = 62 (the EF for F)
EF = ES + duration = 62 + 0 = 62

G: ES = 62 (the EF for F)
EF = ES + duration = 62 + 8 = 70

H: ES = 30 (the EF for C)
EF = ES + duration = 30 + 14 = 44

I: ES = 44 (the EF for H)
EF = ES + duration = 44 + 10 = 54

J: ES = 62 (the later of the EFs for the two preceding activities, the dummy and I)
EF = ES + duration = 62 + 6 = 68

K: ES = 68 (the EF for J)
EF = ES + duration = 68 + 12 = 80

L: ES = 80 (the later of the EFs for the two preceding activities, G and K)
EF = ES + duration = 80 + 6 = 86

The forward pass makes it possible to draw up a schedule of earliest start and finish times for the activities. The earliest finish time, 86 weeks, for the final activity, L, is the shortest time in which the project can be completed. Because the network takes into account the fact that certain activities can be tackled simultaneously, 86 weeks is very different from the result of just adding up the times of the activities (128 weeks – see Table 6.2).

Backward pass

To calculate latest start and finish times a backward pass through the network is needed. The analysis then goes through the network activity by activity backwards starting with the final activity, L. Based on the shortest project completion time, 86 weeks, the latest finish and start times are calculated. These are put onto the network (together with the float) in brackets underneath the earliest start and finish times. For example:

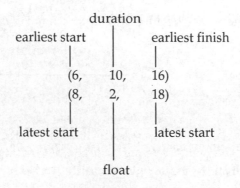

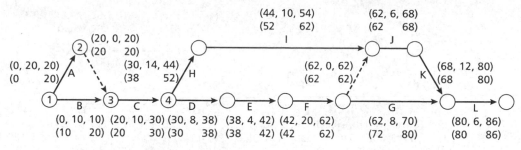

Figure 6.8   Backward pass for health centre

The outcome for the health centre excluding the float is shown in Figure 6.8. Activity by activity:

(LS = latest start; LF = latest finish)

L: Since this is the last activity,
LF = shortest project completion time
= 86
LS = LF − duration = 86 − 6 = 80

K: LF = 80 (the LS for L)
LS = LF − duration = 80 − 12 = 68

J: LF = 68 (the LS for K)
LS = LF − duration = 68 − 6 = 62

Dummy: LF = 62 (the LS for J)
LS = LF − duration = 62 − 0 = 62

I: LF = 62 (the LS for J)
LS = LF − duration = 62 − 10 = 52

H: LF = 52 (the LS for I)
LS = LF − duration = 52 − 14 = 38

G: LF = 80 (the LS for L)
LS = LF − duration = 80 − 8 = 72

F: LF = 62 (the earlier of the LSs for the 2

succeeding activities, the dummy and G)
LS = LF − duration = 62 − 20 = 42

E: LF = 42 (the LS for F)
LS = LF − duration = 42 − 4 = 38

D: LF = 38 (the LS for E)
LS = LF − duration = 38 − 8 = 30

C: LF = 30 (the earlier of the LSs for the two succeeding activities, D and H)
LS = LF − duration = 30 − 10 = 20

B: LF = 20 (the LS for C)
LS = LF − duration = 20 − 10 = 10

Dummy: LF = 20 (the LS for C)
LS = LF − duration = 20 − 0 = 20

A: LF = 20 (the LS for the dummy)
LS = LF − duration = 20 − 20 = 0

Latest start and finish times can now be added to the latest start and finish times on a schedule of activities.

Calculating float

An activity's float is the difference between its earliest and latest start times (or earliest and latest finish times) and measures by how much the activity's start can be delayed or duration prolonged without affecting the completion time for the whole project. The float times have been added to the network in Figure 6.9.

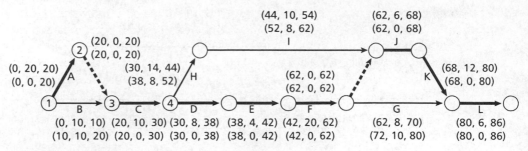

Figure 6.9   Activity floats and critical path

Table 6.3   Activity schedule for health centre

Activity	Start Earliest	Latest	Finish Earliest	Latest	Float
A Design	0	0	20	20	CRITICAL
B Obtain outline pp	0	10	10	20	10
C Obtain full pp	20	20	30	30	CRITICAL
D Tender/select	30	30	38	38	CRITICAL
E Excavate	38	38	42	42	CRITICAL
F Build structure	42	42	62	62	CRITICAL
G External decor	62	72	70	80	10
H Consult medics	30	38	44	52	8
I Contract occupants	44	52	54	62	8
J Accommodation	62	62	68	68	CRITICAL
K Internal decor	68	68	80	80	CRITICAL
L Commission	80	80	86	86	CRITICAL

Determining the critical path

A critical activity is one for which the float is zero. If the start of any of these activities is delayed, or their duration is longer than anticipated, the project will take longer than the expected 86 weeks to complete. All such activities form a critical path through the network, as shown in bold on Figure 6.9.

The critical path comprises the activities: A—C—D—E—F—J—K—L.

Table 6.3 shows a full schedule for all activities in the project. As the project unfolds the project planner will monitor the network and schedule. If critical activities are delayed at all or if non-critical activities are delayed by more than their float, he or she will investigate the possibility of transferring resources in order to recover time. If this is not possible the network will be re-analysed to find the new project completion time and to see if any previously non-critical activities are now critical.

HANDLING UNCERTAINTY

The analysis of the health centre network was based on the assumption that the activity durations were accurate and certain. Sometimes this is the case, for example where an activity has been carried out many times before and there is a record of how long it has taken on each occasion. For instance, the time to decorate a building of standard design can be estimated with high precision. Other activities will be more uncertain, either because they are brand new activities about which little is known or because they are inherently more variable. For example, liaison with medical practitioners depends on the cooperation and whims of those involved and is bound to vary considerably from one health centre to the next. In building projects the weather always introduces an element of uncertainty.

Uncertainty can be handled through *sensitivity analysis*. The network is analysed several times, each time changing one or more of the durations and recording what happens to overall completion time, critical path and schedule. This is a feasible, although time-consuming, way of testing the effect of uncertainty.

A more elegant approach is to build uncertainty into the estimates of the durations. The customary way to do this, originally part of PERT only but now used in most techniques, is to specify for each activity *optimistic, most likely* and *pessimistic* durations. As a method for expressing variability in activity duration this has the advantage that it is easy to understand. Managers involved in a project usually know intuitively what the terms optimistic, most likely and pessimistic mean in practice, whereas statistical terms such as standard deviation might seem like jargon. The project planner will therefore find it easier to persuade managers to make such estimates.

To use information in this form a number of statistical assumptions have to be made. The first is that the activity times follow a *beta distribution*. This assumption is made for the sound reason that this distribution has a shape (unimodal and non-symmetrical) which is commonly found in practice for activities in large projects. However, this is an assumption and statisticians can, and do, debate its validity. Having made the assumption it is not necessary to know the underlying statistical details and its practical use is as follows.

1. An average or *expected* time for each activity is calculated from the beta distribution formula:

$$\text{Expected duration} = \frac{\text{Optimistic} + (4 \times \text{Most likely}) + \text{Pessimistic}}{6}$$

The 'expected duration' is used to analyse the network in the same way that the single duration time has been used up to now, i.e. to work out an expected project completion time, critical path and to draw up a schedule.

2. A *variance* for each activity is calculated from the beta distribution formula:

$$\text{Variance} = [(\text{Pessimistic} - \text{Optimistic})/6]^2$$

This is used as a measure of the variability of each individual activity.

3. A *variance* for the whole project is calculated from the general statistical formula (the variance sum theorem):

$$\text{Variance of project} = \text{Sum (variance of each critical activity)}$$

4. The *standard deviation* for the whole project is the square root of the variance:

$$\text{Standard deviation} = \sqrt{\text{Variance}}$$

5. *Confidence limits* for the completion time of the whole project are calculated. If the whole project is made up of many separate, independent activities, then the distribution of the completion time for the project will have a normal distribution whose mean is the expected completion time and whose standard deviation is as calculated in stage 4 above. This is a consequence of the *central limit theorem* which states that the distribution of the sum of several independent variables becomes increasingly normal as the number of variables included in the sum increases (consult a statistical textbook for details). This is true whatever the distribution of the individual variables.

Confidence limits can then be based on the rule that 95 per cent of a normal distribution lies within plus or minus two standard deviations of the mean. In other words, the 95 per cent confidence limits for the project completion time are:

Expected project duration +/− 2 × standard deviation

If other or more precise confidence limits are needed, normal curve tables have to be used.

The use of the normal distribution explains why it is usual to calculate the 'expected duration' of an activity from the optimistic, most likely and pessimistic times, rather than just using the most likely value. The normal distribution is centred on the mean not the mode (= most likely time). However, there are some doubts hanging over the use of the normal distribution.

1. The central limit theorem only applies if the times of the activities are independent. In practice it might well be the case that the cause of delay for one activity, for example the inefficiency of a subcontractor or a spell of very bad weather, might also result in delays to other activities which involve the same subcontractor or are taking place at the same time.

2. The calculation of confidence limits assumes that the critical path stays the same even though durations have changed. In particular, reductions in the durations might cause other activities to become critical, after which further reductions in the original critical path would have no effect on the completion time of the whole project. There is no standard analytical way to overcome these problems; rather the project planner should be aware that they could happen and interpret results with care.

Health Centre example

Optimistic, most likely and pessimistic activity durations for the health centre development are shown in Table 6.4.

The analysis proceeds as follows and the results are shown in Table 6.5.

1. Calculate an expected duration for each activity. The durations shown in Table 6.5 are exactly the times used in the previous analysis of this network (see Table 6.2). Note that this is the form in which the information would have been collected at the outset if uncertainty was to be built into the planning; it is not a question of estimating the expected durations first and then making the optimistic, most likely and pessimistic times fit in with them.

2. Calculate the variances of the activities as a single measure of the uncertainty in their

Table 6.4 Optimistic, most likely and pessimistic durations for the health centre

Activity	Duration (days) Optimistic	Expected	Pessimistic
A Design	12	18	36
B Obtain outline pp	4	9	20
C Obtain full pp	4	9	20
D Tender/select	4	8	12
E Excavate	2	4	6
F Build structure	16	20	24
G External decor	4	6	20
H Consult medics	4	14	24
I Contract occupants	6	9	18
J Accommodation	5	6	7
K Internal decor	10	12	14
L Commission	4	6	8

Table 6.5 Expected durations and variances

Activity	Optimistic	Duration Expected (days)	Pessimistic	Expected (days)	Variance (days squared)
A Design	12	18	36	20	16.0
B Obtain outline pp	4	9	20	10	7.1
C Obtain full pp	4	9	20	10	⁻7.1
D Tender/select	4	8	12	8	1.8
E Excavate	2	4	6	4	0.4
F Build structure	16	20	24	20	1.8
G External decor	4	6	20	8	7.1
H Consult medics	4	14	24	14	11.1
I Contract occupants	6	9	18	10	4.0
J Accommodation	5	6	7	6	0.1
K Internal decor	10	12	14	12	0.4
L Commission	4	6	8	6	0.4

durations. In a large project the planner would be able to see at a glance which activities carried the most time risk.

3. Calculate the variance of the whole project.

$$\text{Variance} = \text{Sum(variances of activities on critical path)}$$

$$= \text{Sum(variances of activities A, C, D, E, F, J, K, L)}$$

$$= 16.0 + 7.1 + 1.8 + 0.4 + 1.8 + 0.1 + 0.4 + 0.4$$

$$= 28.0$$

4. Calculate the standard deviation for the whole project.

$$\text{Standard deviation} = \sqrt{\text{Variance}}$$

$$= 5.3 \text{ weeks}$$

5. Calculate confidence limits for the completion time of the whole project. Since the project is made up of many separate, independent activities, then the distribution of the completion time for the project will have a normal distribution whose mean is the expected completion time (86 weeks) and whose standard deviation is as calculated above (5.3 weeks). 95 per cent confidence limits are that the project will be completed within the interval:

$$\text{Mean } +/- \text{ 2 standard deviations} = 86 +/- 2 \times 5.3$$
$$= 86 +/- 10.6$$
$$= 75.4 \text{ weeks to } 96.6 \text{ weeks}$$

95 per cent confidence means that the project is almost certain to be completed within these limits. Even so, if they are too wide for practical purposes the planner should consider committing more resources to some of the activities. The next section deals with this problem, that of the tradeoff between time and costs.

MAKING TIME–COST TRADEOFFS

Time and cost are usually interchangeable to some degree and the project planner may be able to reduce the project completion time by spending more money. Information on the relationship between cost and time for *each* activity can lead to a graph relating cost and time for the *whole* project. The planner can then read off the cost of saving 1 week, the cost of saving 2 weeks, the cost of saving 3 weeks and so on. This analysis is known as *crashing* the network. It will only be worth doing this, of course, if the expected completion time and the confidence limits suggest that the project will not be finished on time and if the penalties for late completion are stiff.

Crashing begins by drawing a cost–time curve for each activity as in Figure 6.10. 'Curve' is a misnomer since the graph is merely a line connecting two points, the cost and time for normal operations and the cost and time for the absolute minimum time in which the activity can be carried out. The latter are referred to as the crash cost and the crash time. By drawing a line an assumption is being made that in between the normal and crash

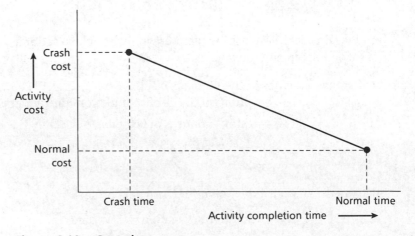

Figure 6.10   Cost–time curve

Table 6.6   Crashing ratios

Activity	Normal time (weeks)	Normal cost (£'000)	Crash time (weeks)	Crash cost (£'000)	Max reduction (weeks)	Ratio cost/ time
A Design	20	300	12	800	8	62.5
B Obtain outline pp	10	100	10	100	0	–
C Obtain full pp	10	100	10	100	0	–
D Tender/select	8	120	6	150	2	15.0
E Excavate	4	1100	4	1100	0	–
F Build structure	20	23 000	10	24 000	10	100.0
G External decor	8	800	8	800	0	–
H Consult medics	14	200	10	250	4	12.5
I Contract occupants	10	600	8	700	2	50.0
J Accommodation	6	100	6	100	0	–
K Internal decor	12	1800	8	1840	4	10.0
L Commission	6	400	6	400	0	–

situations cost increases are proportional to the time saved. From this information, the ratio cost increase/time saved is calculated. This is in effect the 'crashing cost per unit of time' for the activity. It shows which activities can bring about time reductions at the lowest cost and should therefore be considered first when a network is being crashed.

Table 6.6 shows normal and crash costs and times, as well as the crashing ratio, for the activities in the health centre example. The normal cost of the whole project is £28.62 million, obtained by adding up the individual normal costs of all activities.

Crashing involves the original analysed network (Figure 6.9) and the crashing ratios (Table 6.6). Only critical activities are crashed since they are the only ones which can reduce the overall project completion time. The procedure is to examine the activities on the critical path to find the one with the least crashing cost (= lowest crashing ratio). This activity is crashed by reducing its duration either until the maximum possible reduction (as given in Table 6.6) has been made, or until another parallel path is critical.

The critical activities are A, C, D, E, F, J, K, L. Of these K, internal decoration, has the lowest crashing ratio, 10. It can be reduced by the full amount possible, 4 weeks, without altering the critical path – because the parallel activity, G, has a float of 6. The new network is shown

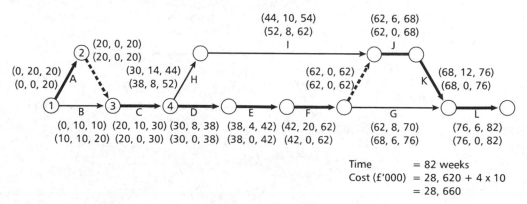

Time   = 82 weeks
Cost (£'000) = 28, 620 + 4 x 10
             = 28, 660

Figure 6.11   Activity K crashed

in Figure 6.11. It has a total duration of 82 weeks (the original 86 minus the reduction of 4) and a cost of £28.66 million (the original £28.62 million plus 4 weeks @ £10 000 crashing cost).

The activities are re-examined to find the next one to crash: that activity on the critical path with the next lowest ratio. This is D, tendering, and it can be reduced by the maximum amount, 2 weeks, without affecting the critical path. Again, the full reduction of 2 weeks can be made because the parallel path through H and I has a float of 6 weeks. The result is shown in Figure 6.12.

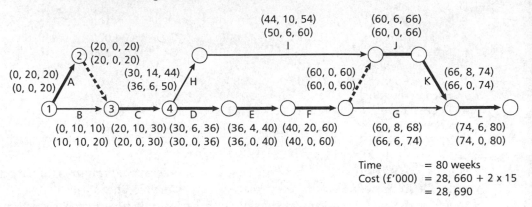

Time   = 80 weeks
Cost (£'000) = 28, 660 + 2 x 15
            = 28, 690

Figure 6.12   Activity D crashed

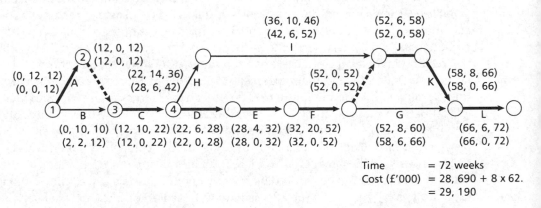

Time   = 72 weeks
Cost (£'000) = 28, 690 + 8 x 62.
            = 29, 190

Figure 6.13   Activity A crashed

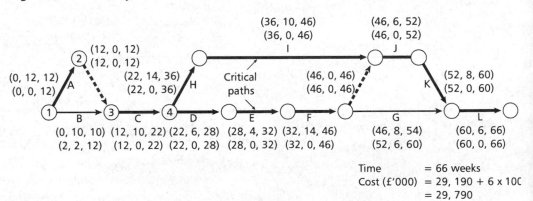

Time   = 66 weeks
Cost (£'000) = 29, 190 + 6 x 10C
            = 29, 790

Figure 6.14   Activity F partially crashed

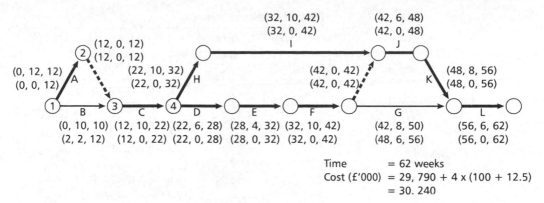

$$Time = 62 \text{ weeks}$$
$$Cost (£'000) = 29,790 + 4 \times (100 + 12.5)$$
$$= 30.240$$

Figure 6.15   Crashing H and F together

The next activity to be crashed is A, design. It can be crashed by the maximum amount, 8 weeks, without affecting the critical path because the parallel path through B has a float of 10 weeks. The result is shown in Figure 6.13. So far the overall time for the project has been reduced to 72 weeks and the cost has increased to £29.19 million.

The sole remaining activity which can be crashed is F, build, up to a maximum of 10 weeks. However, if it were crashed by this amount a parallel path, through activities H and I, would become critical since these activities have a float of only 6 weeks. Reducing activity F by 6 weeks brings about the network shown in Figure 6.14.

If activity F were reduced by more than 6 weeks the path D—E—F will no longer be part of the critical path, which would then take the route A—C—H—I—J—K—L. Further reductions in activity F alone are therefore pointless, since the overall time for the project will not change. To continue crashing the network requires that an activity on the branch H—I be reduced simultaneously with activity F. H has a lower crash ratio than I and thus it is I and F that are reduced. I can be reduced by a maximum of 4 weeks; F can be reduced by another 4 weeks in addition to the 6 week reduction that has already been made. Consequently both are reduced by 4 weeks. The result is shown in Figure 6.15. The duration of the project has been reduced to 62 weeks and the cost has increased to £30.24 million.

Note that the cost of this last reduction has been £112 500 per week, the sum of the crashing ratio of the two activities involved. Had there been another activity elsewhere on the network with a smaller crashing cost, it would have been reduced before H and F. For example, were it possible to crash activity L at a cost of £110 000 per week, then L would have been crashed before the simultaneous crashing of H and F. This is because £110 000, although a higher cost than either £12 500 (for H) or £100 000 (for F), is smaller than the cost of £112 500 for simultaneously crashing H and F.

Once the network of Figure 6.15 has been achieved the project is fully crashed. The only activity not yet crashed is I, but this is on a parallel critical path to D—E—F, all of which are fully crashed. The shortest project duration is therefore 62 weeks achieved at a cost of £30.24 million. Crashing the project could reduce its length by 24 weeks at an additional cost of £1 620 000. The process is summarised in Table 6.7.

Table 6.7 can be converted into a time/cost tradeoff curve by plotting the data in Table 6.7 on a graph as in Figure 6.16. Intermediate time reductions can be achieved since the full time reduction in each activity does not have to be made. For example, a completion

Table 6.7   Summary of crashing process

Crashing sequence	Completion time (weeks)	Total cost (£million)	Critical path
1	86	28.62	A—C—D—E—F—J—K—L
2	82	28.66	A—C—D—E—F—J—K—L
3	80	28.69	A—C—D—E—F—J—K—L
4	72	29.19	A—C—D—E—F—J—K—L
5	66	29.79	A—C—D—E—F—J—K—L or A—C—H—I—J—K—L
6	62	30.24	A—C—D—E—F—J—K—L or A—C—H—I—J—K—L

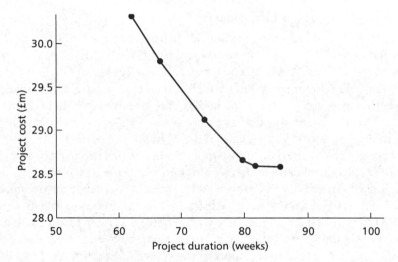

Figure 6.16   Time/cost tradeoff

time of 84 weeks is possible if activity K had been crashed by 2 weeks instead of the full 4 weeks. The project planner can then read off the cost of any particular time reduction. For instance, the cost of the project for completion in 70 weeks would be about £29.4 million.

CONCLUSION

A full network planning analysis, including handling uncertainty and crashing, has the following steps.

1. *List* all activities in the project.

2. *Identify* the predecessors of each activity.

3. *Draw* the network diagram.

4. *Estimate* activity durations as average times or, if uncertainty is to be dealt with explicitly, as optimistic/most likely/pessimistic times.

5. *Produce an activity schedule* by making a forward then a backward pass through the network.

6. *Determine the critical path* by calculating activity floats.

7. *Measure uncertainty* by calculating activity variances, the variance of the whole project and finally confidence limits for the duration of the project.

8. *Draw cost–time curves* for each activity.

9. *Crash the network* and construct a cost–time graph for the project.

As with all other quantitative decision techniques, by even attempting a network analysis a project planner gains the benefit of a clearer understanding of his or her task. For example, listing the predecessors of activities can separate what is possible from what is customarily done and provide insights into the project. At the other end of the scale the planner has the opportunity to make sophisticated analyses, calculating the probability of a project being completed on time and making tradeoffs between time and cost.

In practice, networks of, for instance, major construction projects involve thousands of activities. Drawing and analysing them is a major task which was once done by hand. Now computer programs, especially those for microcomputers, reduce the hard work. These programs can draw the network, analyse it and carry out sensitivity analyses very quickly. Now that the computer takes care of the chores, the planner is free to spend more time on planning issues such as resource allocation and human resource management. This is a prime reason for the recent resurgence of interest in network techniques.

Originally the techniques were PERT (programme evaluation and review technique) and CPM (critical path methods). These differed in that PERT handled uncertainty, by requiring optimistic, most likely and pessimistic estimates of activity duration, whereas CPM had a facility to make time and cost tradeoffs, by reallocating resources. Now both expressions, PERT and CPM, tend to be used generically. Computerised network packages, whether referred to as PERT or CPM, usually include the ability to handle uncertainty and resource allocation.

These techniques are, however, not just used to plan the project before it starts but also to monitor progress as it unfolds. As actual durations turn out to be different from the estimates, because of poor estimation or because a crisis has emerged, the technique can be continually updated to see if the critical path remains the same and to determine which activities currently need management's attention. Twenty years ago updating the plan meant redraughting by hand large charts and pinning them on the wall – with the result that updating was done as infrequently as possible. Computerisation means that it is relatively easy to update the project plan hour by hour, or minute by minute. If the critical path changes, resources can be re-allocated in real time.

CASE STUDIES

CASE STUDY 1

This case is concerned with a company which designs and manufactures radar equipment. The company applies critical path methods in the complex assembly sequence for the equipment. One activity in the sequence is that of attaching a particular integrated circuit to the assembly. The duration of the activity has been estimated as:

- optimistic 4 minutes;
- most likely 6 minutes;
- pessimistic 20 minutes.

1. In analysing the network, what number of days should be used as the single estimate of the activity's duration, i.e. what is its expected duration?

2. What is the variance of the activity?

3. When the variances of the activities are used to calculate confidence limits for the project, what assumptions are being made?

Solutions

1. *In analysing the network, what number of days should be used as the single estimate of the activity's duration, i.e. what is its expected duration?*
The average or expected duration is calculated as:

$$\text{Expected} = (\text{optimistic} + 4 \times \text{most likely} + \text{pessimistic})/6$$
$$= (4 + 4 \times 6 + 20)/6$$
$$= 8 \text{ minutes}$$

2. *What is the variance of the activity?*

$$\text{Variance} = [(\text{Pessimistic} - \text{Optimistic})/6]^2$$
$$= [(20 - 4)/6]^2$$
$$= 64/9$$
$$= 7.11$$

3. *When the variances of the activities are used to calculate confidence limits for the project, what assumptions are being made?*
All three assumptions have to be made in calculating confidence limits. The calculation of the variances are based on the beta distribution. The confidence limits assume that the critical path has not changed. The central limit theorem is applied so that the overall time for the project is normally distributed.

CASE STUDY 2

The BN company is a medium-sized organisation which manufactures small, specialist aircraft. The products are three variants on a 20-seater craft used for flying short distances, usually between a mainland and offshore islands. Many of the aircraft operate in the Caribbean.

BN is an Anglo-French company whose management and design functions are located in the UK. Some manufacturing is carried out in France but to take advantage of cheaper labour rates most assembly work takes place at a subsidiary company, called BN(R), in Eastern Europe. The manufacturing operation works in the following way. The basic sub-components of the aircraft are manufactured by BN and some subcontractors in the south of France. The sub-components are then transported to BN(R) in Eastern Europe, packaged as complete but unassembled aircraft shells. The engines are manufactured in Germany and the internal furnishings and trim are manufactured at the Eastern European plant. BN(R) has to assemble the components, take delivery of and add the engine, and then manufacture and install the trim. Customers wish to have the aircraft customised according to their own requirements and the role the aircraft is to fulfil, so the assembly process differs from order to order.

Although labour is inexpensive in Eastern Europe, the standard of management is not good. BN controls the operation tightly, imposing strict methods to ensure that high levels of efficiency are maintained. A particular problem is that the high degree of customisation means that no one order is like another and BN has to impose its control on assembly operations, which are those of a jobshop rather than mass production. One of the controls is critical path methods.

BN(R) undertakes the following activities once it has received a customer order from its parent company in the UK.

- The first three activities can be carried out simultaneously. (A) Complete formalities and take delivery of sub-components from the UK; (B) verify engine order and take delivery of engine; (C) manufacture trim according to customer instructions.
- After the sub-components have arrived at BN(R)'s factory, activity D is the assembly of the aircraft shell.
- After the shell is complete it is painted (activity E).
- After the engine is received it must be tuned and tested – this is activity F.
- Once the painting operation has been completed the interior trim is added (activity G). This activity also depends on the completion of the trim manufacture.
- After activities E, F and G are finished, activity H, installation of the engine, can be carried out.
- The final activities are finishing in the customer's livery (I) and shipping (J).

The durations of the activities have been estimated by assessing an optimistic, most likely and pessimistic time for each. These estimates are shown in Table 6.8.

1. Make a schedule of the earliest and latest start and finish times for the activities, including their floats and variances.

Table 6.8

Activity		Optimistic	Duration (days) Most likely	Pessimistic
A	Receive components	45	60	75
B	Receive engine	15	45	75
C	Manufacture trim	6	9	12
D	Assemble shell	3	6	9
E	Paint shell	3	6	9
F	Test engine	3	6	27
G	Add trim	3	6	9
H	Insert engine	3	6	18
I	Livery	12	15	36
J	Ship	3	9	24

2. What is the variance for the whole project and what are the 95 per cent confidence limits for its completion time?

Solutions

The stages in a network analysis are:

1. *List* all activities in the project.

2. *Identify* the predecessors of each activity.

3. *Draw* the network diagram.

4. *Estimate* activity durations as average times or, if uncertainty is to be dealt with explicitly, as optimistic/most likely/pessimistic times.

5. *Produce an activity schedule* by making a forward then a backward pass through the network.

6. *Determine the critical path* by calculating activity floats.

7. *Measure uncertainty* by calculating activity variances, the variance of the whole project and finally confidence limits for the duration of the project.

8. *Draw cost–time curves for each activity*.

9. *Crash the network* and construct a cost–time graph for the project.

Steps 8 and 9 are not relevant to this case since crashing the network is not required. Following steps 1–7:

1. A list of the activities is already available.

2. The immediate predecessors can be taken straight from the case description and are shown in Table 6.9.

Table 6.9   Predecessors

Activity		Predecessors	Optimistic	Duration (days) Most likely	Pessimistic
A	Receive components	–	45	60	75
B	Receive engine	–	15	45	75
C	Manufacture trim	–	6	9	12
D	Assemble shell	A	3	6	9
E	Paint shell	D	3	6	9
F	Test engine	B	3	6	27
G	Add trim	C,E	3	6	9
H	Insert engine	F,G	3	6	18
I	Livery	H	12	15	36
J	Ship	I	3	9	24

3. The network diagram is shown in Figure 6.17.

4. An estimate of the expected duration of each activity has to be calculated from the optimistic, most likely and pessimistic estimates. This is shown in Table 6.10.

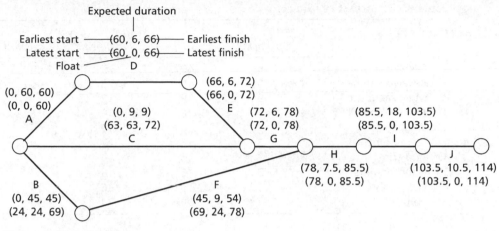

Expected duration

Earliest start ────(60, 6, 66)──── Earliest finish
Latest start ────(60, 0, 66)──── Latest finish
Float   D

(0, 60, 60)
(0, 0, 60)
A

(66, 6, 72)
(66, 0, 72)
E

(0, 9, 9)
(63, 63, 72)
C

(72, 6, 78)
(72, 0, 78)
G

(85.5, 18, 103.5)
(85.5, 0, 103.5)
I

H
(78, 7.5, 85.5)
(78, 0, 85.5)

J
(103.5, 10.5, 114)
(103.5, 0, 114)

B
(0, 45, 45)
(24, 24, 69)

F
(45, 9, 54)
(69, 24, 78)

Figure 6.17   Network

Table 6.10   Expected durations

| | | | Duration (days) | | |
Activity	Predecessors	Optimistic	Most likely	Pessimistic	Expected
A Receive components	–	45	60	75	60
B Receive engine	–	15	45	75	45
C Manufacture trim	–	6	9	12	9
D Assemble shell	A	3	6	9	6
E Paint shell	D	3	6	9	6
F Test engine	B	3	6	27	9
G Add trim	C,E	3	6	9	6
H Insert engine	F,G	3	6	18	7.5
I Livery	H	12	15	36	18
J Ship	I	3	9	24	10.5

Table 6.11   Activity schedule

Activity	Earliest start	Latest start	Earliest finish	Latest finish
A Receive components	0	0	60	60
B Receive engine	0	24	45	69
C Manufacture trim	0	63	9	72
D Assemble shell	60	60	66	66
E Paint shell	66	66	72	72
F Test engine	45	69	54	78
G Add trim	72	72	78	78
H Insert engine	78	78	85.5	85.5
I Livery	85.5	85.5	103.5	103.5
J Ship	103.5	103.5	114	114

Table 6.12   Activity variances

Activity	Optimistic	Most likely	Duration (days) Pessimistic	Expected	Variance (days²)
A Receive components	45	60	75	60	25
B Receive engine	15	45	75	45	100
C Manufacture trim	6	9	12	9	1
D Assemble shell	3	6	9	6	1
E Paint shell	3	6	9	6	1
F Test engine	3	6	27	9	16
G Add trim	3	6	9	6	1
H Insert engine	3	6	18	7.5	6.25
I Livery	12	15	36	18	16
J Ship	3	9	24	10.5	12.25

5. A forward followed by a backward pass through the network gives the results shown in Figure 6.17. The results can be used to produce the activity schedule shown in Table 6.11, giving the earliest and latest starts and finishes of each activity.

6. The float for each activity (earliest start − latest start) is shown in Figure 6.17. The critical path is those activities with zero float and is therefore:

A—D—E—G—H—I—J

7. The variance of each activity is calculated from the formula:

$$\text{Variance} = [(\text{Pessimistic} - \text{Optimistic})/6]^2$$

The results are shown in Table 6.12.

The variance of the whole project is calculated as the sum of the variances of the activities on the critical path:

$$\text{Variance of project} = 25 + 1 + 1 + 1 + 6.25 + 16 + 12.25$$
$$= 62.5$$
$$\text{Standard deviation} = \sqrt{62.5}$$
$$= 7.9$$

The 95 per cent confidence limits for the duration of the project are the expected completion time plus or minus two standard deviations:

$$= 114 +/-(2 \times 7.9)$$
$$= 98.2 \text{ to } 129.8 \text{ days}$$

QUESTIONS

1. Which of the following statements about activities in a network diagram are correct?

(a) An activity is represented as a line connecting two nodes.

(b) Two activities can have the same starting node and the same finishing node.
(c) An activity can have more than one immediate predecessor.
(d) Dummy activities are used in a network to represent activities taking a very short time to complete.
(e) Dummy activities are used in a network to represent delays in the project.

2. A project to implement a multi-media training package has seven activities whose predecessors and durations are given in Table 6.13.

Table 6.13

Activity	Predecessors	Duration (days
A	–	10
B	A	15
C	B	10
D	A	12
E	A	22
F	C,D,E	15
G	C,D,E	10

(a) Draw the network diagram.
(b) What is the shortest time in which the project can be completed?
(c) What are the earliest and latest start times for activity D?
(d) What is the float for activity D?
(e) Which activities lie on the critical path?

3. Speed in getting a new product to the marketplace is of critical importance to high technology companies. Southern Communications has been very successful in developing, manufacturing and marketing a range of telecommunications products, but suffered a recent failure when a competitor was faster in making a new car phone available to consumers. SC decided to look at the process of bringing new products to market and has decided to monitor all such initiatives by means of critical path planning methods. The process of bringing a new product to market involves the following activities.

- The first two activities can be carried out simultaneously: (A) R and D product design; (B) carry out market research.
- Once the R and D is complete, two activities can take place: (C) build prototypes; (D) plan marketing material.
- When the prototype is available, two further activities can be started: (E) large-scale production planning; (F) rigorous testing.
- After the production methods have been finalised and market research is complete, the pricing can be decided and likely production levels decided (activity G).
- The availability of marketing material and prices means that a full marketing plan can be prepared (activity H). This activity also depends on the completion of product tests.
- When the marketing plan is available and production levels decided, full production can commence (activity I).

Table 6.14

Activity	Optimistic	Duration (weeks) Most likely	Pessimistic
A R and D	15	20	25
B Market research	5	15	25
C Prototype	2	3	4
D Marketing material	1	4	7
E Production planning	1	2	9
F Testing	1	6	17
G Pricing	1	2	3
H Market plan	1	2	9
I Full production	4	5	12

The product can be made available to the market once inventory has reached a certain proportion of the expected first year sales. The durations of the activities have been estimated by assessing an optimistic, most likely and pessimistic time for each. These estimates are shown in the Table 6.14.

(a) What is the completion time for the project?

(b) What is the critical path?

(c) What are the 95 per cent confidence limits for its completion time?

4. A defence company, PQ, specialises in developing and producing missiles and artillery It is part of a consortium of companies which has secured a contract from three European governments to produce a new main battle tank. PQ's part of the contract is to develop and produce some secondary weaponry. PQ has secured its role in the contract because of prototype weaponry which its R and D group has already developed but which has not yet been manufactured on a large scale. The contract requires PQ to have produced a first, fully tested batch within 16 months (70 working weeks). There is a penalty of 200 000 ecus per week for late delivery; there is also a bonus of 100 000 ecus per week for early delivery.

The first task for PQ is to make some broad plans for fulfilling its part of the contract. The project can be broken down into several major tasks and CPM is to be used to investigate the financial and human resource implications of the contract. The first of these major tasks is to decide what skills will be needed, who should be assigned to the project team and how the project should be managed. A senior planning group covering a number of departments will carry out this task which is expected to take 3 weeks. Once this is complete the next three tasks can be undertaken concurrently: establishing purchasing and subcontracting requirements (3 weeks), making preliminary production plans (10 weeks), and modifying and adapting the prototype to match the contract specifications (24 weeks).

Once ordered, the subcontracted materials will take a further 30 weeks to be delivered. Once the necessary modifications have been planned it will take a further 18 weeks to adjust and test them. When this is done and materials, equipment, personnel and production plans are all available it will take 4 weeks to train the personnel in quality control requirements and 3 weeks to train them in production techniques. These activities can take place simultaneously. When completed the production phase can start and this will last for 24 weeks. Final preparations and shipping will take a further 5 weeks.

A few of the activities can be crashed (see Table 6.15):

Table 6.15 Activities capable of being crashed

	Normal		Crash	
Activity	Time (weeks)	Cost (Ecu'000)	Time (weeks)	Cost (Ecu'000)
Modify prototype	24	200	12	400
Prelim prod plans	10	150	6	400
Test modifications	18	2400	12	3200
Production	24	2800	14	3600

(a) How long will the project take to complete, without crashing any activities?
(b) What are the critical activities?
(c) The time for the project can be reduced by crashing activities, but this will affect bonus or penalty payments specified in the contract. What schedule of activities is in the best financial interests of the company?

ANSWERS TO QUESTIONS

1. (a) True.   (d) False.
   (b) False.   (e) False.
   (c) True.

2. (a) Figure 6.18 is the correct diagram.

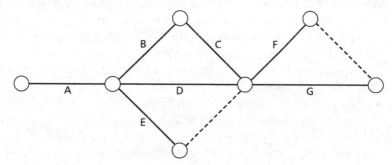

Figure 6.18

(b) The shortest time in which the project can be completed is 50 days.
(c) The earliest and latest start times for activity D are 10 and 23 days respectively.
(d) The float is 13 days.
(e) The critical path is A, B, C, and F.

3. (a) The total completion time is 39 days.
   (b) The critical path is: A—C—F—H—I.
   (c) The 95 per cent confidence limits for the duration of the project are 31.6 to 46.4 days.

4. (a) The project will take 78 weeks to complete.
   (b) The critical path is those activities with zero float and is therefore: A—D—F—G—I—J.
   (c) It is in the best financial interests of the company to crash the network to 59 weeks at a cost 950 000 ecu. This will save 2,700 000 ecu (in penalty costs and bonuses).

CHAPTER SEVEN

Linear programming (LP)

This chapter describes the fundamentals of linear programming (LP). First, it covers formulation – turning a verbal statement of a problem into an algebraic form. Next, the practical application of LP is illustrated with some case examples. The central sections of the chapter show how to solve simple problems graphically and how to interpret the basic output provided by computer packages.

INTRODUCTION

Like decision analysis, linear programming (usually referred to as LP) is a technique which can solve certain types of decision problem. Of course, the type of problem which it can solve has very different characteristics from decision analysis problems. LP is relevant when the problem involves optimising a criterion, for example maximising profit or minimising the use of resources, but where the decision options available are confined by limitations, for example the capacity of a manufacturing plant. LP has been employed in a variety of organisations since the 1950s. The amount of computing power required to solve LP originally confined its use to large organisations which could afford the necessary equipment, but recent substantial improvements in the performance/price ratio of computers have allowed it to be used more widely.

LP's value is not confined to its problem-solving power. As with other decision making techniques, its use brings about a clearer framing and therefore understanding of the problem. In fact, the process of finding a solution usually delivers more benefit than the actual solution. Again, like other decision techniques the solution provides a range of extra management information about the problem, especially in relation to sensitivity analysis and the robustness of the solution.

Every decision problem has two basic elements. The first element is the decision variables. Setting the decision variables at particular levels, for example how many of each product to manufacture, is what the decision is all about. The second element is an objective which measures what the decision maker is trying to achieve, for example making as much money as possible. The objective is a criterion which distinguishes a good decision from a bad decision, a decision which results in a high profit and one which results in a loss. In short, the decision maker is seeking to select production levels which will make the financial return to the organisation as high as possible. In reality such decisions will be surrounded by restrictions and complications. For example, some resource, skilled staff or capital, will probably be in short supply and this might limit the amount and types of product which can be manufactured. In LP these restrictions are known as constraints. The distinguishing characteristic of LP is that the objective and the constraints can be expressed algebraically in terms of the decision variables, and that these mathematical expressions are linear (i.e. they do not contain logarithmic terms, squared, cubed, etc.).

So the overall structure of an LP problem is that it has three parts:

- decision variables;
- objective function;
- constraints.

The objective function and the constraints must be capable of linear algebraic expression in terms of the decision variables.

FORMULATING AN LP PROBLEM

The primary skill in applying LP is to be able to formulate the problem. The initial statement of the problem will be in words and the statement must be recognised as having the characteristics of LP. Formulating the LP problem means isolating the three elements (decision variables, objective function and constraints) and then turning the words into algebra.

Example

The Jacobs Jeans company produces jeans in Eastern Europe for the Eastern European market. Demand is increasing rapidly and, within the limits of its manufacturing capacity, the company can sell whatever it produces. However, materials and skilled staff are in short supply and these factors constrain production. Jacobs Jeans makes two types of jeans, model 321 and model 421, essentially from two resources, manpower and material. The profit per unit of each model is shown in Table 7.1.

The resources required to make the jeans are shown in Table 7.2. To produce one pair of model 321 jeans takes 6 minutes of manpower and 2 units of materials; to produce one pair of model 421 jeans takes 3 minutes of manpower and 5 units of materials.

The availability of manpower is 600 minutes/day and that of materials is 800 units/day.

Table 7.1   Jeans profits

	Model	
	321	421
Profit/unit (£)	16	12

Table 7.2   Resources needed for jeans production

	Model	
	321	421
Manpower(mins)	6	3
Materials	2	5

Jacobs Jeans' problem is to decide how many of each model to produce per day in order to maximise its profit. To formulate the problem as an LP, we need to look at the three basic elements of an LP in turn.

Decision variables

The decision problem is to work out how many of each model to produce. These quantities should therefore be the decision variables:

$$x = \text{the production level of model 321}$$

$$y = \text{the production level of model 421}$$

Objective function

Jacobs' aim is to make as much profit as possible. The function which measures profit in terms of the decision variables must be determined. Taking it in slow stages, it may be helpful to think about the situation if 10 units of model 321 were made and 20 units of 421. The profit would then be:

$$10 \times 16 \quad + \quad 20 \times 12 \quad = \quad 400$$

(Product 321)   (Product 421)

Therefore, when the production levels are the unknown decision variables x and y, the profit is:

$$16x \quad + \quad 12y$$

(Product 321)   (Product 421)

Consequently, the objective function is:

$$\text{Maximise } 16x + 12y$$

If the production levels were known, then substituting these values for x and y in the above equation would give us the amount of profit made.

Constraints

The profit that can be made is of course limited by the availability of resources. Two constraint equations, one for manpower and one for materials, are needed to express these limits in terms of the decision variables. Taking it in slow stages, let us think about the situation if 10 units of model 321 were made, the resources used up would be as follows (see Table 7.2):

$$(10 \times 6) \text{ minutes manpower}$$

$$(10 \times 2) \text{ units of material}$$

Similarly, suppose 20 units of 421 were made, then resources would be used up as follows:

$$(20 \times 3) \text{ minutes manpower}$$

$$(20 \times 5) \text{ units of material}$$

At these production levels, 10 of 321 and 20 of 421, the total resource usage is therefore:

$$(10 \times 6) + (20 \times 3) \text{ minutes manpower}$$
$$(10 \times 2) + (20 \times 5) \text{ units of material}$$

When production levels are the unknown amounts x and y, the resource usages are:

$$6x + 3y \text{ minutes manpower}$$
$$2x + 5y \text{ units of material}$$

The availability of the resources is 600 and 800 respectively, so the constraints may be written as:

$$6x + 3y \leq 600 \text{ for manpower}$$
$$2x + 5y \leq 800 \text{ for materials}$$

These constraints must be in the form of inequalities, demonstrating that the resources do not have to be used up – there may be spare capacity at the optimal production levels.
  The full formulation is:

$$\text{Max. } 16x + 12y$$
$$\text{subject to}$$
$$6x + 3y \leq 600$$
$$2x + 5y \leq 800$$
$$x \geq 0$$
$$y \geq 0$$

Both the decision variables must be non-negative, since negative production levels would not make sense. This is the reason why the final two constraints, $x \geq 0$ and $y \geq 0$, are included.

APPLICATIONS OF LP

LP is a well-established technique which has practical applications in many business situations. Some organisations, for instance the oil companies, have been major users of it for a long time. However, it is the case that LP has proved itself better suited to some types of problems than others. Here are some examples of its use with indications of why it has been successful in that particular situation.

Controlling the operation of an oil refinery

Oil refineries receive crude oil via tankers and through pipelines and convert it into a range of oil products, for example petrol for motor cars, industrial fuel and aircraft paraffins. The crude oil received can vary substantially in quality and type, depending mainly on which part of the world it has come from. This affects the range of products that can be made and the costs of manufacture. Not only does the input, the crude oil, vary daily but also the output, the petroleum products, also varies daily in its profitability because of changes in the market prices of products and global stock levels. LP is used daily to control the conversion process so that the most profitable mix of products is obtained in the context of the crude oil input.

The decision variables are the quantities of each product to make in a given production period; the objective function measures the financial contribution which is to be maximised; the constraints include the amount of crude available, its quality and characteristics, the capacities of the refinery processes, and the available storage for products.

Oil refining is a capital-intensive, continuous-production process which is substantially under the direct and immediate influence of the refinery operators. When the LP suggests changes in the output, buttons can be pressed and dials turned to implement the new production plan. The immediacy and tightness of control is the reason that LP has been used so successfully to regulate the production process. Contrast this with the next application, where external factors mean that management cannot exercise an immediate and direct influence and therefore LP is used for planning rather than control.

Short-term planning for a distribution system

A supplier to food retailers has manufacturing plants at several locations throughout the country. The output of each plant is transported by road to the regional storage warehouses of the major food retailing chains, which are of course at different locations. From the warehouses the retailers deliver the food products to their stores. Each month the supplier plans how much of each food product will have to be moved daily from each plant to each warehouse. It aims to do this so as to keep costs down and give good service.

The decision variables are the quantities to be sent each day along each of the possible routes between plants and warehouses; the objective function is the cost of the distribution which has to be minimised (note that LP is used for maximisation *and* minimisation); the constraints are the forecast demands to be met at warehouses, the production available at plants and the transport capacities along each of the routes.

The distribution is not under such immediate and direct influence of the supplier's management as was the case in the oil refining example. Lorries break down, drivers are ill, the retailers change their forecasts and so on. Management is not able to make instantaneous changes in any plan. For this reason LP is used to plan the month ahead in general terms rather than to exercise day-to-day control.

Ingredients of a pet food product

Another early example of the application of LP was in formulating the content of a brand of pet food. Any such product has certain minimum requirements in regard to the nutrition it provides and these are spelt out by stipulating the proportions of protein, fat etc. it must contain. At the same time maximum limits are set on the amounts of other elements such as fibre and ash. The product can be made up from various basic ingredients, for example sago flour, meat meal and skimmed milk. However, all these ingredients and others contain different amounts of protein, fat, fibre, ash etc. The problem is to decide a 'formula' for the product which meets the minimum and maximum requirements. LP can solve this by showing how much of each ingredient should be used so that the requirements are all met but the cost is kept to a minimum.

The decision variables in the LP are the percentages of each ingredient (sago, meat meal, etc.) the pet food is to contain. The objective function is the cost of a given amount (say,

1 ton) of the pet food, based on the cost of the ingredients. The constraints are the minimum and maximum requirements for the proportions of protein, fat, etc. contained in the product.

An example of the formulation of this type of problem provides one of the cases at the end of the chapter. LP is also applied to the formulation of other food products and consumer goods.

GRAPHICAL SOLUTION

Formulating an LP problem is an important skill, but once formulated the LP still has to be solved and this is not a trivial task. The solution of an LP problem cannot be achieved by the simple means used for decision analysis. Dantzig first developed an algorithm (meaning a method of solution) for LP problems in the late 1940s, but achieving a solution to even a simple problem was still a lengthy process which took up hours, or days, of time on early computers. Over the decades the increasing power of computers has changed this. By the 1960s oil companies were solving large problems overnight on their IBM 360 mainframe computers. Now even large LP problems can be solved on personal computers, although the time they take continues to be an issue in some cases.

Dantzig's algorithm is known as the *Simplex method*. Simplex, or modern variations of it, is still used to solve even the largest-scale problems (with thousands of decision variables and thousands of constraints). Many off-the-shelf computer packages are now available to solve LP in user-friendly ways which do not require the decision maker to know anything about Simplex.

In spite of the complexity of LP algorithms, certain smaller and very simple problems can be solved graphically. The graphical method gives insights into LP which will help the decision maker to interpret and understand the output and economic information provided by computer solutions. To gain these insights we will now solve our earlier simple example concerning jean manufacture by the graphical method (but we are doing so only for the insights – the solution itself would in practice come from a computer).

The formulation was:

$$\text{Max } 16x + 12y$$
$$\text{subject to}$$
$$6x + 3y \leq 600$$
$$2x + 5y \leq 800$$
$$x \geq 0$$
$$y \geq 0$$

Stage 1

We must search for a value of x and a value of y which satisfy the constraints and simultaneously make the objective function take the highest value possible within those constraints. The first step is to represent the constraints graphically and show the area of x and y values in which we can look for a solution. The non-negativity constraints ($x \geq 0$, $y \geq 0$) restrict the search to the shaded area shown in Figure 7.1, the whole of one quadrant of the graph. Only in this area are both x and y non-negative.

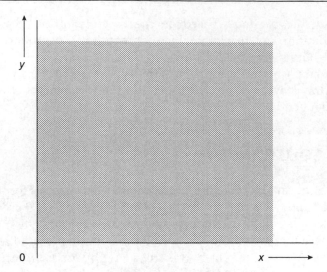

Figure 7.1   Non-negativity constraints

Stage 2

For the first resource constraint ($6x + 3y \leqslant 600$) the line $6x + 3y = 600$ is drawn by the following method:

1. Let $x = 0$. When $x = 0$, $3y = 600$ or $y = 200$. So the line must go through the point ($x = 0$, $y = 200$), i.e. the line crosses the y axis at 200.

2. Let $y = 0$. When $y = 0$, $6x = 600$ or $x = 100$. The line therefore crosses the x axis at 100.

3. Join the two points on the axes to give the line $6x + 3y = 600$.

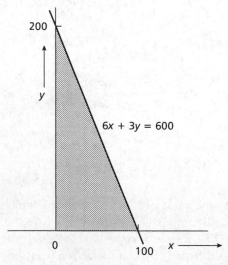

Figure 7.2   One resource constraint added

To satisfy the constraint, any pair of x, y values (in other words, any point) must fall on or below this line. Together with non-negativity constraints, the search area is now restricted to the shaded area shown in Figure 7.2.

Stage 3

For the second resource constraint ($2x + 5y \leqslant 800$), draw the line $2x + 5y = 800$. As before, we can do this by finding the points at which the line crosses the two axes. For this line the points are ($x = 0$, $y = 160$) and ($y = 0$, $x = 400$). To comply with this constraint, any point must fall on or below this line. Together with the previous constraint, this means that the search for the optimal point is restricted to the shaded area shown in Figure 7.3. This area is called the *feasible region*. Any point (pair of x, y values) within the feasible region satisfies all the constraints. The task is now to find which point in this area gives the objective function ($16x + 12y$) its highest possible value.

Stage 4

It will help us to understand Stage 4 if we experiment with the objective function to see how it relates to the feasible region. First, choose an arbitrary value for the objective function and draw the corresponding line on the graph. If we choose 960, the line $16x + 12y = 960$ will be as shown in Figure 7.4. All points on this line give the objective function the same value of 960 (the value of 960 was chosen arbitrarily, but also to make the numbers as easy as possible). Since the line passes through the feasible region, there are many feasible points giving an objective function value of 960. In real world terms this means that there are many combinations of production levels which are achievable given the availability of resources and which will result in a profit of 960.

Continuing the experiment choose, again at random, another objective function value, say, 6000. In Figure 7.5, the line $16x + 12y = 6000$ has been drawn. All points on this line

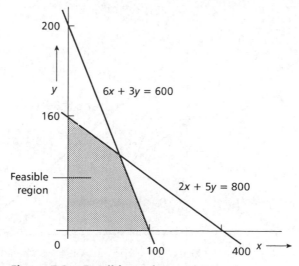

Figure 7.3   Feasible region

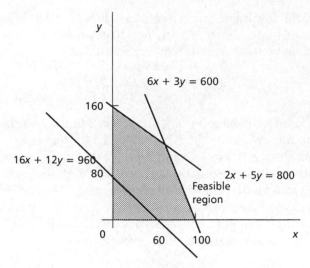

Figure 7.4 Objective function = 960

give the same objective function value of 6000. This is a much-improved level of profit, but since this line does not pass through the feasible region, there is no point which satisfies the constraints and gives the objective function a value of 6000. A profit of 6000 is therefore impossible given the current availability of resources.

Let us return to the first *isoprofit line* $16x + 12y = 960$ (any line whose points give the same objective function value is called an isoprofit line). If we were to move it, as in Figure 7.6, parallel to itself in a north-easterly direction ($16x + 12y = 960 \rightarrow 16x + 12y = 1200 \rightarrow 16x + 12y = 1500 \rightarrow$, etc.) the objective function value would gradually be increased. If it were moved far enough the line would eventually coincide with the second isoprofit line above, $16x + 12y = 6000$. However, we do not want to move the line so far that it leaves the feasible region. We want to move it as far as possible without

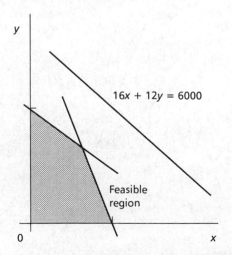

Figure 7.5 Objective function = 6000

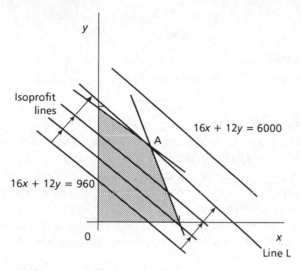

Figure 7.6   Varying the objective function

it leaving the feasible region. This line will give the largest objective function value that is still consistent with the constraints; the point (or set of points) which does remain within the feasible region will give a pair of x, y values which satisfy the constraints and maximise the objective function. In other words, this point (or set of points) is the solution to the LP problem.

Figure 7.6 shows that the line labelled L is the furthest an isoprofit line can be moved yet still intersect the feasible region; point A is the only point on this line which is within the feasible region. Any other isoprofit line either has a lower objective function value (for example $16x + 12y = 960$), or has no points within the feasible region (for example, $16x + 12y = 6000$).

The optimal point is A (the intersection of $6x + 3y = 600$ and $2x + 5y = 800$). The x and y values of A can be found by reading off from the graph or by simple algebra (the method of simultaneous equations). The algebraic approach is as follows.

The point of intersection of two lines is to be found, i.e. x and y values which satisfy two equations at the same time:

$$6x + 3y = 600$$

$$2x + 5y = 800$$

The method of simultaneous equations requires us to combine the two equations into one equation which contains only one of the variables. So, we multiply the second equation by 3 and subtract the first equation, which has been left alone, from it.

$$6x + 15y = 2400$$
$$\underline{6x + 3y = 600}$$
$$12y = 1800$$

Therefore, $y = 150$.

$$\text{Put } y = 150 \text{ into one of the original equations:}$$

$$6x + 3y = 600$$

$$6x + (3 \times 150) = 600$$

$$6x = 600 - 450$$

$$x = 25$$

The optimal point A is therefore ($x = 25$, $y = 150$).

The method of simultaneous equations is based on the general principle of multiplying one or both the original equations by constants, so that when the resulting two equations are added or subtracted one of the variables is eliminated. In the above example the second equation was multiplied by 3 so that when the first equation was subtracted from it the terms involving x disappeared.

When we have found the optimal point, the x and y values are substituted into the objective function to give the optimal value. Putting $x = 25$, $y = 150$ into $16x + 12y$ gives:

$$16 \times 25 + 12 \times 150 = 2200$$

The solution to the example problem is therefore to produce 25 model 321 jeans and 150 of model 421. This production mix will give a profit of £2200.

COMPUTER SOLUTION

The graphical method is not the way to solve an LP problem in practice – it is used to illustrate some of the principles underlying LP. In any case it can only be used for problems with no more than two variables. A computer package is fast and easy, printing out the optimal values of variables and objective functions without any need for graphs or simultaneous equations. However, to understand how a computer solution works it is helpful to think in terms of the graphical method.

The first issue concerns the location of the optimal point: point A is not always the optimal point. If, in the jeans example, the objective function had not been $16x + 12y$ but had been $160x + 12y$, then the graphical solution would have looked like Figure 7.7. The change to the objective function means that its slope is steeper. The last point at which the objective function line leaves the feasible region is B ($x = 100$, $y = 0$) which is the new optimal point. Substituting this in the objective function, its optimal value becomes 16 000.

However, one of the corner points of the feasible region is always an optimal point. Whatever the equation of the objective function, as the objective line is moved north-easterly out of the feasible region, it must always be a corner point which is the last point of contact between objective line and feasible region. The exception to this is when the objective line is parallel to a relevant constraint. Then two corner points and the points on a line between them are all optimal points.

This is also true when the feasible region is different. LP is *linear* programming and the equations involved must be linear, i.e. look like straight lines on a graph. Consequently, however many constraints there are the shape of the feasible region will always be a polygon and the corners will 'stick out'. This would not be the case if one or more of the constraints were curved. So for LP one of the corner points is always an optimal point.

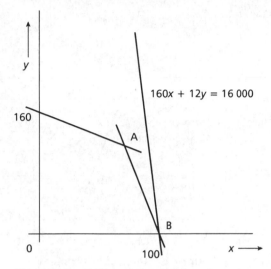

Figure 7.7   Different optimal point

The Simplex method on which computer solutions are based makes use of this fact. The method starts with a 'trial' solution at one corner of the feasible region. It then looks at the objective function values at adjacent corners and moves to the corner which brings the biggest increase in the objective function. The process continues until no further movement can lead to an increase in the objective: the optimal point has then been found.

The Simplex method can solve an LP quickly because it does not consider the whole of the feasible region, just corner points and then only a small number of them. When the LP has a large number of constraints the number of corner points will be large, and therefore the Simplex method represents a considerable saving even over the alternative of evaluating the objective function at all corner points.

Computer packages provide solutions to an LP problem, giving the optimal values of decision variables and objective function. However, a variety of messages and much additional information can also be provided. Most of this extra output will be explained in the next chapter but some basic output is described below, together with some concepts which are useful in solving an LP by computer.

Infeasibility

On the other hand, an LP problem may not always have a solution. Two situations can arise in which there is no solution. The first is when the problem is *infeasible*, which means that it is impossible to satisfy all the constraints at the same time and therefore no feasible region exists.

For example, the problem involving the model 321 jeans and model 421 jeans could well have had an extra constraint, say that production of model 321 had to satisfy orders already received. If there were advance orders for a total of 120 of this product, then the additional constraint would be:

$$x \geqslant 120$$

i.e. the minimum value x can take is 120.

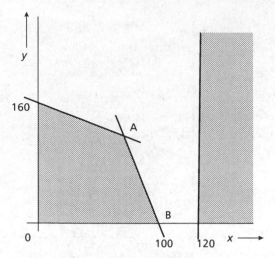

Figure 7.8   Infeasible problem

The problem now becomes:

$$\text{Max } 16x + 12y$$
$$\text{subject to}$$
$$6x + 3y \leqslant 600$$
$$2x + 5y \leqslant 800$$
$$x \geqslant 120$$
$$y \geqslant 0$$

A graphical representation of this is shown in Figure 7.8. No point within the original feasible region satisfies the new constraint and so the problem is infeasible.

Unboundedness

The second situation where there is no solution to an LP problem is when it is *unbounded*. This means that the 'solution' which does exist is infinite. For example, suppose that the jeans problem has, as well as the advance orders constraint for model 321, a further constraint for advance orders of 200 for model 421. Then an extra constraint would have to be added:

$$y \geqslant 200$$

For the sake of the example, suppose also that the constraints on the resources were omitted, either because there were no limitations on these resources or, in error, they were forgotten. The problem would then be:

$$\text{Max } 16x + 12y$$
$$\text{subject to}$$
$$x \geqslant 120$$
$$y \geqslant 200$$

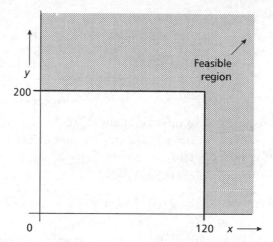

Figure 7.9   Unbounded problem

Figure 7.9 is the result of representing the problem graphically. The feasible region stretches without limit to infinite values of x and y and boundless increases in x and y are possible. As a result the objective function too can be increased to infinity and all the while the constraints are still satisfied. The problem is unbounded.

Given the usual, but unfortunately not negligible, provisos that the data have been put into the computer correctly and that the computer is working, the output of the package will be to provide a solution to a problem or state that it is infeasible or unbounded.

Redundancy

Although personal computers now have great power and LP algorithms are designed to work quickly, the solution to a large problem can still be lengthy and expensive in terms of computer time. It makes sense to do whatever can be done to reduce the size of the problem before it is entered into the computer. One way to do this is to check the constraints for redundancies. Redundancy occurs when one constraint is always weaker than another. For example, suppose two constraints are:

$$x + 4y \leqslant 20 \tag{1}$$

$$x + 4y \leqslant 30 \tag{2}$$

If $x + 4y$ is to be less than 20 then it will certainly be less than 30. So, if the first constraint holds then the second *must* also hold. The second is therefore weaker than the first and is redundant. It will have no effect on the solution and can be omitted from the formulation.

Redundancy also occurs when two constraints are the same. For example:

$$2x + y \leqslant 10$$
$$4x + 2y \leqslant 20$$

If the second constraint is divided by 2 then the first constraint is the result. The two constraints have precisely the same effect and one can be omitted.

On the other hand, we need to be careful before we eliminate too many constraints.

A constraint may be redundant when it is first formulated, but may no longer be so when sensitivity analysis is carried out and/or data are changed. For example, a review of accounting data might result in changes to equations (1) and (2):

$$x + 4y \leqslant 20 \tag{1A}$$
$$2x + 4y \leqslant 30 \tag{2A}$$

With these small but significant changes, (2A) is not always weaker than (1A). For instance, the point $(x = 15, y = 1)$ satisfies 1A but not 2A. A constraint should be omitted only if there is no possibility that sensitivity analysis or data changes will alter its redundant status.

Slack

Besides giving the optimal solution to the problems, an LP package also provides a range of extra management and economic information. This includes indicating whether the constraints are *tight* or *slack*.

A constraint is tight if, for the optimal solution, all of the resource to which the constraint refers is used up. In the jeans example, both resource constraints were tight. For example, the manpower constraint was:

$$6x + 3y \leqslant 600$$

At the optimal point $(x = 25, y = 150)$, all 600 units of the resource were used up since:

$$(6 \times 25) + (3 \times 150) = 600$$

This constraint is therefore tight. A constraint is slack when not all of the resource is used up. For example, had the optimal point been $x = 30, y = 120$, the amount of the resource used up would have been:

$$(6 \times 30) + (3 \times 120) = 540$$

Fewer than the available 600 units have been used up and so the constraint is slack. The amount of the slack, which would be given in the output of a computer solution, is $60 (= 600 - 540)$. A tight constraint is said to have zero slack.

Example

A manufacturer of soft drinks is preparing an overnight production run on two brands, Classic and Regular. There are sufficient ingredients available to make 8000 cans of C (Classic) and 16 000 of R (Regular), but there are only 20 000 cans (both brands use the same type of can). The filling/labelling machine produces 10 cans of C per minute and 25 cans of R per minute. There are two machines and 10 hours' production time is available on each, 20 hours in total. The machines can be used interchangeably for the two brands. The profit is 24p/can for C and 8p/can for R.

To formulate the problem, first isolate the three elements of an LP.

Decision variables

The manufacturer's problem is to decide how many cans of each soft drink it should produce to maximise its profit. The decision variables should be:

$$x = \text{cans of drink C}$$

$$y = \text{cans of drink R}$$

Objective function

The aim is to maximise profit and so the objective function (in £) is:

$$0.24x + 0.08y$$

Constraints

The ingredients for each brand are limited. The first two constraints are to express these limitations:

$$x \leq 8000 \text{ (for brand C)}$$

$$y \leq 16\,000 \text{ (for brand R)}$$

The number of cans available is also limited. Since the cans are suitable for both C and R:

$$x + y \leq 20\,000 \text{ (can availability)}$$

The next constraint concerns the availability of the production machines which fill, label and package the cans. For each can of C, the production time is 1/10 minute (= 10 cans per minute); for each can of R, the production time is 1/25 minute (= 25 cans per minute). Therefore, the total time required on the machines (which can be used interchangeably) for both brands is, in minutes:

$$\frac{1}{10}x + \frac{1}{25}y \leq 20 \times 60$$

Multiplying this equation through by 50, to tidy it up and make it easier to handle, it becomes:

$$5x + 2y \leq 20 \times 60 \times 50$$
$$5x + 2y \leq 60\,000$$

The last constraints restrict the decision variables to non-negative values:

$$x, y \geq 0$$

The fully formulated LP is then:

$$\text{Max } 0.24x + 0.08y$$
$$\text{subject to}$$
$$x \leq 8000$$
$$y \leq 16\,000$$
$$x + y \leq 20\,000$$
$$5x + 2y \leq 60\,000$$
$$x, y \leq 0$$

Table 7.3   Optimal   solution   to canning problem

Variable	Value
x	8000
y	10 000
Objective value = 2720	
Constraint	Slack
1	0
2	6000
3	2000
4	0

A typical computer package would solve this problem very quickly, in a matter of seconds, providing output looking something like Table 7.3.

The output should be interpreted as follows:

1. The optimal production levels are 8000 cans of brand C and 10 000 of brand R.

2. At these production levels the profit will be £2720 (you can check this by substituting $x = 8000$ and $y = 10\ 000$ into the objective function).

3. The column headed 'slack' shows whether each constraint is tight or slack. If a constraint is slack the extent of the spare capacity is the number in this column. For example, the production of brand R is not restricted by the availability of ingredients (constraint 2) – there are sufficient left over to make a further 6000 cans. Similarly, there are 2000 cans left over (constraint 3). The slack values may be checked by substituting $x = 8000$ and $y = 10\ 000$ into each of the constraints. For example, put $y = 10\ 000$ into constraint 2: $10\ 000 + \text{slack} = 16\ 000$ i.e. the slack is 6000. Constraints 1 and 4 show '0' slack: these constraints are tight, so there are no surplus resources. For example, all the available 20 hours of production time are used up (constraint 4). Again, this can be checked by putting $x = 8000$, $y = 10\ 000$ in the equation.

MINIMISATION PROBLEMS

LP is capable of solving a range of practical problems, but the basic technique can be extended in a number of directions to cover a wider range. Most of these extensions will be described in the next chapter but one should be dealt with now.

LP can be used on minimisation as well as maximisation problems. Typically these will have objective functions in terms of costs. The formulation of minimisation problems is the same as for maximisation, except that the minimisation constraints tend to be 'greater than or equal to' rather than 'less than or equal to', but are not exclusively so. Graphical solution proceeds by drawing the feasible region and then moving the objective function lines ('isocost' lines) in a south-westerly (as opposed to a north-easterly) direction to find the optimal point.

Computer packages handle minimisation problems very easily. Most of them require the user to declare at an early stage whether a problem is of maximisation or minimisation, then everything proceeds as before and the output has the same interpretation in both cases. The values of the decision variables are those which optimise the objective (whether maximum or minimum); the objective function value is that maximum or minimum; the slack for each constraint is the difference between how much of that resource is available and how much has been used. In the case of 'greater than' constraints, the slack is referred to as a surplus. For example, if constraint 1 were:

$$y \geqslant 10$$

and the optimal value of this variable is 12, then the output would show:

Constraint	Slack
1	2

This means that there is a surplus of 2 (12 as against the 10 required). Since slack is usually calculated as 'available − used', the slack for a 'greater than' constraint may be shown by some computer packages as '−2'.

CONCLUSION

Like all quantitative decision techniques, and indeed like all quantitative techniques, it is important from a management point of view to regard LP as an *aid* to decision making. It would be a mistake to think of LP as a substitute for decision making. LP is just one of the factors which may contribute to a good decision being taken, the others including softer information such as perceptions, qualitative data and experience. It would equally be a mistake to suppose that, because LP will not be able to capture all aspects of a problem to the last degree, then it cannot be used at all and the problem should be tackled by instinct. Many managers make the best enemy of the good: LP can help but because it is not perfect it is not used. Often it is then substituted by some *ad hoc* method which has no objectivity at all. A balanced approach would be to use LP to deal with quantifiable parts of the problem and so construct a sound information platform on which to build an evaluation of the qualitative factors.

LP contributes to a decision problem by providing, first, a quantitative solution and, second, a range of economic information. It also makes a less direct but equally important contribution, because the formulation of the problem as an LP in itself gives decision makers greater understanding and clearer insights into their problem's structure and the available range of alternative actions.

Examples of LP are usually to do with products and resources, but the technique can be applied to any situation which has the key characteristics indicating an LP. Its application areas include production, distribution, human resource planning and finance.

To summarise, an LP can be recognised by searching for the three factors which constitute the basis of any LP problem:

- decision variables;
- linear objective function;
- linear constraints.

CASE STUDIES

CASE STUDY 1

The case relates to a small furniture workshop and one of its products, double beds. The consortium manufactures two types of bed, standard and decorated. Bed production involves three basic operations: materials manufacture, assembly and finishing. A limited amount of time is available on the machines which carry out these tasks in any one-month planning period. Marketing plans dictate maximum and minimum sales requirements for each type of bed for the month. The new managing director of the workshop is an MBA graduate who has retired early from his career in financial services. He thinks monthly production can be planned using LP.

1. What should the decision variables be?
   (a) The total number of beds to be produced.
   (b) The numbers of each type of bed to be produced.
   (c) The amount of time taken up by each production operation.
   (d) The amount of time taken up by each production operation on each type of bed.

2. What should the objective function be?
   (a) Maximise revenue.
   (b) Maximise contribution (price minus variable costs).
   (c) Minimise costs.
   (d) Minimise time spent on production operations.

3. What should the number of constraints be?
   (a) 3
   (b) 7
   (c) 9
   (d) 12

Solutions

1. *What should the decision variables be?*
The decision variables are the numbers of each type of bed to produce. Answer (a) is not possible since it does not allow a distinction to be drawn between the different costs, prices and production times of the two types of bed. Answers (c) and (d) would make it difficult to devise algebraic expressions for the objective and the constraints.

2. *What should the objective function be?*
The objective function would be to maximise contribution. Answer (a) is incorrect because it ignores costs. The maximum revenue does not usually equate to the maximum profit. Answer (c) is incorrect because it would lead to a solution for which only the minimum sales requirements were produced, ignoring the fact that higher production levels will be more profitable. Answer (d) is incorrect because minimising time on the machines is unlikely to lead to greater financial returns. In any case, we have no information that any machine time saved can be used for anything else.

3. *How many constraints should there be?*
The constraints are:

- Times available for each operation: 3 constraints.
- Minimum sales requirements for each type of bed: 2 constraints.
- Maximum sales requirements for each type of bed: 2 constraints.
- Total = 7 constraints.

Note that non-negativity constraints are not required since they are covered by the minimum sales requirements.

CASE STUDY 2

A small engineering company produces two 'flatpack' workbenches, LD and LS, which are sold in the 'do-it-yourself' market. LD needs 6 minutes of cutting time and 3 minutes of assembly time. LS needs 2 minutes of cutting and 5 minutes of assembly. The time to set up the cutting and assembly machines is negligible. Other products mean that the company has 120 minutes of cutting time available per day and 120 minutes of assembly time. The price the company obtains for the LD workbench is £14 and for the LS £22. Variable costs are £10 per unit for both products. The company can sell as many of each product as it can produce. It wishes to formulate this problem as an LP maximising profit.

1. Formulate the problem as an LP and solve it graphically.

2. What is the slack on the cutter constraint?

Solutions

Stage 1

The decision variables are:

$$x = \text{the quantity of LD to produce}$$
$$y = \text{the quantity of LS to produce}$$

Stage 2

The objective function is:

maximise $4x + 12y$

This objective is the one which maximises contribution.

Stage 3

For the cutter 6 minutes are required by LS and 2 minutes by LD. Thus the total hours used must be $6x + 2y$. This must be no more than the total available, 120. The constraint is therefore:

$$6x + 2y \leqslant 120$$

Each LD requires 3 minutes of assembly time; each LS requires 5 minutes of assembly time. The total assembly time taken is thus $3x + 5y$. This must be no more than the total available, 120. The assembly constraint is:

$$3x + 5y \leqslant 120$$

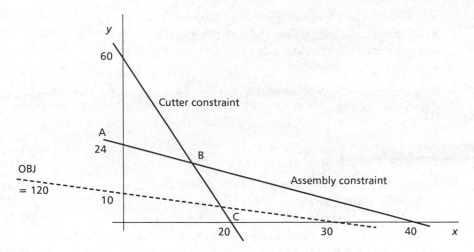

Figure 7.10

In addition, the two variables must be restricted to be non-negative, i.e. $x \geqslant 0, y \geqslant 0$.

The graph in Figure 7.10 shows the feasible region and the objective function when the objective function value is 120.

The optimal point is $x = 0, y = 24$, i.e. no LDs should be made, but 24 LSs should be made. The graph of the feasible region and objective function shows that as the objective increases, the line will move upwards and the last point at which it leaves the region will be point A.

Substituting $x = 0, y = 24$ in the objective function gives an optimal objective of 288.

The cutter constraint is $6x + 2y \leqslant 120$. Substituting $x = 0, y = 24$ shows that 48 of the available 120 minutes are used and therefore the slack is $120 - 48 = 72$.

QUESTIONS

1. Are the following statements true or false?
    (a) Every decision problem has at least one decision variable and an objective.
    (b) A decision problem which has decision variables, an objective function and constraints can be solved by L.P.
    (c) In practice, LP problems with two decision variables are solved by graphical means, larger problems by computer.
    (d) In practice, there are LP applications with thousands of decision variables and thousands of constraints.
    (e) If the objective function is £s then all the constraints must be in £s.
    (f) An LP should have all constraints $\leqslant$, or all constraints $\geqslant$.
    (g) For a $\leqslant$ constraint having a right-hand side in hours, the expression on the left of the $\leqslant$ must be in hours.
    (h) Decision variables must have the same unit of measurement as the objective function.

2. In the following formulation, which constraint is redundant?

$$Max\ 4x + 5y$$
$$subject\ to$$
$$x + 4y \leqslant 12$$
$$2x + 3y \leqslant 20$$
$$x \geqslant 15$$
$$x, y \geqslant 0$$

3. A smallholder owns 20 acres of land and has to decide what proportion to plant with flowers and what proportion with fruit. Although the land may yield more than one crop per year, each acre is devoted to either fruit or flowers for the full year. He calculates the average contribution to be £600 per acre per year for flowers and £800 per acre for fruit. However, the time he has available for cultivation and picking is limited by other activities and the availability of suitable labour, and the labour requirements by season are as in Table 7.4 (in manhours per acre):

Table 7.4

Crop	Winter	Season Spring	Summer	Autumn
Flowers	20	80	0	20
Fruit	20	40	100	20
Labour available (hours)	500	1200	1200	500

Formulate the smallholder's problem as a LP and decide the best pattern of crops to grow.

4. The Blueco organisation manufactures two types of clothes washing machine, Deluxe (D) and Regular (R), which are assembled on the same production line. Both machines use a common steel shell, but have different wiring systems and computer chips. The daily availability of these three sub-units is limited by Blueco's own production facilities. 400 shells are ready for use; a maximum of 250 and 320 timing mechanisms and 180 and 360 wiring mechanisms are available for types D and R respectively. The total

Table 7.5

Resource	Type A	Type B	Availability
Shells	1	1	400
Timer (D)	1		250
Timer (R)		1	320
Chips (D)	1		180
Chips (R)		1	360
Labour	0.3	0.5	150

labour hours required to assemble the machines are 0.3 for D and 0.5 for R. There are 20 assembly workers each contributing a 7.5-hour day. The daily input requirements for the machines can be summarised as in Table 7.5.

In addition, sales requirements mean that a minimum of 100 of D and 80 of R should be produced. The contribution/unit is £80 and £50 respectively.

Formulate the production mix problem as an LP and solve graphically.

5. A timber company wants to make the best use of its wood resources in one of its forest regions which contains fir and spruce trees. During the next month 80 000 board-feet of spruce are available and 90 000 board-feet of fir.

The company owns mills which produce lumber and plywood. Producing 1000 board-feet of lumber requires 1000 board-feet of spruce and 2000 board-feet of fir. Producing 1000 square feet of plywood requires 2000 board-feet of spruce and 1500 board-feet of fir. Firm orders mean that at least 10 000 board-feet of lumber and 12 000 square feet of plywood must be produced during the next month. The profit contributions are £100 per 1000 board-feet of lumber and £250 per 1000 square feet of plywood.

The production decision is taken on the basis of an LP model.

(a) Formulate the problem as a contribution-maximising LP.

(b) Solve the LP graphically.

(c) When solved by computer the following printout results (Table 7.6). What should be in place of the question marks?

Table 7.6

Variable	Value
L	?
P	?
Objective value = 9750	

Constraint	Slack
Spruce availability	?
Fir availability	?
Lumber orders	?
Plywood orders	?

ANSWERS TO QUESTIONS

1. (a) True.
   (b) False.
   (c) False.
   (d) True.
   (e) False.
   (f) False.
   (g) True.
   (h) False.

2. $x \geq 15$ is redundant.

3. Maximise $600x + 800y$

subject to

$$20x + 20y \leqslant 500$$
$$80x + 40y \leqslant 1200$$
$$100y \leqslant 1200$$
$$20x + 20y \leqslant 500$$
$$x + y \leqslant 20$$
$$x, y \geqslant 0$$

The farmer should therefore plant 8 acres with flowers and 12 with fruit to obtain a return of £14 400.

4. Maximise $80x + 50y$

    subject to

    $$x + y \leqslant 400$$
    $$y \leqslant 320$$
    $$x \leqslant 180$$
    $$3x + 5y \leqslant 1500$$
    $$x \geqslant 100$$
    $$y \geqslant 80$$

    The optimal point is: $x = 180, y = 192$
    Optimal objective value $= 24\ 000$

5. (a) Formulation:

    $$\text{Max } 100L + 250P$$

    $$\text{subject to}$$
    $$L + 2P \leqslant 80$$
    $$2L + 1.5P \leqslant 90$$
    $$L \geqslant 10$$
    $$P \geqslant 12$$

    Where   L = amount of lumber produced (in '000 board-feet)

    P = amount of plywood produced (in '000 square feet).

    (b) Make 10 000 board-feet of lumber and 35 000 square feet of plywood.

    (c) The computer printout should be as in Table 7.7.

Table 7.7

Variable	Value
L	10.00
P	35.00
Objective value = 9750	

Constraint	Slack
Spruce availability	0
Fir availability	17.50
Lumber orders	0
Plywood orders	23.00

CHAPTER EIGHT

Extensions to linear programming

Chapter 7 dealt with the fundamentals of LP, giving a platform for a more advanced look at the technique. The basic ideas can be extended, both in terms of generating further information and of applying them to problems that do not appear at first sight to be LPs. Some underlying assumptions on LP can be relaxed if more complex methods such as integer and non-linear programming are used.

INTRODUCTION

Linear programming can help solve decision problems concerned with optimising an objective such as profit, but where the actions which can be taken are limited by constraints, such as the quantity of skilled staff available. Mathematically the decision is represented by decision variables, such as the amount of each product to manufacture. If the objective and the constraints can be expressed algebraically in terms of decision variables, and if these mathematical expressions are linear (they contain no logarithmic, squared, cubed, etc. terms) then LP has the potential to solve this problem by showing what the optimal values of the decision variables are.

This basic idea, as described in the last chapter, is just the beginning. In applying the technique it can be extended in many directions. LP can:

- produce a much richer set of management information than the bare solution to a problem;
- deal with a much wider set of problems than may be apparent at first sight;
- be adapted to solve problems for which the assumptions of LP, such as linearity, are not met;
- solve problems in which some or all the variables can take only whole number values;
- be applied to problems where there is uncertainty, in the sense that some decision variables may have a statistical distribution, for example when the variable describes weather conditions such as rainfall.

This chapter describes all these extensions to the concept of LP.

MANAGEMENT INFORMATION FROM LP

There are four broad categories of management information which an LP solution produces: dual values, right-hand side ranges, reduced costs and coefficient ranges.

Dual values

When a computer algorithm such as Simplex solves an LP problem it provides, besides the optimum values of the decision variables and the objective function, other information which can be used among other things to perform sensitivity analysis. The information shows what would happen to the optimal solution if the basic assumptions or input data of the problem were changed. For example, a new quarter's accounting data can vary profit margins and cost levels, and the decision maker needs to know whether the optimal solution is likely to be affected. Most important in this extra information are probably dual values, sometimes called shadow prices. Dual values are concerned with constraints, not variables. Each constraint has a dual value which is a measure of the increase in the objective function if one extra unit of the resource associated with the constraint were available, everything else being unchanged.

The example used in the last chapter was concerned with the Jacobs Jeans company which produces jeans in Eastern Europe for the Eastern European market. Jacobs makes two types of jeans, brand 321 and brand 421, from two resources, manpower and material. The profit per unit of each brand is shown in Table 8.1.

The resources required to make the jeans are shown in Table 8.2. To produce one pair of brand 321 jeans takes 6 minutes of manpower and 2 units of materials; to produce one pair of brand 421 jeans takes 3 minutes of manpower and 5 units of materials.

The availability of manpower is 600 minutes/day and that of materials is 800 units/day. Jacobs Jeans' problem is to decide how many of each model to produce per day in order to maximise its profit.

The formulation of the problem is:

$$\text{Max } 16x + 12y$$

subject to

$$6x + 3y \leqslant 600$$
$$2x + 5y \leqslant 800$$
$$x \geqslant 0, y \geqslant 0$$

Table 8.1   Jeans profits

	Model	
	321	421
Profit/unit (£)	16	12

Table 8.2   Resources required for the jeans

	Model	
	321	421
Manpower(mins)	6	3
Materials	2	5

Table 8.3

Constraint	Dual value
$6x + 3y \leqslant 600$	2.33 (manpower)
$2x + 5y \leqslant 800$	1.00 (materials)

The solution was: $x = 25$, $y = 150$; objective function $= 2200$. The dual values, which would be given as part of the computer output, are shown in Table 8.3.

The dual values are interpreted as follows. If the available manpower were 601 instead of 600, the optimal value of the objective function would be increased by 2.33 to 2202.33. So, if Jacob Jeans could take on extra labour, for example by recruitment, at the same cost as the previous 600 (the cost already included in the objective function), the company should do this because the profit can thereby increase by 2.33. If the extra manpower costs an extra amount, for example because it comes from overtime, then no more than 2.33 should be paid for it because beyond this level the extra labour becomes unprofitable. An extra unit of materials, 801 being available instead of 800, would increase the optimal objective function value by 1.0 to 2201.

Dual values are therefore measures of the true worth of resources to the decision maker and there is no reason why they should be the same as the price paid for the resource, or its market value. In essence they measure the value which the decision maker can derive from them, not the state of the external market. The dual values are produced as part of the output of an algebraic solution of an LP problem and require no extra calculations once the LP has been solved.

Frequently, dual values are equal to zero, meaning that no extra value can be derived from extra amounts of that resource. In the jeans example, both constraints were tight, meaning that the total availability of each resource was used up. You can check this by substituting the optimal x, y values in the constraints. In some circumstances the total availability of a resource might not be fully used up. If not all the resource is used up the constraint is said to be slack and the associated dual value (of that constraint only) must be zero. Since units of that resource are available but are not being employed, extra units of it can have no value to the decision maker, i.e. when the slack is non-zero then the dual value is zero.

A dual value can be calculated graphically by re-solving the problem with the right-hand side of the constraint increased by 1 (see Figure 8.1). The amount by which the objective function increases in the new solution is the dual value. In the example, the dual value of manpower can be calculated by solving the problem as before, but with manpower availability increased. To make the numbers easier to handle, let the availability be increased by 120:

$$6x + 3y \leqslant 720$$

Then, the optimal point is the point of intersection of:

$$6x + 3y = 720$$
$$2x + 5y = 800$$

The optimal point is no longer A, but is A.[1] Using the method of simultaneous equations

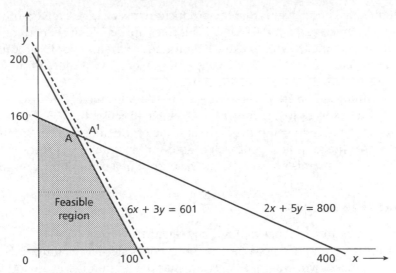

Figure 8.1   Calculating a dual value graphically

as before:

$$6x + 15y = 2400$$
$$6x + 3y = 720$$
$$\overline{12y = 1680}$$
$$y = 140$$

Substituting in the materials constraint:

$$2x + 5(140) = 800$$
$$2x = 100$$
$$x = 50$$

So, $x = 50$, $y = 140$.

Substituting in the objective function:

$$16(50) + 12(140) = 2480$$

The improvement in the objective function is therefore 280 (2480 − 2200). This occurred because the availability of manpower was increased by 120. The dual value, however, is the improvement in the objective function for an increase in the right-hand side of the constraint of *one* unit.

The dual value of manpower is therefore:

$$\text{Dual value} = (2480 - 2200)/120$$
$$= 2.33$$

At first sight it may seem strange that an extra minute of manpower could be used at all. In the original solution all 600 manpower minute and all 800 units of material were being used. Since both brands 321 and 421 require a combination of both resources, how could the extra minute of manpower be used since there is no material with which to combine it? The answer is that the production mix changes: fewer units of brand 421 are made (*y* decreases from 150 to 140). This frees up some units of both resources which can then be combined with the extra 120 minutes of manpower to produce more of brand 321 (*x* increases from 25 to 50). The new production mix is more profitable by 280 – hence the positive dual value or shadow price.

The dual value works in both directions. A dual value of 2.33 also means that one unit *less* of the resource would lower the objective function by 2.33. The same approach can of course be used to compute the dual value of the materials constraint, which is 1.0. In both cases the graphical approach is used for illustrative purposes. In practice the dual values of constraints are taken from the output of a computer package.

Right-hand side ranges

Dual values are marginal values. They refer to a very small – i.e. 'marginal' – increment in a resource and are not guaranteed to hold over larger ranges. For example, if the decision maker were offered 1000 extra manpower minutes at an additional price of 2.0, the first few minutes should be accepted since 2.0 is less than the dual value of 2.33, but this does not mean that all 1000 should be accepted. Fortunately we can find out the range for which the dual value holds. This is known as the right-hand side range and most computer packages print it out automatically. For the manpower constraint the right-hand side (RHS) range – the range over which the dual value holds – is 1800. In other words, the objective function increases by 2.33 per minute for 1800 extra minutes.

Again, the graphical approach helps us understand how an RHS range is calculated. In Figure 8.2, as the number of minutes available is increased, the constraint is moved outwards. For the first few increased minutes the optimal point, the intersection of the two constraints, moves. The objective function increases just as it did when the optimal point moved from A to A[1] in calculating the dual value: each unit increase in the resource results in the same 2.33 increase in the objective function. The dual value is therefore constant at 2.33.

However, when the constraint has reached the situation where it goes through point

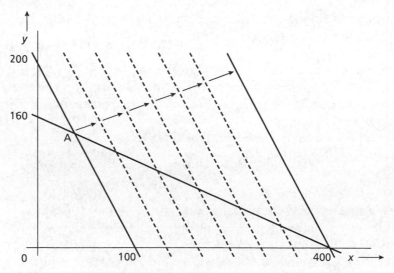

Figure 8.2   Right-hand side range

B (which is then the optimal point), no further changes are possible. If the constraint were moved further, the feasible region would no longer change and the optimal point would no longer move since it cannot go below the x-axis where the y values are negative. Therefore the optimal point will stay at B however much further the resource is increased and the constraint is moved. Therefore no further increases in the resource lead to improvements in the objective function and consequently the dual value must be zero.

Point B has $y = 0$ since it is on the x-axis. Since it is also on the materials constraint:

$$2x + 5y = 800$$
$$2x + 0 = 800$$
$$x = 400$$

When $y = 0$ and $x = 400$, the manpower minutes used are:

$$6x + 3y = (6 \times 400) + 0$$
$$= 2400$$

The manpower minutes were therefore increased from 600 to 2400 before the dual value dropped to zero. The RHS range for manpower is 1800 (2400 − 600). If extra manpower minutes can be made available at a cost less than the dual value of 2.33, up to 1800 of them can be accepted and profit should still increase. More than 1800 and no further improvements in profit will result.

In a similar way the RHS range for *decreasing* manpower minutes, and for increasing and decreasing materials, can be calculated. Computer packages usually produce RHS ranges automatically as part of their output. In this example the output would be as in Table 8.4.

Table 8.4 means that profit can be increased by 2.33 (the dual value) for each extra manpower minute up to a total of 2400 (including the original 600), and decreased by 2.33 for each manpower minute taken away until manpower minutes are reduced to 480. Sometimes tables of RHS ranges show upper and lower limits of the resources (as above) and sometimes they show allowable increases and decreases (1800 and 120 in this example). Similarly, the dual value for materials applies to each added or subtracted unit up to a total of 1000 or down to 200 (an allowable increase of 200 and an allowable decrease of 600). Dual values, and associated RHS ranges, apply to the variation in one constraint at a time, the others being unchanged.

Reduced costs

So far the non-negativity constraints, $x \geq 0$, $y \geq 0$, have not been mentioned, but they are constraints just like the others. What about their dual values? Confusingly, they are known as the *reduced costs* of the decision variables. If the optimal value of a variable is not zero, then its non-negativity constraint is slack and the reduced cost (= dual value) is zero. For example, the optimal value of brand 321 jeans is 25, so a constraint saying

Table 8.4   Right-hand side ranges

Constraint	Initial value	Up to	Down to
Manpower minutes	600	2400	480
Materials	800	1000	200

$x \geqslant 1$ instead of $x \geqslant 0$ would not make any difference to the objective function and the reduced cost is zero.

If, on the other hand, the optimal value of a decision variable is zero then the non-negativity constraint is tight. Forcing this variable to be non-zero will affect the optimal solution and objective function. In this case the variable will have a non-zero reduced cost, which is the amount by which the objective will change if the variable is forced to be non-zero. For example, if the optimal value for the production of brand 321 jeans were zero, but the marketing manager decreed that some should be produced so that a full product range could be offered to customers, the reduced cost of brand 321 jeans is the per unit cost of doing so. If the reduced cost were £15 and 20 pairs were to be made, then the loss compared to the optimal objective function would be £300(= 20 × £15).

Coefficient ranges

Coefficient ranges do for the objective function coefficients what RHS ranges do for the right-hand sides of constraints: they show by how much an objective function coefficient can change before the optimal values of the decision variables change. The graphical solution to the electronics example, Figure 8.3, illustrates what this means.

In the Jacob Jeans example we found the optimal point A by moving the objective function line outwards (north-easterly) until it reached its last point of contact with the feasible region. If the slope of the objective function line had been very different then the optimal point would have been B or C, but as long as it was within a limited range the optimal point would still have been A. Coefficient ranges tell us what this limited range is.

Changing the coefficient values is the same as varying the slope of the line, so the coefficient ranges show by how much the coefficients can be varied while the optimal point remains at A. If they change by small amounts the slope of the line will not be sufficiently different for the optimal point to move away from A; if they change by large amounts the slope may be sufficiently different to change the optimal point. The coefficient ranges are the amounts by which each coefficient of the objective can be varied before the optimal point does move away from A to B or C. Although small changes in

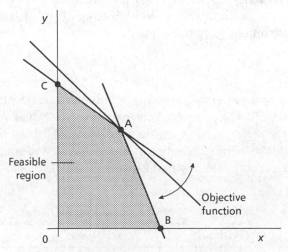

Figure 8.3 Coefficiency ranges

Table 8.5 Coefficient ranges

Coefficient of	Initial value	Up to	Down to
Brand 321	16	24	4.8
Brand 421	12	40	8

a coefficient may not move the optimal point, the optimal objective function value will of course be different.

For the Jacobs Jeans example the computer output would be as in Table 8.5.

The table is interpreted as follows. Profit per unit for Brand 321 can vary between 4.8 and 24 and the optimal production will still be 25 of 321 and 150 of 421. Similarly, the profit per unit of Brand 421 can vary between 8 and 40 without disturbing the optimal point. These ranges apply to the variation of one coefficient at a time, the other being kept at its original value.

Example

In Chapter 7 the following problem was formulated and a basic solution found.

A manufacturer of soft drinks is preparing an overnight production run on two brands, Classic and Regular. There are sufficient ingredients available to make 8000 cans of C (Classic) and 16 000 of R (Regular), but there are only 20 000 cans (both brands use the same type of can). The filling/labelling machine produces 10 cans of C per minute and 25 cans of R per minute. There are two machines and 10 hours' production time is available on each, 20 hours in total. The machines can be used interchangeably for the two brands. The profit is 24p/can for C and 8p/can for R.

The formulation is:

$$\text{Max } 0.24x + 0.08y$$
$$\text{subject to}$$
$$x \leqslant 8000$$
$$y \leqslant 16\,000$$
$$x + y \leqslant 20\,000$$
$$5x + 2y \leqslant 60\,000$$
$$x, y \geqslant 0$$
$$\text{where } x = \text{production of C}$$
$$y = \text{production of R}$$

Typical computer output would look something like Table 8.6.

The output is interpreted as follows:

1. The optimal production levels are to make 8000 cans of drink C and 10 000 of R.

2. At these production levels the profit will be £2720.

3. The column headed 'slack' indicates the extent to which resources are unused. There are, for example, sufficient ingredients for drink R left over to make a further 6000 cans.

Table 8.6   Optimal solution to canning problem

Variable	Value	Reduced Cost		
x	8000	0		
y	10 000	0		

Objective value = 2720

Constraint	Slack	Dual Value	Upto	Down to
1 Ingredients C	0	0.04	12 000	6666.67
2 Ingredients R	6000	0	infinity	10 000
3 Cans	2000	0	infinity	18 000
4 Time	0	0.04	64 000	40 000

Objective coefficient	Original	Up to	Down to
Brand C	0.24	infinity	0.20
Brand R	0.08	0.096	0

4. Slack constraints (2 and 3) have a zero dual value. Constraint 1 (ingredients C) is tight and has a dual value of 0.04. If ingredients for an extra can were available, 4p could be added to total profit.

   Constraint 4 is also tight, with a dual value of 0.04. This dual value is harder to interpret because it is not immediately clear what it is that is worth an extra 4p. We must go back to the constraint itself: $5x + 2y \leq 60\,000$. The dual value is the increase in the objective function if the right-hand side of the constraint is increased by 1 from 60 000 to 60 001. Originally this constraint was that the time available on the machines was less than 20 hours. When the constraint was formulated, hours were turned into minutes so that the right-hand side was 20×60. To get rid of some fractions the constraint was multiplied through by 50 so that the right-hand side became $20 \times 60 \times 50 = 60\,000$. The units are therefore one-fiftieths of a minute, i.e. 1.2 seconds. The dual value means that if extra time were available on the machine each extra 1.2 seconds would be worth 4p. The extra time might be gained by use of overtime and then each 1.2 seconds would be worth 4p, each minute would be worth 200p, each hour would be worth £120. It is worth using overtime if the cost is less than £120/hour, over and above the cost of normal-time working included in the objective function.

5. The columns headed 'up to' and 'down to' are the RHS ranges showing the limits within which the dual values hold. Constraints 2 and 3 (ingredients R and cans) are slack and therefore they have zero dual value. This would continue to be the case no matter how much extra of these resources were available, hence the right-hand side can be increased up to 'infinity' without changing the dual values. Likewise, the right-hand sides can be reduced by the amount of the slack and the dual values will remain zero.

   For ingredients for C, the dual value is 4p per can from 8000 cans up to 12 000 and from 8000 down to 6667. For machine time the dual value is 4p per 1.2 secs (= £120 per hour). This applies for an additional 4000×1.2 secs (= 80 minutes) and for a reduction of $20\,000 \times 1.2$ secs (= 400 minutes).

6. The bottom section of Table 8.6 relating to objective coefficient ranges shows that while the profit for soft drink C is in the range 20p and above (but assuming the profit for

R is unchanged at 8p), the optimal decision will still be to make 8000 of C and 10 000 of R. Similarly, the optimal decision is unchanged while per unit profit of R is no greater than 9.6p (assuming the profit for C stays at 24p).

7.   The optimal values of both decision variables are non-zero so their reduced cost (the cost of forcing them to have non-zero values) must be 0.

DECISION PROBLEMS WITH LP ASSOCIATIONS

The LP problems used as examples and cases in these chapters would be solved very quickly indeed by almost any computer package. In some real world applications, however, the size of the LP is so great that the time and expense involved in obtaining a solution are important factors in deciding how to tackle the problem. There is no point in taking so long to solve an LP that the information it gives is out of date by the time it is ready for use; nor should the cost of finding a solution exceed the value of the information to the decision maker. For example, the large LPs used by oil companies can have hundreds or thousands of constraints and take several hours to solve even on large mainframe computers. The information will therefore be several hours old before it can be used and there is also a high opportunity cost associated with using a large mainframe for so long.

Deciding how often to re-run the programme when new data becomes available is a big issue and it can then become important to look for short-cut solution methods. Some LP problems have particular characteristics which enable them to be solved by special algorithms which take significantly less computer time. *Transportation problems* are an example of this.

For example, a supermarket chain has its yoghurt products manufactured at several different suppliers, each located in a different place. The yoghurts are then taken to any of its many regional warehouses where they are stored prior to distribution to the retail stores. The cost of transporting the products from factory to warehouse differs, of course, according to the locations involved. The problem for the supermarket chain's logistics manager is to decide how much of each supplier's output to send to each of its warehouses so that the cost of distribution is minimised but bearing in mind capacity limitations (perhaps because of the other products that have to be transported) on each route. The problem is represented diagrammatically in Figure 8.4. For simplification, only three suppliers and eight warehouses are shown.

To demonstrate that the problem has the form of an LP some artificial data will be used. Suppose each supplier has a planned monthly output and each warehouse has an estimated demand schedule for yoghurt, as shown in Table 8.7. For example, Table 8.7 shows that Supplier A plans to produce 30 000 cases next month and Warehouse 1 is likely to require 6000 cases. The cost per case of moving yoghurt between the different locations is also shown in Table 8.7. For example, the cost per case of transporting yoghurt from Supplier A to Warehouse 4 is 12p. In this example the total outputs are exactly equal to the total demands, but this does not have to be the case. In a more complicated problem allowance would be made for storage at the suppliers' factories and the warehouses.

This logistics problem can be formulated as an LP.

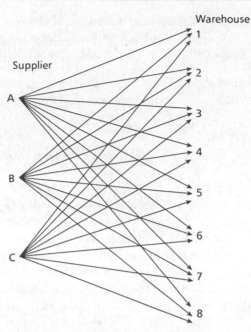

Figure 8.4　Transportation problem for a supermarket chain

Table 8.7　Costs, outputs and demands

	Output	Warehouse							
	('000 cases)	1	2	3	4	5	6	7	8
Demand ('000 cases)		6	11	8	14	5	10	8	14
Cost (p per case)									
Factory　A	30	11	43	9	12	25	32	18	56
B	18	24	22	76	28	5	43	48	16
C	28	54	14	40	33	38	29	33	8

Decision variables

These are the quantities to be transported along each route. There are 24 routes (3 suppliers × 8 warehouses) and therefore 24 decision variables.

xAl, xA2, ... xA8 are the cases taken from supplier A to warehouses 1, 2, ... 8

xB1, xB2, ... xB8 are the cases taken from factory B to warehouses 1, 2, ... 8

xC1, xC2, ... xC8 are the cases taken from factory C to warehouses 1, 2, ... 8

Objective function

The objective is to minimise the total cost of distribution for all outputs and demands over all possible routes. The cost per case for each route is taken from the body of Table 8.7.

Minimise $\quad 11xAl + 43xA2 + \ldots + 56xA8 \quad$ (supplier A)

$$+ 24xBl + \ldots + 16xB8 \quad \text{(supplier B)}$$

$$+ 54xCl + \ldots + 8xC8 \text{ (factory C)}$$

Constraints

The first type of constraint says that, in the absence of storage facilities, all output must go somewhere. For example, one constraint is that all the 30 000 cases produced by supplier A have to go to warehouses. Therefore:

$$xA1 + xA2 + \ldots + xA8 = 30$$

The output could go to just one warehouse (in which case one variable would be equal to 30 and the rest 0) or it could be shared in some way between some or all of them. There are similar constraints for the other two warehouses:

$$xB1 + xB2 + \ldots + xB8 = 18 \text{ (factory B)}$$
$$xC1 + xC2 + \ldots + xC8 = 28 \text{ (factory C)}$$

The second type of constraint is that all demands must be met, i.e. for the sake of the example it is assumed that there will be no stockouts at the warehouses. For example, a total of 6000 cases must be delivered to warehouse 1 from the factories.

$$xA1 + xB1 + xC1 = 6$$

The whole 6000 cases could come from just one factory or from different sources. There are similar constraints relating to the other warehouses:

$$xA2 + xB2 + xC2 = 11 \text{ (warehouse 2)}$$
$$xA8 + xB8 + xC8 = 14 \text{ (warehouse 8)}$$

Apart from non-negativity constraints, these 11 constraints constitute the full list. The problem as formulated could now be solved by LP to show how much yoghurt should be sent from each supplier to each warehouse. In fact the optimal decision is:

$xA3 = 8$
$xA4 = 14$ — output from supplier A goes to warehouses 3, 4, 7
$xA7 = 8$

$xB1 = 6$
$xB2 = 7$ — output from supplier B goes to warehouses 1, 2, 5
$xB5 = 5$

$xC2 = 4$
$xC6 = 10$ — output from supplier C goes to warehouses 2, 6, 8
$xC8 = 14$

This solution, using a standard personal computer package, took just a few seconds, but in a larger problem solution time might be a much more significant consideration. Then the fact that transportation problems have a special structure which enables them

Table 8.8 Press shop assignment problem

£	Piece of work				
Press	1	2	3	4	5
A	2.1	3.5	1.8	2.0	4.2
B	3.0	4.2	3.0	2.7	3.9
C	2.5	3.1	2.3	2.3	3.3
D	3.5	3.8	3.4	2.9	4.8
E	3.4	3.6	2.9	3.1	4.1

to be solved by a short-cut method and thereby reduce computer time could bring about a worthwhile saving. The special structure is that the coefficients of all the variables in all the constraints have the coefficient '0' or '1'. When a problem has this characteristic a *transportation method algorithm* can be used.

Usually it is easier to recognise a transportation problem from the nature of the problem (transporting from 'factories' to 'warehouses') rather than from the mathematical formulation. However, not all transportation problems are concerned with distributing products from their place of manufacture to warehouses or the point of sale. For example, a regional police authority has at least one patrol car attached to each of its 80 police stations. Within the area there are three vehicle centres where the cars are serviced and repaired. To which centre should the cars of each station be sent? This is a transportation problem. The service centres are the 'factories' and their vehicle capacities the 'outputs'. The police stations are the 'warehouses' and the numbers of cars attached to them their 'demands'. The cost of servicing a car at one centre rather than another is related mainly to the distance between centre and station.

Besides transportation problems other situations exhibit special characteristics which allow a short-cut solution method to be used. *Assignment* problems are an example. An illustrative example is that of a metal-pressing shop where there are, say, five different pieces of work to be done and each must be allocated to one of the five different presses. The cost of doing each piece of work on each press is shown in Table 8.8.

The problem is that of assigning each piece of work to a press. When formulated as an LP this problem has characteristics which allow an assignment algorithm to be used to solve it and thereby reduce computer time as compared to standard LP-based methods. An assignment problem is like a transportation problem with the additional feature that the demand at each 'warehouse' is exactly 1, as is the supply at each 'factory'.

INTEGER PROGRAMMING

An integer is a whole number. For example 1, 2, 3, 4, 5 . . . are integers, as are −1, −2, −3 . . . Decimals and fractions, on the other hand, are not.

LP assumes that the decision variables are continuous, that is, they can take on any values subject to the constraints, including decimals and fractions. Therefore LP cannot be applied to problems in which any of the variables must be restricted to integer values only. An example will show when this might occur.

Suppose a shipping company is planning the tonnage it needs in the future. Linear programming could be used to indicate the tonnage required on each route in order to maximise future profit subject to a number of constraints on, say, manpower, finance, demand levels, port capacities, etc. It would not matter if the answers were whole numbers or not. The tonnages are approximate indications of what is needed and an answer of 63.7 thousand tonnes would be acceptable. On the other hand, the problem could have been formulated to decide the number of ships required, not the tonnage. Now it is necessary for the variables to be integer since it would be difficult to interpret an answer such as 2.5 ships. Integer programming would have to be used to solve this problem.

Integer programming uses a different solution method from LP. The algorithm is more complicated and takes longer to solve by computer. Because of the greater difficulty and expense in applying integer programming, 'tricks' are used so that linear programming can be applied. For example, 2.5 ships could be interpreted as owning 2 ships while chartering 1 ship for six months of the year.

Integer programming also has financial applications. For example, a company has a series of opportunities for capital investment which have different returns and cashflow profiles. Only a limited amount of money is, of course, available and also the company has certain cashflow requirements through time. In which of the opportunities should the company invest? The problem can be handled by LP. The decision variables are the amounts of money to invest in each opportunity; the objective is to maximise return; the constraints are the money available and the cashflow requirements through time. Some of the opportunities can have variable amounts invested in them, such as for example the purchase of stocks and shares. Other opportunities, however, require all-or-nothing investments, such as the purchase of a motor vehicle or the construction of a new plant. An answer of investing £20 000 in new vehicles when the vehicles cost £15 000 each would not make sense. The investment must be for £0, £15 000, £30 000, etc. This situation requires integer programming.

NON-LINEAR PROGRAMMING

The term 'non-linear programming' refers to a general category of programming problem where the requirement for equations to be linear is relaxed. For example, the objective function may incorporate squared, cubed or logarithmic terms, allowing for a curved relationship between profitability and output. Only certain types of non-linear problem can be solved, and those that can be solved generally require a large computer capacity.

Quadratic programming is for problems whose objective functions are quadratic, i.e. squared terms are involved. For example, suppose the quantity of a product purchased depends on its price, as is usually the case in practice. The demand function, probably estimated by applying regression analysis to past data or market research information, might be:

$$\text{Quantity purchased} = 10\ 000 - 3 \times \text{Price}$$

$$Q = 10\ 000 - 3P$$

$$\text{Then, Revenue} = \text{Price} \times \text{Quantity}$$

$$= P \times Q$$

$$= P(10\ 000 - 3P)$$

$$= 10\ 000P - 3P^2$$

Table 8.9   Non-linear programming methods

Programming method	Characteristics	
	Objective function	Constraints
Quadratic	Linear and squared	Linear
Geometric	Both non-linear (terms are products of decision variables e.g. max $6xy + 7x^2y^3$)	
Separable	Linear	Non-linear but can be approximated by linear expressions

This is a quadratic equation since it involves P and P^2. If such an expression appeared in an objective function the problem would no longer be one of *linear* programming. Solution methods which assume that the objective function is linear cannot be applied. For example, the graphical approach used thus far is not possible because a curved objective function means that the optimal point is not necessarily a corner point of the feasible region. It is not necessary, in a managerial context, to investigate the nature of the algorithm required in a quadratic programming problem since a computer package would always be used. However, for a manager who is likely to need to solve such problems it is important to check that the software purchased has the capability to handle quadratic programming.

Quadratic objective functions might occur in situations where unit costs are variable. For instance, economies of scale might result in unit costs which decrease according to a quadratic equation as the number produced increases. They might also occur in purchasing problems where there are quantity discounts.

Quadratic programming deals with the particular situation where the objective function is quadratic but the constraints remain linear. Different programming methods have to be used when a problem is non-linear in some other way. Table 8.9 summarises other programming methods and the circumstances in which they are used.

PROGRAMMING UNDER UNCERTAINTY

The programming problems we have encountered up to now have been based on the assumption that all the data are known with certainty: unit costs, sales demands, resource availabilities etc. are supposed to be true and exact. In other words, the coefficients and constants in the problem formulation are fixed. Such a formulation, or model, is said to be *deterministic*. In practice, financial, marketing and other information is likely to have come from estimation and forecasting procedures and will therefore be, to some degree, uncertain. More explicitly, it is extremely likely in most situations that we will be unsure that the data is accurate. We will now look at three ways of handling such uncertainties.

The first is by use of *sensitivity analysis*. This means changing selected items of the input data and then re-solving the problem to see what happens to the optimal solution. For example, the right-hand side of a 'minimum sales' constraint might be a demand of 5000. Sensitivity analysis would re-solve the problem several times, each time changing the 5000 up by steps of 1000 and down by steps of 1000. Carried out exhaustively, this will show which data have a big influence on the results and which a negligible influence. The use of dual values, RHS ranges, coefficient ranges and reduced costs would also fall under the heading of 'sensitivity analysis'.

Some computer packages are able to carry out *parametric programming*, which is a systematic form of sensitivity analysis. In parametric programming a coefficient is varied continuously over a range around its original value and the effect on the optimal solution displayed. For example, in an LP to decide the capital expenditure on each of three projects, one constraint might impose a limit of £10 million on total expenditure. It would be of the form:

$$\text{Investment in project 1}$$
$$+ \text{Investment in project 2}$$
$$+ \text{Investment in project 3} \leqslant 10\ 000\ 000$$

The optimal solution might be:

$$\text{Amount to invest in Project 1: £5.5m}$$
$$\text{Amount to invest in Project 2: 0}$$
$$\text{Amount to invest in Project 3: £4.5m}$$

Parametric programming might vary the 10 million through the range 5 million to 18 million and produce results as in Table 8.10.

However, parametric programming and other forms of sensitivity analysis, although they are based on the idea that the data is uncertain, do not use any probability information which may be available. For example, market research might have shown demand for a new product in the form of some statistical distribution, but sensitivity analysis would not use this information. It is merely a question of trying different demand levels and seeing the effect.

The second approach to dealing with uncertain data in a programming problem is *stochastic programming*. This is the name for the general class of solution methods which deal with uncertainty by formulating the problem in a way which incorporates any probability information which might be available (such as estimated demand distributions) and then transforming the formulation into one which can be handled by ordinary programming methods.

In the above capital expenditure example, the investments in the projects, if they were the costs of building new plants, might not be known with certainty since they would depend on factors which could only emerge after construction had started. Instead these

Table 8.10   Parametric programming

Total Investment Limit	Investment in Project 1	Project 2	Project 3
5 to 8.2	L−4.5	4.5	0
8.2 to 12.6	L−4.5	0	4.5
12.6 to 18	10.3	0	L−10.3

L = investment limit

decision variables might be in the form of normal distributions. One way to handle this would be to treat the variables as the means of the normal distributions and then find the best mix of investments on average. Converting an objective function to be an average value is a simple type of stochastic programming.

The third approach to uncertainty is *chance-constrained programming*, which deals with the situation where some constraints cannot or do not have to be met all the time but only a certain percentage of the time. For example, in a problem to find the optimal size of a water reservoir, constraints will deal with the levels of rainfall. One might express the fact that the minimum rainfall in the area is likely to be 40 inches per annum. However, in some exceptional years the rainfall might be even lower. If there were a 1 in 20 chance that it would be lower the constraint would be written in the form:

$$\text{rainfall} \geq 40 \text{ (with 95 per cent probability)}$$

Chance-constrained programming can deal with constraints in this form to provide an answer which has a high probability of being the best.

CONCLUSION

Extending LP to problems such as integer and non-linear programming greatly increases the range of applications. Further extensions are made possible by the use of 'tricks' – methods to get round, rather than overcome, some of the restrictions on LP. For example, LP requires that decision variables be greater than or equal to zero: negative numbers are not allowed. We can get round this restriction by writing a variable x in two parts:

$$x = x1 - x2$$

x can take on negative values although its two constituent parts, $x1$ and $x2$, are always greater than or equal to zero. Whenever x should appear in the LP formulation it is substituted by $x1 - x2$ and LP proceeds as normal, but of course the output has to be interpreted carefully.

Other variants on LP allow the decision maker to tackle slightly different types of problem. For example, *goal programming* is concerned with setting decision variables at levels which bring the decision maker as close as possible to a set of objectives. Goal programming is therefore a type of minimisation problem, minimising the distance between what is feasible and what is being aimed at. It is an example of the general class of *multicriteria* methods which handle the problem of there being more than one objective.

Other types of programming method have been mentioned to illustrate the ways in which LP can be extended and applied to a wider range of circumstances. Research and development work is continuing and the area is now very large and highly specialised. Beyond LP, however, only small problems of this type (in terms of numbers of decision variables and constraints) are solved in practice. The reason is that these other methods require much more computer power than LP. Even with present-day large computers, the cost of obtaining solutions to large problems can be prohibitive. The decision maker has to be very sure that the expenditure is going to be worthwhile.

Perhaps a more fundamental problem with the more sophisticated types of programs is that they are harder for lay people, especially senior managers, to understand. This may not be a problem with technical applications, but for general management applications it may be difficult for the output to be properly used as a decision aid if users feel intimidated by its complexity. In deciding what is going to be the more effective, a tradeoff between an approximate but comprehensible answer and a complex but more accurate solution is required. According to military generals, a modest plan well implemented is nearly always better than a brilliant plan badly implemented.

CASE STUDIES

CASE STUDY 1

A small engineering company produces two 'flatpack' workbenches, LD and LS, which are sold in the 'do-it-yourself' market. LD needs 6 minutes of cutting time and 3 minutes of assembly time. LS needs 2 minutes of cutting and 5 minutes of assembly. The time to set up the cutting and assembly machines is negligible. Other products mean that the company has 120 minutes of cutting time available per day and 120 minutes of assembly time. The price the company gets for the LD workbench is £14 and for the LS, £22. Variable costs are £10 per unit for both products. The company can sell as many of each product as it can produce. It has formulated this problem as an LP maximising profit.

The decision variables are:

$$x = \text{the quantity of LD to produce}$$
$$y = \text{the quantity of LS to produce}$$

The objective function is:

$$\text{maximise } 4x + 12y$$

The constraints are:

$$6x + 2y \leqslant 120 \text{ (cutting)}$$
$$3x + 5y \leqslant 120 \text{ (assembly)}$$
$$x \geqslant 0, y \geqslant 0$$

The computer print-out of the solution is shown in Table 8.11

1. If an extra hour of assembly time were available, what would the new optimal value of the objective function be?

Table 8.11

Optimal objective function is 288

Optimal decision variables: $x = 0, y = 24$

Constraint	Slack	Dual	RHS range
Cutting		72	
Assembly	0	2.4	0 to 300

Coefficient ranges

LD	0 to 7.2
LS	6.7 upwards

2. What is the dual value of cutting time?

3. A subcontractor offers the use of its assembly shops, making a total of 200 additional hours available. By how much could the profit be increased?

4. A recalculation of the profitability of LD and LS by the finance department shows that the true profit per unit of LS is 10 instead of 12. The objective function should therefore really be $4x + 10y$. What is the new optimal value of the objective function?

Solutions

1. *If an extra hour of assembly time were available, what would the new optimal value of the objective function be?*
The dual value for assembly time is 2.4. This means that if an additional assembly hour were available, the objective function would increase by 2.4, i.e. to become 290.4.

2. *What is the dual value of cutting time?*
Since 72 hours (the slack value) of cutting time are already unused, the value of an additional hour (and this is the dual value) must be 0.

3. *A subcontractor offers the use of its assembly shops, making a total of 200 additional hours available. By how much could the profit be increased?*
The right-hand side range for the assembly constraint shows that the dual value (2.4 for each extra hour) applies as the available hours are increased from 120 up to 300. Only the first 180 of the 200 subcontractor hours therefore carry the dual value of 2.4. The total extra profit is $180 \times 2.4 = 432$.

4. *A re-calculation of the profitability of LD and LS by the finance department shows that the true profit per unit of LS is 10 instead of 12. The objective function should therefore really be $4x + 10y$. What is the new optimal value of the objective function?*
The ranges for the objective function coefficients show that the coefficient for LS can be decreased to 6.7 without altering the optimal values of the decision variables. If the new value of this coefficient is 10, the solution to the LP is still $x = 0$ and $y = 24$. The new optimal value of the objective function must then be $(4 \times 0) + (10 \times 24) = 240$.

CASE STUDY 2

A farmer has to decide how much fertiliser to apply to his root vegetable fields. A soil analyst has advised him that each acre will require the following minimum amounts: 60 lb nitrogen compounds, 30 lb phosphorus compounds and 36 lb potassium compounds. There are two major types of fertiliser available. The first is JDJ which comes in 40 lb bags at £10 per bag and which comprises 20 per cent nitrogen compounds, 5 per cent phosphorus and 20 per cent potassium. The second, PRP, comes in 50 lb bags at £7 each and comprises a 10 per cent–10 per cent–6 per cent mixture.

1. Formulate the problem as an LP which minimises cost.

2. How many bags of each product should the farmer use per acre? Use a graphical solution.

3. Being a cautious farmer he wishes to have a second opinion from another soil analyst.

The second analyst suggests that 6 lb less phosphorus compounds are required per acre, so how much will the farmer save per acre? What is the shadow price of phosphorus?

4. What is the maximum saving that could be made by reducing the amount of phosphorus used?

Solutions

1. *Formulate the problem as an LP which minimises cost.*
This is a minimization problem.

Decision variables

$$x = \text{number of bags of JDJ}$$
$$y = \text{number of bags of PRP}$$

Objective function

The objective is to minimise total costs:

$$\text{Min } 10x + 7y$$

Constraints

There are constraints for the requirements of each of nitrogen, phosphorus and potassium. If x bags of JDJ are used, then $40x$ lb of JDJ are used (40 lb per bag). Since JDJ contains 20 per cent nitrogen compounds, the quantity of nitrogen applied will be 20 per cent of $40x$, i.e. $8x$ lb. Similarly, the nitrogen in y bags of PRP is 10 per cent of $50y$, i.e. $5y$ lb. The total amount of nitrogen applied will therefore be:

$$8x + 5y$$

This must be greater than the amount required, which is 60 lb. The constraint must be:

$$8x + 5y \geqslant 60$$

The other two constraints can be worked out in the same way:

$$2x + 5y \geqslant 30 \text{ (phosphorus)}$$
$$8x + 3y \geqslant 36 \text{ (potassium)}$$

Non-negativity constraints are also required.
The complete formulation is:

$$\text{Min } 10x + 7y$$
$$\text{subject to}$$
$$8x + 5y \geqslant 60 \text{ (nitrogen)}$$
$$2x + 5y \geqslant 30 \text{ (phosphorus)}$$
$$8x + 3y \geqslant 36 \text{ (potassium)}$$
$$x, y \geqslant 0$$

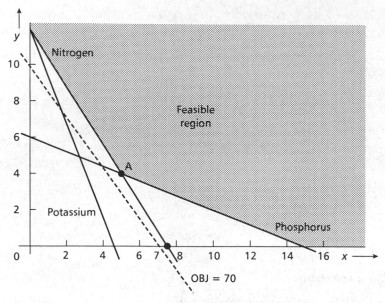

Figure 8.5

2. *How many bags of each product should the farmer use per acre?*
The graphical solution is shown in Figure 8.5. Note that when a constraint is 'greater than', the feasible area defined by it is on the opposite side of the line than for a 'less than' constraint. Similarly, the objective line is moved downwards in the minimising process. A carefully drawn graph shows that the optimal point is A, at the intersection of the constraints for nitrogen and phosphorus. Its coordinates can be calculated by the method of simultaneous equations:

$$x = 5, y = 4$$

The answer to the problem is to use 5 bags of JDJ and 4 bags of PRP per acre at a cost of £78/acre.

3. *Being a cautious farmer he wishes to have a second opinion from another soil analyst. The second analyst suggests that 6 lb less phosphorus compounds are required per acre, so how much will the farmer save per acre? What is the shadow price of phosphorus?*
If 6 lb less of phosphorus is required the constraint becomes:

$$2x + 5y \geqslant 24$$

The graphical solution is in Figure 8.6. The optimal point is B, still at the intersection of the nitrogen and phosphorus constraints. From Figure 8.6 or from simultaneous equations, point B is:

$$x = 6, y = 2.4$$

The new objective function value is $(6 \times 10) + (2.4 \times 7) = £76.8$. The farmer will therefore save £1.2/acre if the second analyst's advice is thought to be correct.

The dual value for phosphorus is the change in the objective function if the requirement for phosphorus is changed by 1. In fact it has been changed by 6 (from 30 to 24), for which the objective function changed by £1.2. The dual value of phosphorus must therefore be:

$$£1.2/6 = £0.20$$

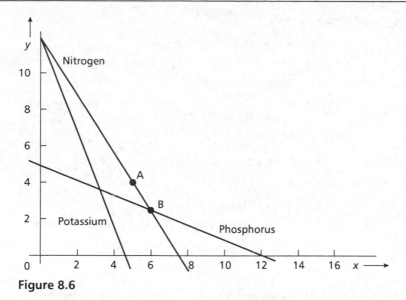

Figure 8.6

4. *What is the maximum saving that could be made by reducing the amount of phosphorus used?*

As the phosphorus requirement decreased the optimal point moved from A down towards B. Figure 8.6 shows that it could be moved until point B is on the *x* axis, at *x* = 7.5. Any further decrease would not affect the feasible region, so this is the maximum decrease that is cost effective. At *x* = 7.5 (and *y* = 0) the usage of phosphorus, from the constraint, is 15 lbs. The maximum saving is found by putting *x* = 7.5 into the objective function which becomes:

$$10 \times 7.5 = 75$$

The maximum saving is therefore £3 per acre (the original objective value, 78, − 75).

CASE STUDY 3

Leisure Products produces garden equipment. The main products of its garden furniture division are a lawn chair, a bench and a garden table. Currently the contribution received from the manufacture and sale of one unit of each is £30 for a chair, £30 for a bench and £50 for a table.

There are two stages in production: tube bending and welding. Table 8.12 gives the total capacity for each stage and also the times (in hours) required by each item for each stage.

The company is confident that it can sell any number of all three products. However, for the coming season, production is limited by a shortage of the main raw material, tubing,

Tablet 8.12

		Product		
	Chair	Bench	Table	Capacity
Operation		(hours)		
Tube bending	1.2	1.7	1.2	1000
Welding	0.8	0	2.3	1200

Table 8.13

Objective function	27666.7		
Decision variables	1	Chair	700.000
	3	Table	133.333
Slack in constraints	2	Welding	333.333
Shadow prices for constraints			
	1	Bending	11.667
	3	Supply	8.000
Reduced costs for decision variables			
	2	Bench	−13.8333

Ranges on coefficients in objective function:

Variable	Lower bound	Current value	Upper bound
1. Chair	22.2	30.0	50.0
2. Bench	Unbounded	30.0	43.8
3. Table	30.0	50.0	67.5

Ranges on constraint limits:

Constraint	Lower bound	Current value	Upper bound
1. Bending	533.33	1000.00	1200.00
2. Welding	866.67	1200.00	Unbounded
3. Supply	1666.67	2000.00	2555.55

All items not listed in Table 8.13 have zero value.

because of a long strike. Currently, 2000 lb of tubing are available, the requirements being 2 lb per chair, 3 lb per bench and 4.5 lb per garden table.

In an attempt to decide the best production mix, the production manager has produced the following linear programming formulation:

Let x_1, x_2 and x_3 be the numbers of chairs, benches and tables produced

maximise contribution $3x_1 + 3x_2 + 5x_3$

subject to

constraints   1. $1.2x_1 + 1.7x_2 + 1.2x_3 \leqslant 1000$ (bending)

2. $0.8x_1 + 2.3x_3 \leqslant 1200$ (welding)

3. $2.0x_1 + 3.0x_2 + 4.5x_3 \leqslant 2000$ (supply)

The computer output for the solution of this LP is shown in Table 8.13.

1. What is the best production mix and what contribution will it bring?

2. Leisure Products has been offered an additional supply of tubing at an additional cost of £6 a lb. Should the company buy it? If so, by how much would the contribution increase if 500 lb were bought?

3. The marketing manager suggests that at least 100 benches should be made to balance the production line. How would this affect contribution?

4. Leisure Products can sell some of its capacity in tube bending at a fee of £15 per hour. How would contribution be affected if it sold 200 hours at this price?

5. Because of a promotional campaign, contribution on chairs will drop to £25. What will be the optimal production mix and what contribution will result?

Solutions

1. *What is the best production mix and what contribution will it bring?*
The optimal production mix is 700 chairs, 133 tables and no benches. This will give a contribution of £27 667.

2. *Leisure Products has been offered an additional supply of tubing at an additional cost of £6 a lb. Should the company buy it? If so, by how much would the contribution increase if 500 lb were bought?*
The shadow price for tubing is £8, compared with the additional purchase price of more tubing of £6. Therefore some should be bought. The constraint ranges show that an additional 556.7 lb can be bought before the dual value changes. Leisure Products should buy all 500 lb offered and the extra contribution will be:

$$= 500 \times (8 - 6) = £1000$$

3. *The marketing manager suggests that at least 100 benches should be made to balance the production line. How would this affect contribution?*
The optimal mix suggests that no benches should be made, but the marketing manager is insisting on at least 100. The reduced cost for benches is £13.83, consequently making 100 will reduce the contribution by £1383.

4. *Leisure Products can sell some of its capacity in tube bending at a fee of £15 per hour. How would contribution be affected if it sold 200 hours at this price?*
The shadow price for tube bending is £11.67 per hour. Since this resource can be sold for £15 per hour, Leisure Products can sell it profitably. The constraint ranges table shows that the available time can be reduced from the present 1000 hours to 533 hours without affecting the dual values. Therefore Leisure Products can sell 200 hours and increase contribution by:

$$= 200 \times (15 - 11.67) = £667$$

5. *Because of a promotional campaign, contribution on chairs will drop to £25. What will be the optimal production mix and what contribution will result?*
Coefficient ranges show that the contribution on chairs can be reduced to £22.2 before the optimal production mix will change. If the contribution is reduced to £25, the optimal production mix will not change but the overall contribution will decrease by:

$$= 700 \times (30 - 25) = £3500$$

QUESTIONS

1. Which of the following statements are true?
   (a) Every decision variable in an LP has a dual value associated with it.
   (b) The dual value of a resource is always greater than the market price of the resource.
   (c) A transportation problem is a type of LP problem with special characteristics which make it easier to solve.

(d) In integer programming the objective function can only take whole number values.

(e) In integer programming the right-hand sides of the constraints can only be whole numbers.

(f) In integer programming at least one of the decision variables can take only whole number values.

(g) Programming techniques other than LP tend not to be greatly used because they are time consuming and expensive.

2. An LP which maximises profit is used to help plan the facilities at a fast-food restaurant. The output from the computer package includes the line below which refers to the constraint for a barbecue grill on which 120 hours per week were available.

Constraint	Slack	Dual	RHS Range
Grill	0	20	75 to 190

If an additional grill were purchased, making 120 more hours available, what would be the additional profit?

3. A furniture company has two major products: chairs and tables. They are purchased in kit form from suppliers and subcontractors and then assembled and finished in the company's workshop. To produce a chair requires 4 hours of assembly time and 2 hours of finishing time. The corresponding times for a table are 3 hours and 5 hours. There are 100 hours of assembly time available per week and 120 hours of finishing time. The contribution (revenue minus variable costs) for a chair is £50 and for a table £70.

(a) What weekly production levels will maximise total contribution?

(b) If overtime is used, extra assembly time can be made available. This costs £4 per hour over and above the normal labour cost which is already included in the contribution data. Should overtime be used? If so, how much overtime?

4. This question is a continuation of question 5 in Chapter 7.

A timber company wants to make the best use of its wood resources in one of its forest regions which contains fir and spruce trees. During the next month 80 000 board-feet of spruce are available and 90 000 board-feet of fir.

The company owns mills which produce lumber and plywood. Producing 1000 board-feet of lumber requires 1000 board-feet of spruce and 2000 board-feet of fir. Producing 1000 square feet of plywood requires 2000 board-feet of spruce and 1500 board-feet of fir. Firm orders mean that at least 10 000 board-feet of lumber and 12 000 square feet of plywood must be produced during the next month. The profit contributions are £100 per 1000 board-feet of lumber and £250 per 1000 square feet of plywood.

The production decision is taken on the basis of an LP model. The formulation of the problem and the resulting computer output is as follows:

Formulation:

$$\text{Max } 100L + 250P$$
subject to
$$L + 2P \leq 80 \text{ (spruce)}$$
$$2L + 1.5P \leq 90 \text{(fir)}$$
$$L \geq 10 \text{ (lumber orders)}$$
$$P \geq 12 \text{ (plywood orders)}$$

Table 8.15   Computer printout

Variable	Value
L	10.00
P	35.00

Objective value = 9750

Constraint	Slack	Dual	Current RHS	RHS Range
Spruce availability	0	125.00	80.00	34.00 to 103.33
Fir availability	17.50	0	90.00	72.50 to infinity
Lumber orders	0	−25.00	10.00	0 to 24.00
Plywood orders	23.00	0	12.00	0 to 35.00

Variable	Current objective	Coefficient Ranges
L	100.00	0 to 125.00
P	250.00	200.00 to infinity

Where L = amount of lumber produced (in '000 board-feet)

P = amount of plywood produced (in '000 square feet).

(a) How much lumber and how much plywood should be produced?
(b) How much contribution is lost if the amount of spruce that arrives at the mills is found to be only 78 000 board-feet?
(c) How much more spruce could be accepted at the mill (assuming there is sufficient processing capacity) before it is no longer profitable to accept more?
(d) What would be the optimal production mix if the contribution of plywood dropped to £230?
(e) What would be the total contribution (objective function) if the contribution of plywood dropped to £230?

ANSWERS TO QUESTIONS

1. (a) False.   (e) False.
    (b) False.   (f) True.
    (c) True.   (g) True.
    (d) False.

2. 1400.

3. (a) 10 chairs, 20 tables.
    (b) 140 hours.

4. (a) 10 000 board-feet of lumber, 35 000 square feet of plywood.
    (b) 250.00.
    (c) 23 330 board-feed.
    (d) Unchanged.
    (e) 9050.

CHAPTER NINE

DEA (data envelopment analysis) in a major bank

This chapter is a case study of the application of DEA to a major clearing bank. The author is P. D. Stone, FCA, formerly a senior manager of the bank.

INTRODUCTION

A brief summary of linear programming may ensure the reader is able to get a general grasp of the ideas behind DEA.

The linear programming technique which is most familiar to students is that used to measure the optimum allocation of scarce resources where supply and demand constraints are known or can be measured with reasonable accuracy. There are many excellent examples of such situations with supply and demand constraints formulated as equations and an objective function stated either in terms of maximising profit or minimising costs. A typical example drawn from manufacturing industry might be a paper mill where machine capacities expressed in normal production hours, labour hours available, supplies of suitable grade pulp for paper, direct contribution per unit of output and the likely pattern of demand for a range of different products can be readily quantified, i.e. parameters can be measured.

However, the adaptation of this familiar technique to the problem of measuring the efficient use of resources in service units is generally excluded from many standard texts.

Measuring the efficient use of resources in service units has always presented a problem because it is difficult to quantify capacity – for example, in a branch of a retail bank each day's business must be completed on that day, making the assessment of 'normal capacity' in terms of labour hours employed difficult. Again, the mix of skills required will vary from branch to branch as will the pattern of demand for services, most notably the processing of customer demand for information and advice on financial services generally. Secondly quality, fairly easy to measure in manufactured goods, is more difficult to define and quantify in service industries.

Quality of personal service is important to customers in retail businesses of any sort. It is therefore perhaps unsurprising that, for example, rapid advances in the use of technology to reduce employee costs over the past decade have coincided with a massive increase in the number of complaints of poor service against banks and quasi-banks such as building societies. Any methodology applied by top management to the measurement of performance and setting objectives for a branch network should not rely solely on financial results.

The same can be said of many service industries and public services. The essence of the problem may be summed up in the questions:

- How do we measure capacity?
- How do we measure achievement in terms of cost effectiveness and quantity/quality of service provided?
- How do we measure the influence of factors beyond the control of unit managers?

DEA v financial analysis

Let us extend our banking example in order to highlight the limitations of a financial analysis approach to measuring profitability.

This technique, with its implications for assessing immediate past and targeting future performance, raises important questions at branch level. For instance, how can such a blanket requirement motivate the manager whose branch is situated in an area where the real wealth of the customer catchment area may be declining? Again, what of the manager who is responsible for a prime site branch in a very large city and is mostly concerned with supplying immediate service to commuter customers with accounts held at branches in towns many miles away? Most important of all, accounting techniques cannot reflect the quality element as perceived by the customer. These questions and others of a similar kind are dealt with in greater detail in the case study presented in this chapter.

While it is clear that financial analysis cannot be used to answer precisely the questions posed above, it must be acknowledged that financial managers at head office have to respond to the best of their ability to requests from board level for management information to help with strategic decision making. Furthermore, they have the option to use ratios to make accounting data more informative to non-accountants and, where transaction accounts and account numbers are available, the scope of ratio analysis may be broadened by their use.

Disadvantages can however arise when management starts to focus either on one ratio or a few key ratios, with resultant discord and confusion about their relative importance. At any event, exclusion of uncontrollable factors such as branch catchment area demographic profiles will always put a limit on the reliability of ratio analysis as the principal source of decision support information.

DEA addresses these difficulties by using ratios to determine mathematically relative performance achieved as opposed to absolute performance against a notional standard. Furthermore, it can effectively utilise objective, externally generated information to improve the quality of its measures.

In practice this means that more factors are being used to measure actual performance against a known attainable rather than a theoretical standard. For this reason the DEA measures, or ratings, generate less controversy and therefore can be used with greater confidence.

Its disadvantages, namely that it is a mathematical technique unfamiliar to many in business and public service management and that its results need careful and expert interpretation, may be addressed by creating sound project management structures and by the skilful presentation of results. These matters are dealt with in detail in the Case Study section below.

THE DEA TECHNIQUE

The development of DEA originated from a 1957 paper prepared for the Journal of The Royal Statistical Society by Farrell which outlined the general case. DEA is a complex variant of LP but can be explained briefly in the following terms, using bank branches as an illustrative example.

In summary, DEA measures the efficiency of each branch, based on the standard definition of efficiency as the ratio of output to input. A bank branch has several outputs, for example transactions processed and aggregate balances; it has several inputs, for example staff numbers and direct costs. The branch's efficiency is measured as a ratio of a weighted sum of the outputs to a weighted sum of the inputs. So, the efficiency of branch k is:

$$E_k = \frac{\lambda_1 O_{1k} + \lambda_2 O_{2k} + \lambda_3 O_{3k} + \lambda_4 O_{4k} + \ldots}{\gamma_1 I_{1k} + \gamma_2 I_{2k} + \gamma_3 I_{3k} + \gamma_4 I_{4k} + \ldots}$$

where $O_{1k}, O_{2k} \ldots$ are the outputs of branch k

$\lambda_1, \lambda_2 \ldots$ are weights given to the outputs – these are the decision variables of the LP
$I_{1k}, I_{2k} \ldots$ are the inputs of branch k
$\gamma_1, \gamma_2 \ldots$ are weights given to the inputs of branch k – also decision variables

The LP is run separately for each branch. For branch k:

Decision variables: $\lambda_1, \lambda_2 \ldots \gamma_1, \gamma_2 \ldots$

Objective function: maximise E_k

Constraints: $E_1 \leqslant 1$

$E_2 \leqslant 1$

:

$E_k \leqslant 1$

:

and so on for all branches

The constraints ensure that the efficiency ratios for all branches, including k, cannot be more than 1, i.e. 100 per cent. The way that LP works is to try to find weights for the outputs and inputs so that the efficiency of the selected branch, k, is maximised, i.e. 100 per cent. In other words the LP determines whether, looking at branch k in its most favourable light by choosing the most favourable values for the weights, there is some sense in which branch k can be seen as 100 per cent efficient. This is by no means always possible. For example, if branch 1 had exactly the same inputs as branch k and exactly the same outputs, apart from one output which was better for branch 1, then it would be impossible for branch k to be 100 per cent efficient.

The detail of the information which a DEA LP produces is complex and not described here, but two broad situations can arise.

1. The optimal value of the objective function is less than 1 – branch k is not 100 per cent efficient. In this case the LP output is able to show in what regard it is inefficient. For example, it might highlight another branch with similar inputs but greater outputs. Or it might highlight a branch with similar outputs but lesser inputs.

2. The optimal value of the objective function is 1 – branch k is, at least under this definition (called Pareto efficiency), efficient. In this case the tight constraints (those equal to 1 – the so-called reference set) show which other branches are also efficient and which are not. For those which are not the output can show in what areas they are inadequate.

DEA extends well beyond the simple description above. For example, the measurement of input can also be assessed by dividing input by output. The results in this case are derived from an alternative formulation which produces efficiency ratings greater than 1, but where a higher rating is an indicator of lower performance. Efficient units still have a score of 1 as above.

CASE STUDY

Background

The XYZ Retail Bank operates throughout the country and has approximately 1200 branches ranging from small units employing as few as 5 people to very large units with more than 60 people employed at prestige locations in large cities.

The XYZ Retail Financial Institution (RFI) has increasingly found itself under severe competitive pressure since the mid/late 1980s. XYZ has now recovered, with some official help and by the exercise with other RFIs of monopoly power to the disadvantage of its more solvent customers, from much of the weakness induced by its outstanding relative contribution to the huge bad debts experienced by the RFI sector during the early 1990s. Official sympathy and solvent customers having been exploited to the limit, the board has now decided that the only way at least to stand still in a non-inflationary environment and in a sector suffering from chronic overcapacity is to improve its operating efficiencies. It follows that there has been much internal debate about cost-effective performance at branch level, including the impact of further investment in IT, with the 'profitability analysis' statements the main point of reference as to relative performance.

Not surprisingly, all this deliberation at board level has thoroughly alarmed branch managers who interpret, perhaps with some justification, the expression 'improvement to operating efficiencies' as meaning that their jobs could be on the line. They are firmly defending their long-held view that they cannot be made responsible for improving 'profit' in book-keeping terms when they have no control over:

- the demographics of the catchment area which the branch serves;
- the age of the branch building;
- the location of the branch relative to pedestrian traffic;
- the staff complement, which they are not authorised to vary significantly in numbers or skills mix;
- the occupancy costs of the branch which are largely fixed;
- competition from branches of other RFIs.

The managers point out that all of these factors have a direct bearing on 'profit'. They argue that they strive to the utmost to meet corporate objectives in full, subject to the limitations imposed on performance by the uncontrollable factors. Furthermore, the accountants' trick of distributing branch support and head office costs to branch level when assessing 'profit' has, on this occasion, understandably aroused a greater level of incomprehension and indignation than in prior years.

Finally, they insist to a mildly surprised board that the public really does see an RFI as a network of personal service points where quality at the point of delivery matters significantly; that there is potential advantage to be gained by showing a 'human face' to customers and that failure to do so cannot be compensated by an 'image' conjured up by the bank's PR department and advertising agency.

This line of argument persuades the sensitive board to suspend the cost-cutting axe in mid-air before the downward swing. They perceive that peremptory withdrawal of personal service by a combination of increased automation and branch closure might well be looked on unfavourably by customers, attract unwelcome attention from the media and perhaps backfire by adversely affecting future corporate earnings to the detriment of performance-related executive bonuses.

However that may be, the board is faced with real dilemma. There are too many mutually competitive RFIs forcing up unit costs in a static market and recent improvements in results are mostly attributable to reductions in bad debt provisions. Current demand for loans is far from strong. It follows that operating efficiencies must be improved. On the other hand, staff morale is not high and rumours of closures and redundancies are not helping them to maintain their customary high standards of knowledgeable professionalism in day-to-day dealings with customers. The board recognises that at least for the foreseeable future the bank needs all the support it can get from its customers and employees to maintain goodwill – the managers have made their point.

However, the 'profitability analysis' technique, which has been relied on in the past, is viewed with suspicion by managers and a general feeling prevails that it is a blunt instrument. The board therefore finds an opportunity to display a hitherto unsuspected open-mindedness with a practical knowledge of business mathematics. It makes known its decision to appoint operational research (OR) consultants to resolve the problem of measuring cost-effective performance in the branch network as a prerequisite to formulating a new strategy.

Preliminary considerations

The operational researchers appointed make a preliminary appraisal of requirements and discover that, owing to the initiative of a numerate senior manager at head office, there is hard output data available in a database containing information drawn directly from the daily branch transactions and messages processed history files of the national on-line-real-time (OLRT) customer accounts system. This gives them confidence at an early stage because experience has taught them that OR techniques as an aid to decision making have often failed to live up to promise in the past, not because of any inherent defects, but because adequate 'hard' basic data has not been available internally as input to models. Secondly, it has often been found that there was no senior manager sufficiently numerate and knowledgeable of the business to appreciate the potential advantage of OR techniques in problem solving and able to draw on experience of the business to liaise with and advise consultants as the project proceeds.

But in the case of XYZ Bank this is not so. Investigation reveals that the database holds branch data sets by main retail account type which include numbers of active and dormant accounts with related classified volumes of transactions and messages processed by the

OLRT national banking system. Furthermore the experienced numerate senior manager is still employed at the bank's head office.

The OR consultants decide to proceed by stages. They obtain authority from the board for the senior manager to set up an internal liaison group which includes representatives from corporate planning and marketing, managers with branch network experience, as well as an accountant from head office finance whose main concern, it later transpired, was to obtain assurance for the finance director that the DEA technique did not violate the principle that all credits would equal all debits.

Determining objectives

The consultants and the working group determine from XYZ management that its corporate objective is continued real profit growth from a range of banking and financial services, to be achieved by maximising the interest differential (i.e. the difference between interest earned from lending less interest paid plus service charges) while minimising costs, consistent with, as advised by their public relations department, a satisfactory service to the general public.

The objective at branch level is to maximise retail profits by first offering a competitive current account and money transmission service to a broad customer base. Other products such as notice deposit accounts, fixed-term deposits, housing loans (i.e. mortgages) and personal loans repayable by instalments would be cross-sold to offset the costs of offering an acknowledged loss leader.

Accordingly the consultants identify the following factors which may be used to develop DEA branch efficiency ratings. The variables are classified into 'outputs', which quantify branch achievement and 'inputs' which quantify the cost of that achievement.

Outputs

- Aggregate balances (£ millions) on
  (a) current account (+ and -);
  (b) deposit account;
  (c) mortgage accounts;
  (d) personal lending.
- Transactions and messages volumes processed.
- Branch net profit.

Inputs

- Employee complement.
- Branch direct costs (employee salary and related costs + branch occupancy expense).
- Age of branch.
- Number of teller positions.
- Number of auto-teller units.
- Location grade.
- Local competition from RFIs.
- Catchment area.
- Customer profile.

Location grade is obtained from an index of 'site quality' and local competition is measured by reference to the number of competing RFI branches in the catchment area. Customer profile can be constructed by sampling customer address codes.

Notice that input values are not drawn exclusively from accounting sources and in practice some cannot be found internally. In the case of XYZ Bank it was found necessary to use external sources to profile branch catchment areas adequately and to complete satisfactorily the process of profiling the customer base. Also keep firmly in mind that the outputs and inputs included in this case study example are wholly dependent on corporate and branch-level objectives. The task of defining corporate-level and subsidiary branch-level objectives is therefore a vitally important first step in any DEA exercise – different objectives will require a different selection of inputs and outputs.

Pilot project

The consultants and the working group were realistic and understood the need to produce results which would provide practical decision support information in an understandable form. They were fully aware that introducing a recently developed mathematical technique would arouse suspicion and even resistance in the retail financial business where originality and innovation are not commonplace. Notwithstanding top management support, branch network management and head office middle management, including those represented on the liaison group, would have to be convinced that the DEA exercise was worthwhile and that the technique should be taken seriously as a tool of planning and analysis in future. In these circumstances the consultants and the liaison group decided to proceed by way of a pilot study.

The first step was to examine the ratio analysis data produced by the financial analysts, which indicated that ranking varied significantly depending on which ratio was selected as a measure of performance.

The finance director's department had produced a complete analysis of profitability by branch using the full absorption cost technique. Costs directly attributable to operations, such as salary and related expense and occupancy costs, were allocated directly to the branch. Area support and head office administrative costs were allocated proportion to branch direct costs. Every branch was credited with the 'internal transfer price' value of the deposits it made available to a central pool and was conversely charged with the use of funds relating to loan business it generated. Income from bank charges was directly credited to the branch at which it was earned.

A first schedule to the financial analysis showed a percentage breakdown of all costs and income elements including net profit earned – the 'bottom line'. Ratios using both financial and non-financial data were presented in a second schedule. 'Non-financial' data included staff numbers, account numbers and transaction volumes. The report, termed the 'branch profitability analysis', is considered to be the most important source of internal information for reviewing the immediate past performance of units and their managers and for setting future targets to be included in annual budgets and in medium/long-term financial plans.

The consultants and the working group were aware that the 'bottom line' branch profit/branch income ratio was the standard reference point when branch performance was assessed at head office. So therefore by implication were the ratio branch income/branch costs. They further discovered that the 1200 XYZ branches were very diverse and their number made an initial full-scale analysis impractical. A survey of qualitative factors showed that branches might be conveniently categorised by reference to regional location, staff numbers and location, and simple inspection of available data showed that there was evidence of high correlation between account numbers, numbers employed and current account balances. After various statistical calculations it was decided to select a stratified random sample of 85 branches to represent the network.

This number was arrived at by applying a statistical formula to determine the size of the sample of branches required to measure total current account balances + or −5 per cent at the 90 per cent confidence level.

A detailed consideration of stratified random sampling is outside the scope of this chapter, but its essentials may be briefly illustrated by saying that in this instance a matrix of cell values was constructed so that, if for example, it was found that 6 per cent of the branches employed more than 20 staff and that one-third of such branches were in large city centres in the southern region, then it could be calculated that 2 such branches should be randomly selected from the total of similar branches in that region. The process was repeated for other cells until the matrix was complete and the sample selected.

Building the model

It was decided to build the model step by step. Given that the starting point for measuring efficiency was the 'bottom line' ratio, the consultants examined the information contained in the branch profitability analysis to select 'inputs' and 'outputs' for the model.

The consultants understood that the aim of the board was to find out if cost savings could be achieved throughout the network. They also understood that the ratio total branch revenue/total branch costs was also more significant than the board realised, as it was a rough indicator of efficiency when perceived as the 'revenue-generating ratio'.

A second study of the data therefore had to be made to find the order of correlation of the input factors with this revenue-generating ratio. This was by no means a mechanical process and once the correlation coefficients had been established between the ratio (i.e. the approximate measure of efficiency) and the inputs, it was necessary to examine them in order to determine whether or not a causal relationship could logically be established.

It was found in the case of XYZ Bank that the extensive use by customers of branch facilities as reflected in the transaction and message volume counts correlated strongly and negatively with a low revenue-generator value, owing to the need to deploy more staff at high occupancy cost to cope with demand for personal services. Similarly, correlation with total balance values was positive and strong. Other inputs were on a scale of declining correlation. Transaction volumes and account balances were therefore selected for the first run.

Strictly it is not necessary to use a computer to determine relative efficiency where only two input factors are being used. Readings from an XY plot of the ratio values for account balances/branch costs and transaction and message volumes/branch costs will give the required result. However, this was a first run and it was necessary to gain everyone's confidence in the technique by demonstrating its utility in a simple case.

The next task was again to review the correlations, this time with the transaction and message volume count/branch costs ratio, select an additional input factor which logic would suggest has a determining effect on profitability, and run a revised model. This iterative process continues until all significant causal influences on profit have been included in the model. It is clear that at this stage the use of a computer to determine relative efficiency is essential because the number of variables involved precludes a graphical solution. The model was extended to incorporate other outputs, including a measure of service quality derived from an earlier unconnected survey of customer attitudes by the head office marketing department.

Output and interpretation

The eventual outcome took the form of a schedule of branch efficiency ranking in the range 0.75 to 1.00. It was noticeable that some branches appeared more frequently as elements in reference sets than others – these former were the more efficient branches. A ranking of these 'efficient branches' was then compiled for further study of their cost structure. Secondly, the reference sets of the more inefficient branches contained similar types of branch, confirming that the claim of proponents of DEA to produce measures of relative efficiency is evidenced by practical results – this was important to newcomers to the technique who needed some convincing. Some difficulty arose in determining 'marginal efficiency'. As a broad general view it seemed right to assume that those branches which appeared in just a few reference sets might be considered marginally efficient. On the other hand, some of these branches may have an efficiency rating of between 85 and 90 per cent and could therefore by considered as being good candidates for improvement projects.

While there was some mutual self-congratulation among those responsible for the pilot project, the problem of communicating the findings to the board had to be resolved. After some discussion it was felt that the task would best be achieved by relating the ratings results to a measure with which all board members and the finance function were familiar, namely branch net profit.

The report to management therefore included an explanation of the findings, a simple XY chart plotting ratings against total branch earnings/net profit. This chart demonstrated the need for DEA because it made it easy for management to compare DEA efficiency ratings with a recognised standard measure of performance. The graphs made it plain that the two did not necessarily go together. Some branches, for example, showed a high level of efficiency while earning a low margin. In the case of others the reverse was true.

CONCLUSION

The DEA pilot project was a worthwhile exercise. The project did open up the prospect of eliminating some of the internal friction generated from overreliance by head office staff functions on reports containing information generated from application of the absorption cost accounting technique. The branch managers, who were represented on the liaison group, were satisfied that a technique was available which would more objectively measure the results of their efforts. While obliged to concede that there were indeed inefficient branches in the network and that a comprehensive review might bring about closure in some cases, they were now reasonably satisfied that less reliance was being placed on the 'blunt instrument' of absorption accounting.

The project findings also convinced management at board level that a practical method of realistically appraising efficiency was available, and that intelligent use of the rating data produced with a key traditional measure enhanced their in-depth knowledge network performance. It also resulted in a greater chance of realistic performance standards being set when DEA ratings were used as a point of reference, and meant that difficult planning decisions could in future be made in a clearer light.

To summarise, the network could be managed with more confidence and probably with greater benefit to XYZ Bank as a result of the insights obtained from the use of DEA. For these reasons management decided to include the DEA technique in the portfolio of MIS, generating decision support information on a regular basis.

So far as the consultants were concerned the success of the pilot project was accounted for by an early decision to take a step-by-step approach. Careful analysis, with the liaison group, of internal and external factors relating to performance ensured that a realistic balanced model was eventually formulated, and the knowledge and experience built up by the members of the liaison group who represented the branch managers were invaluable in convincing colleagues that the resultant branch efficiency ratings fairly reflected performance in the real world. Use of sampling techniques to restrict the number of branches involved ensured that the project was not too ambitious in scale, and correspondingly more easily and less conspicuously aborted if unforeseen circumstances rendered its continuance impracticable. Fortunately such circumstances did not arise.

Vitally important to the whole project were the availability of consistent basic performance data retrieved from the OLRT business history files and the sophisticated use of reliable externally generated data. In other words, showing respect for the time-honoured and inviolable Murphy's Law made all the difference between success and failure.

QUESTIONS

1. Why was DEA an appropriate technique for addressing the issue of branch efficiency in the XYZ Bank case? In particular, why was it thought to be superior to alternative approaches?

2. Describe some other situations in which you think DEA could be usefully applied.

3. What general lessons does the case provide about the obstacles which might hinder the successful application of analytical techniques such as DEA? What are the critical success factors in applying such techniques?

PART FOUR

Business Forecasting

Chapter 10 The management of business forecasting

Reviews different approaches to business forecasting and discusses the factors involved in successful forecasting, giving examples of success and failure. Describes surveys comparing different forecasting methods.

Chapter 11 Time series forecasting

Describes basic time series methods such as moving averages, exponential smoothing and decomposition, and gives examples of situations in which they have been shown to succeed.

Chapter 12 Marketing information systems (MKIS): A necessary strategic weapon?

Author: C D Beaumont.
Good forecasting needs good data. Marketing Information Systems are becoming essential for many organisations. This chapter makes particular reference to MKIS in the advertising industry.

Chapter 13 Forecasting methodologies in practice

Author: C D Beaumont.
This chapter describes a range of forecasting methods which have been applied in the advertising industry. Discusses implementation problems and critical success factors.

Chapter 14 Causal modelling

Describes the basic methods of simple linear regression and correlation and their application to forecasting in a range of industries.

Chapter 15 More regression analysis

Continues the ideas of simple linear regression into multiple and non-linear regression.

Chapter 16   Judgemental forecasting

Classifies and reviews qualitative, judgemental methods, including Delphi, scenarios and cross-impact analysis, giving examples of their application.

Chapter 17   Experience of using the Delphi forecasting process

Author: J Raine.
A case study of judgement forecasting in the pharmaceutical industry. Discusses implementation problems and critical success factors.

CHAPTER 10

The management of business forecasting

Business forecasting can be thought of in terms of techniques and data. This view ignores the fact that success or failure in forecasting seems more often to be determined by softer issues concerned with the way forecasting is managed and integrated into the decision-making processes of an organisation. This chapter puts forecasting in a business context, stressing a broad view of forecasting as a management system. The chapter provides a nine-stage set of guidelines for developing forecasts systematically.

INTRODUCTION

The business world of the 1960s and earlier was more stable than it is as present. This view is not merely the product of nostalgic reminiscence: business and economic data of the period reveal relatively smooth series and variations through time. As a result, business forecasting was not the issue it is now. In fact, many managers claim to have done their forecasting on the back of the proverbial envelope. The situation is different today. Uncertainty is evident everywhere in the business world. Forecasting has become more and more difficult. Data, whether from companies, industries or nations, seems to be increasingly volatile. The rewards of good forecasting are very high; the penalties for bad forecasting or for doing no forecasting at all are greater than ever. Even the most non-numerate managers tend to agree that the back of a second envelope is necessary.

As a consequence, interest and investment in forecasting methods have been growing. Organisations are spending more time and money on their planning. Much of this increased effort has gone into techniques. Established techniques are being used more widely; new techniques have been developed. The specialist forecaster's role has grown. Unfortunately, the outcome of this effort has not always been successful. Indeed, some of the most costly mistakes in business have been made because of poor forecasting methods. Analysing these mistakes reveals that in the main they come about not through technical errors, but because of the way that the forecasting was organised and managed.

While attention has rightly been given to the 'kitbag of techniques' of the practitioner (statistician, operational researcher etc.), the roles of non-specialists involved in the process (general managers, accountants, financial analysts, market experts and those who are to use the forecasts to take decisions) have been neglected. These roles are usually concerned with managing the forecasts. However, because they have less technical expertise, non-specialists have tended to hold back and not participate in planning and operating the forecasting system. Their invaluable (though non-statistical) expertise is thereby lost to the organisation. Accordingly, the effectiveness of many organisations' forecasting work has been seriously weakened. The role of the non-specialist is at least as important as that of the practitioner.

The purpose of this chapter is to describe the role of managers and non-specialists in the forecasting process and to show what they can do to improve the forecasting performance of the organisation. This chapter will also provide a context for the more detailed topics later in the book.

THE MANAGER'S ROLE IN FORECASTING

Who should be in charge?

In small organisations forecasting may be done by one person. The individual who needs the forecasts has to produce them. He or she has to cover all aspects of the work. In larger organisations the question arises as to which department should take responsibility. There are three general possibilities:

● user department;
● management services;
● data processing unit.

The third possibility, data processing, is perhaps the most popular, but probably the worst candidate. The user department may well abrogate its responsibility to the 'experts' and as a result never become involved. While the members of the data processing unit will have plenty of technical expertise, they will know little of the wider issues and will be unable to integrate the forecasting system with the decision taking it is intended to serve. The most likely outcome is an isolated and little-used forecasting system.

The second possibility, management services, suffers from some of the problems of the data processing unit in being remote from the decision taking. Yet when the forecasts are for strategic decisions at board level this solution can be successful. Management services, perhaps in the form of a corporate planning unit, is then able to devote itself entirely to the major decisions to be taken. It can make the link between the technicalities of forecasting and the decisions.

The first possibility, the user department, should be the best solution for non-board-level decisions. However, it frequently does not work. The users feel that they have insufficient technical expertise and therefore hand over responsibility to technical experts in another department. As a result they have little involvement in the system which may once again lead to it being underutilised. Bringing non-specialists into the process and maintaining their participation is a key factor for the future of business forecasting. The non-specialists are in the best position to forge the link between techniques and decisions.

Wherever responsibility rests, accountants usually play a part. Frequently the forecasts are financial and accountants are involved as members of the user department. Even when the forecasting is centred on, say, marketing or production control, there are likely to be financial aspects to be considered and financial expertise will be required.

In larger organisations, therefore, forecasting is generally a team activity. Typically, the team members will be a forecasting practitioner, a representative of the user department and a financial expert, although the exact composition inevitably depends on individual circumstances. In small organisations forecasting may be done by one person in whom must be combined all the team's expertise. That person is likely to be someone in a general management position.

In a team, the role of the practitioner is reasonably clear. The roles of the other team members include facilitating access to the user department and providing financial data, but much more importantly, they must include responsibilities for 'managing' the forecasts. This means ensuring that resources (the forecasts) are properly applied to objectives (the intended uses of the forecasts). In carrying this out it is essential to view forecasting as a system and not just as a technique. While the specialist is considering the statistical niceties of the numbers being generated, the manager should be considering the links with the rest of the organisation: what is the decision-taking system which the forecasts are to serve? Is the accuracy sufficient for the decisions being taken? Are the forecasts being monitored and the methods being adjusted? In short, the specialist takes a narrow view of the technique, but the manager takes a broad view of the whole forecasting system. The role of managing the system frequently falls, often by default, to a manager in the user department. It is the most vital role in the forecasting process.

What do you need to know?

The recommended broad view can be broken down into three distinct areas. They show the non-specialist knowledge with which a manager needs to be equipped in order to play an effective part in the system.

- *Being aware of the range of techniques available.* A specialist may have a 'pet' technique. The manager should have a good general knowledge of the full spectrum of techniques so that he or she can make at least an initial judgement on whether they apply to the particular situation. Such knowledge will also increase the manager's confidence and credibility when taking part in discussions with specialists.
- *Incorporating forecasts into management systems* This is the essence of the manager's role. A checklist of things which should be done to integrate a forecasting process with the rest of the organisation will be described later in the chapter.
- *Being aware of past forecasting errors.* Many organisations have made forecasting errors in the past. Most have one thing in common: they are sufficiently simple that, with hindsight, it seems remarkable that mistakes could have been made. Yet errors were made and they are a source of valuable information for the present.

These areas will now be amplified. Practical examples will be used to pinpoint the nature of the manager's contribution in managing a forecasting system and to confirm the importance of this task.

FORECASTING TECHNIQUES

This review describes in outline different approaches to forecasting and provides some general awareness of the range of techniques available. The details will be given in later chapters. Forecasting techniques can be divided into three categories:

- qualitative;
- causal modelling;
- time series methods.

Qualitative methods are based on judgement rather than on records of part data. Popular opinion might suggest that qualitative methods are the best. Stories abound of managers with 'instinct' who made predictions with astounding accuracy. On the other hand, the few surveys which have been done show that qualitative methods are, in general, inferior to quantitative ones. The reason for this anomaly may be psychological. There is a tendency to remember the successes of people and to forget their failures. The man who predicted political revolution in Iran in 1979 is remembered, while the man who said that sliced bread would never catch on is forgotten. The opposite seems to be the case with systems: successes are forgotten, failures remembered.

Even so, some qualitative methods have a successful record. These are the ones which convert judgements into forecasts in a thoughtful and systematic manner. They are different from the instant guesses which are often thought of as qualitative forecasts. More importantly, there are many situations where the qualitative approach is the only one possible. For new products, industries or technologies (developing and retailing micro-computer software, for instance) no past records are available to predict future business; in some countries political uncertainties may mean that past records are not valid. In these situations qualitative techniques provide systematic ways of making forecasts. Qualitative techniques are the subject of Chapter 16.

Causal modelling means that the variable to be forecast is related statistically to one or more other variables which are thought to 'cause' changes in it. The relationship is assumed to hold in the future and is used to make the forecasts. For example, the well-known econometric forecasts of national economies are based on causal modelling, relating one economic variable to another. Policies such as restricting the money supply, and economic assumptions such as the future price of oil, are fed into the model to give forecasts of inflation, unemployment, etc. A further example might be a company trying to predict its turnover on the basis of advertising expenditure, products, prices and economic growth. The value of causal modelling is that it introduces, statistically, external factors into the forecasting. This type of forecast is therefore usually good at discerning turning points in a data series. Causal modelling is the subject of Chapter 14.

Time series methods predict future values of a variable solely from historical values. They involve determining patterns in the historical record and then projecting the patterns into the future. While these methods are not good when the underlying conditions of the past are no longer valid, there are many circumstances when time series methods are the best. They are used when:

1. Conditions are stable and will continue to be so in the future.

2. Short-term forecasts are required and there is not enough time for conditions to change more than a little.

3. A base forecast is needed onto which can be built changes in future conditions.

Time series methods are also usually the cheapest and easiest to apply and therefore can be used when there are many forecasts to be made, none of which warrants a large expenditure. This might be the case in forecasting stock levels at a warehouse dealing in large numbers of small-value items. Time series methods are the subject of Chapter 11.

DEVELOPING A SYSTEM

The key word is *system*. Forecasting should not be viewed as a number-generating technique but as a system. The technique is just one part of the forecasting process which includes many other factors to do with the generation and use of forecasts within an organisation. The process should specify how judgement is to be incorporated, how the effectiveness of the forecast is to be measured, how the system should be adjusted in response to feedback and many other aspects. In addition, a broad view leads to consideration of the links between the forecasting system and other management systems in the organisation. Lack of thought about the nature of these links is often the reason why forecasts may be accurate yet ineffective.

Gwilym Jenkins, joint originator of one of the most sophisticated modern forecasting techniques, the Box Jenkins method, has suggested some guidelines for the development of a forecasting system.

1. *Analyse the decision-making systems* to be served by the forecasts. This involves listing and describing all decisions and actions influenced by the forecasts, the people involved and the links between them. For instance, forecasts of car sales may be required by a manager of an assembly line at a car plant. Primarily, the forecasts will help decide the speed and mix of the line (the total volume produced and the split between different variants of the model). But other decisions will be influenced by the forecasts: the ordering of steel, the production of sub-assemblies, the buying of components and the setting of stock levels, for example. Forecasts for the assembly line should not be made without a thorough analysis of their impact on other areas. The analysis may reveal fundamental flaws in decision systems or organisational structure which must be sorted out before any forecasts stand a chance of being effective. This is a lengthy but essential process.

2. *Define what forecasts are needed.* This comprises determining forecast variables, frequencies, time horizons and accuracy levels. In the car assembly examples it might imply forecasting total demand and variant mix weekly for eight weeks ahead. No more than a medium level of accuracy would probably be required because stocks provide a balancing factor. Defining the forecasts like this prevents the generation of needless forecasts (over-accurate, too frequent, covering too great a time horizon). This can only be done after the decision process has been analysed because, for instance, the ordering of steel may require a greater time horizon than is strictly necessary for the assembly line alone.

3. *Develop a conceptual model* of the forecasting method. This suggests the ideal forecasting method and includes all the factors which might be suspected of affecting the variable being forecasted. It indicates the historical patterns which might influence the future, causal variables, and whether volatile conditions might point to the use of a qualitative method. In the car assembly example the factors might include seasonal patterns, the economic environment, marketing activity levels, stock levels and price changes. The

development of the conceptual model causes thought to be given to the realities of the situation. It should prevent a blind rush into inappropriate statistical techniques.

4. *Ascertain what data is available* (and what is not available). This will indicate the ways in which the actual forecasting method might fall short of the ideal. It might be impossible to split advertising and promotional expenditures or difficult to measure stock levels accurately. Both these factors would affect the car production forecasting method by limiting the variables which could be included.

5. *Develop the actual methods for making forecasts.* This is the technique part of the system, involving the selection of a suitable technique based on forecasts, accuracy required, and the data and resources available. In many organisations it is the only part of the system given any real consideration. The chosen method for car demand might be a causal model (relating demand to an economic variable, perhaps personal disposable income, and marketing variables, perhaps relative price and promotional expenditure) but incorporating an allowance for seasonal effects. Chapters 11 to 16 deal with techniques and their relative advantages.

6. *Test the method's accuracy.* At this stage several techniques might be on the short list. They must be compared on the basis of the past data and the best chosen for use. Statistical methods for making these comparisons are described in the next section. This does not mean that there is one best method for every situation. On the contrary, research has shown that using several methods and combining their output is often more accurate than the single method approach. If at this stage the shortlist of possible methods consists of a time series method and a judgement method, and it is difficult to choose between them, the best action will be to use both and combine the output, probably by taking their average. The 'combining' approach seems to work well when it brings together the different strengths of different forecasting methods.

7. *Decide how to incorporate judgements into forecasts.* Quantitative forecasting models work on the assumption (not always explicitly recognised) that many of the conditions of the past will continue to prevail in the future. This is true for causal modelling just as for time series modelling. The influence of the economic environment on car demand, for example, may be assumed to apply as in the past. Other factors, such as political circumstances, may mean that the future is radically different from the past. It may not be possible to quantify these factors. Qualitative views about such changes should be allowed to influence the forecast. Of course, a remarkably large number of people believe strongly that they have special insights denied to other managers. It is not being suggested here that free rein should be given to the making of instinctive and arbitrary changes.

A systematic method of incorporating judgement should be developed. This may lean on one of the qualitative forecasting methods. It will certainly require people to be accountable for the changes they make. In the car example, the plant manager may take the view that industrial problems are brewing at a rival car maker and that demand may increase as a consequence of the rival's inability to supply. There should be a means of testing this view and, if it seems valid, of allowing it to influence the forecast. If a forecasting method does not allow for such changes then the decision takers may disregard the forecasts and go their own way. The whole system may lose credibility and fall into disuse.

8. *Implement the forecasting system.* This means ensuring in the initial stages that the system is being properly used, correcting problems and answering queries. It is essential that when the system is first used, the designers of the system are available for advice and to check that its operation is understood.

9. *Monitor the performance* of the forecasting system. The operation of the system should be checked continually to verify that all is happening according to the specification, in terms of both the use being made of the system and its statistical performance. Tests of the accuracy of the forecasts should be made with a view to changing the technical structure of the model as its conditions change, and improving the accuracy (rather than allocating blame or giving praise).

The checklist provides the context in which to view the techniques described in later chapters.

To reiterate, a broad view of forecasting must be given. The reason for discussing forecasting as a system and giving a nine-point checklist is that forecasting seems to fail in organisations far more often because of poor management of the forecasting process than because of technical errors. Some of the examples of errors which have occurred are the subject of the next section.

MEASURING ACCURACY

There are two common measures for comparing, quantitatively, the accuracy of forecasting methods, the *mean absolute deviation* and the *mean square error*.

Mean absolute deviation (MAD)

MAD measures forecasting error by calculating the average difference between forecast and actual values.

$$\text{MAD} = \frac{\text{Sum}(|\text{actual value} - \text{forecast}|)}{\text{Number of values}}$$

where | | is the symbol for an *absolute value*, meaning the size of the number ignoring the sign. The MAD is therefore the average forecasting error. For example, if we had been

Table 10.1

Time period	Actual sales	Forecast sales	Error
Week 1	12	11	1
Week 2	11	12	−1
Week 3	14	12	2
Week 4	17	14	3
Week 5	16	16	0
Week 6	15	17	−2
Week 7	15	18	−3
Week 8	18	17	1

Table 10.2

Time period	Actual sales	Forecast sales	Squared error
Week 1	12	11	1
Week 2	11	12	1
Week 3	14	12	4
Week 4	17	14	9
Week 5	16	16	0
Week 6	15	17	4
Week 7	15	18	9
Week 8	18	17	1

forecasting sales (Table 10.1):

$$\text{MAD} = (1 + 1 + 2 + 3 + 0 + 2 + 3 + 1)/8$$
$$= 1.6$$

on average the forecast was 1.6 wrong.

Mean square error (MSE)

MSE measures the average squared error of the forecasts.

$$\text{MSE} = \frac{\text{Sum(actual value} - \text{forecast)}^2}{\text{Number of values}}$$

The MSE of the above sales example is shown in Table 10.2.

$$\text{MSE} = (1 + 1 + 4 + 9 + 0 + 4 + 9 + 1)/8$$
$$= 3.6$$

The average squared error is therefore 3.6.

In comparing forecasts, the method with the lowest MAD or MSE is the more accurate and, statistically, is preferable. Unfortunately the two measures do not have to come to the same conclusion. One forecasting method may have the lowest MAD, another the lowest MSE. The reason for the difference is that the MSE penalises any large errors because this measure uses the squared errors. With the MAD an error of 2 is twice as bad as an error of 1; with the MSE it is four times as bad. So generally the MSE will favour a forecasting method which, on a particular set of data, has few large errors, even though it is on average (as measured by the MAD) not so good. It is up to the decision maker to decide which is preferable in any given circumstances.

Hold-out method

As described above, both the MAD and the MSE are *ex post* measures: they were used after the event when the actual values were known. The hold-out method is a way of assessing the accuracy of forecasting methods *ex ante*, before they are used.

Suppose we have data from 1980 to 1995 and are making forecasts for the next five years. The hold-out method works as follows (see Figure 10.1).

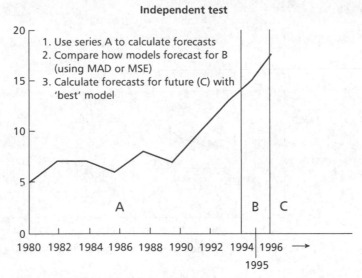

Independent test

1. Use series A to calculate forecasts
2. Compare how models forecast for B (using MAD or MSE)
3. Calculate forecasts for future (C) with 'best' model

Figure 10.1   Hold-out method

The later portion of the data series is 'held out'. In Figure 10.1 the last two years data, 1994–95, are put to one side. Forecasts for 1994–95 are made using the 1980–93 data. These forecasts are then compared with the known actual values for 1994–95 and the accuracy measured, using the MAD or MSE. The technique with the best forecasts for 1994–95, i.e. the lowest MAD and/or MSE, is chosen and used to forecast for 1996–2000 using all of the data 1980–95.

The advantage of the hold-out method is that it gives an independent assessment of accuracy. It is independent in the sense that it is benchmarked against data, in the example 1994–95, which were not used in making the forecasts. Its disadvantage is that the hold-out data may not be typical.

FORECASTING ERRORS – FAMOUS MISTAKES

The history of business forecasting is crowded with expensive mistakes. Some cases are presented here with the positive purpose of helping the reader to learn from others. The mistakes are a guide to the surprisingly simple and usually non-technical things which can go wrong.

Chartering oil tankers

Gwilym Jenkins[1] cites the case of an oil company which lost enormous sums of money by taking too superficial an approach to forecasting. A time series approach was adopted which was unsuited to the circumstances.

Figure 10.2 shows the spot prices for chartering oil tankers for the years 1967–71. Analysing the series and detecting an upwards trend in early 1969, it was assumed that the trend would continue, at least in the short term. The company would therefore save money by current rather than future chartering. Accordingly, charter contracts were taken

---

[1] *See Practical Experiences with Modelling and Forecasting Time Series*, Gwilym Jenkins, GJP Partners, 1980.

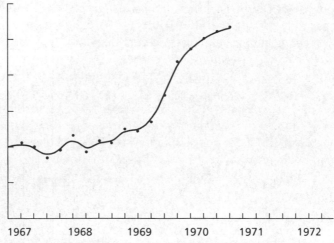

Figure 10.2 Spot prices for chartering oil tankers

out. The spot price continued to rise; more contracts were arranged. No doubt other oil companies, noticing what was happening, became involved. The spot price rose to great heights. When the chartering activity came to a halt in early 1971, the spot price fell to its pre- 1970 level. Contracts taken out this time would have been about one-third of the price of just a few months earlier. The cost to the company of the over-priced contracts has been estimated at £250 million.

Two mistakes had been made. First, the company's intervention in the spot market affected the market mechanism and thus the price. This occurred because the company was very large and because the supply of oil tankers is, in the short term, fixed. This is a conceptual error, which with the benefit of hindsight can be seen with some clarity. The second mistake is more technical. A deeper analysis of the series would have revealed that it had the appearance of a 'random walk': the step from one spot price to the next seemed to be a random one. If it was random, then by definition there was no pattern in the movement of the spot prices. This would mean that time series analysis was inapplicable. The bases of time series analyses is that they determine patterns in historical data and project them into the future. If there are no patterns then time series analysis will fail. Worse still, any patterns determined in subsets of the data will be spurious and may lead to false conclusions.

In the absence of patterns in the series, a different type of forecasting method should be employed. In this case a causal approach would have been better. An investigation of factors likely to cause the spot prices to vary, such as supply of tankers, demand for oil and economical variables, would have had a better chance of bearing fruit.

Airline passenger miles

Distinguishing between the statistical and non-statistical aspects of forecasting, and thinking clearly about both, might have saved an airline from an expensive and embarrassing error. One Sunday the planning director of the airline noticed a graph of the index of UK manufacturing production in the business supplement of his Sunday newspaper.

The thought struck him that the shape of the graph was very much the same as that of 'passenger miles flown' with his airline. On Monday he set his team to work and they developed a causal model linking the two variables. Analysis showed that, statistically, the model was a good one and it was subsequently used to predict future business. It was several months later when it started producing unsatisfactory forecasts and had to be abandoned.

There were two mistakes in this piece of forecasting. First, the strong statistical evidence had demonstrated only that the two variables were associated. It had not shown that the link was causal. Over the period of analysis both variables had risen steadily as the UK economy slowly grew. When the economic situation changed, manufacturing production dropped. At the same time the $/£ exchange rate increased and large numbers of tourists flew off to the USA for their holidays. Consequently passenger miles flown increased at a time when the model was predicting a decrease. There was no causal link between the variables so, when circumstances altered, the model no longer held good.

The second mistake was that in order to forecast passenger miles flown the airline had first to forecast the index of manufacturing production. This in itself was no trivial matter. A direct attempt at forecasting passenger miles flown would have carried an equal chance of success while saving time and effort. While forecasts of economic variables are needed, ones which are readily available should be chosen. Good forecasts of some economic variables, such as gross domestic product, personal disposable income and others, are published regularly by a variety of econometric forecasting institutes.

Production Planning: where a forecast wasn't used

Forecasts are not always monitored for accuracy after the event. A company in the manufacturing industry did check its sales forecasting accuracy and found that predictions were excellent. However, the production planning for which the forecasts were prepared was poor. After investigation it was found that the forecasts, delivered each week in form of large, heavy computer printouts, were never used. The production planners could not understand the output and no one ever explained it to them. They ignored it and used their own judgemental forecasts which were poor (just how poor the production managers did not realise until they were monitored). The fault lay with the designer of the forecasting system. They should have produced their output in a form which the users could understand and discussed its use with those who received it. The forecasting had never been integrated with the decision making which it was intended to serve.

Stories of errors in forecasting are usually about inaccurate forecasts being used, with disastrous results. An equally frequent occurrence may be as in the above example, when accurate forecasts are not used with disastrous results.

These three examples show how easily major mistakes can be made. More especially, they show that the role of the forecasting non-specialist in supervising a forecast effort or as part of a forecasting team is of vital importance. Mistakes are usually non-technical in nature. There is no guaranteed means of avoiding them, but it is clearly the responsibility of the managers in the team to guard against them. The lessons which other organisations have learned the hard way can help them in their task.

DOING YOUR OWN FORECASTING

Managers have a clear role in managing forecasts. The advent of microcomputers (desk-top computers) has made it easier for them to become practitioners of forecasting as well. Management journals have recently been reporting this phenomenon. The low cost of a fairly powerful microcomputer means that it is not a major acquisition; software (the programs) and instruction manuals are readily available. With a small investment in time and money, managers, frustrated by delays and apparent barriers around specialist departments, take the initiative and are soon gathering forecasts themselves. They can use their own data to make forecasts for their own decisions without having to work through management services or data processing units.

This development has several benefits. The link between technique and decision is made more easily; one person has overall understanding and control; time is saved; the forecasts are quickly obtained. But of course there are pitfalls. There may be no common database, no common set of assumptions within an organisation. For instance, an apparent difference between two capital expenditure proposals may have more to do with data/assumption details than with differences between the profitability of the projects. Another pitfall is in the use of statistical techniques which may not be as straightforward as the software manual might suggest. The use of techniques with no knowledge of when they can or cannot be applied is dangerous. A time series method applied to a random data series (such as chartering oil tankers) is an example. The computer will always (well, nearly always) give an answer. Whether it is legitimate to base a business decision on it is another matter.

CONCLUSION

This chapter has advised that the management aspects of forecasting are too often neglected and should be given more prominence. Statistical theory and techniques are of course important as well, but the disproportionate amounts of time spent studying and discussing them gives the wrong impression of their value in relation to other considerations.

One piece of advice might be to avoid forecasting. Sensible people should only use forecasts, not make them. The general public and the world of management judges forecasts very harshly. Unless they are exactly right they are thought to be failures. And they are never exactly right. This rigid and unrealistic test of forecasting is unfortunate. The real test is if the forecast is, on average, better than the alternative, which is often a guess – frequently, not even an educated guess.

A more positive view is that the present is a particularly rewarding time to invest in forecasting. The volatility in data series seen since the mid-1970s puts a premium on good forecasting. At the same time, facilities for making good forecasts are readily available in the form of a vast range of techniques and a wide choice of relatively cheap microcomputers. With the latter, even sophisticated forecasting methods can be applied to large data sets. It can all be done on a manager's desk-top without him or her having to engage in lengthy discussions with experts in other departments of the organisation.

Whether managers are doing the forecasting themselves or are part of a team, they can make a substantial contribution to forward planning. To do so, they need to arm themselves with some background information and to be aware of hidden traps.

QUESTIONS

1. An investment management company has used three-point moving averages to make short-term forecasts of the number of bargains struck per week.

Week	1	2	3	4	5	6	7	8
Bargains ('000s)	8	5	8	6	3	4	6	5
Forecasts ('000s)				7	6.3	5.7	4.3	4.3

   What is the MSE (mean square error) and MAD (mean absolute deviation) of these forecasts?

2. A manufacturer of household electrical equipment has used two forecasting methods, three-point moving averages and exponential smoothing, to make short-term forecasts of the weekly stock levels. The company now wants to choose the more accurate of the two and use it alone to forecast. To do this two measures of accuracy, the MAD (mean absolute deviation) and MSE (mean square error), have been calculated for each method over the last 10 weeks. Which of the following conclusions should be drawn if moving averages has the lower MSE while exponential smoothing has the lower MAD?
   (a) Moving averages is superior.
   (b) Exponential smoothing is superior.
   (c) A calculating error must have been made because such a situation could never arise.
   (d) Exponential smoothing is better on average but probably has more large individual errors.

3. A major soccer club plays some 30 matches at home in the course of a season. The matches vary in importance, depending on a range of factors including the quality of the opposition, the status of the match, the weather and many others. On some occasions the ground is full, with 40 000 fans an hour before kick-off, on others the attendance is less than 20 000. The club, however, has to book staff (ticket issuers, ground stewards, catering staff, security guards) in advance and the cost is high. To lower these costs, the club has decided that it should attempt to forecast attendance and book staff accordingly. Describe briefly how the guidelines for developing a forecasting system might be applied to this situation.

ANSWERS TO QUESTIONS

1. MAD 1.66, MSE 3.62.
2. Exponential smoothing is better on average but has more large individual errors.

CHAPTER 11

Time series forecasting

Time series methods are forecasting techniques which predict future values of a variable solely from its own past record. In various ways they identify patterns in the data and project them into the future. The methods are categorised according to the types of series to which they can be applied. The different types of series are: stationary, trended, seasonal, and seasonal with cycles.

INTRODUCTION

Time series methods are introspective and it may seem that such techniques will inevitably be inferior to both qualitative techniques and causal modelling. When conditions change, time series methods, looking only at the past record, have no way of predicting the change or even responding quickly to it. Both qualitative methods and causal modelling take external factors into account. However, when tested, time series methods have compared favourably to the others and there are distinct situations in which they have proved to be highly successful. Time series methods do well in the following circumstances:

- *In stable conditions.* If these circumstances do not change, it is reasonable to assume that the factors which influenced a variable in the past will continue to influence it in the future, and in the same way. Consequently, the time series approach is likely to provide good forecasts when conditions are stable.
- *For short-term forecasts.* Over a short time horizon there may not be sufficient time for conditions to change except in a minor way. If so, time series methods are likely to provide good forecasts for the reasons given above. In the short term, therefore, most data series may continue just as in the past. What constitutes the short term is difficult to say. It depends what is being forecast. In the fast-moving software market, the short term is very short – perhaps a few weeks. In the shipping industry, when forecasting the world's cargo-carrying capacity, the short term may be measured in years because new ships take a long time to build.
- *As a base forecast.* A 'base' forecast shows what would be expected if the future were exactly the same as the past. Even when conditions are changing, a base forecast can be used as the starting point on which judgements and measures of the impact of changing conditions can be built.
- *For screening data.* Time series methods identify patterns in the past record. If new data is compared with these patterns, a better understanding of current influences can be gained. For instance, a particularly high level of sales one month may be exceptional – the beginning of a spurt in consumer expenditure. Or it may be unexceptional – merely the coincidence of high points in a cycle and in seasonality.

Time series methods have a good track record in all the above situations. Surveys of forecasting performance[1] have frequently shown them to outperform other approaches.

The methods are categorised according to the types of series to which they can be applied:

- *Stationary*: there is no trend in the data, and fluctuations are, on average, roughly the same at different points in time.
- *Trended*: overall there is a consistent movement upwards or downwards in the data.
- *Seasonal*: there is a trend and seasonality (a regular pattern which repeats itself every year).
- *Cyclical*: there is a trend, seasonality and cycles (regular patterns which take more than a year to repeat themselves).

This chapter describes some of the techniques which can deal with these types of data.

STATIONARY SERIES

A data series is stationary if it fluctuates about some constant level and if, while the amount of fluctuation differs from one period of time to the next, there is no general tendency for there to be more fluctuation at one part of the series than at another. Stated in more technical terms, a stationary series has no trend and constant variance.

In the long run virtually no series are stationary, but they may be in the short run. For example, the weekly stock volumes in a warehouse over two years is a long series (104 observations) which may well be stationary. Over five years it would probably not be.

In spite of their limited applicability, knowledge of stationary time series methods is essential because the concepts underlying them are the basis of techniques which deal with non-stationary data. Two techniques for forecasting stationary series are now described – moving averages and exponential smoothing.

Moving averages

Moving averages is a *smoothing technique*. To varying degrees, data series are affected by random fluctuations or 'noise' which obscure the patterns in the series. Smoothing techniques act to smooth out these fluctuations, usually by averaging them, so that the true patterns can be seen and analysed.

Moving averages forms a 'smoothed' series from the original data by replacing each actual observation, or data point, with the average of it and other observations either side of it. If each average is calculated from three actual observations, i.e. if each data point is smoothed by averaging it with the data point on either side of it, it is said to be a three-point moving average; if each is calculated from five actual observations, it is a five-point moving average, and so on. Table 11.1 gives an example of a three-point moving average.

---

[1] See J.S. Armstrong, 'Forecasting by extrapolation: conclusions from 25 years of research', *Interfaces* 14, November/December 1984, pp 52–66. This study reviews 39 academic papers which have used time series methods and concludes that simple methods, i.e. simple time series methods, are just as good as sophisticated ones. Articles in the *Journal of Forecasting* have also shown that simple time series methods perform as well as more sophisticated methods, including approaches to forecasting which are not based on time series.

Table 11.1

Time period	Actual series (x)	Smoothed series (S)
1	8	
2	7	9 = (8 + 7 + 12)/3
3	12	11 = (7 + 12 + 14)/3
4	14	10 = (12 + 14 + 4)/3
5	4	

Smoothed value at time period t =
(actual value at t − 1 + actual value at t + actual value at t + 1)/3
Algebraically, $S_t = (x_{t-1} + x_t + x_{t+1})/3$
For example, $S_3 = (x_2 + x_3 + x_4)/3$

Table 11.2

| | 1994 | | | | 1995 | |
	Q1	Q2	Q3	Q4	Q1	Q2
Data	8	7	12	14	4	
t	1	2	3	4	5	6
Algebraic notation	x_1	x_2	x_3	x_4	x_5	x_6

The notation can be confusing. Table 11.2 shows how the labelling works for a quarterly data series from quarter 1 1994 through to quarter 2 1995.

Moving averages is used in two ways. First, since the averaging process smooths away, to some extent, the random fluctuations in the series, the constant level about which the stationary series is fluctuating can be seen. This is shown in Figure 11.1. Even if the series is not stationary, moving averages can still be used to reveal trends, seasonality and cycles in the data.

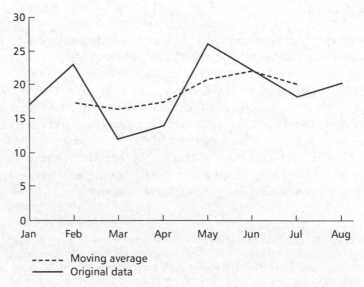

----- Moving average
——— Original data

Figure 11.1   Moving averages

Secondly, moving averages is used to make forecasts. The forecast for *any* future time period is the most recent smoothed value. In the example of Table 11.1 and Figure 11.1, the forecast is 10 for periods 6, 7, 8, 9, . . ., i.e. quarter 2 of 1995, quarter 3 of 1995, quarter 4 of 1995 . . . A constant forecast makes sense because the series is stationary.

Each smoothed value refers to the time period which is at the centre of the moving average. For example, the smoothed value obtained by averaging the data for January, February and March is centred on February. The use of an even number of points in a moving average therefore creates a problem. A smoothed value can no longer refer to a particular time period. It must refer to half-way between the middle of two time periods. For example, a four-point moving average for January, February, March and April is the smoothed value for 'in between' February and March. Specifying the time period to which a smoothed value refers makes no difference with a stationary series since there is no time trend, but it does have an effect in other uses of moving averages. There will be more on this later.

An important question is that of deciding how many points to include in a moving average. The above example used three points but there is nothing special about three. A tradeoff must be made. The average should include sufficient points to smooth the fluctuations – in general the more points, the smoother the data. On the other hand there should not be so many points that the last smoothed value refers to a time period remote from the time periods for which the forecasts are being made. For example, an 11-point average 'lags' five months behind the most recently available data; when the November data is available the most recent smoothed value will be based on the 11 months January to November and will be centred on June. This would mean that the moving average would be slow to respond to recent changes; it would matter if moving averages was being used to spot a trend or if there had been a one-off 'jump' in the constant level of a stationary series.

In practice, three- or five-point moving averages are probably the most common, except where seasonal data is concerned. Seasonal as well as random fluctuations in the data can be smoothed away by moving averages. You might want to do this to see what the trend looked like without the seasonal pattern obscuring it. This is done by including sufficient points in the average to cover the seasonality exactly. For example, seasonal monthly data would be smoothed using a 12-point moving average. Each month is included once and only once in the average and thus seasonal variation will be averaged out.

Exponential smoothing

For a moving average, each value in the average is given an equal weight. For example, in a three-point moving average each value is given the weight of one third. Exponential smoothing is used for the same purposes as moving averages but forms the smoothed values in a way which gives more weight to recent values than those further in the past. How this works is explained in a technical note a little later in the chapter.

An exponentially smoothed series is given by the equation:

New smoothed value = $(1 - \alpha)$ (previous smoothed value)

$+ \alpha$(most recent actual value)

i.e. $S_t = (1 - \alpha)S_{t-1} + \alpha x_t$

where α is a number between 0 and 1

Table 11.3

Time period		t	Actual series (x)	Smoothed series (α = 0.2)*
1994	Q1	1	8	
	Q2	2	7	7.8 = (1 − 0.2)(8) + 0.2(7)
	Q3	3	12	8.6 = (1 − 0.2)(7.8) + 0.2(12)
	Q4	4	14	9.7 = (1 − 0.2)(8.6) + 0.2(14)
1995	Q5	5	4	8.6 = (1 − 0.2)(9.7) + 0.2(4)

* Calculations have been rounded.

The value of the smoothing constant, α, is chosen by the forecaster. The larger the value, the heavier the weighting being given to the recent values. So if the forecaster is using exponential smoothing to spot trends visually and thinks that the trend may be changing, then a relatively high α should be chosen so that recent changes are picked up quickly; if the forecaster believes the trend to be stable then a relatively low value would be chosen to achieve a better smoothing effect. This is analogous to the choice of points to include in a moving average.

Chapter 10 describes how to compare the effectiveness of different forecasting methods and this can also be the basis for choosing the value of α. Exponential smoothing is carried out by using different α values and the results compared as if they came from the different forecasting methods. The α value giving the best results is chosen for the forecasting proper. In practice α is usually in the range 0.05 to 0.5.

Example

The data used in Table 11.1 have been exponentially smoothed in Table 11.3. Since the smoothing equation requires a previous smoothed value to get it started, it is usual to make

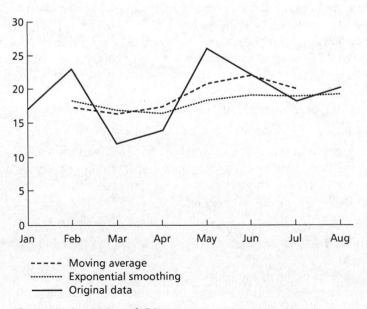

Moving average
Exponential smoothing
Original data

Figure 11.2   MA and ES

the first smoothed value equal to the actual value. This assumption can have a measurable effect on the forecasts, especially if the series is a short one. In a real situation thought must be given to the choice of starting values.

Figure 11.2 shows how exponential smoothing works to average out random fluctuations. As with moving averages, the forecast for future time periods of a stationary series is the most recent smoothed value, in this case 8.6.

Technical note

Some algebra is required to show why exponential smoothing gives different weighting to different time periods. The equation for exponential smoothing is:

$$S_t = (1 - \alpha)S_{t-1} + \alpha x_t \tag{1}$$

From the previous time period:

$$S_{t-1} = (1 - \alpha)S_{t-2} + \alpha x_{t-1} \tag{2}$$

Putting S_{t-1} from equation (2) into equation (1) gives:

$$S_t = (1 - \alpha)^2 S_{t-2} + \alpha(1 - \alpha)x_{t-1} + \alpha x_t \tag{3}$$

Just as S_{t-1} in equation (1) was substituted with equation (2), so S_{t-2} in equation (3) can be substituted by using the smoothing equation for S_{t-2} from a previous time period. Continuing this process eventually gives:

$$S_t = \alpha x_t + \alpha(1 - \alpha)x_{t-1} + \alpha(1 - \alpha)^2 x_{t-2} + \alpha(1 - \alpha)^3 x_{t-3} + \ldots \tag{4}$$

Exponential smoothing is therefore equivalent to giving a string of reducing weights to the past values of the data. The gradual reductions mean that more emphasis is put on the most recent data and this should allow changes in the data patterns (trend, level etc.) to be picked up more quickly. In the case of $\alpha = 0.2$ the weights are:

$$x_t: \qquad\qquad \alpha = 0.2$$
$$x_{t-1}: \qquad \alpha(1 - \alpha) = 0.16$$
$$x_{t-2}: \qquad \alpha(1 - \alpha)^2 = 0.128$$
$$x_{t-3}: \qquad \alpha(1 - \alpha)^3 = 0.1024$$

and so on

There is a neat symmetry in the way exponential smoothing works. If α is 0.2 then the most recent weight is 20 per cent and each preceding weight is reduced by 20 per cent (0.16 is 20 per cent less than 0.2, 0.128 is 20 per cent less than 0.16, etc.). If α is 0.3 then the most recent weight is 30 per cent and each preceding weight is reduced by 30 per cent, and so on.

It is important to distinguish between the concept underlying exponential smoothing (which is to smooth historical data by means of a series of gradually reducing weights) and the most convenient way to calculate the smoothed data (which is the smoothing equation (1)).

Table 11.4 (where time period 13 is 'now' and time period 1 is '13 months ago') illustrates different weighting systems. Note that for low α values the reducing weights theoretically continue indefinitely into the past. Even with a high value such as 0.5, it is some

Table 11.4

Time	Moving average (3-point)	Moving average (5-point)	Exponential smoothing* ($\alpha = 0.2$)	Exponential smoothing* ($\alpha = 0.5$)
1			0.014	0
2			0.017	0
3			0.021	0
4			0.027	0.001
5			0.034	0.002
6			0.042	0.004
7			0.052	0.008
8			0.066	0.016
9		0.2	0.082	0.031
10		0.2	0.102	0.063
11	0.33	0.2	0.128	0.125
12	0.33	0.2	0.16	0.25
13	0.33	0.2	0.2	0.5

time before the weights are reduced to negligible levels. It would therefore often be impossible, as well as a lengthy procedure, to calculate the smoothed data directly from the weights. The 'convenient' method of calculation (equation (1)) overcomes both these difficulties, although it is necessary to impose a starting value, usually the first data of the series, as described above.

SERIES WITH A TREND

Truly stationary series are rare, and the existence of a trend may have been revealed by the use of moving averages or exponential smoothing. Or the trend may have been immediately obvious from a graph without any smoothing. But these simple techniques cannot incorporate a trend into their forecasts and have to be adapted before they can be used on non-stationary data. Several variants of moving averages and exponential smoothing can deal with a trend. The two described here are double moving averages, which is a form of simple moving averages, and Holt's method, which is a form of exponential smoothing.

Double moving averages

Double moving averages works, as the name suggests, by smoothing the series once and then smoothing the smoothed series. The difference between the two is an estimate of the trend. The procedure is illustrated in Table 11.5 (notice that the data is different from Tables 11.1 and 11.3 – there is now a trend).

Table 11.5 assumes that we are now in time period 8, quarter 4 of 1995. The actual data for quarter 3 (17) has just become available and so the smoothed value for quarter 2 (time period 6) can be calculated.

$$S_6 = (10 + 12 + 17)/3 = 13 \text{ (based on the data for quarters 1, 2 and 3)}$$

Table 11.5

Time period		t	Actual	1st MA	2nd MA	Trend
1994	Q1	1	8			
	Q2	2	7	9		
	Q3	3	12	11	10.7 = (9 + 11 + 12)/3	
	Q4	4	14	12	11.7 = (11 + 12 + 12)/3	1.3 = 12 − 10.7
1995	Q1	5	10	12	12.3 = (12 + 12 + 13)/3	0.3 = 12 − 11.7
	Q2	6	12	13		0.7 = 13 − 12.3
	Q3	7	17			

Also when the data for quarter 3 1995 become available the latest doubly smoothed value that can be calculated is for quarter 1 1995 (time period 5).

$$DS_5 = (12 + 12 + 13)/3 = 12.3$$

Subtracting the two most recent smoothed values one from another is, according to the double moving averages technique, the estimate of the trend.

$$\text{Trend } (t = 7) = \text{1st smoothed value } (t = 6) - \text{2nd smoothed value } (t = 5)$$
$$= 13 - 12.3 = 0.7$$

Of course, the trend could have been estimated from the first smoothed series by subtracting adjacent values in the column, but the double smoothing, theoretically, is likely to give greater accuracy.

For stationary series the forecasts were the same for all future periods, but forecasts made for data with a trend using double moving averages must take into account the trend.

Forecast for 1 period ahead = most recent smoothed value + 2 ×trend

Forecast for 2 periods ahead = most recent smoothed value + 3 ×trend

and so on.

For example, taking the data from Table 11.5,

Forecast for Q4,1995 = 13 + (2 × 0.7) = 14.4

Forecast for Q1,1996 = 13 + (3 × 0.7) = 15.1

Forecast for Q2,1996 = 13 + (4 × 0.7) = 15.8

The technique of double exponential smoothing works in a similar way.

Holt's method

As we can see from Table 11.5, the trend is itself affected by fluctuations in the data, making it seem more variable than it really is. Holt's method adds a refinement to the process of calculating the trend by smoothing the trend as well as the data series.

The formula for exponential smoothing is:

$$S_t = (1 - \alpha)S_{t-1} + \alpha x_t$$

If the series has a trend, it should be seen in the smoothed values. Therefore a first way of calculating a trend might be, similarly to double moving average:

Trend = most recent smoothed value − previous smoothed value i.e. = $S_t - S_{t-1}$

Just as random fluctuations in the data can be smoothed, so with the trend. A 'smoothed' trend is obtained by means of a smoothing constant (labelled γ) to combine the most recently observed estimate of the trend with the previous smoothed trend, just as α is used for the data. γ is between 0 and 1, is chosen by the forecaster and may or may not be different from α.

$$\text{Smoothed trend} = (1 - \gamma) \times \text{previous smoothed trend} +$$

$$\gamma \times \text{most recently observed trend}$$

$$\text{i.e. } T_t = (1 - \gamma)T_{t-1} + \gamma(S_t - S_{t-1})$$

How is this estimate of trend used in conjunction with the exponential smoothing formula? First, the basic smoothing formula must be changed so that the previous smoothed value, S_{t-1}, is increased to allow for the trend.

$$S_t = (1 - \alpha)S_{t-1} + \alpha x_t$$

becomes

$$S_t = (1 - \alpha)(S_{t-1} + T_{t-1}) + \alpha x_t$$

Secondly, future forecasts must allow for the effect of the trend. A forecast for the three periods ahead is:

Forecast m periods ahead = most recent smoothed value + m × smoothed trend

$$\text{i.e. } F_{t+m} = S_t + mT_t$$

To summarise, when a time series has a trend, forecasts with Holt's method are based on three equations:

$$S_t = (1 - \alpha)(S_{t-1} + T_{t-1}) + \alpha x_t$$
$$T_t = (1 - \gamma)T_{t-1} + \gamma(S_t - S_{t-1})$$
$$F_{t+m} = S_t + mT_t$$

where x_t = actual observation at time

S_t = smoothed value at time

α, γ = smoothed constants between zero and 1

T_t = smoothed trend at time

F_{t+m} = forecast for m periods ahead

Example

Table 11.6 shows how Holt's method is applied to an annual series of sales figures. The series has been shortened in order to simplify the example. The smoothing constants have

Table 11.6

Year (t)	Sales vol. (x_t)	$\alpha = 0.2$ Smoothed sales* (S_t)		$\gamma = 0.3$ Smoothed trend* (T_t)	
1985	20	20		–	
1986	22	22		2	= 22 – 20
1987	28	24.8	= 0.8(22 + 2) + 0.2(28)	2.24	= 0.7(2) + 0.3(24.8 – 22)
1988	26	26.8	= 0.8(24.8 + 2.24) + 0.2(26)	2.18	= 0.7(2.24) + 0.3(26.8 – 24.8)
1989	37	30.6	= 0.8(26.8 + 2.18) + 0.2(37)	2.66	= 0.7(2.18) + 0.3(30.6 – 26.8)
1990	34	33.4	= 0.8(30.6 + 2.66) + 0.2(34)	2.70	= 0.7(2.66) + 0.3(33.4 – 30.6)
1991	35	35.9	= 0.8(33.4 + 2.70) + 0.2(35)	2.63	= 0.7(2.70) + 0.3(35.9 – 33.4)
1992	40	38.8	= 0.8(35.9 + 2.63) + 0.2(40)	2.72	= 0.7(2.63) + 0.3(38.8 – 35.9)
1993	41	41.4	= 0.8(38.8 + 2.72) + 0.2(41)	2.69	= 0.7(2.72) + 0.3(41.4 – 38.8)
1994	44	44.1	= 0.8(41.4 + 2.69) + 0.2(44)	2.68	= 0.7(2.69) + 0.3(44.1 – 41.4)
Forecasts					
1995		46.78	= 44.1 + 2.68		
1996		49.47	= 44.1 + (2 × 2.68)		
1997		52.15	= 44.1 + (3 × 2.68)		

* There may be rounding errors: calculations were precise but rounded for presentation.

values:

$$\alpha = 0.2$$
$$\gamma = 0.3$$

The choice of these values is based on the same principles as for simple exponential smoothing.

The calculating process needs a starting point for both the data and the trend. The first two data values are used for the first two time periods to start the smoothed data series. The difference between them is used to start the smoothed trend series (located at the second time period – the trend cannot be estimated for the first time period).

SERIES WITH A TREND AND SEASONALITY

Seasonality is defined as a regular pattern of upward and downward movements which repeats itself every year or less. There are several techniques which can deal with a series with trend and seasonality. The one described here is the Holt–Winters method which is an extension of Holt's method.

Holt–Winters method

The Holt's method formulae are:

$$S_t = (1 - \alpha)(S_{t-1} + T_{t-1}) + \alpha x_t$$
$$T_t = (1 - \gamma)T_{t-1} + \gamma(S_t - S_{t-1})$$
$$F_{t+m} = S_t + mT_t$$

Table 11.7

Year	Quarter	Sales	Smoothed $\alpha = 0.4$	Trend $\gamma = 0.3$	Seasonality $\beta = 0.2$
1991	1	23	23		
	2	24	24.0	1.0	
	3	30	27.0	1.6	
	4	28	28.4	1.5	
1992	1	28	29.1	1.3	0.96
	2	34	31.9	1.7	1.07
	3	38	35.4	2.3	1.07
	4	25	32.6	0.7	0.77
1993	1	30	32.5	0.5	0.95
	2	37	33.6	0.7	1.07
	3	45	37.4	1.6	1.10
	4	33	40.6	2.1	0.78
1994	1	34	39.9	1.2	0.93
	2	43	40.7	1.1	1.07
	3	49	42.9	1.4	1.11
	4	38	46.2	2.0	0.79
1995	1	37	44.7	1.0	0.91
	2	47	45.0	0.8	1.07
	3	52	46.2	0.9	1.11
	4	37	47.1	0.9	0.79
		Forecasts			
1996	1	43.76			
	2	52.04			
	3	55.34			
	4	39.80			

where x_t = actual observation at time

S_t = smoothed value at time

α, γ = smoothed constants between 0 and 1

T_t = smoothed trend at time

F_{t+m} = forecast for m periods ahead

Seasonality in a series is manifested in that some time periods (months, quarters etc.) the actual data is always above or always below the corresponding smoothed value. It is measured as a ratio between actual and smoothed values. For any time period:

$$\text{Seasonality} = x_t/S_t$$

Just as the trend was smoothed in Holt's method, so is the seasonality here. Naturally, a further smoothing constant, β, is required. The relevant formula is:

Smoothed seasonality = $(1 - \beta)$. (previous smoothed seasonality) + β.(most recently observed seasonality)

$$I_t = (1 - \beta).I_{t-12} + \beta.(x_t/S_t)$$

The above equation refers to a monthly seasonal pattern. If the calculation is being made for, say, January, then the previous smoothed seasonality refers to the previous January, 12 periods ago. Hence the presence of $t - 12$ in the equation. The complete system of equations for the Holt–Winters method is:

$$S_t = (1 - \alpha)(S_{t-1} + T_{t-1}) + \alpha(x_t/I_{t-12}) \qquad \text{Smoothed data series}$$
$$T_t = (1 - \gamma)T_{t-1} + \gamma(S_t - S_{t-1}) \qquad \text{Smoothed trend}$$
$$I_t = (1 - \beta).I_{t-12} + \beta.(x_t/S_t) \qquad \text{Smoothed seasonality}$$
$$F_{t+m} = (S_t + mT_t)I_{t+m-12} \qquad \text{Forecasts}$$

Comparing these equations with Holt's method:

- In smoothing the original series, allowance is made for the seasonality which is removed from the actual values by dividing by the seasonal effect.
- The trend equation is exactly the same as for Holt's method.
- The seasonal equation has been added as described above.
- Forecasting with Holt–Winters takes the latest smoothed value, adds a trend allowance and then multiplies by the seasonal effect.

Table 11.7 shows the application of Holt–Winters to a quarterly data series. One of the difficulties in using Holt–Winters on a short series such as this is that the starting assumptions have an untoward effect. There are refinements to the method which go some way to overcoming this problem. Note that the smoothing constants have been given relatively large values so that the system adapts quickly and the influence of the starting assumptions diminishes rapidly.

SERIES WITH A TREND, SEASONALITY AND CYCLES

The decomposition method

A cycle is a regular repeating pattern of upward and downward movements greater than one year in length. Contrast this with seasonality in which the patterns repeat in no more than a year. One of the most common methods of dealing with the three elements – trend, seasonality and cycle – is the decomposition method.

The method is based on the supposition that a time series can be separated or decomposed into four different elements:

- Trend;
- Cycle;
- Seasonality;
- Random.

Nothing can be done about the random element since random is by definition unpredictable. However, the first three elements, once separated out, can be re-assembled to make a forecast. The elements are isolated one by one.

Trend

The trend is isolated by regression analysis of the data against time (see Figure 11.3). Regression analysis is described in detail in Chapter 14. The time variable has the value

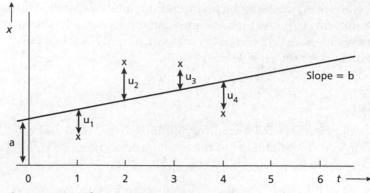

Figure 11.3 The trend in decomposition

1 for the first time period, 2 for the second, 3 for the third . . . The regression equation will be:

$$x_t \qquad = \qquad a + bt \qquad + \qquad u_t$$

actual data   trend element   residuals comprising
seasonality, cycles random
elements

Cycles

The next step is to isolate any cycle in the data. By choosing a suitable moving average (12 points for monthly data, four for quarterly, etc.) the random and seasonal elements can be smoothed away, leaving just the trend and cycle. If S_t is such a moving average, then the ratio between S_t and the trend $a + bt$ must be the cycle. If this ratio is approximately 1 for all time periods then there is no cycle. If it differs from 1 with any regular pattern then the ratio should be inspected to determine the nature of the cycle.

For instance, if the ratio is graphed against time, it might appear as in Figure 11.4. Although not completely regular, this suggests a cycle of period 12 quarters, or three years.

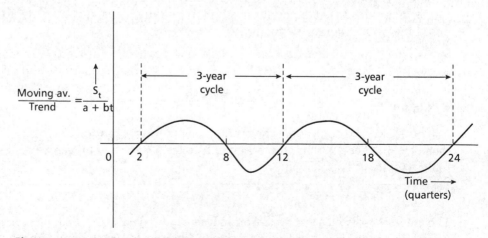

Figure 11.4 Cycles in decomposition

The ratio returns to its starting point after this interval of time. The size of the cyclical effect is measured by calculating the average of the ratio for each point in the cycle. For example, the fifth time period in the cycle (= 6, 18, 30 . . . .)

$$\text{Cyclical effect} = \text{average of } S_6/(a + 6b), S_{12}/(a + 12b), S_{18}/(a + 18b)$$

Seasonality

Seasonality is isolated by an approach similar to that used for cycles. The moving average, S_t, comprises trend and cycle; the actual values comprise trend, cycle, seasonality and random effect. The ratio:

$$\text{actual value/moving average}$$
$$\text{or } x_t/S_t$$

should therefore contain only seasonality and the random effect. As with other time series methods, the way to eliminate random fluctuations is by averaging. Suppose the data are quarterly, then the seasonality for, say, the first quarter is calculated by averaging the ratios:

$$\text{Seasonality for the first quarter} = \text{average of } x_1/S_1, x_5/S_5\ x_9/S_9.$$

The seasonality of the other three quarters can be calculated in the same way.

In making a forecast, the three isolated elements are multiplied together. Suppose the forecast for a future quarter, t = 50, is needed. It will be calculated:

$$\text{Forecast} = \text{trend} \times \text{cycle} \times \text{seasonality} \quad \text{all for } t = 50$$

If the data are quarterly with a cycle of length 12 quarters, t = 50 is the second period of a cycle and the second period of the seasonality. Therefore:

$$\text{Forecast} = (a + 50b) \times \text{cyclical effect for 2nd period} \times \text{seasonal effect for 2nd quarter}$$

Example

A company makes a variety of white consumer goods. The products are of good quality and have been successful in terms of sales volumes. Selling costs, however, have been unacceptable to senior management, mainly because of the stock levels. There is now a company-wide initiative to reduce stocks, starting with washing machines whose value, and therefore stocking cost, is high.

As part of the initiative forecasting methods have to be improved and a major preliminary task is to forecast sales of washing machines. The data is quarterly and sales volumes for the last nine years, 1986–94, are shown in Table 11.8. Since sales of white goods are

Table 11.8

Year									
Quarter	1986	1987	1988	1989	1990	1991	1992	1993	1994
1	14.4	19.8	21.0	30.9	45.3	40.8	58.5	69.3	70.8
2	20.7	28.5	32.4	55.2	56.4	58.2	85.2	93.0	103.8
3	17.7	23.7	27.9	47.4	46.2	53.1	78.0	78.0	93.9
4	24.3	31.8	44.1	59.7	59.1	78.3	103.2	103.2	110.1

influenced by prevailing economic conditions, it is thought that economic cycles might be found in the data and therefore the decomposition method has been recommended as the place to begin. In the first instance quarterly sales forecasts in 1996 are required. Following the decomposition method:

Calculate the trend

A regression analysis is carried out with sales volume as the y variable and time as the x variable:

y:	14.4	20.7	17.7	24.3	19.8	28.5...
x:	1	2	3	4	5	6 ...

The analysis gives: shipments = 8.556 + (2.516 × time)

Calculate the cyclical effect

This effect is calculated as the ratio between a moving average and a trend. The moving average has to be a four-point average to include each of the quarters in every average and thus smooth out seasonality (see column 4 in Table 11.9). The first moving average is 19.27, calculated thus:

$$19.27 = (14.4 + 20.7 + 17.7 + 24.3)/4$$

Since it includes the first four actual observations, for time periods 1, 2, 3, 4, the moving average should really be centred between periods 2 and 3. Because the cyclical effect is calculated for each time period, each moving average must refer to one and only one time period. Arbitrarily, it is taken to refer to the later of the two periods, i.e. time period 3. Period 2 would have been equally valid as an approximation. The second moving average incorporates the actual data from periods 2–5 and is centred on period 4. The last moving average is for period 35 and includes the last four items of actual data (periods 33–6).

Column 5 in Table 11.9 shows the trend, calculated from the regression equation. For example, for 1989, quarter four (time period 16):

$$\text{Trend} = 8.556 + (2.516 \times \text{time})$$
$$= 8.556 + 2.516 \times 16$$
$$= 48.78$$

The cyclical ratio (= moving average/trend = column 4/column 5) is shown in column 6. If this ratio exhibits any pattern, it should be revealed in a graph relating the ratio to time, as in Figure 11.4. The curve is not completely smooth, as in most practical situations, but there does appear to be a cycle. The length is 12 quarters since troughs and peaks both recur at this interval. For each of the 12 periods within the cycle, this effect can be calculated by averaging over all such periods. The first period of the cycle is taken, arbitrarily, to be the first period of the time series. The cyclical effect for, as an example, period 8 of the cycle is calculated (using data from column 6 of Table 11.9):

$$\text{Cyclical effect for period 8 of cycle} = \text{average for periods 8, 20, 32}$$
$$= (0.92 + 0.86 + 0.97)/3$$
$$= 0.92$$

Table 11.9

Year/quarter seasonality (1)		Time (2)	Sales vol. (3)	Moving average (4)	Trend (5)	Cycle (6)	Seasonality (7)
1986:	1	1	14.4	–	11.1	–	–
	2	2	20.7	–	13.6	–	–
	3	3	17.7	19.3	16.1	1.20	0.92
	4	4	24.3	20.6	18.6	1.11	1.18
1987:	1	5	19.8	22.6	21.1	1.07	0.88
	2	6	28.5	24.1	23.6	1.02	1.18
	3	7	23.7	26.0	26.2	0.99	0.91
	4	8	31.8	26.3	28.7	0.92	1.21
1988:	1	9	21.0	27.2	31.2	0.87	0.77
	2	10	32.4	28.3	33.7	0.84	1.15
	3	11	27.9	31.4	36.2	0.87	0.89
	4	12	44.1	33.8	38.7	0.87	1.30
1989:	1	13	30.9	39.5	41.2	0.96	0.78
	2	14	55.2	44.4	43.8	1.01	1.24
	3	15	47.4	48.3	46.3	1.04	0.98
	4	16	59.7	51.9	48.8	1.06	1.15
1990:	1	17	45.3	52.2	51.3	1.02	0.87
	2	18	56.4	51.9	53.8	0.96	1.09
	3	19	46.2	51.8	56.3	0.92	0.89
	4	20	59.1	50.6	58.8	0.86	1.17
1991:	1	21	40.8	51.1	61.3	0.83	0.80
	2	22	58.2	52.8	63.9	0.83	1.10
	3	23	53.1	57.6	66.4	0.87	0.92
	4	24	78.3	62.0	68.9	0.90	1.26
1992:	1	25	58.5	68.8	71.4	0.96	0.85
	2	26	85.2	75.0	73.9	1.01	1.14
	3	27	78.0	81.2	76.4	1.06	0.96
	4	28	103.2	83.9	78.9	1.06	1.23
1993:	1	29	69.3	85.9	81.5	1.05	0.81
	2	30	93.0	85.9	84.0	1.02	1.08
	3	31	78.0	85.9	86.5	0.99	0.91
	4	32	103.2	86.3	89.0	0.97	1.20
1994:	1	33	70.8	89.0	91.5	0.97	0.80
	2	34	103.8	92.9	94.0	0.99	1.12
	3	35	93.9	94.7	96.5	0.98	0.99
	4	36	110.1	–	99.1	–	–

Note: Rounding may result in slight discrepancies.

The effect for all 12 periods of a cycle is shown in Table 11.10.

Calculate the seasonal effect

The seasonality is the ratio of actual to moving average, averaged for each quarter. Table 11.9 shows these ratios in column 7, calculated as column 3 divided by column 4. Average these ratios for the first quarter:

Table 11.10

Time period of cycle	Cyclical effect
1	0.96
2	1.01
3	1.10
4	1.08
5	1.05
6	1.00
7	0.97
8	0.92
9	0.89
10	0.89
11	0.91
12	0.88

Table 11.11

Quarter	Basic seasonal index
1	0.82
2	1.14
3	0.93
4	1.21

Seasonality index for quarter 1:

$$= (0.88 + 0.77 + 0.78 + 0.87 + 0.80 + 0.85 + 0.81 + 0.80)/8$$
$$= 0.82$$

Table 11.11 shows all four seasonal indices, but unfortunately there is a problem with these basic seasonal indices. The overall effect is to change to level of data – because their average is different from 1. From the table:

$$\text{Average seasonal effect} = (0.82 + 1.14 + 0.93 + 1.21)/4$$
$$= 1.025$$

The seasonal index is meant to re-arrange the pattern within a year, not to increase or decrease the overall level of the data. In the above case the level of the data would be increased by 2.5 per cent each year. Consequently the seasonal indices have to be adjusted so that their average is 1. This is done by dividing each index in Table 11.11 by 1.025 to give the adjusted seasonal indices of Table 11.12.
The average seasonal effect is now neutral since:

$$(0.80 + 1.11 + 0.91 + 1.18)/4 = 1.00$$

Make the forecasts

The original series has been decomposed into trend, cycle and seasonality. To make forecasts for 1996, the three elements are re-assembled. The forecasts are shown in Table 11.13.

Table 11.12

Quarterly	Adjusted seasonal indices
1	0.80
2	1.11
3	0.91
4	1.18

Table 11.13

Quarter	Trend	Cycle	Seasonality	Forecast
1	111.7	1.05	0.80	93.8
2	114.2	1.00	1.11	126.8
3	116.7	0.97	0.91	103.0
4	119.3	0.92	1.18	129.5

Note: Rounding may result in slight discrepancies.

- The trend is 8.556 + (2.516 × time). The four quarters of 1996 are the time periods numbered 41–44. The trend for the first quarter is therefore:

$$\text{Trend} = 8.556 + (2.516 \times 41)$$
$$= 111.7$$

- Each cycle lasts for 12 periods. Starting at the first quarter of 1986, the cycles are 1986–88, 1989–91, 1992–94. Consequently, the four quarters of 1996 are time periods 5–8 of a cycle. The cyclical effects for these periods are taken from Table 11.10. They are 1.05, 1.00, 0.97, 0.92 respectively.
- The seasonal effect for each quarter is taken from Table 11.12.
- The forecast is the product of the three elements, e.g. for 1996, quarter 1:

Forecast	= 111.7	×	1.05	×	0.80
	(trend)		(cycle)		(season)
	= 93.8				

Table 11.13 shows the 1996 forecasts in full.

CONCLUSION

This chapter has tried to show the types of data with which time series methods can deal and where the time series approach is most likely to be successful. The techniques described are just a few of the many which are available. Furthermore, the basic ideas can be extended to allow for a variety of circumstances. In particular, smoothing methods are capable of a wide range of applications. For example, they can cover the incorporation of judgement into the forecast, as in the *Harrison–Stevens method*. The *Trigg–Leach tracking signal method* (which is described in the next chapter) is a system for monitoring forecasting errors and checking whether they are random; *adaptive response rate* is a means of setting the smoothing constant automatically and altering it as time goes by and new data become available.

In spite of the flexibility of time series methods and the fact that surveys have demonstrated how effective they can be, they are often undervalued. The reason is that, since a variable is predicted solely from its own historical record, the methods have no power to respond to changes in organisations and their business environment. They work on the assumption that future circumstances will be as in the past.

Nevertheless their track record is good, especially for short-term forecasting. In addition, they have one big advantage over other methods. Because they work solely from the historical record and do not necessarily require any element of judgement or forecasts of other causal variables, they can operate automatically. For example, a large warehouse holding thousands of items of stock has to predict future demands and stock levels. The number of items, which may be of low unit value, means that it will not be practicable or economic to give each variable individual attention. Time series methods will provide good short-term forecasts by computer without needing managerial attention. Of course, some initial research would have to be carried out, for instance to find out the best overall values of smoothing constants. But once this research was done, the forecasts could be made automatically. All that would be needed would be the updating of the historical record as new data became available. This should cause little difficulty if the stock system is computerised.

The conclusion is, therefore, that time series methods should not be underestimated. They have advantages of cost and, in the short term, of accuracy over other methods.

CASE STUDIES

CASE STUDY 1

A mail order company has just installed a new computerised inventory control system. The stock levels for the first seven weeks under the new system were:

Week	1	2	3	4	5	6	7
Stock (£ million)	10	14	12	11	9	13	12

1. For budgeting purposes a three-point moving average forecast for period 8 is calculated. What should this forecast be?

2. In carrying out sensitivity analysis, an exponential smoothing ($\alpha = 0.2$) forecast for period 8 is also prepared What is this forecast?

Solutions

1. *For budgeting purposes a three-point moving average forecast for period 8 is calculated. What should this forecast be?*

Week	Stock	Moving average		Forecast
1	10			
2	14	12	[=(10 + 14 + 12)/3]	
3	12	12.3	[=(14 + 12 + 11)/3]	
4	11	10.7	[=(12 + 11 + 9)/3]	12
5	9	11	[=(11 + 9 + 13)/3]	12.3
6	13	11.3	[=(9 + 13 + 12)/3]	10.7
7	12			11
8				11.3

The forecast is 11.3.

2.   *In carrying out sensitivity analysis, an exponential smoothing ($\alpha = 0.2$) forecast for period 8 is also prepared. What is this forecast?*

Week	Stock	Exponential smoothing		Forecast
1	10			
2	14	10.8	[= 0.8(10) + 0 2(14)]	
3	12	11.0	[= 0.8(10.8) + 0.2(12)]	10.8
4	11	11.0	[= 0.8(11.04) + 0.2(11)]	11.0
5	9	10.6	[= 0.8(11.03) + 0.2(9)]	11.0
6	13	11.1	[= 0.8(10.63) + 0.2(13)]	10.6
7	12	11.3	[= 0.8(11.1) + 0.2(12)]	11.1
8				11.3

The forecast, as with the moving average, is 11.3.

CASE STUDY 2

One of the best-selling products of a chain retailer of do-it-yourself goods has for five years been a range of 'minimum cleaning' paint brushes. Because of the high sales levels, stock levels are correspondingly high and the director of distribution is determined to reduce the warehousing costs. However, this has proved difficult because production schedules have been continually changed on account of substantial variations in demand from quarter to quarter. The distribution director is trying to improve the situation and, much against his natural inclinations, has decided to adopt a scientific approach to forecasting the demand. He asked his latest recruit, a business graduate, to take on the assignment. Her first move was to apply the decomposition method to the available quarterly data covering 1990–95. The separation of the elements of this time series revealed:

(a) The trend was: demand = 3600 + 50t, where t = 1, 2, 3 etc. and t = 1 represents Quarter 1, 1990.

(b) There was no cycle.

(c) The seasonal factors (calculated as actual/moving average) were:

	Q1	Q2	Q3	Q4
1990	–	–	80	101
1991	116	106	77	105
1992	108	110	78	103
1993	112	109	74	102
1994	111	106	78	101
1995	113	109	75	106

We are now in the first quarter of 1996 and forecasts are needed for the remaining quarters of the year, i.e. Q2, Q3, Q4 of 1996.

1.   What should the forecasts be?

2. Should the schedule be delayed until the results for the current quarter are available, i.e. is the actual demand for the first quarter likely to affect the forecast?

3. If the method proves unsatisfactory in practice, what other forecasting methods could be used?

Solutions

1.   *What should the forecasts be?*
First, calculate the average of each quarter's seasonal factors to see if their level needs to be adjusted. Quarterly seasonal averages:

	Q1	Q2	Q3	Q4
1990	–	–	80	101
1991	116	106	77	105
1992	108	110	78	103
1993	112	109	74	102
1994	111	106	78	101
1995	113	109	75	106
Average	112	108	77	103

The average of these averages is exactly 100, so no adjustment is necessary.
  Classical decomposition splits a time series into three elements:

Trend

For Q2, 1996, t = 26 and the trend factor is:

$$3600 + 50 \times 26 = 4900$$

For Q3, 1996, t = 27 and the trend factor is:

$$3600 + 50 \times 27 = 4950$$

For Q4, 1996, t = 28 and the trend factor is:

$$3600 + 50 \times 28 = 5000$$

Cycle

No cycle was found.

Seasonality

For the second quarter the seasonal factor is 108. For the third quarter the seasonal factor is 77. For the fourth quarter the seasonal factor is 103.

Forecasts

The forecast for Q2, 1996 is 4900 × 1.08 = 5292. The forecast for Q3, 1996 is 4950 × 0.77 = 3811.5. The forecast for Q4, 1996 is 5000 × 1.03 = 5150.

2. *Should the schedule be delayed until the results for the current quarter are available, i.e. is the actual demand for the first quarter likely to affect the forecast?*

Data from the first quarter of 1996 will affect the forecasts very little. First, the trend will be adjusted, but since the record covers 24 quarters the effect of adding the 25th will not be great. Secondly, the seasonal element will be unchanged, since first quarter data cannot affect the second, third and fourth quarters' seasonal factors.

3. *If the method proves unsatisfactory in practice, what other forecasting methods could be used?*

The series is a seasonal one, therefore a method to handle seasonality is needed. Holt–Winters is a suitable time series method. If the main factors affecting demand can be found (perhaps a variable measuring economic activity, one measuring marketing expenditure, etc.) and measured, regression analysis could be used.

QUESTIONS

1. Which of the following statements are true?
    (a) Time series forecasting methods are for stationary data series only.
    (b) Time series forecasting methods are based on regression analysis.
    (c) Time series forecasting methods forecast the future of a variable from its own past record.
    (d) Time series forecasting methods are most useful in a stable situation.
    (e) Time series forecasting methods are most useful where the historical data record is very short.
    (f) A stationary series has no trend.
    (g) In Holt's method the two smoothing constants should be the same.
    (h) In Holt–Winters method seasonality is measured as actual/trend.
    (i) In decomposition the cycle is measured as moving average/trend.

2. A supplier of gardening materials for retail garden centres has just installed a new computerised inventory control system. The stock levels for the first six weeks under the new system were:

Week	1	2	3	4	5	6
Stock (£ million)	26	31	26	23	21	25

    (a) What are the smoothed values of this series, using three-point moving averages, and what is the three-point moving average forecast for period 7?
    (b) To help to check and compare this forecast, calculate an exponential smoothing (α = 0.3) forecast for period 7.
    (c) What are the mean square errors and mean absolute deviations for both sets of forecasts?

3. The accountants of a car hire company have been looking at various costs with a view to eliminating the ones which they believe to be unjustified. One cost on which the accountants seized was a long-running advertising campaign in local newspapers. As a result the campaign has been terminated on the grounds that the campaign was having little impact. However, since it has been stopped the demand for hire cars has dropped.

Table 11.14

Week	Demand
1	148
2	168
3	137
4	175
5	174
6	161
7	133
8	180
9	143
10	163
11	156
12	161

Until an agency can be engaged and advertising relaunched, completely new production and sales plans are having to be drawn up. To do this some short-term demand forecasts need to be made, but it is not certain which method might be the best.

The demand record for car hires over the short period since the advertising campaign was terminated is shown in Table 11.14. The data refer to the number of days car hire per week.

(a) One forecasting method for the data might be to take the average of the whole series and use this as the forecast. Why is this likely to be less accurate than moving averages or exponential smoothing?

(b) Make a forecast of demand for week 13 using three-point moving averages and another using exponential smoothing ($\alpha = 0.1$).

(c) Which of these methods is likely, on average, to give better forecasts?

4. The senior financial management of a group of fast-food restaurants has realised the

Table 11.15

Trend coefficients:		Intercept = 9.7	Slope = 1.6
Seasonality:	Q1	0.90	
	Q2	1.05	
	Q3	1.10	
	Q4	0.95	
Cycle (over three years):	1		1.0
	2		1.06
	3		1.10
	4		1.20
	5		1.08
	6		1.03
	7		0.98
	8		0.90
	9		0.84
	10		0.88
	11		0.95
	12		0.98

need to re-assess its working capital requirements. Difficulties with its cashflow in recent years have meant that the chain will have to seek substantial sums of additional finance from its bankers. A business plan has been prepared showing its cashflow needs and the underlying soundness of the business. The basis of the plan is quarterly sales forecasts produced with the decomposition method. However, the bankers have asked for further details on the way in which the forecasts have been prepared. In millions of pounds, the statistics in Table 11.15 have been estimated from the historical data record.

What are the forecasts for each quarter of the next year? Quarter 1 is $t = 21$ and is the fifth period of the cycle.

ANSWERS TO QUESTIONS

1. (a) False.   (d) True.   (g) False.
   (b) False.   (e) False.   (h) False.
   (c) True.   (f) True.   (i) True.
2. (a) 27.7, 26.7, 23.3, 23: 23.
   (b) 24.57.
   (c) Moving average: MAD 4, MSE 18.88.
       Exponential smoothing: MAD 2.75, MSE 10.6.
3. (a) Smoothing methods are likely to be better because they reflect recent movements in the time series.
   (b) Moving average forecast 160.
       Exponential smoothing forecast 155.5.
   (c) MADs 15.4, 14.7. The MAD measures average error. In the past the exponential smoothing has had a lower MAD and thus this method is likely to give the better forecasts on average.
4. 42.1, 48.6, 50.1, 41.1.

Marketing Information Systems (MKIS): A necessary strategic weapon?

'Forecasting in business, is like sex in society; everybody does it but nobody knows which is the best approach'

High-quality data is a prerequisite for high-quality forecasting. This chapter deals with marketing information systems, with particular reference to consumer decision making. The author is Chris Beaumont, a senior manager with McCann-Erickson.

INTRODUCTION

The business enterprise has two – and only two – basic functions: marketing and innovation. Marketing and innovation produce results; all the rest are costs.

(PETER F. DRUCKER)

Information means power. Power to out-think one's competitors and provide appropriate products/services to fulfill the needs and aspirations of your customers. As markets become more fragmented and competitive, and consumers more sophisticated, marketers need to adopt a more scientific approach to understanding marketing complexity, to deliver long-term, dependable and controllable growth.

Companies across all industries are facing the pressure of increasing competition, whether it is from technological development, modified regulation or market globalisation. Many commentators have highlighted the power of information technology, but today senior management are still daunted by its unrealised potential.

The computing power on people's desks today is equivalent to the power of the mainframe of about eight years ago. Guru James Martin expects desktops of a few years' time to be roughly equivalent in power to the largest mainframe in existence today. To be really reliable the desktop needs to access corporate data. The end-user should not be concerned with where the information is located. Flexibility is the key characteristic. Today, most networks are corporate networks, confined to one organisation. Tomorrow, there will be more inter-corporate networking, such as manufacturers linked directly with their suppliers, customers, retailers and distributors.

We have now moved away from the 'computer era' with its emphasis on internal/administrative applications to the 'information era', with an emphasis on external and strategic applications. Information can be a source of competitive advantage, and it

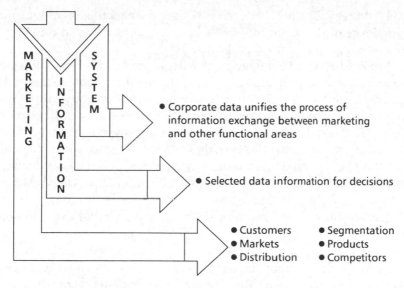

Figure 12.1   MKIS

is a significant additional weapon in the marketer's armoury. Against the backcloth of intensifying competition, the increasing importance of the marketing function as an integral element of business strategy is now being recognised.

In this chapter, the appropriateness of a marketing information system (MKIS) as a 'desktop consultant' is considered. From our experiences, particularly as the dangers of 'data overload' grow with advances in data capture technologies, the statistical methods familiar to market researchers can have an important role in the design, specification and implementation of an MKIS. Generally, with regard to computer-based information systems, too much attention has been given to database management and (graphical) report presentation at the neglect of the necessary analytic engine to transform raw data into useful information which will guide action. This is particularly true in the case of short-term business forcasting, which is the focus of the next chapter.

Throughout the discussion, our orientation is on what the marketer requires, rather than on what the analysts may want to produce. Our focus on MKIS is that it should be driven by (marketing) demand, rather than (IT) supply. Our MKIS is seen as a tool for management support, providing opportunities for future competitive advantage. By so doing, it should be an integral component of a company's competitive strategy, because it provides necessary customer support. Unfortunately, discussions of information technology usually focus on technologies *per se*, rather than on the use of technologies to generate relevant information for decision making. As Figure 12.1 illustrates, it is possible to break down the individual elements of a marketing information system, while simultaneously emphasising the application dimensions.

CONTEXT

The planning of MKIS development has a number of problems/constraints. The lack of commitment from top (Board-level) management and the lack of integration within an overall corporate business strategy are the main problems. (Or, indeed, there is simply no IT strategy.) Furthermore, the generally poor reputation of information services and experience of unfulfilled promises, linked to an inability to consider the nuances of IT investment, can be serious problems.

A major failure is the apparent inability to create simple techniques to ensure a return on investment. It seems that as IT is mentioned the common standards of business practice are forgotten. This situation in part is a symptom of the difference between the DP motivation for computing during the 1970s and 1980s and the current strategic dimension to IT expenditure. When computer systems were solely used to handle invoicing, stock control, payroll and ledgers, they offered the potential to carry out monotonous yet structured tasks and thereby reduce the workforce; clear cost-reduction arguments could be provided. Such a cost-based approach is not possible when systems are developed to handle relatively unstructured and new tasks; the difficulties were compounded when IT became cheaper and more accessible to those people working outside the DP environment.

In our view, it is unrealistic to attempt to justify a strategic IT expenditure by restricting the analyses/justification to the concept of productivity. For marketing information systems, it is necessary to consider explicitly the benefits (rather than merely costs). It is essential to attempt to quantify the argument and derive a return as the ratio of some perceived benefit for a given investment. Although an investment proposal to improve productivity may gain acceptance or at least be comprehended relatively easily, there is no simple evaluation of improved services which produce competitive advantage. Any resource should be invested in a priority area which generates the greatest 'return'. It is necessary to ensure that strategic importance is addressed. The investment decision should consider:

- What is being proposed?
- What are the benefits?
- What are the real costs?
- What are the risks and how should they be managed?
- Who is responsible and who is the product champion?
- What is the action plan, milestones and timetable?

For any business, it is necessary for management to be able to plan and control effectively. An MKIS is deemed to be a decision support tool which can have a number of advantages, including:

- improving coordination and confidence across the company;
- enhancing marketing effectiveness;
- performing as a monitoring system.

It is important to recognise that today most companies have an inability to handle their own database for competitive advantage. In any MKIS, raw data are transformed into information which can be used for making specific decisions. Central to the idea of a corporate database are the establishment and maintenance of a customer database; it is customers to whom marketeers sell products and services. Figure 12.2 identifies changes in the orientation of a customer database. In terms of marketing, concern involves a range of dimensions of interest, such as markets, customers, products and services, distribution channels and competitors. In practice, the information provided is selected as appropriate for the types of decision that a marketer has to make. Moreover, it is essential to

	1960s	1970s	1980s	1990s
MARKETING PURPOSE	Separate channel of distribution	Cost-effective, measurable communications	Cross-selling maximum value of existing base	Maintain and increase customer loyalty
METHOD	Mail order	Direct mail	Direct mail to customers	Integrated communicating mail, telephone (in) sales staff
IMPACT ON DATABASE	Database essential basis for business	Database optional 'junk-mail'	Rationalise Develop for targeting and control	Database essential to manage customer relationships

Figure 12.2   MKIS: a marketing information weapon

recognise that there is a corporate database which is used not only by the marketing function but also by other functional areas.

The development of an MKIS should be driven by marketers, but must involve personnel from other functions. The interrelated elements of MKIS are:

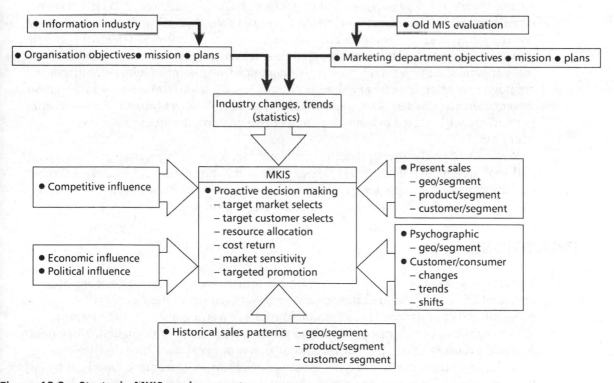

Figure 12.3   Strategic MKIS environment

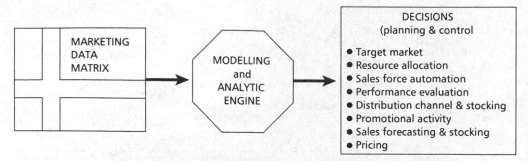

Figure 12.4   For data to be information it must relate to decision making

- strategy and marketing;
- systems and networks;
- communications.

Any successful MKIS must be an integral part of the overall corporate business strategy, whether this strategy is cost leadership, product differentiation or market focus (see Figure 12.3). An essential element is a suitable marketing data matrix, comprising different dimensions of customers, products, services and channels, which will change over time.

Any information system is only as good as the data which are input and updated. However, with advances in data capture technologies, it is clear, that there is a need for greater modelling and analysis to generate information from data. Indeed, while many commentators highlight that there is enormous potential, it should be realised that there are real dangers of 'data overload' unless data are properly structured, collected, collated, stored, and so on. For example, electronic point of sales (EPOS) and the recent use of Nielsen's Scan Track systems generate enormous amounts of raw data which can provide information for stock control, merchandising and branch-level marketing. However, the real dangers of 'data overload' are being experienced, and some retailers/manufacturers are now only using data from a sample of branches for their management information systems; clearly, this raises new analytic issues of sample selection and representation, particularly with regard to branches' competitive position, product range and changes over time.

While we strongly believe that the modelling (the focus of other chapters in this text) and analytic engine are important elements of the transformation of raw data into practical information for marketers, it is of paramount importance that any analysis is undertaken within the context of their decision-making requirements (see Figure 12.4).

APPLICATIONS

The analysis of data to create information has long been viewed as a basic function in organisations and a primary rationale for organisational structure. As the business environment and organisations become more complex, careful planning of the information system, which is becoming the 'central nervous system' of an organisation, is essential. Any MKIS must be able to provide the information to support marketing decision making.

To illustrate the need for analysis, we consider a number of common problems facing most marketers. These all consider the future, but do not necessarily employ statistical forecasting techniques:

- *Sales force automation* – can we sell more effectively?
- *Targeted customer service* – who? what? where?
- *Advertising effectiveness* – how should we spend our promotion budget?
- *Channels of distribution* – what is the balance between direct and indirect demands?
- *Pricing* – how should we price?
- *Forecasting and control* – can we integrate sales and market forecasts company-wide and produce a management monitoring system?

Each of these problem areas is discussed briefly in turn below. The reader should consider how linear programming, project management and other techniques discussed elsewhere in the text may be employed to address the issues described below.

Sales force automation

In terms of sales forces, the usual situation is a lot of data and paper, covering sales reports, core reports, training information, product fliers and so on. Moreover, the databases related to markets, customers, products and services are scattered, difficult to update, incomplete, inaccurate (or simply wrong!). They are primarily in hard copy form and difficult to integrate and much data redundancy exists. Thus, information which would be truly valuable is often buried, not easily accessible and requires reworking for effective use by a sales force.

There is a need to convert data and paper into information which can guide action, focusing on:

- strategy and tactics;
- selling aids;
- decision support;
- competitive intelligence.

The process required to automate the sales force process is dependent on a number of building blocks, which are summarised in Figure 12.5.

Advances in communications and computing capabilities, especially in relation to mobility, have been important. From our evidence the structured capture of field-

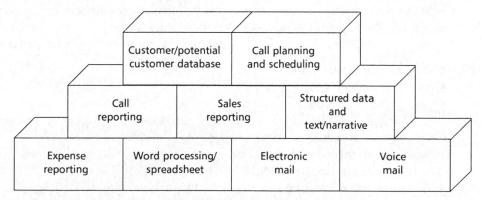

Figure 12.5   Marketing intelligence: building blocks

Benefit category	Example	Characteristics	Observations	Measurement
Efficiency	Allocation of time spent in field	What are we doing?	Direct	● Activity levels ● Costs
Effectiveness	Context and perception of face-to-face market presentations	How do we do it?	Indirect	● Revenue ● Market share ● Competitive perception
Adaptability	Sales support Product information	We can do it!	Indirect Direct	● Customer perception ● Activity levels ● Profitability

Figure 12.6　Setting realistic expectations for benefits

level competitive and market information can lead to:

- improved/focused sales;
- timely market analysis;
- appropriate product/service analysis;
- sensible human resource management;
- desirable accountability and control.

Benefits can be translated into increased productivity and real bottom line advantages such as increased revenue topped by reduced costs and avoidance of unnecessary calls. Figure 12.6 summarises the benefits of sales force automation. Simply stated, salespeople can spend more time selling.

Targeted customer service

The mass marketing of the 1950s and 1960s has been replaced by today's niche marketing, with its great emphasis on customer segmentation and product/service differentiation and on likely future trends on individual customers' lifestyles.

For any targeted customer service, the process can be divided into two stages:

- describe the target market;
- locate the target market.

A number of basic questions should be asked:

- who – should our customers be?
  - – are our customers?
  - – are our competitors?
- what – new/existing products should we develop?
  - – new/existing markets should we enter?

- where – should we develop?
  - – are our customers?
  - – should we distribute our products?
  - – are our competitors?

Given this problem, the solution process is usually in terms of defining customer profiles estimating local market expenditure and then forecasting sales or market share for individual outlets, recognising that the distribution channel could be conventional branches or direct marketing, teleshopping and so on. While location is an important dimension, this must be complemented by merchandising.

The benefits of effective customer service include:

- identification of 'cross-selling' opportunities to existing customers;
- monitoring existing performance;
- sensible merchandising;
- appropriate promotional activity;
- (proactive and reactive) new site appraisal;
- market-led business development.

Advertising effectiveness

'How effective is advertising?' is a pertinent question in the UK given the relatively high costs of TV advertising. Advertising is, depending on your point of view, considered to be wasteful, expensive, communicating information, persuading people to buy goods they do not really want, or what makes watching the TV worthwhile! Yet even this service community is having to justify its high fees to clients requiring a more critical assessment of their advertising spend. Essentially, the issue is that advertising, as an element of the marketing mix, consumes significant resources, with sometimes unclear, indirect returns. There is concern over the efficacy and effectiveness of this marketing tool, especially as there are other strategic and tactical weapons (for example, other forms of promotion, price, packaging).

Variables which need to be considered are not only product value, volume and market share, but also competitors' value and volume and how the structure of the market is changing through the company's own proactive activity and as a consequence of competitors' actions. Evaluation can therefore look at a single campaign idea, a fundamental change in advertising strategy, a change in the amount spent on advertising (for example increasing TV hours) or a change in media (a recent trend as people have recognised the high cost of television and the fact that it only has the potential of mass marketing). It is important to recognise that, within the broader elements of the marketing 'mix', it is necessary to take into account not only the effects of advertising dynamics but also changes in price, packaging, channels of distribution, and so on. In addition, given that one is trying to cultivate an attitude and therefore an action orientation, any effectiveness study must consider the question of ensuring that the particular brand/product strategy has been confirmed.

A flexible and robust process for monitoring advertising effectiveness has been developed which incorporates a number of distinct facets (see Figure 12.7). The context and problem definition need to be investigated in order to provide a description of the environment. Observations of the marketplace can be drawn from an understanding not only

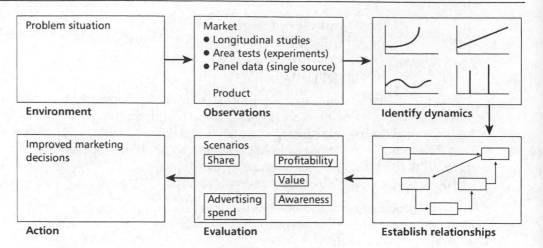

Figure 12.7   Marketing modelling: adding value to data

of the specific product(s) under consideration in terms of functionality and fashion, but also through analysis of longitudinal data, panel data or focus groups, and in certain instances via area tests (pseudo experimentation).

The complexity of the market and the nature of its dynamics should determine the analytical process. Figure 12.8 describes a six-stage, flexible (both in terms of modeling methodology and information analysis) process, which enables one to look at the effectiveness of advertising. It should be noted that this iterative, interactive, action-oriented approach focuses on the marketing environment and the situation within which advertising strategy and decisions are made. We have found that this modelling approach works best when the market being studied has certain characteristics.

The question of data (see Table 12.1), especially data variability and data consistency, needs to be considered in more detail than space permits in this chapter. With regard to the nature of the quantitative information, the questions of continuity and frequency of the historical record must be specified as well as the coverage. Moreover, the timing of

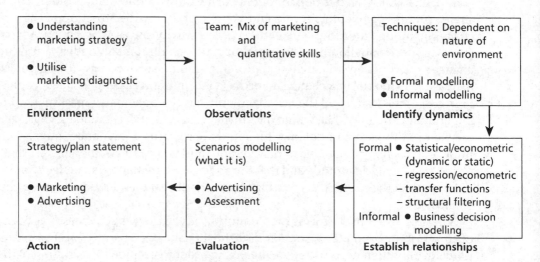

Figure 12.8   Marketing modelling: some comments

Table 12.1   Data requirements

Quantitative	
Nature	● continuous/frequency
	● historical
Coverage	● sales (volume, value)
	● market share(s)
	● prices (relative, constant, real)
	● distribution
	● advertising spend, volume measures (GRPs), by medium
	● sales promotion levels
	● total market and major competitor data on above
Quantitative	
	● product/market positioning
	● marketing and advertising objectives
	● creative/media strategy
	● media shifts
	● agency changes
	● awareness, usage, attitude data

the information should not only be consistent with the decision-making processes within the parent organisation, but also reflect the dynamic characteristics in the marketplace. In practice, modelling and preliminary data analysis are facilitated by recent technology advances in personal computer-based modelling.

Channels of Distribution

Across a number of different sectors, for example the IT marketplace and the retail services environment, the different economics and need to serve a fragmented customer base have led to the issue of the role of the third party (for example original equipment manufacturers). For the manufacturer the crucial issue is to control the balance of direct and the indirect channels, ensuring that in the mind of the end-user there is no conflict of interest.

Thus, within the marketing information system, there is a need not only to understand the motivations, business risks and opportunities which face the individual yet separate third party, but also to hold one's own data in a manner which facilitates control of the channel.

For example, both in terms of the negotiations of discount levels and particularly of the longer-term relationships between the manufacturer and the ultimate customer base, it is inadequate simply to monitor sales performance (volumes and revenues) by products and/or markets. A fundamental dimension is by channel/key account, and it is necessary to incorporate the different costs of distribution and so focus on marginal profitability.

Pricing

With regard to pricing, the most immediate management task for most companies is to establish the market-driven yet economic price for any particular product or service. Conceptually this is not difficult, since at two extremes you have a lower limit which is determined by the cost of production and servicing of the marketplace, and an upper limit which is a realistic premium above which sales are most unlikely. Thus, the price needs to be between these limits; the exact price should reflect market forces, rather than production and cost considerations *per se*.

Figure 12.9 provides a hierarchy of data needs within the retail environment, factors which need to be taken into account when considering the issue of price. This visual representation has three core elements identified by the outer, middle and inner rings. The

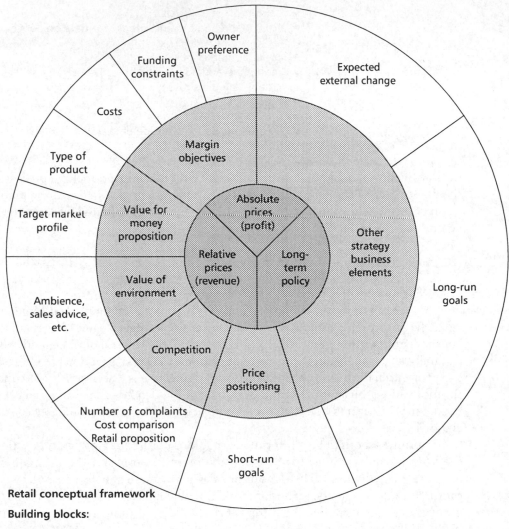

Retail conceptual framework

Building blocks:

Key:
INNER CIRCLE
– elements of pricing policy
MIDDLE CIRCLE
– key influences on pricing policy
OUTER CIRCLE
– main parameters

Figure 12.9   Marketing decisions: pricing

outer circle identifies the main parameters in terms of not only the business and product short-term profitabilities, but also the positioning and distribution of the individual products or brands. Taking this further down the hierarchy, one needs to become concerned with the notion of value for the customer, the point in terms of a money proposition or the environment in which the purchase takes place (for example, note the difference in prices that one can charge for toiletries according to whether they are purchased in a local convenience store, a discount store, a chain store or a special cosmetics department within a major department store). There will necessarily be objectives on margin, which reflect the funding and cost constraints which drive the business, and other strategic issues reflecting competitive action need to be considered in the price determination, if only from a tactical perspective. Thus, the inner circle elements of the pricing policy seek to ensure that a necessary level of revenue and thus absolute profit comes from any long-term policy.

Forecasting and control

A central problem for most companies is to predict the future or reduce uncertainties. Any marketing information system must have a facility for forecasting, which also helps in management control. The key issue that both characterises the manager's dilemma and dominates the academic literature is the question of which forecasting technique to employ. In our experience this is quite a naive and inappropriate view.

The key issue as represented in the Figure 12.10 is the interface between objective analytic techniques and the level of managerial judgement and experience which needs to be incorporated to derive predictions of the future. Within the idealised product life cycle, it is apparent that data-rich analysis is only applicable as the primary analytic tool in one of a subset of life cycle states. Moreover, it is evident from empirical studies that

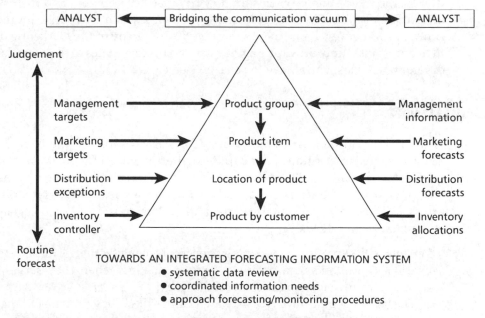

Figure 12.10   Forecasting: methods and decision flows

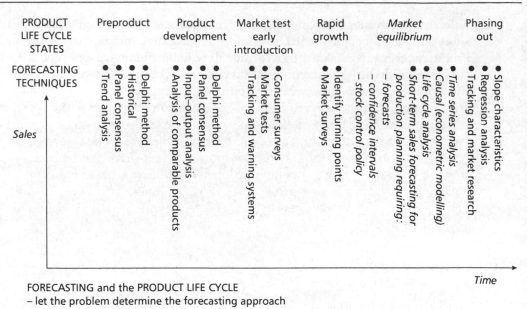

PRODUCT LIFE CYCLE STATES	Preproduct	Product development	Market test early introduction	Rapid growth	*Market equilibrium*	Phasing out

FORECASTING and the PRODUCT LIFE CYCLE
– let the problem determine the forecasting approach

Figure 12.11   Marketing decisions: sales forecasting

the subjective input of managerial expertise into the preparation of forecasts is itself a very *ad hoc* approach.

It is this balancing between quantitative and qualitative information that is the real added value which modelling brings to the marketing information system. What is implicitly indicated in the problem of forecasting within the information system is the need for integrated and systematic reviews of data availability and information needs, coordinated across the business functions of an organisation to a consistent basis for monitoring. Clearly, the forecasting problems for new product development and the risks involved are completely different to the forecasting problems which are routine for the inventory controller. Moreover, as one moves through the hierarchy of the marketing department, then one is not simply providing aggregates and disaggregates of the same data for other, different decisions which have to be taken (see Figure 12.11).

CONCLUSION

Without doubt MKIS is a real opportunity for many companies and is the facilitator for action-oriented forecasting systems. Indeed, there is a need for greater analysis as better quality data becomes available. Data is only useful if it is in the form of information which will guide action. We would envisage a marketing services group, providing a service across all brand teams, in a matrix organisation. The nature and scope of such a service is summarised as follows:

Persons with expertise in marketing science, employed either as full-time staff or as external consultants, can improve decision making when they serve as liaison between the manager and the new technology.

The liaison people have two very important skills. They understand the business and strategic problems that management faces. They also understand enough about data analysis, statistical analysis and modelling to make sure that appropriate checks and questions have been asked when a recommendation based on computer analysis is made. These people should report directly to top and middle management as part of staff groups. That way they will control the quality of the analysis being done. We cannot emphasise enough the importance of having someone who understands data analysis and review management's decisions on strategy.

Source: Lodish, L M and Reibstein, D J (1986) 'Keeping informed – new goldmines and minefields in market research, *Harvard Business Review* 86(1), pp. 168–82.

The real test of being able to integrate internal performance data with marketing research information is clear objective setting and a vision of how the marketing function will evolve. MKIS can be/should be an integral tool, but it has to be carefully developed and implicitly related to the marketing/brand organisational form and the existing decision-making processes. In implementing MKIS, realistic expectations and achievable short-term goals are necessary – it is a tool which improves marketing decision making only if there is an evolution, and not a revolution.

The next section goes to a quite different level of detail and reviews the statistical methodologies appropriate for short-term business forecasting. However, the reader must note that business success is not about statistical acumen. To misquote Disraeli's 'lies, damned lies and statistics', in today's IT environment we have lies, damned lies, statistics and spreadsheets.

QUESTIONS

1. Why are MKIS particularly important in the advertising industry? Discuss the benefits an MKIS can bring in the context of the frameworks presented in the chapter.

2. Choose another industry, for example retailing or insurance, and suggest some applications for an MKIS.

3. What are the critical success factors for implementing an MKIS? Give examples of these factors in the context of an industry or organisation of your choosing.

CHAPTER 13

Forecasting methodologies in practice

'Forecasting is hazardous particularly in relation to the future.'

The range of forecasting methods available is wide. This chapter describes some methods used in brand management, discussing implementation problems and the factors which promote successful forecasting. The author is Chris Beaumont, a senior manager with McCann-Erickson.

INTRODUCTION

This chapter takes the discussion of marketing information systems to the practical level and outlines operationally how forecasts can be generated and business performance monitored. It is divided into three separate yet interrelated sections, for ease of monitored discussion:

- non-time-series based procedures;
- statistical methods for short-term forecasting;
- statistical techniques for monitoring forecasting/performance as the future occurs.

In well-run companies forecasting, in many different manifestations, is pivotal to good management, profitability and controllable growth. In making many commercial decisions there is at least an implicit, if not explicit, recognition of what the future might be. Within the corporate environment there is a need for objectivity and clarity, recognising the difficulty of using personal judgement to address complex and interrelated (as well as political) issues. Forecasting should involve most functions in a company: sales and marketing (volume, value, share); production; distribution; finance (cashflow, etc.); personnel/human resources, etc. A non-trivial management issue is to ensure that forecasts from different functional departments are coherent.

With modern computer processing the forecaster's dilemma is management dissemination of this information, rather than analytic computation. For this reason discussion of the statistical techniques will concentrate on the pitfalls of analysis and interpretation, rather than computation. Microcomputer based software provides a 'user-friendly' environment in which the methodologies described can be readily used. Moreover, computer graphics facilitate interpretation and dissemination within a company by non-technical staff.

The most common techniques of short-term forecasting are based on historical (sales) data. These are often referred to as *time series* methods. Two quite distant approaches are employed:

- extrapolative (Chapter 11);
- causal (Chapters 14 and 15).

Only the former will be discussed in this chapter.

NON-TIME-SERIES BASED PROCEDURES

The choice and application of specific techniques should be governed by the sort of business you are in, and the degree of marketing orientation.

Forecasting techniques, of varying degrees of mathematical and statistical sophistication, have proved particularly successful in the chemical and other industries, where demand is largely dictated by the natural (macro) forces of commerce. However, if you supply products (for example, fast moving consumer goods such as soap powder, tea) to a marketing-oriented environment, then consumer demand is effected by marketing stimuli (price, promotions, advertising, direct mail, etc.). Any mathematical model requires historical data as a base for its forecasts, and this data should be 'cleaned up' (adjusted) in order to isolate and remove the impact of marketing factors (your own and your competitors') which have influenced sales.

In categories where demand is influenced by marketing initiatives, statistical forecasts often lose the richness of understanding about the marketplace. A good forecast is one which makes the best use of all of the information available.

That is not to discount the statistical methods discussed in the next section. Rather, one employs them to provide a more macro baseline forecast of market sizes, or to evaluate the effectiveness of an advertising campaign, for example. In such market categories, the forecaster should have reservations, for practical reasons, about the more detailed areas of product line sales on a month-to-month basis.

So how can one forecast? It is necessary to approach a forecast from two directions. First, use simple statistical techniques of forecasting, discussed in the next section, to extrapolate sales performance to the year ahead; the period breakdown is estimated by arriving at a common-sense base level and adjusting the line to compensate for proposed marketing activity and seasonality. Secondly, the first stage of developing an annual forecast is carried out by extrapolating the total market size and forecasting (simple techniques) a brand share. The period breakdown is derived as for the first method.

FMCG companies make extensive use of market and consumer research data to help them arrive at forecasts, and particularly to help overcome practical problems encountered en route. Dialogue with the consumer is a constant one. They use information in any one year which has been derived from interviews with consumers and in-store checks. With existing or ongoing brands this research is designed to monitor the attitudes of the consumer towards products or brands and to detect any changes in consumer usage of them. In this way, the aim is to be able to detect trends in the marketplace, sometimes even before they are reflected in sales data.

One useful procedure is a *retail audit*. A retail audit takes a representative sample of stores in whichever sector of the trade is being examined (e.g. supermarkets, grocers, chemists, off-licences) and, by checking invoices against stock within defined periods of time, is able to provide information about consumer sales, retailer purchases, shop and sterling distribution, brand share, stock cover, out of stock and so on. It should also provide this information by area and by different types of outlet (for example multiples, cooperatives and independents in the grocery trade). This information is particularly valuable in monitoring competitive activity, isolating problem sales areas, and determining the effectiveness of promotional activity. It is also helpful to forecasters. If the sales of a product suddenly start to decline the reasons can be manifold, and it is a brave person who calls it a trend and predicts forward without knowing the reasons behind the decline.

The retail audit enables the forecaster to identify some of the possible reasons. The actions necessary and the resulting forecasts of sales would be very different, depending on which of the reasons was felt to be appropriate. Some of these reasons could be short term and would wield far less influence on forecasts than the others. These audits are very useful also in helping to assess the effects of promotional activity. One naturally expects different weights of promotion to have differing impacts. By having such promotional stock separately itemised, one can see the rapidity of sell in and sell out, and from that gauge the amounts required and, just as important, go some way to assessing the subsequent effect on future sales.

As an adjunct to the retail audit, which provides a trade perspective, it is also invaluable to undertake a *consumer audit*. The principle is similar: a sample of households is regularly audited to monitor their purchases in certain product fields. From this one can derive (1) the *volume* of products bought, (2) the *frequency* with which they are purchased, (3) the *share* of the consumers' purchases in relation to competitors. Simple cross-tabulation of such data can reveal a multitude of useful facts to the marketer. We shall come back to this type of audit when discussing new product forecasting, but it also has application to established brands.

How can this help? Imagine that one has identified the problem with a hypothetical product to be a consumer one from the retail audit. From consumer audit data it is possible to determine why one is losing sales. There are three ways in which this can happen: consumers stop buying, buy less, or buy less of your brand and more of others. Again, the factors which one isolates as being most important will undoubtedly influence the decisions one makes and the view one takes about sales in the future. Other analyses of this data enable one to analyse more precisely the effect on sales of trade behaviour; for example, do consumers go to another outlet to buy their favourite brand if it is not available in their normal store? Similarly, one can establish the demographics of the consumers who buy specific products, or of consumers who buy other products in the market, and that information can be used to direct more precisely advertising or consumer promotions.

A third audit which is commonly used is a U/A (usage and attitude) benchmark 'Monitor'. For a long time researchers have classified people by fairly obvious criteria such as age, sex, marital status, number of children, working or non-working housewife and occupation of head of household. Monitor postulates that attitudes towards life and living can also be important influences on behaviour and to an extent are determining factors in purchasing decisions (see Figure 13.1). By using this *continuous* study of social trends

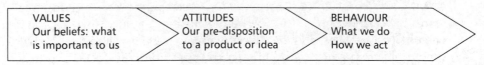

Figure 13.1

to establish which attitudes or groups of attitudes exist, and then establishing how these relate to purchasing behaviour, one has a valuable extra indicator of how purchasing habits may be expected to change. One example of this would be the share of markets which own-label products will take.

Finally, in relation to existing products, it is appropriate to briefly discuss various other types of *ad hoc* consumer research which can be helpful to the forecaster. Broadly, they can be labelled 'diagnostic' and their use is in determining whether or not the remedy will restore sales or, in the case of an upward trend, to what degree it is likely to be sustained.

To summarise, although the above discussion has not focused on sophisticated forecasting techniques, considerable use of sophisticated analyses help a company to understand the markets in which it trades and the consumers who buy products. Through these analyses one pieces together, rather like a jigsaw puzzle, a picture of the marketplace. However, to continue the analogy, this futuristic puzzle always has a few pieces missing and it is the forecaster who has to predict what the final piece (the actual outcome in a specific time period) will look like. The paradox for the forecaster in a marketing environment is that one of the purposes of the forecasts is to enable managers to take corrective action when the forecast trend is unfavourable, and perhaps to economise on costly activities when the forecast trend is more favourable. For this reason, the good forecaster suffers from an insoluble problem. The more attention a manager pays to the forecast, the less likely it is to occur; managers will try to defeat a forecast which they find unacceptable and, by default, may ease their efforts where the forecast indicates probable success.

Consider now the forecasting of new products. A new product passes through several stages before an 'idea' becomes a national brand. At each stage a forecast has to be made. Quite simply, is it worth proceeding with the project? New product forecasting divides into (1) new products in existing markets and (2) new products in new markets. Reliable background information can be found or purchased for the majority of existing markets. This provides invaluable baseline data for approaching the forecast. From this information one can usually determine market size in volume and value, brand share, distribution, rate of sale, penetration (number of people who have ever bought) and frequency of purchase data. With this information one can draw the parameters of the market one hopes to enter.

Another most valuable input is the reaction of the consumer to the product one proposes launching – using consumer research in a predictive rather than diagnostic fashion is a far more difficult proposition. Nevertheless, a great amount of work has been done by a number of companies in fast moving non-durables in this field. There are two stages. The first is to establish a set of questions which will cover the appropriate decision areas in the purchasing motivation of the consumer; to devise questions in forms which will accurately measure consumer response to new product ideas and to concepts at a relatively early stage of their development.

The second stage is to establish norms for these scales. The classic manner of testing new products among consumers is by placing them in a representative sample of households, leaving them with the respondent for a set period of time, and then returning to question them about their opinions of, and reactions to, the product. It is the kinds of questions one asks within that framework which are all important to the forecaster. Basically, one attempts to measure reactions to the concepts both before and after testing, reactions to the price, a scale which combines both of these into a propensity to serve or purchase, and finally a scale designed to give added dimensionality in terms of frequency of purchasing occasions. It is the pattern of results which is of greater importance than any individual mean score. Over time one has been able to identify a level of scores above which the product in question should be capable of marketplace success. The mean scores above which success should be possible have become known as the norms. In addition, if one is launching into an existing market, it is possible to assess the performance of a product in a blind or branded test against the competition; knowing the rate of the sale and rate of purchase variables of the competitive product provides a yardstick for assessing probable performance of one's own brand.

Establishing norms allows one to be informed about the market at which one is aiming and the product intended for launch. In addition, one must make some further assessments: the ability of the sales force to gain distribution; the level of marketing support; whether the price is right; whether the trade margin is adequate; the penetration of other brands in the market.

Finally, it is necessary to examine the situation where one is called on to forecast for new products which will themselves create a market. We have demonstrated the way in which consumer research can help the forecaster in more straightforward situations. It can be of even greater help here. The logic in attempting to forecast these new products is the same as for those in existing markets. The same factors are important and must be considered; the problem is that there is no market or market norm to act as a guide. The potential market has first to be created and the growth of that market and the particular brand within it has to be forecast. In the main one attempts to gather together information about the potential target audience – which is where consumer research comes in. What products similar in concept to this one do they currently use; how loyal are they to those products; how often do they find themselves in the situation where one envisages this product is going to be used, and so on. This kind of circumstantial information is combined together with the kind of assumption made about the sector and a forecast is derived.

A major aid to the forecasting of future sales of a new product is a test market. This can be defined as 'a real life trial of a marketing mix on a small scale where the trade and consumer can be observed in normal market conditions'. In other words, a test market attempts to replicate fully the conditions which the product or proposition will experience on full sale, but to do it in such a way as to enable the effect of controlled inputs (the product and its marketing mix) to be measured. Although costly to undertake, by both improving the quantification of the opportunity and enabling potential improvements to be diagnosed, a test market leads to better forecasts and reduces or limits the degree of risk in marketing (or business) decision making. It does, however, give direct information to competitors!

The foregoing discussion has demonstrated that forecasting in practice is not so much a science, but an art. The art is to bring together, in an intelligent way, a multiplicity of marketing intelligence information to make an objective assessment the future. *All* forecasts are wrong; it is the good forecaster who understand the measure of the uncertainly and is able to plan in such circumstances. No approach can obviate risk. Statistical procedures of data analysis provide the probabilistic framework to quantify uncertainty and these are discussed in the next section. A forecaster who says both Products A and B will sell 100 million units next quarter is not doing a good job. To provide the appropriate guidance to management it is necessary to put forecasting *confidence limits* around these 'average' forecasts. To say you are 95 per cent confident that Product A will sell between 95 and 105 million units next quarter, whereas you believe Product B will sell between 80 and 120 million units, is far more informative. It does not mean necessarily that you have less knowledge about Product B, rather that the product sells in a more volatile marketplace.

STATISTICAL METHODS FOR SHORT-TERM FORECASTING

In time series analysis, we take a historical time series and attempt to construct a simple mathematical model which describes its behaviour. The analysis consists of identifying and measuring trends, patterns and changes in both of these entirely on the basis of the past behaviour of the series. The trends, patterns and rates of change are projected forward to forecast the future. Although the underlying mechanism generating the time series is *not* understood, one assumes that future behaviour will be much like that in the past (the past, the present and the future are synonymous). Since this is more likely to hold in the short term, time series analysis is more often used for the short as opposed to medium term. Forecasts based on projections cannot *anticipate* changes and in particular cannot predict 'turning points'.

In causal modelling, one attempts to understand more and gain some insight into the underlying mechanism generating a time series. One tries to explain the behaviour of the time series in terms of other variables. The analysis focuses on relationships between variables and on constructing the structural rules which best generate the observations. The main statistical tool is regression analysis. Since the underlying causation is modelled, forecasts can often be made with more confidence and further into the future. If all the crucial determinants of the time series have been captured correctly in the model, it should be possible to forecast turning points satisfactorily. However, to forecast with such models needs forecasts of *all* explanatory variables! Building such a model for a time series is clearly a much more sophisticated and costly activity than merely projecting trends and patterns observed in the past into the future. Moreover, when the basic structure of a market changes (a new entrant or channel of distribution, for example), historical relationships modelled by regression analysis may in themselves fall down. (Reflect on the discussion in the previous section.)

The main focus in this section is on short-term forecasting of a routine nature and hence on simple time series analysis and projection. For example, in controlling inventory sales of tens of thousands of items, very large number of forecasts of demand are required relatively frequently (say monthly).

Consider the different time series illustrated in Figures 13.2–13.4. Looking at these examples, we can see the major components making up a time series:

- *Trend* – this is the long-term movement of the series, either upwards (growth) or downwards (decline). It results from long-run influences usually of an economic, brand, social or political nature.
- *Periodic variation* – often groups of causes which function periodically and not continuously affect a time series. The most common type of periodic oscillation is a *seasonal effect*. Seasonal effects are oscillations which are annual in period and are explainable in terms of a seasonal phenomenon.

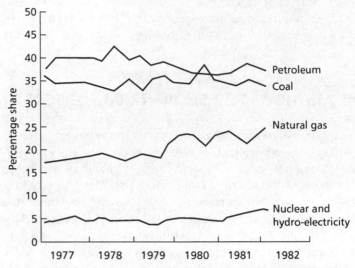

Figure 13.2   Percentage share of total inland energy

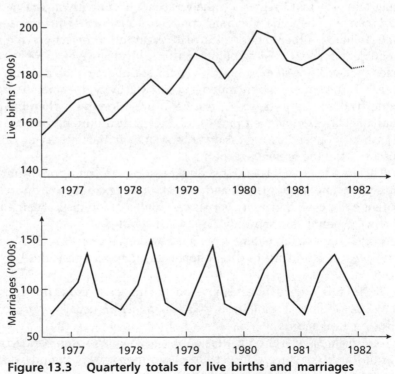

Figure 13.3   Quarterly totals for live births and marriages

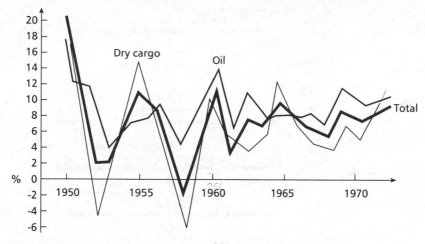

Figure 13.4   Percentage yearly change in world trade 1950–70

- *Cyclical movements* – these differ from periodic movements in that they are usually longer than a year in period and are often irregular in periodicity. For example business cycles, which are not random oscillations as the business activity in one quarter (or year) influences activity in following quarters, etc. Some long-term business cycles are said to correspond to political cycles in government. In practice, the most important fact to understand is that if one wishes to estimate cycles accurately they have to have repeated themselves at least three times. Some of the data, if available, will be very old and possibly irrelevant.
- *Random variation* – these are the unsystematic oscillations, owing to a variety of causes which are essentially irregular in effect.

Finally, in all the series we have examined there is still some residual movement from period to period, even after we have isolated the main trend, seasonal and cyclical movements. One hopes this is random – has no structure. This is the random component, which results from irregular, unpredictable, once-and-for-all events. The size of this component indicates the uncontrollable element and the level of uncertainly associated with any forecast.

In what is the most important contribution to statistical forecasting in the last three decades, Professors G.E.P. Box and G.M. Jenkins, in their book *Time Series Analysis, Forecasting and Control*, gave an excellent synthesis of the theory and properties of a flexible class of linear models for time series analyses. More importantly, this exposition was within a practical forecasting methodology. Their philosophy was that any reasonable approach to model building and forecasting needs to be interactive and self-learning. They proposed that it should be conducted in three discrete yet closely interpolated stages, prior to using the fitted model for forecasting (Figure 13.5). This assumes that the preliminary stage when the actual class of model is stipulated has been undertaken, which in the strictest sense should not be done. This philosophy is appropriate for any modelling approach.

The remainder of this chapter will be devoted to illustrating the analysis and forecasting of a single time series of AIRLINE passenger data (Figure 13.6). The methods applied to this historical series are principally exponential smoothing and Box–Jenkins, having obtained a feel for the structure of the time series by employing decomposition and other

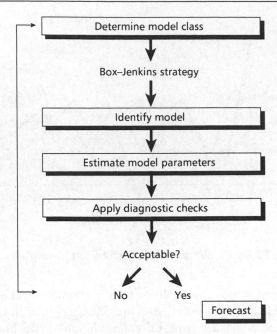

Figure 13.5   Towards the development of a forecasting model

simple models. The underlying precept is that the forecasting model has to be able to produce forecasting confidence intervals, since the forecaster has to be able to quantify his or her uncertainty. This requires an emphasis not on the generation of forecasts but on assessing the appropriateness of the model to the historical data. As such, the discussion below will focus on a battery of diagnostic tools to understand the model's efficacy. All the forecasting models described in this chapter and their diagnostic statistics are typically available in PC-based forecasting software. An understanding of the implication of the diagnostic tools is especially critical with today's software, which is able to produce forecasts automatically. The reader should note that (from com-prehensive empirical studies of real commercial data) *there is so single best forecasting technique*.

From a visual inspection of the monthly AIRLINE series (Figure 13.6) it is evident that there are both a trend and a seasonal component. Since the within-year valuation in absolute terms tends to increase with the trend, one can conclude that a *multiplicative* model is appropriate. This is the most common form of trend-seasonal interaction. (The other common assumption is the *additive* model – visually the seasonal pattern would be completely independent of the trend level.) The multiplicative model is assuming that proportionately the sales in January February, . . . December remain constant. The form of trend-seasonal interaction is important, since this determines the type of forecasting model to be applied whether one uses Box–Jenkins or exponential smoothing. The basic features of the AIRLINE services are summarised below:

Depend variable AIRLINE

Length 144	Minimum 104.000	Maximum 622.000
Mean 280.299	Standard deviation 119.549	

Classical decomposition (multiplicative)

Trend cycle: 91.25 per cent	Seasonal: 8.16 per cent	Irregular: 0.59 per cent

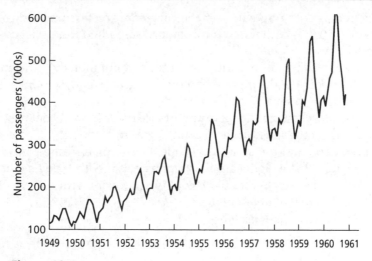

Figure 13.6

Smoothing models by their very name seek to 'smooth out' the minor period-to-period fluctuations in a historical series to provide a smooth extrapolation. One of the simplest smoothing models for a series $X_t\{X_1 \ldots X_n\}$ of observations is to take a k-point *moving average* X_t.

$$\mathrm{MA1} = \frac{X_1 + X_2 + \ldots + X_k}{k}$$

$$\mathrm{MA2} = \frac{X_2 + X_3 + \ldots + X_{k+1}}{k}$$

If the series is seasonal it is important to ensure that no seasonal bias is incorporated in any projection. One fundamental problem with such equally weighted moving averages is that old data is given as much importance as the most recent information. Intuitively this is unreasonable, and empirically it has been demonstrated to be less accurate than exponential smoothing models.

Exponential smoothing techniques are the most popular methods for short-term forecasting because they are computational efficient, robust to fluctuations in data, accurate and very easy to understand.

The most common methods of exponential smoothing are referred to as the Holt–Winters family. The time series is assumed to be modelled by one, two or three elements to represent level, trend and seasonality respectively. If the model includes a trend it is usually forecasted linearly into the future, or occasionally using a damped exponential that eventually dies out to a constant level. The seasonal component can be either multiplicative or additive, to reflect its relationship with the trend.

In simple exponential smoothing, the only element is the level of the series. This assumes that the data are irregular variations around a relatively stable level. Such a model is inappropriate when the data exhibits either a trend and/or seasonality. When there is a trend, the Holt two-parameter model is appropriate – it assumes fluctuations about a level that is changing with some linear trend. For seasonal series, the Holt technique is extended (Holt–Winters) to incorporate a smoothed multiplicative or additive seasonal index.

Whatever the model form, each uses computationally efficient recursive equations which smooth out the model components (level, trend, season) as necessary. Each equation has its own smoothing parameter which takes any value between 0 and 1. This is the *exponential* weight, giving more importance to the more recent past in generating updates (forecasts) of the series. If the weight(s) are large, the most recent past is very important in prediction and the series is volatile, or adaptive. Some consideration in other texts is given to what weights are most appropriate. With today's computer power this is a non-issue; the weights should be optimised (over a grid search) on the basis of the best historical fit to the time series.

Simple exponential smoothing

$$S_t = \alpha X_t + (1 - \alpha)X_{t-1}$$

with the k-step ahead forecast

$$\hat{X}_t(k) = S_t$$

Holt (two-parameter; α, β) exponential smoothing has a forecasting equation:

$$\hat{X}_t(k) = S_t + KT_t$$

with smoothing equations for

level: $$S_t = \alpha X_t + (1 - \alpha)(S_{t-1} + T_{t-1})$$

trend: $$T_t = \beta(S_t - S_{t-1}) + (1 - \beta)T_{t-1}$$

In the damped trend form of this Holt model, forecasts are developed as a damped exponential rather than linear trend:

$$X_t(k) = S_t + (\phi + \phi^2 + \ldots + \phi^n)T_t$$

Otherwise the model is identical to the basic Holt form (indeed when $\phi = 1$ they are equivalent).

Holt–Winters three-parameter (α, β, γ) exponential smoothing assumes that each observation is based on a de-seasonalised value and a seasonal index for each month (quarter). The de-seasonalised values one models by the Holt model above. It has a forecasting equation in the multiplicative form with the smoothing equations:

level: $$S_t = \alpha \frac{X_t}{Se_{t-s}} + (1 - \alpha)(S_{t-1} + T_{t-1})$$

trend: $$T_t = \beta(S_t - S_{t-1}) + (1 - \beta)T_{t-1}$$

season: $$Se_t = \gamma \frac{X_t}{Se_t} + (1 - \gamma)Se_{t-s}$$

where s is the number of seasonal periods.

Table 13.1   Forecast model for AIRLINE

Multiplicative Winters: Linear trend, multiplicative seasonality

Component	Smoothing weight
Level	0.265
Trend	0.0205
Seasonal	0.7929

Indexes for periods	1–12	0.91	0.85	0.94
		0.989	1.01	1.14
		1.31	1.29	1.07
		0.948	0.804	0.886

Standard diagnostics

Sample size 144	Number of parameters 3
Mean 280.3	Standard deviation 120
R-square 0.922	Adjusted R-square 0.9919
Durbin–Watson 1.436	**Ljung–Box (18) = 35.84 P = 0.9926
Forecast error 10.81	BIC 11.27
MAD 7.968	RMSE 10.7

Forecasts of AIRLINE from base period 1960–12

Period	Lower 2.5	Forecast	Upper 97.5
1961–01	424.811	446.890	468.970
1961–02	396.929	419.802	442.675
1961–03	443.269	466.940	490.611
1961–04	469.953	494.426	518.899
1961–05	481.565	506.844	532.123
1961–06	549.484	575.573	601.663

For the AIRLINE series the only appropriate model to consider because of the seasonality present is Holt–Winters. The results of estimating and forecasting such a model are shown in Table 13.1.

As well as checking whether a particular model is acceptable or not, prior to using the model to produce forecasts it is also efficient to utilise the same battery of diagnostic techniques to compare the relative fit, to the historical data, of different models. The fundamental assumption is that the best-fitting model will also provide the best forecasts.

In summarising the fit of the Holt–Winter model to the AIRLINE series, a number of different summary statistics were given. These show the efficacy (or otherwise) of a particular estimated model. It is sensible to employ the same diagnostic for different model classes so that two comparisons can be made. Essentially these diagnostics focus on analyses of the residuals of the series after the model has been fitted to the time series. There are broadly two components to such analyses, addressing (1) whether the series is random (all consistent patterns have been modelled); and (2) the magnitude of the uncertainly (and by implication the size of the forecasting errors). The standard numerical diagnostics include:

Random?

- Durbin–Watson
- Ljung–Box

Uncertainty?

- R-square ((un)adjusted)
- Forecast error
- MAPE
- MAD
- BIC

These are commonly used in conjunction with graphical auto-correlation techniques (see below). Indeed, Durbin–Watson and Ljung–Box are themselves diagnostic statistics based on the residual auto-correlation foundations under the assumption that all auto-correlation coefficients are zero (no structure). The Durbin–Watson test concentrates on the first lag auto-correlation, while the Ljung–Box diagnostic looks at the sum of usually the first 20 auto-correlations. The former therefore looks at a specific lag, while the latter is concerned with the overall fit of the model.

With regard to the overall fit of a model, the R-square statistic (unadjusted) provides a descriptive measure of the historical variation explained by the model. The adjusted R-square takes into account how many parameters there are in the model to obtain this degree of explanation. The basic tenet is to attempt to keep the forecasting model as simple as possible (with as few parameters as possible). That being said, the most straightforward diagnostic of 'best' model is the BIC which is based on information theory. The 'best' model is that which minimises the BIC. However, this diagnostic really is too mathematical for many business forecasters (who quite rightly do *not* wish to understand the mathematics behind the procedures employed). For this reason the mean absolute percentage error (MAPE) and mean absolute deviation (MAD), whose names are self-explanatory, are often used to compare the efficacy of different models.

In their seminal forecasting text, Box and Jenkins utilised *auto-correlation* techniques as a mechanism for identifying the particular form of the model class they proposed. (Now commonly referred to as Box–Jenkins models, these are the ARIMA (autoregressive integrated moving average) family of stochastic processes). In fact, this procedure is also an important diagnostic tool for detecting whether a residual series is random. Correlation analysis seeks to quantify (in a standardised form) the magnitude of a relationship between two variables – for example, temperature and sales of ice-cream. Auto-correlation analysis measures the relationship *within* a time series between observations at different lags. Auto-correlation coefficients range between −1 and +1; values around zero imply no structure at a specific lag. For a random series all auto-correlation coefficients at any lag should not be significantly different from zero. The simplest way of interpretating auto-correlations is visually in the form of a *correllelogram* (Figure 13.7).

Exponential smoothing models are relatively adaptive (high smoothing parameters) models, but if the structure of the time series is relatively stable then Box–Jenkins models tend to be more accurate. In context, one would intuitively expect macro market sales data to be more stable than individual product histories in the same category.

While exponential smoothing models are simple in form and readily understood, the mathematical form of even the simplest ARIMA models does not lend itself to communication with the end-user of the forecasts. Moreover, the ARIMA models require at least 40 observations before the auto-correlation structure can be robustly estimated and used to identify the appropriate ARIMA model. It is beyond the scope of this chapter to describe in any detail the forms of ARIMA models. The reader should note that modern computer

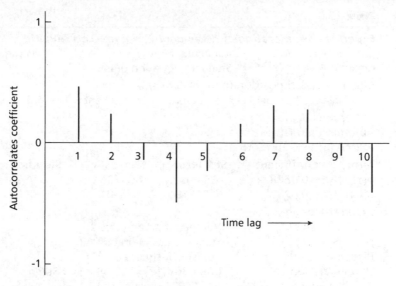

Figure 13.7   A correllelogram

software is able to identify the most appropriate model form automatically. Although this runs counter to the original thesis of Box–Jenkins, if they are used carefully and their efficacy compared with the exponential smoothing, then they have become a practical alternative. The process of residual analyses is as described for exponential smoothing.

Returning to the AIRLINE series, the summary in Table 13.2. is the diagnostic fit and forecasts produced by an automatically identified ARIMA model. The generic form of the

Table 13.2

Forecast model for AIRLINE
Automatic model selection
ARIMA (1, 1, 0)*(0, 1, 0)$_{12}$

Term	Coefficient	Std. error	t-statistic	Significance
a[1]	−0.3142	0.0826	−3.8043	0.9999

Standard Diagnostics

Sample size 131	Number of parameters 1
Mean 295.6	Standard deviation 114.8
R-square 0.9895	Adjusted R-square 0.9595
Durbin–Watson 1.958	Ljung–Box (18) = 18.54 P = 0.5794
Forecast error 11.75	BIC 11.92
MAD 9.013	RMSE 11.7

Forecasts of AIRLINE from base period 1960–12

Period	Lower 2.5	Forecast	Upper 97.5
1961–01	420.942	444.314	467.686
1961–02	389.875	418.215	446.556
1961–03	412.492	446.246	480.001
1961–04	450.164	488.237	526.309
1960–05	457.195	499.240	541.284
1961–06	516.594	562.239	607.883

Table 13.3

Expert data exploration of dependent variable – Log AIRLINE

Length 144	Minimum 4.644	Maximum 6.433
Mean 5542	Standard deviation 0.440	

Classical decomposition (multiplicative)

Trend cycle: 91.55 per cent	Seasonal: 7.92 per cent	Irregular: 0.53 per cent

Forecast model for
Automatic model selection
ARIMA (0, 1, 1)*(0, 1, 1)

Term	Coefficient	Std. error	t-Statistic	Significance
b[1]	0.3878	0.1116	3.4733	0.9995
B[12]	0.6203	0.01719	8.6301	1.0000

Standard diagnostics

Sample size 131	Number of parameters 2
Mean 5.613	Standard deviation 0.3968
R-square 0.9916	Adjusted R-square 0.9915
Durbin–Watson 1.972	Ljung-Box (18) = 17.48 P = 0.5099
Forecast error 0.03651	BIC 0.0376 (Best so far)
MAPE 0.005156	RMSE 10.03623
MAD 0.02857	

Forecasts of AIRLINE from base period 1960–12

Period	Lower 2.5	Forecast	Upper 97.5
1961–01	6.036	6.110	6.183
1961–02	5.969	6.056	6.142
1961–03	6.081	6.179	6.276
1961–04	6.091	6.199	6.306
1960–05	6.114	6.231	6.347
1961–06	6.244	6.369	6.494

ARIMA class of model is ARIMA (p, d, q) (P, D, Q)s where p, d, q reflect the within-year auto-correlation structure and P, D, Q form the seasonal(s), between-year structure.

However, the robustness of the Box–Jenkins model suggests that it may be necessary to *transform* the original series prior to fitting a model. The fact that the season–trend interaction of the AIRLINE series is multiplicative necessitates a logarithmic transformation, since the seasonal variation is in proportion to the level of the series. The process of modelling of the transformed series is as with the original series; forecasts are produced, once the residuals have been checked, in the transformed scale and then adjusted back to the original units. Transformations in practice tend to worry management since they often perceive it to be an unnecessary complexity. The best software tends to tell the user whether a transformation is necessary or not, but often such software does not retransform the forecasts back to the original units. This is clearly rather frustrating and practically very inconvenient.

MONITORING AND CONTROL

In the author's experience the generation of forecasts should only be the first stage in the process of effective business planning. Forecasts are there to be beaten, for example by proactive and imaginative marketing initiatives. The original forecasts produced provide

Table 13.4

Week	Forecast	Actual	Error	% Error	CUSUM
1	80	80	0	0.0	0
2	80	88	8	9.1	8
3	80	92	12	13.0	20
4	80	76	−4	−5.3	16
5	80	67	−13	−19.4	3
6	80	90	10	11.1	13
7	80	85	5	5.9	18
8	80	76	−4	−5.3	14
9	80	65	−15	−23.1	−1
10	80	80	0	0	−1
11	80	71	−9	−12.7	−10
12	80	86	6	7.0	−4
13	80	88	8	9.1	4
14	80	74	−6	−8.1	−2
15	80	76	−4	−5.3	−6
16	80	74	−6	−8.1	−15
17	80	85	5	5.9	−7
18	80	82	2	2.4	−5
19	80	81	1	1.2	−4
20	80	76	−4	−5.3	−8
21	80	80	0	0.0	−8
22	80	92	12	13.0	4
23	80	90	10	11.1	14
24	80	76	−4	−5.3	10
25	80	69	−11	−15.9	−1
26	80	68	−15	−17.6	−13
27	80	74	−6	−8.1	−19
28	80	76	−4	−5.3	−23
29	80	78	−2	−2.6	−25
30	80	74	−6	−8.1	−31
31	80	91	11	12.1	−20
32	80	80	0	0.0	−20
33	80	74	−6	−8.1	−26
34	80	82	2	2.4	−24
35	80	74	−6	−8.1	−30
36	80	68	−12	−17.6	−42
37	80	82	2	2.4	−40
38	80	84	4	4.8	−36
39	80	72	−8	−11.1	−44
40	80	81	1	1.2	−43
41	80	76	−4	−5.3	−47
42	80	78	−2	−2.6	−49
43	80	82	2	2.4	−47
44	80	84	4	4.8	−43
45	80	72	−8	−11.1	−51
46	80	82	2	2.4	−49
47	80	81	1	1.2	−48
48	80	87	7	8.0	−41
49	80	67	−13	−19.4	−54
50	80	84	4	4.8	−50
51	80	82	2	2.4	−48
52	80	71	−9	−12.7	−57

the basis on which managerial actions can be objectively assessed. This section briefly describes two alternative statistical approaches which can be employed to compare actual performance (when it occurs) with earlier forecasts. Since almost all market categories have a structure and business practices are relatively disciplined and not schizophrenic, such comparisons should not simply compare forecasts and actuals separately for each time period (every month, say). Where there are even large differences this can in fact be a random (and therefore uncontrollable) deviation, rather than a good (or bad) sign for the company. All too often managers look at each month's data in isolation, and by not monitoring cumulative month-on-month differences from the forecasts tend to change their activities very often, leading to considerable inefficiencies both internally through the misuse of company resources, and externally by maintaining excess (or inadequate inventories) in the marketplace.

The two techniques described below are quite different in how they allow managers to control the forecasting process and monitor business performance. The first, called the *CUSUM* (cumulative sum) technique, is a single simple measure of cumulative difference from forecasts, analogous to how golfers remember their scores (to par) during a round of golf. (This analogy is particularly relevant to executives.) The second approach is to build a forecasting model which itself can automatically adjust its model parameters as new actual data becomes available. This approach uses a technique referred to as *Trigg's tracking signal*.

CUSUM is based on the cumulative sum of the forecast errors, set to zero at the outset:

$$\text{CUSUM}_t = \text{CUSUM}_{t-1} + (\text{Actual}_t - \text{Forecast}_t)$$

$$= \text{CUSUM}_{t-1} + \text{Error}_t$$

In the example in Table 13.4 a car rental company wished to track utilisation rates at a depot near an international airport. (Therefore there should be no seasonality and/or trend.) To meet their financial targets they had to achieve an average utilisation of 80 per cent. The table summarises their achievement during a year. How well did they do?

Inspection of the weekly error figures hides a systematic trend of underperformance. During the early part of the year the achieved utilisation did seem to fluctuate around the goal. However, inspection of the CUSUM demonstrates an increasingly worse situation from about week 25 (when they began not to keep to par), when action should have been taken to control their business. Simply plotting their actual performance (Figure 13.8) would not have demonstrated this worsening situation as easily as a simple chart of the weekly CUSUM statistics (Figure 13.9).

A popular monitoring device, usually used with the simple exponential smoothing model described earlier, is *Trigg's tracking signal*. This is based on similar principles to the basic precept of the exponential smoothing model, but focuses on the forecast's errors. Rather than look at the individual errors it calculates a smoothed error, which is a weighted sum of past forecast errors. As in the forecasting model more weight is given to the more recent errors by employing an exponential weight, α (usually for convenience the same as in the forecasting equation). This smoothed error is then standardised (to take value between -1 and $+1$) so that the forecast does not have to take into account the units of the data. Computationally this device is very simple to implement. Table 13.5 shows the equations which could be readily incorporated into any spreadsheet environment.

Absolute values of the tracking signal (T_t) close to 1 indicate errors which are large and

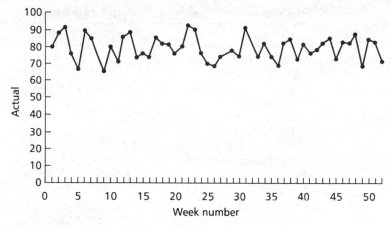

Figure 13.8   Actual performance

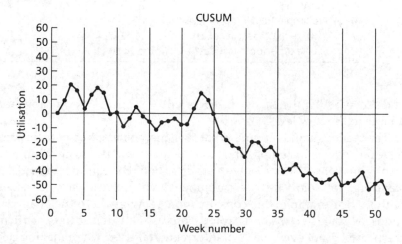

Figure 13.9   CUSUM

the model is out of control. You will recall that when a series is relatively volatile then the most appropriate exponential weight is close to 1. This led to the development of a truly adaptive exponential smoothing model where the smoothing weight (α) changes from period to period, being equal to the modulus of T_t / T_t. In such instance the adaptive simple exponential smoothing equation becomes

$$S_t = |T_t|X_t + (1 - \alpha)X_{t-1}$$

This model tends to be too volatile since it reacts to every change immediately, some of which can be random fluctuations. A far more robust form is to set the value of (α) equal to the previous value of the tracking signal $|T_{t-1}|$. In which case the adaptive form of the simple exponential smoothing equation takes the form:

$$S_t = |T_t|X_t + (1 - |T_t|)X_{t-1}$$

The advantage of this form of the forecasting model is that it has one time period to 'look

Table 13.5   Exponential smoothing + Trigg's tracking signal

Row	Description	Formulae
1	Current demand value	X
2	Current forecast	$\hat{X}_t$
3	Error	$e_t = X_t - \hat{X}_t$
4	Squared error	e^2_t
5	Cum. sq. error	Σe^2_t
6	Alpha * error	$\alpha \times e_t$
7	1 − alpha * past sm. error	$(1\alpha)\bar{e}_{t-1}$
8	Current smoothed error	$\bar{e}_t = \alpha * e_t + (1 - \alpha) * \bar{e}_{t-1}$
9	Alpha− * $\|e_t\|$	$\alpha * \|e_t\|$
10	(1 − alpha) * past MAD	$(1 - \alpha) * MAD_{t-1}$
11	Current MAD	$MAD_t = \alpha * \|e_t\| + (1 - \alpha) * MAD_{t-1}$
12	Current st. dev	$e_t = 1.25\ MAD_t$
13	Trigg's signal	$T_t = \bar{e}_{t-1}/MAD_t$
14	Cumulative error	Σe_t
15	Alpha	α
16	Alpha * current demand	αX_t
17	$(1 - \alpha)$ * past forecast	$(1 - \alpha) * \hat{X}_t$
18	Next period's forecast	$\alpha X_t + (1 - \alpha)\hat{X}_t$

and see' whether the change is real or not. If there is a significant change then it quickly adapts to the new level.

The reader should recognise that such mathematical approaches to monitoring do not have any way of including other knowledge about the reasons things are changing significantly. In reality, such objective measures should be considered as just one input to understanding the competitive environment. No forecasts should be judged in isolation without, for example, due consideration being given to the change in consumers' attitudes, as discussed in this chapter. 'Forecasting is hazardous, particularly in relation to the future' if not every piece of information is used when making decisions.

QUESTIONS

1. The chapter describes some time series forecasting methods not covered in Chapter 11. Compare them with the methods of Chapter 11 and discuss their advantages and disadvantages.

2. What do the author's experiences suggest are the critical success factors in using analytical forecasting methods in an organisation?

3. In many organisations and industries the use of analytical forecasting methods is limited. Based on the author's experiences, and your own, give reasons (both valid and invalid) why this is so.

CHAPTER FOURTEEN

Causal modelling

Causal modelling is about the existence and nature of relationships between variables. It has two parts: correlation *measures the strength of a relationship;* regression analysis *determines the mathematical formula which expresses the form of a relationship. Correlation shows whether a connection exists; regression finds what the connection is. Causal modelling is used for forecasting, for establishing the existence of relationships and for quantifying the influence of one variable on another.*

INTRODUCTION

Causal modelling is a group of methods which work on historical data to analyse how variables influence one another. It considers two aspects of these influences. *Correlation* addresses the issue of how strong the influences are, while *regression analysis* is concerned with discovering the mathematical forms of the influences.

For example, we might have the last 10 years' data for the quarterly sales volume of a product together with the quarterly expenditures for advertising it. Correlation can use this data to measure the extent to which sales volume appears to have been influenced by advertising expenditure. It can show whether a high level of sales has usually corresponded with a high advertising expenditure in the same quarter (and low with low), i.e. it can measure the strength of the relationship between sales and advertising.

Regression can provide the formula linking sales with advertising. The formula might look like:

$$\text{Sales volume} = 3000 + 3.1 \times \text{Advertising expenditure}$$
$$\text{(thousands)} \qquad\qquad\qquad \text{(£ thousands)}$$

This information can be used in three main ways. First, the existence of a very strong correlation would tell us that advertising really was critically important to the business; likewise a low correlation would bring the value of advertising expenditure into question. Secondly, the regression equation could forecast sales in a future quarter for which the advertising level had been decided. Or it could indicate what level of advertising expenditure would be needed in order to meet sales targets. Thirdly, the equation would reveal the marginal return on advertising expenditure, i.e. the above equation suggests that an extra £1000 spent on advertising should produce an extra 3100 sales. In general, correlation and regression have three purposes: to forecast, to establish the existence of relationships, and to quantify the influence of one variable on another.

In studying causal modelling we will have to use some technical and statistical terms.

Sales is the *dependent* or *left-hand side* (LHS) *variable*; advertising expenditure is the *independent* or *right-hand side* (RHS) *variable*. '3000' is the *constant*; '3.1' is the *coefficient* of advertising expenditure.

APPLICATIONS

Forecasting sales of children's clothing

A national chain store predicts the sales of children's clothing in the catchment area of each of its 300 stores by carrying out regression analyses relating the quarterly sales for children of a particular age group to the birth rate in the catchment area an appropriate number of years earlier. For example, it would forecast sales of clothing for three-year-olds at a particular store by looking at the regression formula linking sales to the birth rate in the store's catchment area three years earlier. Figure 14.1 shows the historical data record graphically, known as the *scatter diagram*. It indicates a strong straight line relationship between the variables.

The forecast for a future quarter is calculated by putting the appropriate birth rate into the regression equation. Of course, this regression analysis is not by itself an adequate means of making forecasts since there are many other influences on sales. This example is of *simple linear regression* and has been used as an illustration of the basic concepts of regression analysis. 'Simple' means that only two variables, sales and birth rate, are involved; 'linear' means that the regression equation is a straight line when graphed and has the mathematical form of a straight line. All straight lines have an equation similar to that shown below where 'A' and 'B' are constants. Essentially all regression analysis does is to determine the values of these constants.

$$\text{Sales} = A + B \times \text{Birth rate}$$

The variable of the birth rate is called a *leading indicator* for the obvious reason that it 'leads' the variable being forecast, sales, by three years.

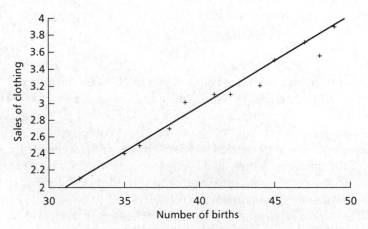

Figure 14.1 Sales of three-year-old children's clothing

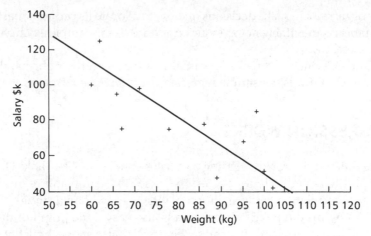

Figure 14.2 Salaries and weight

Explaining the link between salary and weight

A research group at a US business school investigated the relationship between the salaries and weights of US executives. It collected data from a sample of US organisations and carried out a correlation analysis. The scatter diagram is shown in Figure 14.2. The data are *cross-sectional* because they relate to different people at one point in time. In contrast, the data in Figure 14.1 are *time series* because each observation relates to a different point in time.

Figure 14.2 shows that in general high salaries are associated with low weights, and vice versa. However, the relationship is not a strong one because the points are not very close to a straight line. Since high salaries are associated with low weights, the correlation is *negative*. If high salaries had been associated with high weights then the correlation would be *positive*.

Clearly this analysis is used to improve understanding and to explain, rather than to forecast: the idea is not to tell an executive how many kilograms he or she should lose in order to secure a 20 per cent rise in salary. The correlation analysis would be just the start of a qualitative investigation into why heavy people appear to be paid less.

Estimating the return on advertising expenditure for drug products

Promotional expenditure on drug products is high and pharmaceutical organisations tend to use a variety of different promotional methods – advertising in different media, introductory offers, workshops, conferences and so on. By regressing the sales of a product against expenditures on different promotional vehicles, the return for each £ spent on advertising can be estimated. For example, the regression equation might be:

Sales = 2000 + 2.7 × Journal advertising + 2.3 × workshops + 4.2 × salespeople's visits

('000s)　　　　　　　　　　　(£'000s)　　　　　　　　　(£'000s)　　　　　　　(£'000s)

The equation suggests that every £ spent on journal advertising results in a 2.7 increase in sales, in volume terms; each £ spent on workshops results in a 2.3 increase in sales; each £ spent on salespeople's visits results in a 4.2 increase in sales. This information can help the organisation make decisions on how to allocate its promotional budget. However, the situation is inevitably not as straightforward as this simple example suggests, as we shall see later.

The existence of three independent variables on the right-hand side of this equation means that this is not simple regression, it is *multiple regression*.

HOW REGRESSION WORKS

The data record for advertising and sales could look like Table 14.1. When plotted on a graph the result is Figure 14.3. In this case correlation and regression are easy. There is perfect correlation because all the points lie exactly on a straight line; it is just a matter of joining up the points. Regression is also easy – the graph of the line has to be interpreted as a mathematical formula. Figure 14.3 also shows how the equation of the line is related to the graph of the line. The '3000' is the constant, the point where the line meets the vertical axis; the '3.1' is the coefficient, the slope or gradient of the line.

Normally the points will only lie *exactly* on a straight line by a fluke, or by cheating. It

Table 14.1 Sales and advertising I

Year	Quarter	Sales ('000s)	Advertising (£'000s)
1993	1	3310	100
	2	3372	120
	3	3248	80
	4	3620	200
1994	1	3341	110
	2	3465	150
	3	3310	100
	4	3775	250

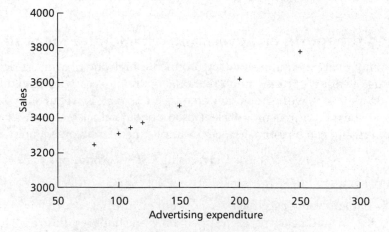

Figure 14.3 Table 14.1 in graphical form

Table 14.2   Sales and advertising II

Year	Quarter	Sales ('000s)	Advertising (£'000s)
1993	1	3420	100
	2	3472	120
	3	3181	80
	4	3500	200
1994	1	3512	110
	2	3470	150
	3	3450	100
	4	3670	250

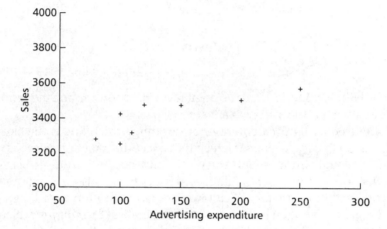

Figure 14.4   Graph of Table 14.2

would be more realistic for the data to look something like Table 14.2 and the graph like Figure 14.4.

Correlation and regression are much more difficult with the data from Table 14.2 because there is no line that could be drawn *through* all the points but several which could plausibly be drawn *near* the points. The question is, which of all these lines is the best? This is the question that regression answers. Its starting point is that the best line is the one which, in some way, is closest to the points. To operationalise this obvious concept we need to define *residuals*.

Whichever line we draw, most of the points will not fall on it. The vertical distance between the point and the line is the residual. Figure 14.5 illustrates this.

Figure 14.5 is a scatter diagram of some data points. Let us suppose that after some trial and error, the line, $y = 10 + 5x$, which seems close to the points, has been drawn through them. Point A is one of the data points for which $x = 1$ and $y = 17$. '17' is the *actual y value*. The point B is the point on the line immediately below A. Its y value is calculated from the equation of the line.

$$y \text{ value at B} = 10 + (5 \times 1) = 15$$

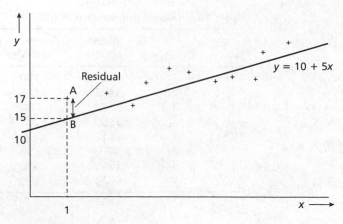

Figure 14.5   Residuals

'15' is the *fitted y value*. The residual is therefore:

$$\text{Residual} = \text{actual } y \text{ value} - \text{fitted } y \text{ value} = 17 - 15 = 2$$

Each point has a residual. If the point falls exactly on the line the residual is zero, if above it is positive, if below it is negative.

One frequently used criterion for deciding which line is the closest is to define the regression line as the one for which the *sum* of the *squared residuals* is the smallest for any line that could be drawn. This criterion is known as *ordinary least squares* (OLS) (the reasons for the popularity of OLS are discussed later). Fortunately, the mathematical implications of this definition are not difficult to work out (although we will not go into the details) and regression is then just a series of mathematical formulae for calculating the constant and the slope (3000 and 3.1 in the example) based on the OLS definition of closeness. The formulae are:

$$\text{Slope:} \qquad B = \frac{\Sigma(x\text{-mean}(x))(y\text{-mean}(y))}{\Sigma(x\text{-mean}(x))^2}$$

$$\text{Intercept:} \qquad A = \text{mean}(y) - B.\text{mean}(x)$$

These formulae are built into sophisticated calculators and computer software and so in practice they do not need to be used manually. However, applying them can help to reinforce the underlying concepts – and check out the software.

Example

Pharmaceutical companies spend heavily to promote their products, especially in the period before patent expiry. This is because during this time profit margins are at their highest and also, in the absence of competitors, they are able to establish products and build a platform of regular customers to carry them through the fiercely competitive times after patent expiry. The data in Table 14.3 shows quarterly volume sales and promotional expenditure over two years for the fictitious drug Divopan which is manufactured by the equally fictitious Clinico pharmaceutical company. What is the regression equation linking sales and promotional expenditure?

Table 14.3   Sales and promotional expenditure for Divopan

Year	Quarter	Sales (millions)	Promotions (£millions)
1993	1	3	5
	2	4	4
	3	6	5
	4	5	4
1994	1	8	5
	2	10	6
	3	9	4
	4	11	7

Since sales are to be forecast, this is the 'y' or dependant variable; promotional expenditure is the 'x' or independent variable. The least squares formulae require the means of both variables to be calculated.

$$\text{Mean}(y) = (3 + 4 + 6 + 5 + 8 + 10 + 9 + 11)/8 = 7$$
$$\text{Mean}(x) = (5 + 4 + 5 + 4 + 5 + 6 + 4 + 7)/8 = 5$$

The least squares formula for the slope is:

$$\text{Slope:} \qquad B = \frac{\Sigma(x\text{-mean}(x))(y\text{-mean}(y))}{\Sigma(x\text{-mean}(x))^2}$$

$$B = \frac{\begin{matrix}(3-7)(5-5)+(4-7)(4-5)+(6-7)(5-5)+(5-7)(4-5)+(8-7)(5-5) \\ +(10-7)(6-5)+(9-7)(4-5)+(11-7)(7-5)\end{matrix}}{(5-5)^2+(4-5)^2+(5-5)^2+(4-5)^2+(5-5)^2+(6-5)^2+(4-5)^2+(7-5)^2}$$

$$= \frac{(-4)(0)+(-3)(-1)+(-1)(0)+(-2)(-1)+(1)(0)+(3)(1)+(2)(-1)+(4)(2)}{(0)^2+(-1)^2+(0)^2+(-1)^2+(0)^2+(1)^2+(-1)^2+(2)^2}$$

$$= \frac{0+3+0+2+0+3-2+8}{0+1+0+1+0+1+1+4}$$

$$= \frac{14}{8}$$

$$= 1.75$$

The formula for the intercept is:

$$\text{Intercept: } A = \text{mean } (y) - B \text{ mean } (x) \qquad A = 7 - 1.75(5)$$
$$= -1.75$$

The regression equation is therefore:

$$\text{Sales} = -1.75 + 1.75(\text{promotional expenditure})$$

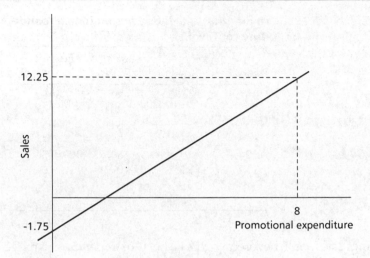

Figure 14.6   Divopan sales and promotions graph

If in a future quarter promotional expenditure was 8, then the forecast for sales is:

$$\text{Sales} = -1.75 + 14 = 12.25$$

This is illustrated in Figure 14.6.

The particular way in which the least squares criterion defines 'closest' may seem unnecessarily complex because of squaring the residuals, but there are good reasons for doing this. First, the act of squaring the residuals penalises any points that are a long way from the regression line: 2^2 is 4, 4^2 is 16 and so on. Therefore if one point is *twice* as far from the line as another it will count for *four times* as much in the 'sum of squared residuals'. Secondly, squaring means that there is no need to worry about positive and negative residuals since both positive and negative numbers, when squared, become positive. Thirdly, there are technical reasons why, according to statistical theory, the squaring gives better estimates of the intercept and slope.

These formulae mean that, unfortunately, regression analysis always works. Provided

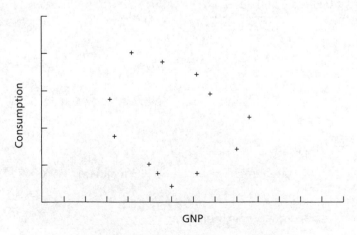

Figure 14.7   Sales of Scotch whisky and GNP

suitable data is available it is always possible to find the regression equation which links two variables. Why 'unfortunately'? The problem is that the regression formulae produce an equation even when the graph shows that a straight line does not remotely fit the data. Figure 14.7 is a scatter diagram of the UK sales of Scotch whisky and the UK's GNP (gross national product). There used to be a school of thought that believed that sales of Scotch whisky, being a luxury product, were affected by the health of the economy. Figure 14.7 shows that this is not the case. However, it is still possible to find the 'best fit' straight line through the points, even when it makes no sense to consider a straight line in the first place. What is needed, alongside regression, is a method of determining how strong the straight line relationship is. This method, known as correlation, is the subject of the next section.

HOW CORRELATION WORKS

Correlation measures the strength of a relationship by calculating a statistic called the 'correlation coefficient' or 'R-squared' which is a number between 0 and 1. If it is 1 there is perfect correlation: the points all lie exactly on a straight line, as in Figure 14.8. If it is 0 the points are a random jumble, not at all like a straight line.

In practice R-squared is rarely 0 or 1 and will be somewhere in between. In general we are looking for as high an R-squared as possible: the higher the R-squared the better and more accurate the regression equation. Figure 14.9 gives some examples of different R-squared values.

The way R-squared works is rather complex. Broadly it splits the variation in the dependent variable (e.g. the general up and down changes in sales) into two parts. One part is 'explained', the movement that can, because of the regression, be attributed to advertising; the other part is 'unexplained', the movement – as seen in the residuals – that cannot be attributed to advertising. R-squared is the proportion of the original variation in sales that is attributed to advertising. When R-squared is 1 all the variation can be attributed to advertising, i.e. the points lie exactly on the line; when R-squared is 0 none of the variation, according to regression analysis, can be attributed to advertising.

It works like this. The variation in the dependent variable, or any variable for that matter, is given by its variation about its mean. This is called the total variation.

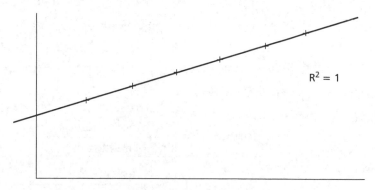

Figure 14.8   Perfect correlation

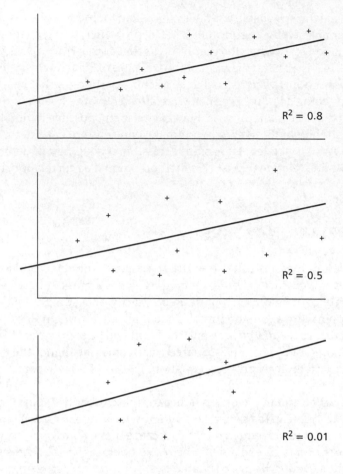

Figure 14.9   Examples of correlation coefficients

$$\text{Total variation} = \Sigma(y - \text{mean}(y))^2$$

It is this variation that is split into two parts. The part that is 'unexplained' is the variation that is 'left over', i.e. the variation in the residuals. So,

$$\text{Unexplained variation} = \Sigma(\text{residual})^2$$

The part that is 'explained' is the difference between the total variation and the unexplained variation.

$$\text{Explained variation} = \Sigma(y - \text{mean}(y))^2 - \Sigma(\text{residual})^2$$

Therefore the correlation coefficient is:

$$\text{R-squared} = \frac{\text{Explained variation}}{\text{Unexplained variation}}$$

$$= \frac{\Sigma(y - \text{mean}(y))^2 - \Sigma(\text{residual})^2}{\Sigma(y - \text{mean}(y))^2}$$

After some unpleasant and tedious algebra this becomes:

$$\text{R-squared} = \frac{[\Sigma(x - \text{mean}(x))(y-\text{mean}(y))]^2}{\Sigma(x - \text{mean}(x))^2 \cdot \Sigma(y - \text{mean}(y))^2}$$

Example

The example used is the one of the Clinico company and its product Divopan which illustrated the regression equation. The data are given in Figure 14.6. What is the correlation coefficient?

The calculations made previously are helpful now. They were as follows.

$$\text{Mean}(y) = 7$$
$$\text{Mean}(x) = 5$$
$$\Sigma(x\text{-mean}(x))(y\text{-mean}(y)) = 14$$
$$\Sigma(x\text{-mean}(x))^2 = 8$$

To calculate R-squared we also need to calculate:

$$\Sigma(y - \text{mean}(y))^2 = (3 - 7)^2 + (4 - 7)^2 + (6 - 7)^2 + (5 - 7)^2 + (8 - 7)^2$$
$$+ (10 - 7)^2 + (9 - 7)^2 + (11 - 7)^2$$
$$= 16 + 9 + 1 + 4 + 1 + 9 + 4 + 16$$
$$= 60$$

$$\text{R-squared} = \frac{[\Sigma(x - \text{mean}(x))(y\text{-mean}(y))]^2}{\Sigma(x - \text{mean}(x))^2 \cdot \Sigma(y - \text{mean}(y))^2}$$

$$= \frac{14^2}{8 \times 60}$$

$$= 196/480$$

$$= 0.408$$

There is no more than a weak correlation between sales and advertising in this example, since only about 40 per cent of the variation in sales has been explained by advertising. The question of whether 40 per cent is good enough, and what defines the boundary between an acceptable and an unacceptable R-squared, must be left for the statistical methods of the next chapter.

EXAMINING THE RESIDUALS

Once the regression equation has been calculated and the correlation checked, the next step is to examine the residuals. They are important not just because they are the basis of the least squares criterion, but also because they can give guidance on whether the variables are *linearly* related. The correlation coefficient indicates whether the relationship is strong, the residuals whether it is linear. We must look to see if the residuals are random.

Figure 14.10 is a scatter diagram in which the residuals are not random. The correlation coefficient may be high, but a straight line is not the best representation of the link

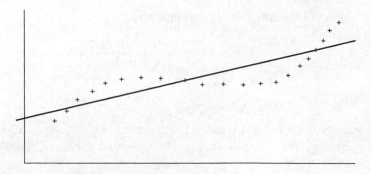

Figure 14.10   Non-random residuals

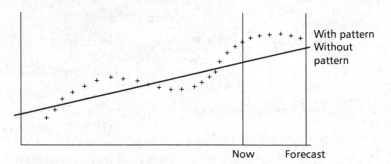

Figure 14.11   Forecasting with non-random residuals

between the variables. Figure 14.11 shows the error that would occur if the regression equation were to be used for forecasting.

There is a clear pattern in the data of Figures 14.10 and 14.11 which is evidence of some other effect which should be incorporated into the 'model' of the data. If the x variable is 'time' then the pattern may be a seasonal variation or a cycle, as described in Chapter 11.

The essence of the matter is this. If the unexplained variation (the residuals) in the forecast variable is random then it is by definition unpredictable. If unpredictable then there is nothing more we can do to reduce the unexplained variation. The current regression equation, whether good or bad, has come as far as it can. However, if the residuals are non-random, i.e. there is a pattern in them as in Figure 14.10, then the current regression equation can be improved by incorporating the pattern, in some way, into the equation. Examining the residuals for randomness is thus a second check, after the correlation coefficient, that the regression equation is a good representation of the link between the variables.

The residuals can be calculated by subtracting the fitted y values (calculated from the regression equation) from the actual y values.

Example

The example is the previous one concerning the Clinico company. The regression equation was found to be:

Table 14.4 Residuals for Divopan regression

Year	Quarter	Sales (millions)	Promotions (£millions)	Fitted y values (from regression)	Residuals (sales-fitted)
1993	1	3	5	7[=−1.75 + 1.75(5)]	−4
	2	4	4	5.25[=−1.75 + 1.75(4)]	−1.25
	3	6	5	7[=−1.75 + 1.75(5)]	1
	4	5	4	5.25[=−1.75 + 1.75(4)]	−0.25
1994	1	8	5	7[=−1.75 + 1.75(5)]	1
	2	10	6	8.75[=−1.75 + 1.75(6)]	1.25
	3	9	4	5.25[=−1.75 + 1.75(4)]	3.75
	4	11	7	10.5[=−1.75 + 1.75(7)]	0.5

$$\text{Sales} = -1.75 + 1.75(\text{promotional expenditure})$$

The calculation of the residuals is shown in Table 14.4.

It is not difficult to see from the numbers in Table 14.4 that these residuals are not random. Apart from one major exception, for low x values the residuals tend to be negative and for high x values positive. The regression line is too high to start with but too low later, suggesting that a curved relationship may be better than a straight line.

This can be seen directly if the residuals are plotted along with the regression line, as in Figure 14.12. In fact, we could have spotted the curve from a scatter diagram of the data. So why bother with the calculations? First, the situation is not always as clear as it is in the situations represented by Figures 14.10 and 14.12. The numbers allow us to carry out some statistical tests, as will be demonstrated in the next chapter. Secondly, it is not possible to plot the regression line for multiple regression because three or more variables are involved.

The inability to plot regression lines for multiple regression means that a visual examination of residuals is usually carried out by plotting the fitted points against the residuals. Figure 14.13 is a plot of fitted points against residuals which appear to be random.

There are two principal types of non-randomness. The first is *serial correlation*, when

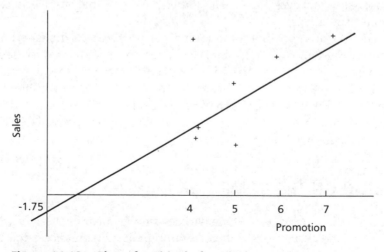

Figure 14.12 Plot of residuals for Divopan

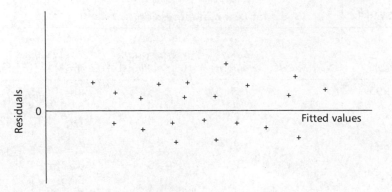

Figure 14.13   Fitted vs residual: random residuals

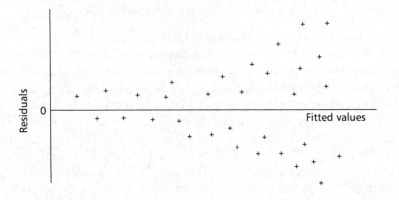

Figure 14.14   Fitted vs residual: heteroscedasticity

each residual is related to the previous one. In other words, if you know what the previous residual is you can make a better forecast of it than if you did not. Serial correlation would normally be found in a situation when the x variable is time and some pattern, such as seasonality or a cycle, has been omitted from the analysis. Figure 14.8 is an example of serial correlation.

The second type of non-randomness is *heteroscedasticity*, where the residuals vary in size at different parts of the line, i.e. the residuals are related to the x value. Figure 14.14 is an example of hetroscedasticity. It is likely to occur in cross-sectional data. For example, in a study relating profitability to company size, it may well be that the residuals are smaller for small companies than they are for the larger ones. In other words, the unexplained part or error is roughly proportional to company size. Thus the residuals are related to the x value.

REGRESSION ON THE COMPUTER

The situations described so far have been simple linear regressions with few observations. Even so, the calculations were tedious. In practice regression and correlation are carried out on a computer. Standard packages are available for personal computers and in fact

Table 14.5   Regression output from Lotus

Constant	−1.75
Std. err. of Y est.	2.432419
R-squared	0.408333
No. of observations	8
Degrees of freedom	6
X coefficient(s)	1.75
Std. err. of coef.	0.859990

normal spreadsheet packages have now developed quite sophisticated regression capabilities. The skill is no longer that of accurate number crunching but the ability to understand and interpret the output.

Example

For the Clinico pharmaceutical example, the output from, for instance, *Lotus 1-2-3* is as shown in Table 14.5. It can be interpreted as described below, although a fuller explanation of some of the concepts will have to wait until the next chapter when the statistical ramifications of regression and correlation are described.

1. The regression equation uses the 'constant', −1.75, and the 'X coefficient', 1.75.

$$Sales = -1.75 + 1.75(promotion)$$

2. The correlation coefficient uses the 'R-squared' value 0.408333, i.e. 41 per cent.

3. The 'no. of observations' is 8 = 2 years and 4 quarters per year.

4. The 'degrees of freedom' is only needed when statistical tests are to be conducted. It is calculated:

Degrees of freedom = no. of observations − no. of items estimated in the
regression equation
= 8 − 2 (the 'constant' and the 'X coefficient')
= 6

5. The 'std. err. of Y est.' is the standard error of the forecast. A rough interpretation is that the 95 per cent confidence limits for the forecast are +/−2 times this amount, i.e. +/−2 × 2.432419 = +/−4.86. In other words we can say we are '95 per cent confident' that what actually happens will lie in the range 'forecast − 4.86' and 'forecast + 4.86'.

6. The remaining figure given in the output is the 'std. err. of coef.' This gives us the 95 per cent confidence limits for the estimate of the X coefficient, i.e. +/−2 × 0.85999 = +/−1.72. In other words we can say we are 95 per cent confident that the true value of the coefficient (as opposed to the estimate obtained from just a few observations) will lie in the range 'estimate − 1.72' and 'estimate + 1.72'.

Computer packages can also produce visual output – the graphs and plots that are the basis of scatter diagrams to gain a first understanding of the data and to examine the residuals for randomness. Most packages, including spreadsheets, can produce scatter diagrams as well as doing the calculations.

There are a variety of software packages which can carry out a regression analysis. Most people start with something simple, such as a spreadsheet, and then, as their needs for more sophisticated methods and outputs increase, they move on to a specialist package.

STATISTICS VS COMMON SENSE

So far we have dealt with the numerical aspects of regression and correlation, but the way we interpret and use the results is potentially more important. Even when a relationship between variables satisfies all the statistical tests, we must still use management experience and common sense to know what conclusions can be drawn. Here are some discussions of the more relevant issues.

Causality

Perhaps the most important point to remember is that while the statistical results show whether the variables are *associated*, i.e. the numbers show similar movements, they do not tell us that there is a *causal* link between them, i.e. that changes in one variable cause changes in the other. Some extreme examples can illustrate this point.

For example, there is a close association (high correlation etc.) between the price of rum and the level of remuneration of the clergy. This does not mean that a rise in salary for the clergy will be spent on rum, thereby depleting stocks and causing a rise in the price. What it probably means is that there is a third factor (perhaps inflation or a general increase in society's affluence) which affects both variables, so that in the past clergy's salaries and the price of rum have moved together. It would be a mistake to suppose that if conditions were to change the relationship must continue to hold. For example, if the clergy, for some good philanthropic purpose, agreed next year to take a salary cut, then the situation is substantially different from anything that has gone before. The price of rum would continue to change in response to inflation or whatever the third factor was, and the association would be broken. Had the relationship been a causal one, then manipulating one variable would have caused a corresponding change in the second variable.

The existence of causality over and above statistical association is nearly always difficult to determine. The most notorious case is the alleged link between lung cancer and smoking. There is certainly a strong statistical association between the two, but causality is a different matter. The tobacco companies say there is a third factor, perhaps the level of stress in society, which makes people smoke more while at the same time causing greater incidence of lung cancer. If this were true, then telling people to stop smoking would not only not affect their likelihood of suffering from lung cancer, but would make them less able to cope with life's stresses (supposing smoking does help in this regard).

Usually the question of causality can be advanced by collecting new data from new situations and showing that the relationship still holds. For instance, data on women smoking shows a link with lung cancer even though the numbers of women smoking, unlike men, were very low until after the Second World War. New data like this does not furnish proof, but strengthens existing evidence.

Regression and correlation are probably at their most useful when testing relationships whose causality is suggested by some theory. For example, if a medical mechanism by which smoking could cause lung cancer were suspected, then regression and correlation would supply strong supporting evidence.

Extrapolation

Extrapolation is the use of regression information outside the range of data or conditions on which the regression equation was estimated. For example, if the relationship between the sales of Divopan and promotional expenditure was based on advertising levels in the region £1.5 million to £2 million, it would be over-optimistic to expect the regression to predict the effect of increasing the level of advertising to £5 million.

Spurious regression

Regression and correlation results are spurious when they are not what they seem at first sight because of some logical quirk in the structure of the regression. For example, a regression study investigated the relationship between the profitability and size of organisations. The result was a negative correlation, i.e. high profitability seemed to be associated with small size and vice versa. However, the variables had been defined in the following way.

$$\text{Profitability} = \text{net profit/net assets}$$
$$\text{Size} = \text{net assets}$$

Consequently the equation looked like:

$$\frac{\text{Net profits}}{\text{Net assets}} = A + B(\text{net assets})$$

'Net assets' therefore appeared on both sides of the equation. Companies with large net assets would inevitably have a small y variable and a large x variable. There was in-built bias towards a negative correlation and the results were spurious.

Choice of data

Statistically, regression always works: it is always possible to find the regression equation. However, the equation might not make much sense if one looks at the data on which it was based. For example, the data in Figure 14.15(a) may have quite a high correlation coefficient, hiding the fact that two separate straight lines (Figure 14.15(b)) would be more appropriate. This highlights the need to pay careful regard to the data, including studying the scatter diagram.

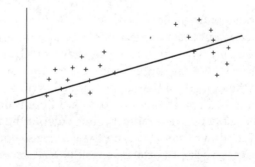

Figure 14.15(a)

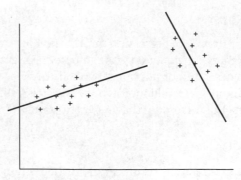

Figure 14.15(b)

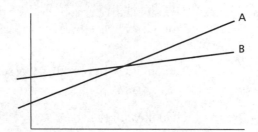

Figure 14.16   Lines with similar R-squared values

Over-precision

The least squares criterion combined with a computer package can be misleading by being over-precise. The two lines, A and B, in Figure 14.16 may have very similar R-squared values although their equations are very different. Least squares picks out one equation from many as being the best and specifies the coefficients to 6 or 7 decimal places. This can give the impression that the 'best' equation is clearly the best. For all practical purposes, however, other equations may be just as good. They may even be better when non-statistical factors are considered. Prior knowledge, previous work or just common sense will almost certainly be more relevant than the third or fourth decimal place in R-squared in deciding between equations A and B.

Which is x, which is y?

Before embarking on regression analysis, we have to choose which variable is x, which is y. We then carry out the a regression of y *on* x, minimising the sum of residuals in the y direction (vertically on a standard scatter diagram). The distinction is important because if the two variables were interchanged and we carried out a regression of x *on* y, minimising the sum of residuals in an x direction (horizontally), then a different regression equation would emerge. It would be a different line with different intercept and different slope. Only by the remotest chance would the two lines coincide.

Usually it is clear which way round the variables should be. The variable being forecast should be the y variable because its residuals are being minimised – and if the y residuals (or errors) are minimised then the forecast will be as accurate as possible.

The correlation coefficient is unaffected by the choice of y and x variable. The formula for R-squared shows that it would make no difference if y and x were the other way round.

CONCLUSION

Regression and correlation are fundamental techniques for understanding and predicting data relationships in budgeting, corporate planning, costing, economics, manpower planning, sales and many other areas of business and administration. So far we have dealt with four steps in executing the techniques.

1. Inspect the scatter diagram.

2. Calculate the regression and correlation coefficients.

3. Examine the residuals.

4. Make predictions, with confidence limits.

Software can handle the complex calculations easily, but the importance of the scatter diagram should definitely not be underestimated. It is the first rough guide to the sort of analysis that might be appropriate – is there any indication of a strong relationship? Is it linear? Could other variables be used? Is the data a single set or should some be discarded? At any stage of the analysis it is also a check that the statistical analysis and common sense are pointing in the same direction.

Such checks are always important. The statistical aspects have great depth, as will be seen in the next chapter when the statistical underpinnings are described, and this depth can in itself cause problems. The technicalities can easily dominate thought processes to the exclusion of more relevant management concerns. Major mistakes can be made when the statistical and management aspects are not held in balance.

General managers, the users of the forecasts, have a crucial role to play in making sure these issues remain on the agenda. Paradoxically, they can only do this if they have a reasonable grasp of the basic statistical principles – without being expert statisticians. Only when they have equipped themselves with this knowledge will they be able to make proper use of the facilities which software packages offer and be able to participate fully in discussions with experts, should experts be called upon.

Techniques such as regression and correlation, especially when used in forecasting, have a mixed track record in organisations. A key success factor seems to be proper management involvement in order that common-sense issues are addressed and to make sure that there is proper 'ownership' of the results.

CASE STUDIES

CASE STUDY 1

In preparation for privatisation, a railway company is investigating the productivity of its booking clerks. As a first step a pilot study has been carried out at eight offices to investigate the number of transactions performed per day, on average, at the different offices. The results are shown in Table 14.6.

Table 14.6

Office	Clerks	Transactions (hundreds)
1	3	11
2	1	6
3	3	10
4	4	15
5	6	22
6	7	19
7	3	12
8	5	17

To help understand these pilot results, a regression analysis is to be carried out.

1. Draw a scatter diagram. Does the data seem linear?

2. Calculate the regression equation.

3. Calculate R-squared. Does the correlation seem strong?

4. Calculate the residuals. Do they seem random?

Solutions

1. *Draw a scatter diagram. Does the data seem linear?*
The scatter diagram is in Figure 14.17. The data looks reasonably linear.

2. *Calculate the regression equation.*
The computer output is shown in Table 14.7 (or the calculations could be done manually). The regression equation is:

$$\text{Transactions} = 3.69 + 2.58 \times \text{Clerks}$$

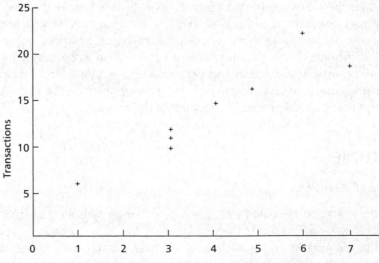

Figure 14.17 Scatter diagram

Table 14.7

Constant	3.69
Std. err of Y est.	1.80
R-squared	0.90
No. of observations	8
Degrees of freedom	6
X coefficient(s)	2.58
Std. err of coef.	0.35

3. *Calculate R-squared. Does the correlation seem strong?*
R-squared shows that 90 per cent of the variation in transactions is explained by the number of clerks, i.e. the correlation is strong.

4. *Calculate the residuals. Do they seem random?*
The residuals are calculated as shown in Table 14.8. A plot of residuals against fitted values is shown in Figure 14.18. There are too few observations for it to be easy to spot any

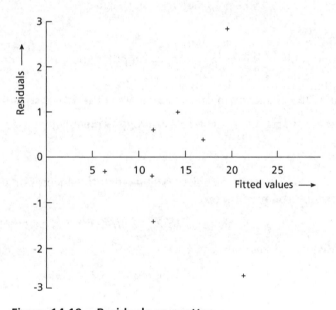

Figure 14.18   Residuals vs scatter

definite patterns, but there does seem to be some evidence of heteroscedasticity – larger residuals for larger fitted values. In other words, the model is less reliable in offices where there are a greater number of clerks.

Table 14.8

Office	Clerks	Transactions (hundreds)	Fitted (from regression)	Residuals (actual fitted)
1	3	11	11.4	−0.4
2	1	6	6.3	−0.3
3	3	10	11.4	−1.4
4	4	15	14	1.0
5	6	22	19.2	2.8
6	7	19	21.7	−2.7
7	3	12	11.4	0.6
8	5	17	16.6	0.4

Table 14.9

Variable	Coefficient
Advertising expenditure	8.3
Constant	16.2
R-squared	0.60
Sum of squared residuals	800

CASE STUDY 2

The data in Table 14.9 is output from a computer linear regression package relating sales volume and advertising expenditure:

1. What is the prediction of sales volume when the advertising expenditure is 4?

2. What is the total variation in sales: sum $(y − mean(y))^2$?

Solutions

1. *What is the prediction of sales volume when the advertising expenditure is 4?*
The regression equation is:

$$\text{Sales volume} = 16.2 \times 8.3(\text{Advertising expenditure})$$

When advertising expenditure is 4, then:

$$\text{Sales volume} = 16.2 \times 8.3(4)$$

$$= 49.4$$

2. *What is the total variation in sales: sum $(y − mean(y))^2$?*

$$\text{R-squared} = \text{Explained variation/total variation}$$

$$= (\text{total variation} − \text{unexplained variation})/\text{total variation}$$

$$0.60 = (tv − \text{sum of squared residuals})/tv$$

$$0.6tv = tv − 800$$

$$0.4tv = 800$$

$$\text{Total variation} = 2000$$

QUESTIONS

1. Which of the following statements are true?
   (a) Correlation and regression are synonymous.
   (b) Correlation would establish whether there was a linear relationship between the weights of one sample of business executives and the salaries of another sample of business executives.
   (c) Annual sales figures for each of a company's 17 regions is a set of cross-sectional data containing 17 observations.
   (d) If high values of one variable are associated with low values of a second and vice versa, then the two variables are negatively correlated.
   (e) The residuals of a regression line are the perpendicular distances between actual points and the line.
   (f) The residuals of a regression line are the differences between actual and fitted y values.
   (g) The residuals of a regression line are all zero for a 'best fit' line.
   (h) The relationship between the ages of husbands and wives is likely to show strong positive correlation.
   (i) Research has shown that there is a strong positive correlation between age at death and the number of times, as an adult, a patient has visited the doctor, and therefore it is right to conclude that visiting a doctor prolongs life.
   (j) Simple regression means that one y variable is related to one x variable; multiple regression means that several y variables are related to several x variables.

2. A chain of retail kiosks sell shirts at railway stations. The owners of the chain have decided to embark on a strategy of expansion and open several new kiosks. As part of the expansion planning process a project team is carrying out an investigation to find out how to forecast the sales levels at the new kiosks. One approach has been to use regression analysis, relating the average level of sales per week (y) for each existing kiosk (12 in all) with estimates of the number of people passing by the kiosk in the course of an average day. Data for the 12 kiosks is shown in Table 14.10.

Table 14.10

Kiosk	Average sales (£'000)	Passers-by (000s)
1	23	67
2	28	75
3	21	66
4	34	79
5	39	96
6	32	80
7	27	70
8	29	71
9	35	85
10	22	59
11	18	42
12	25	63

Table 14.11

Variable	Coefficient
Passers by	0.4338
Constant	−3.0866
Correlation coefficient: R-squared	0.88
Residual standard error:	2.2836

The computer output for regressing average sales against the numbers of passers-by is shown in Table 14.11.

(a) What is the estimated relationship between sales and passers-by? What sales level would be predicted for a kiosk in a railway station where there would be approximately 70 000 passers-by?

(b) How good is the fit of the linear equation to the data?

(c) Use the residual standard error to suggest what the maximum level of accuracy achieved by the model is likely to be.

(d) What are the non-statistical reservations connected with forecasting sales in this way?

3. There is a high correlation between the number of storks migrating to Scandanavia in summer and the birth rate in Scandinavia. What conclusions do you draw?

ANSWERS TO QUESTIONS

1. (a) False.   (f) True.
   (b) False.   (g) False.
   (c) True.   (h) True.
   (d) True.   (i) False.
   (e) False.   (j) False.

2. (a) 27 279.
   (b) Good – high R-squared, random residuals.
   (c) +/−4.567.
   (d) Data measurement problems, need for more explanatory variables.

CHAPTER FIFTEEN

More regression analysis

This chapter extends casual modelling and discusses its application to a wider range of situations. It also introduces the underlying statistical theory, which can be highly complex. The amount of prior statistical knowledge required to understand the chapter has been minimised, but two topics may cause difficulty: logarithms and exponents, significance tests and the t distribution. If you have problems when reading the chapter you should consult an elementary statistical text.

INTRODUCTION

Regression is a big subject. There seems almost no limit to the ways in which it can be extended and to the complexity it can involve. For a manager the line has to be drawn somewhere and this chapter attempts to draw it. A manager should know enough to discern where causal modelling can be applied, and enough of the theory to read reports and to manage in-company experts and consultants.

The chapter deals with two extensions to basic regression analysis, multiple and non-linear regression. It also outlines the underlying statistical theory and how statistical tests can be used, for example in assessing whether residuals are random. Finally, to bring everything together, there is a step-by-step summary of the whole regression process.

MULTIPLE REGRESSION ANALYSIS

An example of regression analysis in the previous chapter looked at the relationship between sales, the dependent variable, and promotional expenditure, the independent variable. This is *simple* regression. But you do not need any special knowledge to know that factors other than promotional expenditure are affecting sales – the general economic situation, advertising expenditure, the size of the sales force, actions by competitors and so on. These other factors are brought into the equation by means of *multiple* regression. In simple linear regression the equation is of the form:

$$Y = a + bx$$

In multiple regression the basic idea is extended to two or more variables on the right-hand side of the equation. For example, three 'x' variables:

$$Y = A + Bx + Cz + Dt$$

There are three independent (also called 'x' or 'right-hand side') variables x, z, t; their coefficients are B, C, D; the constant is A. This is still a linear equation because it includes only

y, x, z and t but no squared, cubed, logarithmic etc. terms. If y is the sales of a pharmaceutical product and x is promotional expenditure, then z could be an economic measure such as personal disposable income and t could be the number of sales people in the sales force. The a and b in the first equation will not be the same (except by a remote chance) as A and B in the second equation. When additional variables are added the coefficients of existing variables will be re-calculated with multiple regression formulae and there is no reason why they have to take their original values.

Similarities and differences between simple and multiple regression

The criterion for the 'best fit' equation in multiple regression, i.e. the basis on which A, B, C, and D are calculated, is the same as for simple regression. It is the *least squares criterion* by which the sum of squared residuals is minimised. Naturally the formulae for calculating A, B, C, D are more complicated, but this makes no apparent difference if a computer is being used. However, the formulae are too complex to be given here and we will have to work on the assumption that some computing power is available for multiple regressions and leave the formulae in their black box.

Just as in simple regression, and for the same reasons, it would be expected that, for a good model, the residuals would be random. Beyond these basic principles – the least squares criterion and the randomness of the residuals – there are important differences.

Scatter diagrams

A scatter diagram is two-dimensional and therefore it is not possible to draw one involving several variables. At the outset of the analysis a scatter diagram for each variable has to be drawn – one scatter diagram for the y variable combined with each of the x variables. The intention is just as for simple regression, that is to gain a rough idea of whether and how the variables are related.

Correlation coefficient

In simple regression, the correlation coefficient, R-squared (R^2), measures the proportion of variation in the y variable explained by the regression and is a means of quantifying the closeness of fit of the regression equation. In multiple regression, a more sensitive measure is needed for the following reason.

Following our usual example of a simple regression model:

$$\text{Sales} = a + b \times \text{Promotional expenditure}$$

to improve the accuracy of the model, a second x variable, personal disposable income (PDI), is added and the multiple regression equation becomes:

$$\text{Sales} = A + B \times \text{Births} + C \times \text{PDI}$$

The difficulty is that it is not possible for R^2 to decrease when PDI is added. Even if PDI had no influence whatsoever on Sales, R^2 could not fall because the multiple regression could 'choose' A and B to be equal to their original values, a and b, and C to be equal to 0. Then the multiple regression would be the same as the simple regression with the same R^2. Since least squares acts to minimise the sum of squared residuals and thereby maximises R^2, the new R^2 can do no worse than equal the old one. In practice a new x variable will always have at least some small influence on the y variable, even if it is spurious, and so R^2 will almost certainly rise to some extent. It will then appear that the closeness of fit has improved.

In multiple regression, a more sensitive measure of closeness of fit is the adjusted correlation coefficient squared, $\bar{R}^2$ (said R-bar-squared). This does the same job as R^2 but the formula is adjusted to make allowance for the number of x variables included. If a new x variable is unconnected with the y variable, then $\bar{R}^2$, unlike R^2, will fall. It is not necessary to know the exact nature of the adjustment since most computer packages usually print out $\bar{R}^2$ in preference to R^2. R-bar-squared is used in just the same way as R-squared, as a measure of the proportion of variation explained and thereby as a quantification of the closeness of fit. To summarise, $\bar{R}^2$ is based on R^2 but adjusted to make allowance for the unfair advantage bestowed when increasing the number of right-hand side variables included in the equation.

Collinearity

Imagine what would happen if the same x variable were included twice in the regression equation. In other words, suppose that in the equation below z and t were the same variable included twice by mistake.

$$y = a + bz + cz + dt$$

The computer package would not be able to make the calculations. However, if z and t were almost but not quite identical then the regression could proceed and c and d would be estimated. These estimates would have little value because the two variables were virtually the same. Nor would it be easy to make sense of which variable had the greater influence on the y variable.

This, in simple form, is the problem of *collinearity* (sometimes referred to as *multicollinearity*). This occurs when two (or more) of the x variables are themselves highly correlated with each other. In these circumstances the two variables are contributing essentially the same information to the regression. Because of this the regression equation is highly sensitive to small changes. Slight variations in the observations can produce large changes in the coefficient estimates which are therefore unreliable: regression finds it difficult to discriminate between the effects of the two variables. While the equation overall may still be used for forecasting, it cannot be used for assessing the individual effects of the two variables.

In multiple regression we should test for collinearity by inspecting the correlation coefficients of all x variables taken in pairs. If any of these R-squareds are high, then the corresponding two variables are collinear.

There are three remedies for collinearity:

1. *Use only one of the variables.* Which to use and which to exclude is a matter of common sense, i.e. a subjective choice of what appears to be the more relevant variable, and of which variable has the higher correlation with the y variable.

2. *Amalgamate the variables.* For example, they could be added together if the amalgamated variable is meaningful. This would be the case if promotional expenditure and advertising expenditure were added to form a 'marketing expenditure' variable.

3. *Substitute the variables with new variables.* The new variables should have a similar meaning to the original ones but without being highly correlated. For example, that part of promotional expenditure which related to magazine and television promotions (as opposed to advertising) might be removed from 'promotional expenditure' and combined with 'advertising expenditure'.

The remedies for collinearity are not precise and depend on some creative thought. The importance of collinearity is that we should be aware of the problem and the restrictions it places on interpretation.

Example

A high street retailer of household electronic goods is forecasting weekly sales of its main product lines by using multiple regression with three explanatory variables. The explanatory variables are 'gross domestic product' (GDP, reflecting the influence of the economic environment on sales), 'weekly advertising expenditure on television' and 'weekly advertising expenditure in newspapers'.

The regression analysis should follow these stages:

Inspect scatter diagrams

This is to see whether approximate linear relationships do exist. There will be three: sales against GDP, sales against TV advertising, sales against newspaper advertising.

Carry out regression analysis by computer

The computer will ask for the data values for the dependent variable, then those for the independent. The printout will look something like Table 15.1.

The equation predicting sales is:

$$\text{Sales} = 7.48 + 4.52 \times \text{GDP} + 0.65 \times \text{TVadv} + 1.89 \times \text{Newsadv}$$

Contrast this with the regression output for simple regression involving only sales and GDP (Table 15.2).

Table 15.1

	Coefficient		
GDP	4.52	R-bar-squared	0.94
TV advertising	0.65	Residual standard error	5.60
Newspaper advertising	1.89		
Constant	7.48		

Table 15.2

	Coefficient		
GDP	8.86	R-squared	0.72
Constant	11.59	Residual standard error	8.41

A number of differences have emerged.

1. The coefficient for GDP is now 4.52, whereas for simple regression it was 8.86. The addition of an extra variable changes the previous coefficients, including the constant.

2. R-bar-squared has risen to 0.94 from 0.72. The presence of the advertising expenditures has therefore noticeably increased the proportion of variation explained. This is a real increase since the adjusted correlation coefficient has been used and this makes allowance for the presence of extra variables.

3. The residual standard error has decreased. In other words, the residuals are generally smaller, as would be expected in view of the increased R-bar-squared.

Check the residuals

This process is exactly the same as for simple regression. A scatter diagram of residuals plotted against fitted y values is inspected for randomness.

Check for collinearity

Most computer packages will print out the correlation matrix showing the correlations between the x variables taken in pairs. For example, see Table 15.3.

There is a fairly high correlation (0.6) between the two advertising variables and so they appear to be collinear. Their coefficients will not be reliable and could not be used with confidence to compare the effectiveness of the two types of advertising. To overcome the problem the possibility of amalgamating the variables to form a combined advertising expenditure variable should be investigated.

The other remedies for collinearity would probably not be used. Since the correlation between them is far from perfect (0.6, and so the variables do contribute some separate information), it would be wrong to drop one of the variables completely. It is unlikely that the third remedy for collinearity (finding substitutes) could be applied because the meanings of the two variables are already narrow and precise.

However, if the purpose of the regression is solely to predict sales the equation could still be used as it stands. Values for GDP and advertising would be inserted in the equation to give a predicted value for sales.

Dummy variables

Some data have a 'two-category' definition, for example male/female employees, yes/no responses to a questionnaire, and are represented by dummy variables. A dummy vari-

Table 15.3

Variable	1	2	3
1	1.0	0.1	0.3
2		1.0	0.6
3			1.0

able takes just two values, 0 and 1, and is used in multiple regression in exactly the same way as any other variable.

For example, a study of capital expenditure by government departments used regression analysis to relate the expenditure in any one year to two other variables: last year's expenditure and the amount by which last year's expenditure request had been cut. The data covered 20 years, i.e. there were 20 observations. The purpose of the study was to investigate whether departments employed 'budget strategies' to maximise the amount they would be allowed to spend. For example, did they ask for much more than they needed to anticipate expected cuts in their request? Did the level of their requests reflect what had happened to the previous year's request?

It was thought that the political party in power at the time might be an important factor and this was represented in the regression by a dummy variable. There were two main parties and therefore the dummy took the value '0' for the years in which one of the parties was in government and '1' for the years when the other was in government.

The regression calculated a coefficient for the dummy variable. This was interpreted as the amount by which capital expenditure changed when the second party (for dummy = 1) was in power. The sign of the coefficient showed whether the change was an increase or decrease.

Dummy variables can be used whenever data are in 'two-category' form. The situation is more complicated when the data can take more than two categories. For example, if three political parties were to be represented, it would not be possible to use 0 for the first, 1 for the second and 2 for the third. This would imply a ranking, for example that the third party had twice the effect of the second.

NON-LINEAR REGRESSION ANALYSIS

The previous section was concerned with the extension of simple regression to multiple regression. In this section we consider the extension from *linear* to *non-linear* regression. In other words, the equations expressing the relationship between the variables will no longer always be of a linear form such as:

$$y = a + bx + cz$$

In non-linear regression the right-hand side variables may appear in squared, cubed, logarithmic and other forms; a scatter diagram need no longer approximate to a straight line. The usual ways of carrying out a non-linear regression are based on converting or *transforming* the non-linearity so that it appears to be linear. Two examples of linear transformations are now described.

Curvilinear regression

In curvilinear regression, squared, cubed etc. terms in an x variable are treated as separate variables in a multiple regression. For example, the non-linear equation:

$$y = a + bx + cx^2 \tag{1}$$

is a curved relationship. For example, Figure 15.1 shows the graph (for $x = 0$ to 6) of the

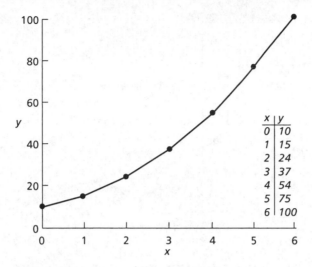

Figure 15.1   Graph of $y = 10 + 3x + 2x^2$

equation:

$$y = 10 + 3x + 2x^2$$

Curvilinear regression treats such an equation as (1) (a quadratic equation) as if it were of the form:

$$y = a + bx + cz$$

x^2 is treated as if it were an entirely separate variable, z, rather than the square of x. Multiple regression is then used to estimate the coefficients a, b and c. After estimation x^2 is restored to the equation which can then be used for forecasting.

Example

The data in Table 15.4 relate to the production of children's shoes by a manufacturer who is a supplier to major chains of shoe retailers. The manufacturer has ten production plants in different locations. y is the productivity (in '000 units per person p.a.) and x is the capital employed (in £ million, for production equipment only) at each of the 10 production plants. Find the curvilinear regression equation linking the data.

Figure 15.2 shows a scatter diagram of the data The relationship does not appear to be linear. The shape looks similar to that in Figure 15.1 and a curvilinear regression involving x and x^2 seems to be a reasonable starting point for the analysis.

To carry out the regression a 'new' variable equal to x^2 must be created. The data fed into the computer regression package will be for three variables (Table 15.5).

The output for this regression is of the form shown in Table 15.6.

Table 15.4

y	8	9	12	16	21	39	43	53	65	79
x	2	3	3	4	5	7	7	8	9	10

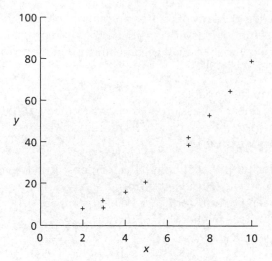

Figure 15.2 Productivity and capital employed in manufacture of children's shoes

Table 15.5

y	8	9	12	16	21	39	43	53	65	79
x	2	3	3	4	5	7	7	8	9	10
z	4	9	9	16	25	49	49	64	81	100

Table 15.6

Variable	Coefficient
x	−0.50
z	0.80
Constant	5.10
R-bar-squared = 0.99	
Residual standard error = 1.57	

From the output, the regression equation is:

$$y = 5.1 - 0.5x + 0.8z$$

The correlation coefficient is high (R-bar-squared = 0.99). The residual should also be inspected for randomness. Restoring x^2 to the equation in place of z:

$$y = 5.1 - 0.5x + 0.8z^2$$

The equation can now be used to forecast values of y given values of x.

Transformation

A variable is *transformed* when some algebraic operation is applied to it. For example, a variable x is transformed when it is turned into its square (x^2), or its reciprocal ($1/x$), or its logarithm (log x). Many other transformations are possible, and some are even useful. The principle behind the use of transformations in regression is that a non-linear relationship between two variables may become linear when one (or both) of the variables is transformed. The process is:

- transform the variable(s);
- perform linear regression on the transformed variables;
- de-transform the equation to its non-linear form;
- make forecasts.

The principle is that although the relationship between y and x seems to be non-linear, it may be possible to find a transformation of either y or x or both such that the relationship between the transformed variables is linear.

For example, a relationship of the form:

$$Y = a.e^{bx} \qquad (2)$$

is non-linear between y and x. This is the *exponential function* which is characterised by the fact that each time x increases by 1, y increases by a constant proportion or percentage of itself. A linear function ($Y = A + BX$), on the other hand, is characterised by the fact that each time X increases by 1, Y increases by a constant amount (= B). Linear means a *constant* increase (or decrease); exponential means a *constant percentage* increase (or decrease). For instance, if the sales increase of some product were thought likely to be 20 per cent per year, the relationship between sales and time would be exponential. Were the increase thought likely to be a constant amount, say £500 000 each year, the relationship would be linear.

The practical issue in the particular case of non-linear regression where an exponential function is involved is this. Suppose that two variables are thought to be related by an exponential function and that some historical data are available. How can the equation relating the variables (i.e. the values of a and b in equation (2)) be found when the regression formula applies only to linear relationships?

Figure 15.3a shows the graph of the exponential function. A transformation can make it linear. If natural logarithms (to the base e) are taken of each side of the equation and some algebra applied using the rules for manipulating logarithms. The result is:

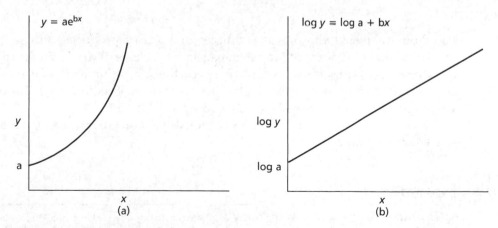

Figure 15.3   The exponential function

$$y = a.e^{bx}$$
$$\log y = \log(a.e^{bx})$$
$$\log y = \log a + b.x$$

The new equation has the linear form:

$$Y = A + BX$$

with

$$Y = \log y$$
$$A = \log a$$
$$B = b$$
$$X = x$$

If a graph relating log y and x is drawn (Figure 15.3b) it will be linear. The regression formulae can now be applied to the transformed variables, log y and x, since they are linearly related. The coefficient estimates obtained from this equation are equal to log a and b. If the antilog of the former is taken, the exponential function (2) has been completely determined. Given a value for x, the corresponding value for y can be calculated. Logarithms to bases other than to the base e can be used, but the slope coefficient in the transformed equation is no longer simply equal to b in the untransformed equation.

The situation can be summarised as follows. Two variables, x and y, are, it is thought, related by an exponential function. The y variable is transformed by taking its logarithmic values. Linear regression is applied to log y and x as if they were two new variables. The coefficient estimates obtained from this linear regression can be translated into the coefficients of the exponential function, which can then be used to forecast.

It is important to be clear that the underlying relationship between y and x is not itself being altered. There is no sense in which this curved relationship is being forced to be linear. It is the way the relationship is expressed mathematically that is changed. The 'trick' of expressing the same relationship in a different form makes it possible to use regression analysis.

Example

Based on experience with previously successful software products and sales data from the first few months of a new project management package (PM), the marketing director of a well-established software company expects the sales volume of PM to grow rapidly, according to an exponential pattern, for three years from its launch date. The retail sales volumes for PM for the first 12 months were as in Table 15.7.

Use regression analysis to find the exponential equation linking sales and time. Predict sale volume for the next 3 months.

Table 15.7

Sales volume	y	12	14	17	20	24	28	34	41	48	56	66	76
Month	x	1	2	3	4	5	6	7	8	9	10	11	12

Table 15.8

Log y	2.48	2.64	2.83	3.00	3.18	3.33	3.53	3.71	3.87	4.03	4.19	4.33
x	1	2	3	4	5	6	7	8	9	10	11	12

Table 15.9

Variable	Coefficient
x	0.17
Constant	2.32
R-bar-squared	0.99
Residual standard error	0.02

An exponential equation is of the form:

$$y = a.e^{bx}$$

Fitting an equation of this type to the data amounts to estimating the values of a and b. In order to use linear regression formulae, the equation must first be transformed to a linear one. Taking logarithms of both sides, the equation becomes:

$$\log y = \log a + b.x$$

The regression is performed on $\log y$ and x. To do this the logarithms of the sales must be found (Table 15.8).

Putting these two variables into a regression package, the output is as shown in Table 15.9. From the output the linear equation is:

$$\log y = 2.32 + 0.17x$$

i.e.

$$b = 0.17 \text{ and } \log a = 2.32$$

Taking the anti-logarithm of 2.32:

$$a = 10.2$$

The exponential function relating to y and x is therefore:

$$y = 10.2e^{0.17x}$$

The usual checks on the correlation coefficient and the residuals should be carried out at this point just as for standard linear regression analysis.

The next three time periods are for $x = 13, 14, 15$. Substituting these values in the estimated exponential equation gives the following predictions for y (Table 15.10).

Two factors were the main reasons why transformation worked in the above case. First, there was a belief, founded on marketing experience, that sales in the product were increasing by a constant percentage each year and would continue to do so, i.e. there was

Table 15.10

y	93.0	110.2	130.6
x	13	14	15

good reason for applying the exponential function. Secondly, having decided to use the exponential function it was fortunate that it is one of the relatively few non-linear relationships that can be made linear by applying a transformation to both sides of the equation. Most non-linear relationships cannot be made linear in such a neat, and theoretically valid, way.

In (most) other situations such good fortune will not apply. There will not be such a good basis for using transformations and trial and error must be substituted instead in determining whether a transformation will turn non-linearity into linearity. In these situations transformations can be helpful in a different way. The scatter diagram is the starting point. It may show a curve of some sort, but it may be difficult to go further and suggest possible non-linear equations that fit it. It may then be necessary to try several transformations by using the squares, square roots, reciprocals, logarithms etc. of one or both of the variables to find the scatter diagram of transformed variables which looks most like a straight line. Equally, regression analysis may be carried out with several types of transformation to find the one which gives the best statistical results, highest R-squared, random residuals, etc.

This approach, although sometimes necessary, can be dangerous. If enough transformations are tried it is usually possible, eventually, to come up with one that appears satisfactory. However, there may be no sound business reason for using the transformation. The model may be purely associative. If at all possible it is better to base the choice of transformation on logic, theory and experience rather than on exhaustive trial and error.

For example, take a manufacturer with several plants all manufacturing the same product. The unit cost of production (y) will vary with the capacity of the plant (x). The relationship is unlikely to be linear because of economies of scale. Finding a transformation that expresses the relationship in linear form could be based on trial and error. Several transformations of y and x could be tried until one is found which appears (from the scatter diagram or regression results) to make the relationship linear. But it would be preferable to have a sound reason for trying particular transformations. The 'law' of economies of scale suggests that unit costs might be inversely proportional to capacity. This is a good reason for transforming capacity to 1/capacity and considering the relationship between unit cost of production (y) and 1/capacity ($1/x$). If this relationship appears to be linear then statistics and logic are working together.

When this is the case then the statistics are in the position of confirming the logic. Otherwise there will be no underlying basis for using the transformation and the statistics will be in isolation from the real situation. The dangers of confusing causality and association and of producing spurious correlations, as discussed in the last chapter, will arise. Or attempts will be made to rationalise the structure of the situation to fit in with the statistics. This might of course lead to the discovery of new theories – this is, after all, where Newton, Boyle and Einstein all made their mark. The conclusion must be that the trial and error approach to transformation should not be ruled out, but it should be used with caution.

STATISTICAL BASIS OF REGRESSION AND CORRELATION

Calculating the 'best fit' line or curve through a set of points and judging its strength have been described so far in this chapter and the previous one in a non-rigorous fashion. The statistical basis of regression and correlation gives more depth to the subject. It allows causal models to be tested statistically rather than visually or by rule of thumb. For example, the randomness of residuals, up to now, has been judged by inspection. A statistical perspective, based on sampling, allows their randomness to be tested more precisely. For the moment we will restrict the discussion on the underlying statistical theory to simple linear regression.

If it is believed that two variables are linearly related, then the statistician supposes (or, more technically, hypothesises) that, in the population of all possible observations on the two variables, a straight-line relationship does exist. Any deviations from this (the residuals) are caused by minor random disturbances, measurement errors, etc. A sample is then taken from the population and used to estimate the equation's coefficients, the correlation coefficients and other statistics. This sample is merely the set of points upon which calculations of a, b, and R-squared have been based up to now.

However, the fact that these calculations are made from sample data means that a, b and R-squared are no more than estimates. Had a different sample been chosen, different values would have been obtained. Were it possible to take many samples (in theory it is possible, in practice it is never done), distributions of the coefficients would be obtained.

These distributions (of a, b, R-squared and other statistics) are the basis of significance tests of whether the hypothesis of a straight-line relationship in the population is true. They are also the basis for determining the accuracy of regression predictions. The statistical approach has several practical implications.

Measuring closeness of fit

Correlation is measuring the strength of a relationship. So far this has meant looking at R^2 or, in multiple regression, R-bar-squared, and making a judgement on whether it is high enough. By use of *ANOVA* and the *F statistic* it is possible to carry out a statistical test. If you remember, R-squared acts as a measure of correlation by considering the total variation in the y variable before regression:

$$\text{Total sum of squares} = \text{Sum}(y - \text{mean }(y))^2$$

After regression this can be split into two parts:

$$\text{Total SS} = \text{Explained SS} + \text{Unexplained SS}$$

where,

$$\text{Explained sum of squares} = \text{variation which is explicable because of regression}$$
$$= \text{Sum(fitted } y - y)^2$$

$$\text{Unexplained sum of squares} = \text{variation left unexplained}$$
$$= \text{variation in residuals}$$
$$= \text{Sum(residuals)}^2$$

The correlation coefficient squared is:

$$R^2 = \frac{\text{Explained variation}}{\text{Total variation}}$$

Hence R^2 measures the proportion of variation explained by regression. This can be turned into a significance test of whether the regression explains a statistically significant amount of variation by applying *analysis of variance* (known as *ANOVA*). 'Statistically significant' is defined as meaning that such a degree of explanation is unlikely (by convention, less than 5 per cent likely) to have happened purely by chance. In other words, some explanatory power is at work.

Analysis of variance splits total variation into parts attributable to different sources and then tests whether such variations could be expected purely by chance, i.e. whether the explanatory variable really has no influence but by dint of the particular sample data chosen appears to have an influence. In regression the total variation is split into that attributable to regression (explained) and that forming the residuals (unexplained). Analysis of variance then tests whether 'explained' variation is larger than would be expected by chance. If so, it is concluded that the regression equation does have a significant effect in explaining correlation. Analysis of variance is a complex topic which is only outlined here in order to explain references to ANOVA in some computer outputs.

ANOVA tests are based on the *F statistic* and ANOVA output will typically say something like 'F is significant with p = 1.2 per cent'. This means that the regression equation does explain a significant amount of variation in the y value and that the likelihood of this happening by chance is only 1.2 per cent.

The level which R-squared needs to reach to be statistically significant depends on the number of explanatory variables used and the number of data observations used in making the regression estimates. We have already seen how the addition of further explanatory variables tends to increase R-squared. The number of observations are also important because it is easier to fit a straight line and keep the residuals small when there are three points (even when they lie on a circle) than it is to 100 points lying on the same circle. The threshold for statistical significance is therefore higher for few observations than for many.

In summary, R-squared (or R-bar-squared) tells us the proportion of variation explained by the regression; ANOVA tells us whether this proportion is statistically significant.

Testing that the residuals are random

The statistical approach to regression hypothesizes a true linear relationship. Any deviations from it are minor random disturbances. Not only is the randomness part of the hypothesis, it is also intuitively reasonable. If the residuals are not random, then they must have a pattern in them. If they have a pattern then the linear model is not adequate and should be in some way revised or altered to incorporate it. If they are random then the linear model must be the best pattern that can be obtained from data.

Many statistical tests for randomness exist. The *Durbin–Watson* test is a common example and one that is incorporated in many computer printouts. The DW statistic measures *serial correlation*, the relationship between each residual and its predecessor. It takes on values between 0 and 4 and should, if there is no serial correlation, equal or be close to 2. The DW test can give one of three results:

1. Accept the hypothesis that there is no serial correlation. This occurs when the statistic is close to 2.

2. The test is inconclusive. This occurs when the statistic is further from 2, whether above or below.

3. Reject the hypothesis of no serial correlation. This occurs when the statistic is close to 0 or 4.

The exact boundaries between these outcomes vary, depending on the number of observations and the number of right-hand side variables. Durbin–Watson tables must be used to define the critical values in each situation.

Deciding which variables to retain

Multiple regression allows more than one right-hand side variable to be included in the regression equation and examples earlier in the chapter have included two or three x variables. But why stop at three? There is nothing to prevent the inclusion of any number of x variables and, with the aid of a computer, the complexity of the formulae is no barrier. How can we decide how many explanatory variables to include?

The criterion is that we should include any x variable provided it has a *significant* (in the statistical sense) effect on the y variable. Taking the statistical perspective on regression analysis allows us to carry out a significance test for each variable. For any x variable the hypothesis is that it has no influence on the y variable. In other words, the coefficient of the variable is in reality zero but the fact that the coefficients were estimated from a particular sample of data has resulted in a non-zero coefficient purely by chance. If the significance test shows that the estimated coefficient is *not* significantly different from zero then the hypothesis is accepted and it is concluded that this x variable *has no effect* on the y variable. This x variable can be discarded from the regression equation. If the test shows that the estimated coefficient *is* significantly different from zero then the hypothesis is rejected and it is concluded that this x variable *has an effect* on the y variable. This x variable has been included in the equation correctly (see Figure 15.4).

Technical note[1]

The basis of the test is that the coefficient of each right-hand side variable follows a *t distribution*. The statistical reasons for this and t distribution theory will not be discussed here. But this fact gives the test its name – the *t test*. Like all significance tests, the t test has five stages.

1. *Hypothesise* that the variable does not influence the y variable and that therefore its true coefficient is zero.

2. *Collect evidence.* This is the set of observations from which, among other things, the coefficient of the variable and its standard error will have been estimated.

3. Set the *significance level*, usually at 5 per cent. This implies that we are prepared to

[1] This is a brief review of the theory behind a t test. For a detailed description, consult a book on elementary statistics.

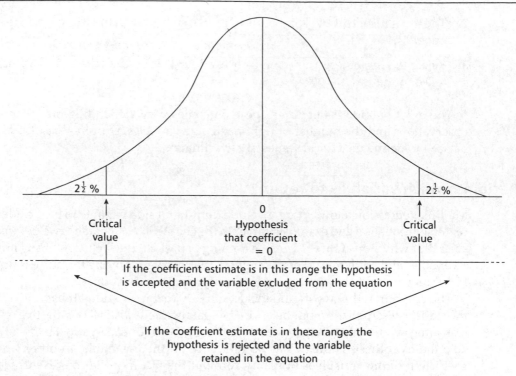

Figure 15.4   t test for variable coefficient

accept no more than a 5 per cent chance of incorrectly accepting the hypothesis that the x variable has no influence on the y variable.

4. *Calculate* the ratio:

$$t = \frac{\text{Coefficient estimate} - 0}{\text{Standard error}}$$

Conventionally this ratio is referred to as the 'observed t ratio'.

5. *Compare* the observed t ratio with the critical value and decide whether to accept or reject the hypothesis that the variable has no influence on the y variable (see Figure 15.4). The critical value depends on the significance level and the degrees of freedom.

Degrees of freedom = number of observations (i.e. number of data points)

− number of coefficients in the equation which were estimated from the data.

For example, if there were two years of monthly data and there were three x variables and a constant in the regression equation, then:

Degrees of freedom = 24 − 4 = 20

When the degrees of freedom are known then the critical t value can be found from a t distribution table (see the *t*-distribution table in the Appendix). For 20 degrees of freedom and a 5 per cent significance level (2.5 per cent in either tail), the critical t value is 2.086.

Table 15.11

	Coefficient	Std. error	t value
GDP	4.13	0.60	6.88
Advertising	0.76	0.25	3.04
Promotions	3.66	2.40	1.53
Constant	4.74	2.00	2.37
R-bar-squared		0.98	
RSE		2.0	
Degrees of freedom		42	

Most computer packages print out the t ratio automatically as the ratio between coefficient estimate and standard error.

Example

An earlier example was of a high street retailer of household electronic goods, forecasting the weekly sales of its main product lines by using multiple regression with three explanatory variables. The explanatory variables were 'gross domestic product' (GDP), 'weekly advertising expenditure on television' and 'weekly advertising expenditure in newspapers'. The second and third variables were then combined, because of collinearity, into one variable, 'advertising expenditure'. Suppose a third variable is now added. It is a dummy variable which takes the value '0' when there are no special promotions in the week, '1' when there are. The computer printout is as shown in Table 15.11.

Are all the three variables, GDP, advertising and promotions, correctly included in the regression equation?

The computer output shown above is more extensive than the examples we have seen up to now since it includes coefficient standard errors and t values. Most packages would show at least this much information.

To answer the question, a t test must be carried out on the coefficients for each of the variables. Because the observed t ratios have been printed out this can be done very easily. In each case the critical t value is 2.02 (for a 5 per cent significance level and 42 degrees of freedom).

For 'GDP' and 'advertising', the t ratios exceed the critical value. These variables therefore must both have a significant effect on 'sales' and are correctly included in the equation. The observed t ratio for 'promotions' is 1.5, less than the critical value. According to the statistical test, 'promotions' does not have a significant effect on 'sales'. The variable could be eliminated from the equation.

Accuracy of forecasts

The forecast corresponding to an x value is found by putting the x value into the equation and calculating y. This y value is called a *point estimate*, but it is of limited value if you do not also have some assessment of how accurate it is likely to be and what level of accuracy is needed in the decisions for which it is to be used. So how accurate is a point estimate likely to be?

The residuals are the basis for measuring the accuracy of a prediction. Intuitively this makes sense, because the residuals are the historical differences between the actual values and the regression line. It might be expected that actual values in the future will differ from the regression line by similar amounts. Therefore the variation in the residuals, as measured by their standard error, is an approximate indication of forecasting accuracy. If the residuals are normally distributed, as we have been assuming, then the approximate *95 per cent confidence limits* for the point estimate forecast are:

Point estimate +/−2 × residual standard error

(because 95 per cent of a normally distributed variable lies within +/−2 standard errors).

The confidence limits are interpreted as meaning that we are 95 per cent confident that the true value of the sales, for example, which we are trying to forecast will lie within this range.

The residuals are what is 'left over', outside a regression equation. However, there is also error within the regression model – the inaccuracy in the estimation of the coefficients of the variables and the constant. This inaccuracy is measured through the standard errors of the coefficient estimates.

The overall uncertainty in a prediction comes therefore from two areas:

● what the regression does not deal with – the residuals;
● uncertainty in what the regression does deal with – the error in the estimate of the x variable coefficients.

Both types of error are combined in the *standard error of predicted values*, often shortened to *SE(Pred)*. The formula for this standard error is a complicated one, integrating as it does the standard errors mentioned above. However, most computer estimates have the capability to print it out automatically.

Once calculated, SE(Pred) is used to determine confidence intervals for predictions. Provided we are prepared to accept the normal distribution assumption, 95 per cent of future values of the variable are likely to lie within +/−2 SE(Pred) of the point estimate. 95 per cent confidence limits define what is sometimes called the *forecast interval*. This is used to decide whether the level of accuracy is sufficient for the decisions being taken.

Suppose an organisation is forecasting its profit in the next financial year in order to take pricing decisions. The point forecast is £100 million, the SE(Pred) is £8 million. We are therefore '95 per cent confident' that the profit will turn out to be in the range £84 to £116 million.

SE(Pred) is different for each different set of x values used to make the prediction. A simple regression example can demonstrate this. Since the x value is multiplied by the slope in making the prediction, any inaccuracy in estimating the x variable coefficient must vary as the x values vary. Figure 15.5 shows how the forecast interval varies for different x values. The interval is wider for x values which are further from the centre of regression.

In many regards, SE(Pred) is the most important measure in a causal forecasting model. Whatever the statistical indications of the regression model – R-squared, t values etc. – the real question is whether a prediction is sufficiently accurate to be useful to the decision maker. In the pricing example above, the question is whether radically different decisions would be taken if the profit were at different parts of the forecast interval. Is the forecast interval so wide that the forecast gives no reliable guide to determining which pricing

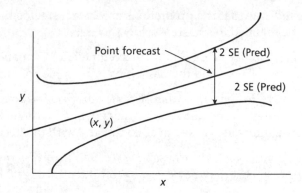

Figure 15.5   Variation in the forecast interval

decisions should be taken? If this is the case, then the search must go on for more accurate predictions, and therefore better regression models; if the forecast does indicate which pricing decisions should be taken, then what would be the benefit of further refinement of the model? In summary, the forecast interval is the final determinant of whether the regression model is satisfactory.

REGRESSION ANALYSIS SUMMARY

The necessary components for carrying out a regression analysis are now available. The purpose of this section is to bring them all together into a coherent form and provide a structured approach to a regression problem. The steps suggested below assume that the problem to be tackled is one of making predictions, whether time related or cross-sectional, rather than just establishing the existence of a relationship.

1. *Propose a tentative model.* Use scatter diagrams to decide, initially, what the regression equation might be. This stage involves some tentative decisions as to which x variables to include and which transformations to use to handle any curvature. It will also consider the extent and type of data available.

2. *Run the regression and check the closeness of fit.* A computer printout would provide R-bar-squared and thereby show whether a high proportion of the original variation in the y variable had been explained.

3. *Check the residuals.* The residuals should be random. A scatter diagram between residuals and fitted values will demonstrate this visually; the Durbin–Watson statistic will permit the check to be made statistically.

4. *Decide whether any x variables could be discarded.* A t test on each x variable coefficient will indicate if the variable has a significant influence on the y variable. If not, the variable could be discarded, but this decision should also be based on experience and common sense. For example, if there were a good non-statistical reason for including a particular x variable then a t value of, say, 1.4 should not automatically lead to its elimination. This situation arose in the earlier example of the high street electronics retailer where the t value of the coefficient of 'special promotions' was 1.5. If sales

reports indicate that the promotions are in fact having an effect, then the variable should be retained in spite of the low t value.

5. *Check for collinearity.* A correlation matrix for all the *x* variables will show which, if any, of them are collinear and therefore have unreliable coefficient estimates.

6. *Decide if the regression estimates are accurate enough for the decision.* For the point estimate corresponding to any particular *x* value(s), SE(Pred) will be the basis of calculating confidence intervals. These can be contrasted with the decision which is being taken.

7. *If necessary, formulate a new regression model.* Should any of the checks have given unsatisfactory results, it may be necessary to return to stage 1 and try again with a new model.

CONCLUSION

The intention of this chapter has been to extend the ideas of simple linear regression by removing the limitations of 'simple' and 'linear'.

First, multiple regression analysis makes the extension beyond simple regression. It tries to explain changes in one variable (the *y* variable) by relating them to changes in several other variables (the *x* variables). Multiple regression analysis is based on the same principle, the least squares criterion, as simple regression. However, the addition of the extra *x* variables does bring about added complications. Table 15.12 summarises the similarities and differences between the two cases as far as their practical application is concerned.

The second extension beyond regression is to 'curved' relationships between variables. This is done by transforming one or more of the variables so that the equation can be handled as if it were linear. The range of possible transformations is wide, allowing regression analysis to be applied to a variety of non-linear relationships.

It may seem that all these possibilities of many explanatory variables and many types of equation will be highly advantageous to the decision maker, but they do lead to a danger. This is that more and more regression variations will be tried until one is found which just happens to fit the set of observations that are available. Indeed, there is a technique called *stepwise regression* which is a process for regressing all possible combinations of variables and selecting the one that, statistically, is the best. The selection is made automatically by the computer. The risk with stepwise regression and similar approaches is

---

Table 15.12

Similarities
1.   Substitution of *x* values in regression equation to make predictions.
2.   R-bar-squared to measure closeness of fit.
3.   Checking of residuals for randomness.
4.   Use of SE(Pred) to measure accuracy.

Differences
1.   Adjustment of correlation coefficient to allow for degrees of freedom.
2.   t test to determine variables to leave out.
3.   Check for collinearity.

that causality will be forgotten. Ideally the role of regression should be to confirm some prior belief, rather than to find a 'belief' from the data. This latter process can of course be successful, but it is likely to lead to many purely associative relationships between variables. In multiple and non-linear regression analysis it is more important than ever to ask the question: Does it all make sense? This question should be asked even when, or especially when, the statistical checks are satisfactory.

The theoretical background to regression has also been introduced. The whole subject is large and complex and we have done no more than scratch the surface. The next logical step would have been to look at criteria other than that of least squares. The theoretical aspects led to consideration of statistical tests for regression analysis. The ones mentioned in the chapter are just a few of the many available.

Fortunately computer packages, so essential to all but the smallest of problems, can carry out these tests automatically. But this in itself brings a problem, because when a package carries so much information it is difficult to understand and interpret the computer output. A major problem faced by new users of regression analysis is that, while they may have a good understanding of the topic, their first sight of a computer printout may despondency, even despair, to set in. The answer is not to be put off by the initial shock, but to persevere and learn to select from the output just those parts that are essential. Computer packages are trying to satisfy a wide range of users at all levels of sophistication, and their output tends to include everything that any one person could reasonably ask for.

Perhaps the best advice in this statistical minefield is to make the correct balance between statistical and non-statistical factors. The profusion of complex data produced by a regression package can promote a spurious sense both of accuracy and of the importance of the statistical aspects. It is not unknown for experts in regression analysis to make mountains out of statistical molehills.

CASE STUDIES

CASE STUDY 1

The computer output in Table 15.13 is from a multiple regression analysis relating sales volume to three types of promotional expenditure – advertising spend (£'000), promotional spend (£'000) and the number of people in the sales force.

1. What are the t values for the three variables?

2. How many observations was the regression analysis based on?

Table 15.13

Variable	Coefficient	Standard error
Advertising	8.0	1.2
Promotion	10.3	7.0
Force	35.0	5.6
Constant	8.5	1.4
Degrees of freedom = 36		

3. Why, statistically, should the variable relating to promotional spend be eliminated from the regression equation?

Solutions

1. *What are the t values for the three variables?*
A t value is the ratio between the coefficient of a variable and the standard error of the estimate of the coefficient. Therefore the t values are:

Advertising spend: 8.0/1.2 = 6.67
Promotional spend: 10.3/7.0 = 1.47
Sales force: 35/5.6 = 6.25

2. *How many observations was the regression analysis based on?*
The degrees of freedom are 36 and four factors (the coefficients of the three variables and the constant) were estimated from the data. Therefore, from the definition of degrees of freedom, there must have been 40 observations.

3. *Why, statistically, should the variable relating to promotional spend be eliminated from the regression equation?*
Its t value is 1.47, less than the critical level of approximately 2.0. Therefore, statistically, it does not have a significant influence on sales. However, there may be non-statistical reasons for keeping it in the regression equation.

CASE STUDY 2

A national government analyst is investigating the fuel consumption of a popular make of car when it runs on a new 'environment friendly' unleaded petrol. The preliminary data

Table 15.14

Trip	Miles/ gallon (mpg)	Average speed (mph)	Altitude ('00)	Passenger weight ('00k)
1	34	55	0	2
2	37	40	1	3
3	26	40	3	2
4	26	50	4	4
5	31	30	1	3
6	26	45	5	4
7	22	50	3	5
8	35	30	0	2
9	32	45	1	3
10	25	55	2	3
11	23	50	4	4
12	24	50	2	2
13	30	45	3	2
14	39	35	0	2
15	31	45	1	3

Table 15.15

Variable	Coefficient	Std error
mph	−0.2	0.12
altitude	−2.0	0.7
weight	−0.5	1.2
constant	43.7	
R-bar-squared 0.70		
Standard error of residuals 3.3		

shown in Table 15.14 were collected from 15 trips of similar length in the same car. The evidence collected from each trip consisted of the fuel consumption in miles per gallon, the average speed in miles per hour, the average altitude in hundreds of metres and the total weight of passengers and luggage in the car in hundreds of kilos.

In an attempt to measure the effect on fuel consumption of speed, altitude and load, multiple regression analysis was used, relating fuel consumption to speed, altitude and load. The results (rounded) are shown in Table 15.15.

1. What is the regression equation linking fuel consumption to the other variables? What consumption would you predict for a trip at an average speed of 40 mph, at an altitude of 300 metres and with total passenger weight 200 kilos?

2. Calculate the values of the residuals. Is there a pattern in the residuals?

3. Should any of the variables be excluded from the regression equation?

4. Approximately, using the standard error of the residuals from the computer output, what is the accuracy of the prediction you made in question 1?

5. How might the analysis be improved?

Solutions

1. *What is the regression equation linking fuel consumption to the other variables? What consumption would you predict for a trip at an average speed of 40 mph, at an altitude of 300 metres and with total passenger weight 200 kilos?*
The regression equation is:

$$\text{mpg} = 43.7 - 0.2 \times \text{speed} - 2 \times \text{altitude} - 0.5 \times \text{weight}$$

When speed = 40, altitude = 300 and weight = 200,

$$\text{mpg} = 43.9 - 0.2 \times 40 - 2 \times 3 - 0.5 \times 2$$

$$= 28.9$$

2. *Calculate the values of the residuals. Is there a pattern in the residuals?*
There seems to be no particular pattern in the residuals: the negative residuals and the larger residuals seem to be spread across all the trips.

Table 15.16

Trip	Residual	
1	2.3	= 34 − (43.7 − 0.2 × 55 − 2 × 0 − 0.5 × 2)
2	4.8	= 37 − (43.7 − 0.2 × 40 − 2 × 1 − 0.5 × 3)
3	−2.7	= 26 − (43.7 − 0.2 × 40 − 2 × 3 − 0.5 × 2)
4	2.3	= 26 − (43.7 − 0.2 × 50 − 2 × 4 − 0.5 × 4)
5	−3.2	= 31 − (43.7 − 0.2 × 30 − 2 × 1 − 0.5 × 3)
6	3.3	= 26 − (43.7 − 0.2 × 45 − 2 × 5 − 0.5 × 4)
7	−3.2	= 22 − (43.7 − 0.2 × 50 − 2 × 3 − 0.5 × 5)
8	−1.7	= 35 − (43.7 − 0.2 × 30 − 2 × 0 − 0.5 × 2)
9	0.8	= 32 − (43.7 − 0.2 × 45 − 2 × 1 − 0.5 × 3)
10	−2.2	= 25 − (43.7 − 0.2 × 55 − 2 × 2 − 0.5 × 3)
11	−0.7	= 23 − (43.7 − 0.2 × 50 − 2 × 4 − 0.5 × 4)
12	−4.7	= 24 − (43.7 − 0.2 × 50 − 2 × 2 − 0.5 × 2)
13	2.3	= 30 − (43.7 − 0.2 × 45 − 2 × 3 − 0.5 × 2)
14	3.3	= 39 − (43.7 − 0.2 × 35 − 2 × 0 − 0.5 × 2)
15	−0.2	= 31 − (43.7 − 0.2 × 45 − 2 × 1 − 0.5 × 3)

Table 15.17

Variable	Coefficient	Std. error	t value
mph	−0.2	0.12	−1.67
altitude	−2.0	0.70	−2.86
weight	−0.5	1.2	−0.42

3. *Should any of the variables be excluded from the regression equation?*
To see if variables should be excluded, the t values have to be calculated (see Table 15.17).
  There are 11 degrees of freedom (15 observations − four estimates). The critical t value for 11 degrees of freedom and a 5 per cent significance level is, from the t table, 2.201. Altitude has a t value that is less than −2.2 and is rightfully included. There is some doubt about speed since its t value is not less than −2.2. However, other evidence (on the working of internal combustion engines) suggests that it should be retained, especially since the t value is not far short of the critical value. Weight presents more of a problem since its t value is close to zero. It could probably be eliminated. We know that weight must affect the petrol consumption (again from the workings of the internal combustion engine), but perhaps the weight variation in the trials is not sufficient to make an appreciable difference.

4. *Approximately, using the standard error of the residuals from the computer output, what is the accuracy of the prediction made in question 1?*
Approximately, the accuracy of the forecast (95 per cent confidence limits) in question 1 is given by 2 × residual standard error,

$$\text{i.e. } +/-6.6$$

5. *How might the analysis be improved?*
R-bar-squared is 70 per cent so that 30 per cent of the variation in fuel consumption has not yet been explained. We should try to improve the correlation either by including other variables (for example for wet or dry conditions, or for temperature) or by eliminating other

variations (for example by ensuring that the style of driving (or the driver) does not change from trip to trip), and checking that the terrain is approximately the same for each trip, i.e. the same mixture of urban and rural. In any case more trials should be conducted: 15 observations are too few when there are 3 independent variables.

QUESTIONS

1. Are the following true or false?
   (a) R-bar-squared is a better measure of closeness of fit than the unadjusted R-squared because it makes allowance for the number of x variables included in the regression equation.
   (b) In the curvilinear regression on the equation $y = a + bx + cx^2$ the independent variables are b and c.
   (c) In using a transformation in non-linear regression an approximation is being introduced, since a curved relationship is being approximated by a linear one.
   (d) To carry out a regression analysis based on the equation $y = ae^x$ a linear regression is performed on log y and x.

2. The computer output in Table 15.18 comes from a regression analysis relating a company's annual revenue to three independent variables. The results are to be used to predict future revenue as part of the corporate plans.
   (a) What does R-bar-squared mean?
   (b) What are the t values for the three variables?
   (c) From the statistical point of view, should the variable 'marketing expenditure' be eliminated from the regression equation?

Table 15.18

Variable	Coefficient	Standard Error
Gross domestic product	5.6	0.8
Previous year's profit	0.8	0.2
Marketing expenditure	12.6	20
Constant	10.4	2.2
R-bar-squared 0.89		
Residual standard error 2.4		

3. In a market research project, 1200 consumers were asked to give a score (from 1 to 7) for their overall perception of the quality of a new washing powder which, it was claimed, improved the 'smell' of clothes after washing. This score was regressed against their assessments for four other variables. The results of the regression, which are shown in Table 15.19, are to be used to review the product and its marketing.
   (a) What is the difference, in concept, between R-squared and R-bar-squared? How much of the variation in consumers' overall perceptions is explained by the regression analysis?
   (b) What are the t values for the variables? And which of them, statistically, should be

Table 15.19

Variable	Coefficient	Standard Error
Value for money	0.48	0.12
Packaging	0.06	0.03
Image	1.20	0.15
Odour	0.84	0.80
Constant	0.63	0.09
R-squared 0.68		
R-bar-squared 0.62		

retained in the regression equation? And which of them seems to have the greatest influence on consumers' overall perception of the product?

4. The Golden Disc Company markets compact discs (CDs) by mail order and through selected retail outlets, often hypermarkets. The company deals only with CDs that have a large sales potential. Usually they are by well-known middle-of-the-road singers. Golden Disc advertises in newspapers and magazines. The expenditure varies from week to week depending upon the CDs the company is launching and the magazines published during the period. When sales are thought to be disappointing, Golden Disc boosts its advertising by using television commercials. Financial data for the last eight weeks are shown in Table 15.20.

Table 15.20

Week	Gross revenue (£'000)	Newspaper advertising (£'000)	Television advertising (£'000)
1	180	5	1
2	165	3	2
3	150	3	3
4	150	3	3
5	185	5	2
6	170	4	1
7	190	6	1
8	200	6	0

In an attempt to measure the effect of advertising and compare newspaper and TV, regression analysis was used, relating gross revenue to newspaper advertising. The results are in Table 15.21.

Table 15.21

Variable	Coefficient	t-value
Newspaper advertising	10	3.7
TV advertising	−5	−1.5
Constant	138	
R-bar-squared = 0.92	D–W = 2.59	

(a) What is the equation linking the variables?
(b) Calculate the values of the residuals.
(c) Is the regression fit a good one?
(d) Could the model be used to forecast revenue?
(e) How could the model be improved?

ANSWERS TO QUESTIONS

1. (a) True.   (c) False.
    (b) False.   (d) True.

2. (a) The regression explains 89 per cent of the variation in the past record of revenue.
    (b) 7.0, 4.0, 0.63.
    (c) Yes.

3. (a) 62 per cent.
    (b) 4.0, 2.0, 8.0, 1.05. All should be retained except 'odour'.

4. (a) Revenue = 138 + (10 × news advertising) − (5 × TV advertising).
    (b) −3, 7, −3, −3, 7, −3, −3, 2.
    (c) Yes.
    (d) Yes.
    (e) More data; other factors, for example, economic performance; seasonal analysis.

CHAPTER SIXTEEN

Judgement forecasting

Judgement forecasting is based on qualitative data such as comment, opinion and instinct rather than numerical data. The essence of techniques of judgement forecasting is that they bring this qualitative data together in a systematic way to form forecasts which are more likely to be of directions, turning points and boundaries than of numerical point estimates.

INTRODUCTION

Unlike the techniques we have seen so far, judgement forecasting techniques are not based mainly on numerical data. They are methods of combining qualitative information such as experience, views, intuition and so on to make a forecast. Although it is much used in everyday management tasks including forecasting, qualitative information can be slippery. Unless it is handled carefully the forecasts will be little more than wild guesses. Consequently, the essence of the techniques is that they are systematic. The best techniques are able to distil the real information in, say, a manager's experience from the surrounding 'noise' of personality and group pressures, directing it to the making of the forecasts. For example, the Delphi technique is a way of obtaining a forecast from a group of people without the process being influenced by the usual group pressures of personality, status and vested interest.

Qualitative forecasting uses a different approach from that of quantitative forecasting. The former is more concerned with defining the boundaries or directions in which the future will lie; the latter is concerned with making point estimates of the future values of variables. For example, qualitative techniques might predict the most profitable product areas and countries of operation for an organisation, whereas quantitative techniques would try to forecast the actual levels of profit. This may make it seem as if the quantitative techniques are clearly superior. An old (and possibly true) forecasting story demonstrates that this is not necessarily so. In 1880 it was forecast that by 1920 London would be impassable to traffic under a three-foot layer of horse manure. Qualitative techniques might have avoided this error by considering changes in the technology of road transport corresponding to the fast-developing railway network and the development of the internal combustion engine.

This last example also illustrates why judgement forecasting is sometimes referred to as technological forecasting. In this sense, qualitative techniques try to predict turning points and new directions of business activity. A feature of the last decade has been that the business environment is rapidly changing and that there is turbulence all around us in politics, economics, social change and technology. This has resulted in a corresponding need to predict technological and other types of change and this is undoubtedly behind the recent increase in the use of these techniques. And of course, there are situations in which the lack of quantitative data means that qualitative techniques are all that can be used.

This chapter looks first at the sort of situations in which qualitative techniques are used. It then goes on to describe several such techniques. Those included are by no means an exhaustive list, nor are they necessarily the ones most frequently used. Rather, they are intended to convey the scope of the techniques available. Many qualitative techniques are at an early stage of development and the extent of their application is unclear. The advantages and disadvantages of qualitative techniques are discussed at the end of the chapter.

WHERE QUALITATIVE TECHNIQUES ARE SUCCESSFUL

Managers appear naturally to associate formal forecasting with quantitative rather than qualitative techniques. As a subject, forecasting is seen as a numerical and analytical process. However, in practice managers do not usually employ quantitative techniques. They tend to prepare forecasts based on opinion and hunch but generally not on any systematic basis. In other words, even though managers are prepared to use qualitative data, few of them are prepared to use a qualitative technique in doing so. We must ask how managers can be motivated to use qualitative techniques. We must also ask why the use of these techniques is now starting to increase rapidly from its former low base. Two motives lie behind the use of qualitative techniques.

The first motive is that the forecaster's choice is restricted because there is a lack of adequate data. Quantitative techniques work from a historical data record, and preferably a long one. A lack of data may occur simply because no record exists. The organisation may be marketing an entirely new product or exporting to a region in which it has no experience. Alternatively, data may exist but be inadequate. This may be because data have been recorded incompetently; more likely, it will be because the circumstances in which the data are generated are changing rapidly. For example, the political situation in an importing country may be unstable, making past records of business an unreliable base for future projections. Recently this problem has occurred because of the changing business environment in Eastern Europe, where enormous markets which were previously closed have now opened up. Another example is the information technology industry, where events happen so quickly that historical data are soon out of date. For instance, microcomputer software sales are difficult to forecast quantitatively because product developments occur frequently and the rate of growth of sales can be steep then quickly drop. Quantitative techniques are generally poor at dealing with such turbulent situations.

The second motive for using qualitative techniques is a more positive one: the factors affecting the forecast may be better handled qualitatively. You may recall from Chapter 10 that an important step in a systematic approach to forecasting is to develop a conceptual model in which the influences on the forecast are listed. But the most important influences may be ones which are not easily quantified. Such influences could give rise to quantum leaps in the forecast variable. For example, in the 1990s forecasts of business activity in Hong Kong must be influenced in a major way by the agreement between the United Kingdom and the People's Republic of China regarding Hong Kong's future. The nature of this agreement and the way it is implemented would be difficult to deal with quantitatively, yet nothing is likely to have a greater bearing on future business activity as can be seen by the violent movements in the Hang Seng stockmarket index. It would probably be better to try to estimate the effect of this influence on business qualitatively. It is therefore by no means always the case that qualitative techniques are second best to qualitative ones; in many situations they will reflect actual circumstances more closely.

As to why there has been a recent increase in the use of qualitative techniques, the answer lies in the second of the above motives. The business environment seems recently to have been changing more rapidly than previously, whether for technological, social or political reasons. The situations in which the qualitative techniques are seen to have advantages are occurring more frequently. The micro-electronic revolution is a clear example of this, but the boundaries are wider. Since the start of the 1980s business data have tended to be more volatile, showing greater variability than previously. This has meant that rewards for accurate forecasting have increased, but it also means that previously established forecasting models performed less well. The need both to plan successfully and to consider new techniques has resulted in a greater use of forecasting techniques, in terms of the number of organisations that have a forecasting system and of the range of techniques employed.

The next section outlines some of the major qualitative forecasting techniques and gives examples of their application.

QUALITATIVE TECHNIQUES

Several of the most common qualitative forecasting methods hardly deserve the title technique, although they have been given pseudo-scientific labels. They are included here if only for the sake of completeness before moving on to more serious contenders.

Visionary forecasting

Visionary forecasting involves a purely subjective estimate (or guess, or hunch, or stab in the dark) made by one individual. Many managers believe themselves to be good at this; or believe that someone else in the organisation is good at it. Most organisations like to believe that they have a forecasting hero tucked away on the third floor. Sadly, when the forecasts are properly monitored, the records usually show visionary forecasting to be inaccurate. The reason for this paradox seems to be that visionary forecasting is judged on its occasional successes. The senior manager who, in 1986, predicted the fall of the USSR will be well remembered in company folklore. On the other hand, economic pundits frequently make erroneous predictions – on the timing of interest rate rises, foreign exchange rates, for example – but they (the predictions, not the pundits) seem to be forgotten.

There are undoubtedly people who are good visionaries, but they are few in number and their records need to be carefully monitored.

Panel consensus

Panel consensus forecasting is probably the most common method used in business. This refers to a meeting of a group of people who, as a result of argument and discussion, produce a forecast. One would think that this method should provide good forecasts because, in theory, it brings together the expertise of several people. You might also judge it to be successful because, in practice, managers spend so much time in meetings – if they spend so much time on it they must know that it works. Again, the record suggests otherwise. Panel forecasts consensus are generally inaccurate. The reason is that the forecasts are dominated by group pressures. The status, personality, strength of character and vested interests of the participants all influence the forecast. As a result the full potential of the gathered experience is not brought to bear and the forecast may turn out to be little different from that of the strongest personality working alone – and that will probably not be good. Some improvements can be gained by using structured group meetings in which different people are given distinct responsibilities – organising the meeting, providing background information etc. – and in which it is ensured that people with distinct capabilities (ideas generation, critical objectivity, an eye for detail, financial analysis etc.) will be present.

Brainstorming

Brainstorming is a technique which is perhaps better known for producing ideas rather than generating forecasts. It is based on a group meeting, but with the rule that every suggestion must be heard. No proposal is to be ridiculed or put aside without discussion. In forecasting, brainstorming is used first to define the full range of factors which influence the forecast variable and then to decide on a forecast. When properly applied it is a useful technique, but the process can degenerate into an ill-disciplined panel consensus forecast.

Market research

Market research also falls within the area of qualitative forecasting. It is an accurate but expensive technique. This extensive subject involves a large number of distinct skills such as statistical sampling, questionnaire design and interviewing. It is more usually described within the context of marketing.

Delphi forecasting

Named after the oracle of Ancient Greece, this technique is based on the panel consensus method but has characteristics which enable it to overcome the ill effects of group pressures. It does this by not allowing the members of the group to communicate with one another. The group can therefore be physically in the same place or at the end of telephones. The most important role is that of the chairperson who conducts the proceedings. The process is as follows:

1. The chairperson asks each member of the group to make a forecast of the variable in question for the relevant time period. This forecast, along with an idea of what the participant believes are the major factors affecting the variable, is written down and passed (or phoned) to the chairperson.

2. The chairperson collects the submissions of all participants and summarises them. A typical summary may comprise the average and range of the forecasts plus a list of major factors. The chairperson relays the summary back to the group. At no time are

the participants told anything about the individual response of the other participants. In other words, the feedback is anonymous.

3. The chairperson asks the group to reconsider their forecasts, taking into account the information presented to them in the summary. Again, the forecasts are submitted to the chairperson for summary and relay.

4. This process is repeated until the group has reached (approximately) a consensus or until the participants are no longer prepared to adjust their forecasts further.

5. The final consensus is the Delphi forecast. If there is no consensus, then the median of the individual final forecasts is the overall forecast. However, if the individual final forecasts still cover a wide range then it will probably be necessary to examine the reasons for the spread, resolve them and start the process again. Or, the spread may be the basis for forming scenarios (see below).

By keeping the participants apart, the intention is that effects such as personality and rank are minimised. The final forecast is then a distillation of the views of the entire group. Even better, each participant will have had the opportunity to re-adjust his or her views in response to worthy suggestions from others. If some persist in deviating from the norm then the onus is on them to explain and defend their views to the chairperson.

When tested, the Delphi technique has produced good results. But it has some disadvantages. It can be expensive, especially when the group is assembled in the same physical place. Also, it is possible to cheat by indulging in some game playing. One participant, knowing the likely views of the other participants can submit unrealistic forecasts in order that the averaging process works out as he or she wants. For example, in an attempt to forecast sales, a financial executive may substantially understate her view so that the optimistic view of the sales manager is counterbalanced; as a result, she achieves her aim of holding down stock levels. It is the job of the chairperson to filter out such reactions. Chapter 17 is a case study describing the implementation of Delphi forecasting in a practical situation.

The technique can be unreliable since different groups of people might well produce different forecasts. The results can also be sensitive to the style of questions which the group is asked. Table 16.1 summarises the strengths and weaknesses of the technique.

Table 16.1   Strengths and weaknesses of Delphi technique

Strengths	Weaknesses
Removes effects of prejudice and peer pressure	Could get different results from different groups
Good track record	Cost and time
Can be conducted by post or telephone	Requires skilful/unbiased chairperson
No special resources needed	Risk of 'game playing'

Scenario writing

Scenario writing is not concerned with single estimates of the future. It is the construction of several sets of circumstances which could plausibly arise. Each set of circumstances is called a scenario and stems from a series of assumptions about the future. In other words, scenario writing is a translation of several different sets of assumptions into pictures of what the future might look like. There are then several alternative futures rather than one single view. The essence of scenario writing is the expression of a wide range of situations which could apply in the future and which describe the boundaries within which contingency planning can take place.

For example, suppose an exporting company is trying to forecast sales of its products in a South East Asian country over the next 10 years. One set of assumptions could be that at that time there would be a pro-Western government and a strong world economy. In addition, there may be specific assumptions about inflation rates, exchange rates, technological changes etc. These assumptions are translated into a scenario which shows the sales, prices, costs, staffing and competition relating to the products which might be associated with these assumptions. A second scenario is formed from another, different set of assumptions. The process continues and more scenarios are formed until all sets of assumptions which could reasonably be expected to apply have been exhausted.

Scenario writing is not a detailed technique, nor does it pretend to be accurate in terms of the numbers it produces. Rather, it involves a new approach to forecasting. The difficulty of making a definite forecast is recognised. Instead, the emphasis is on covering the range of possibilities and forming flexible plans which can cope with all of them. Its advantage is that it leads to a realistic perspective on future uncertainty. It can also be combined with more detailed techniques for translating assumptions into quantified scenarios. It is particularly useful in the most difficult type of forecasting, for example where the time horizon is long and there are many uncertainties.

Cross-impact matrices

Cross-impact matrices in themselves do not produce forecasts. They are a means of providing estimates of the likelihood or probabilities of future events which can be used as part of the planning process. Special emphasis is placed on cross-influences between different events, by considering how the occurrence of one event might affect the probability of another. Thus the technique gets its name: 'cross-impact'. The 'matrix' part of the name derives from the way the probabilities are written down, in a matrix.

The technique consists of the following steps, which are illustrated by the previous example of a company forecasting its business activity in South East Asia.

1. Make an extensive list of all the factors which might affect the plans to be made. In this example, this would include all the developments which could occur with regard to the political situation, the economic climate, technology breakthroughs, product innovation, competition and so on. For instance, three developments in the political situation might be used: a pro-Western, a Marxist or an independent government.

2. Estimate the probabilities of these developments. They would each have to be assessed subjectively using say, the Delphi method.

3. Form a matrix with each row representing one of the developments and each column

Table 16.2   A cross-impact matrix

| | | *Then the probability (%) of* | | | | |
If this development happens		A	B	C	D	E	F
Pro-Western govt.	(A)	–	0	0	50	40	10
Independent govt.	(B)	0	–	0	30	50	20
Marxist govt.	(C)	0	0	–	5	35	60
Economy grows 5%	(D)	30	65	5	–	0	0
Economy grows 1%	(E)	15	60	25	0	–	0
Economy declines	(F)	10	25	65	0	0	–

also representing a development. Each cell of the matrix is the new probability for the development in that column, given that the development of that row has taken place.

In the example, a section of the completed matrix might appear as in Table 16.2. The matrix is formed by taking the most likely developments first and adjusting the probabilities of all the other developments in that column. Then the second most likely development is considered, then the third and so on. If the most likely development is almost certain, then the adjusted probabilities may be used to determine the second most likely.

4. Using the original probabilities and the cross-probabilities, the overall likelihood of different developments can be calculated. This may involve simulation. For example, given the probabilities of all other developments, the relative frequency of occurrence of, say, the successful launch of some new, as yet non-existent, product can be calculated.

The essence of cross-impact matrices is that they are a means whereby the planner can juggle with a whole series of uncertain developments, and in particular their influences on each other. The cost of the technique may only be justified when the list of developments is long. In these circumstances the whole process may be computerised, with the formulae being the basis of adjustment of the probabilities. How all the probabilities are used is not a part of the technique. They may be used formally in further calculations or they may be used informally in making judgements about the future. They may well be used as part of scenario writing to formulate the most realistic scenarios.

Although a sales example has been used to illustrate these steps, the technique is at its best when dealing with technological uncertainties. In fact, one of the earliest reports of its application was to the development of the US Minuteman system.[1]

The advantage of the system is that it provides a tool for the difficult task of dealing with a wide range of complex events and interactions in a relatively straightforward manner. Its disadvantages are that it is expensive, and that the forecaster must be capable of interpreting the probabilities produced.

Analogies

When forecasting a variable for which there is no data record, a second variable, the history of which is completely known and which is supposed to be similar to the first, is

[1] See T. J. Gordon and H. Hayward, 'Initial experiments with cross impact matrix method of forecasting', *Futures* vol. 1., no. 2, December 1968.

used as an analogy. Because of conceptual similarities between the two, it is assumed that as time goes by the data pattern of the first will follow the pattern of the second – and the data history of the second is already known.

For example, the company forecasting sales of a new product in South East Asia might choose as an analogy the sales of a previous new product with similar characteristics marketed in that country or a similar country in the recent past. The growth record of the previous product is the basis for the forecast of the current one. The forecast does not have to be exactly the same as the analogy. The record may be adjusted for level and scatter (or confidence limits). For instance, the sales volume of the current product may be thought to be double that of the previous one and to have greater month-by-month variations. To forecast, the growth record of the analogy does not have to be exactly like the forecast variable, but similarities in the products and the marketing environment should be sufficient for the forecaster to believe that the data patterns will be comparable. When the first sales data starts to become available it should be checked to confirm that the correct level has been chosen. It will take longer to be able to confirm that the pattern is also correct.

The advantage of the technique is that it provides a cheap but comprehensive forecast in a way that makes sense to marketing managers. The analogy is not restricted to business. Biological growth can provide the basis for analogies in business and social sciences. The underlying philosophy of the technique is that there may be social laws just as there are natural laws. Although the laws themselves in, say, marketing, may not be fully or even partially understood, data records are the evidence that some laws exist and can be used in forecasting.

The main problem with the technique is that there must be at least one but not too many analogies to choose from. If the situation is totally new to the organisation no analogy may be available. On the other hand, there may be several plausible analogies and great arguments may develop over deciding the right one to use. For example, a wines and spirits company was planning the launch of a new product about which high hopes were held. But it was extremely difficult to decide which of several previously successful products should be the analogy. All had been successful yet their growth patterns differed considerably. The problem was resolved by making a subjective decision in favour of one but agreeing to monitor the forecast variable's record closely to see if at some point the marketers should revert to a new analogy.

Catastrophe theory

Most forecasting techniques, whether qualitative or quantitative, are based on the assumption that changes in the forecast variable will be, more or less, continuous. In other words, although the variable may exhibit gradual trends or steep growth or decline, it will not jump from one level to another. Catastrophe theory deals with the possibility that a variable may jump from one level to another. It does not refer to catastrophe in the sense of disaster but as in a sudden alteration of behaviour.

There are plenty of examples of this type of behaviour in non-business fields: in psychology, the change of mood from, say, fear to anger; in chemistry, the changes of a substance from a solid to a liquid and from a liquid to a gas; in atomic physics, the ideas of quantum theory. In business the examples may not be so clear-cut but there are plenty of possibilities to think about: a rapid take-off in the sales of a product, a turn-around in a company's profitability, corporate failure, a sudden change in the price of a commodity.

Catastrophe theory is not a quantitative technique. It does not calculate the expected size of jumps. Rather, it is a systematic way of determining whether a catastrophe is likely in a given situation. The technique comprises a series of questions to answer and characteristics to look for, which will indicate the nature of the situation being investigated.

Catastrophe theory is relatively new and there is not much in the way of a track record to judge its success. However, it certainly fills in a gap in the range of forecasting techniques and is growing in use. The reason for its importance and the interest it has created is that while companies can usually take emergency action to deal with continuous changes (whether rapid or not), sudden jumps or reversions in behaviour often leave no time for evasive action. The potential of catastrophe theory is thus that it may be able to predict circumstances with which companies have no way of dealing unless they have advance warning.

Relevance trees

The techniques described so far have all started with the present situation and put out 'feelers' to see what the future might look like. These techniques can be described as *exploratory*. The relevance tree technique is different. It starts in the future with a picture of what the future should ideally look like and works back to determine what must occur to make this future happen. Such an approach is described as *normative*.

The technique starts with a broad objective, breaks this down into sub-objectives, further breaks down the sub-objectives through, perhaps, several different levels until specific technological developments are being considered. This structure is a relevance tree. The elements of the tree are then given relevance weights, from which it is possible to calculate the overall relevance of the technological developments which are most important or relevant to the achievement of the higher level of the tree. The outcome of the technique is a list of those developments which are most important or relevant to the achievement of the higher level objective and sub-objectives.

There seven steps in the application of relevance trees. They will be described using as an example a much simplified case of the design of a new passenger airliner.

1. Draw the relevance tree. For the airliner it might appear as in Table 16.3.

2. Establish criteria for determining priorities. In a purely financial case there might be only one criterion – money. In the more usual technological applications there are several criteria which are the dimensions along which achievement can be measured. In the airliner example the criteria might be:
    (a) Passenger comfort.
    (b) Safety.
    (c) Cost.
    (d) Route capability.

3. Weight the importance of each criterion relative to the others. A group of experts, knowledgeable about the situation, would have to carry out this task by answering questions such as: 'What is the weight of each criterion in achieving the highest level objective?' In the airliner example the weights might be assigned as in Table 16.4.

Table 16.3   A relevance tree

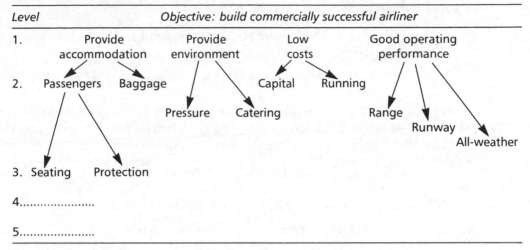

Level	Objective: build commercially successful airliner

1. Provide accommodation · Provide environment · Low costs · Good operating performance

2. Passengers · Baggage · Capital · Running · Pressure · Catering · Range · Runway · All-weather

3. Seating · Protection

4. ....

5. ....

Table 16.4

	Weight
(a) Passenger comfort	0.10
(b) Safety	0.35
(c) Cost	0.40
(d) Route capability	0.15
	1.00

4. Weight the sub objectives at each level (referred to as the elements of the tree) according to their importance in meeting each criterion. The question posed might be: 'In order to meet criterion (c), what is the relative importance of each element at level 3?' At each level a set of weights for each criterion must be assessed. For the airliner example, the process might work as shown in Table 16.5. The first column, for example, shows the assessed relevance of the four elements at level 1 to the criterion of comfort. Accommodation is weighted 0.20, environment 0.65, and so on. Since the table gives the relative relevance of the elements to the criterion, each column must

Table 16.5   Assessing a set of weights for each criterion at level 1

	Criteria			
	Comfort	Safety	Cost	Route
Criterion weight	0.10	0.35	0.40	0.15
Elements at level 1:	Element weights			
Accommodation	0.20	0.35	0.05	0.05
Environment	0.65	0.25	0.05	0.05
Low costs	0.05	0.05	0.75	0.25
Performance	0.10	0.35	0.15	0.65
	1.00	1.00	1.00	1.00

sum to 1. The process of assessing weights is carried out for each level of the relevance tree.

5. Calculate partial relevance numbers. Each element has a partial relevance number (PRN) for each criterion. It is calculated:

$$PRN = \text{criterion weight} \times \text{element weight}$$

It is a measure of the relevance of that element with respect only to that criterion (hence 'partial'). For the airliner example the partial relevance numbers are shown in Table 16.6. For instance, the PRN for accommodation with respect to comfort is:

$$= 0.2 \times 0.1 = 0.02$$

PRNs are calculated for each element at each level for each criterion.

6. Calculate a local relevance number (LRN) for each element. The LRN for each element is the sum of the PRNs for that element. It is a measure of the importance of that element relative to others at the same level in achieving the highest-level objective. For the airliner example the LRNs are shown in Table 16.7. The LRN for accommodation is 0.17 (= 0.0200 + 0.1225 + 0.0200 + 0.0075). There is one LRN for each element at each level.

7. Calculate cumulative relevance numbers (CRNs). There is one for each element. Each is calculated by multiplying the LRN of an element by the LRNs of each associated element at a higher level. This gives each element an absolute measure of its relevance. In the airliner example, at level 3 the CRN for seating is calculated:

$$CRN \text{ (seating)} = LRN \text{ (seating)} \times LRN \text{ (passengers)} \times LRN \text{ (accommodation)}$$

By this means the bottom row of elements (specific technological requirements) will have overall measures of their relevance in achieving the objective which was the starting point at the highest level of the tree. This should lead to discussions about the importance, timing, resource allocation etc. of the tasks ahead.

Table 16.6   Calculating partial relevance numbers

| | Criteria | | | |
	Comfort	Safety	Cost	Route
Criterion weight	0.10	0.35	0.40	0.15
Elements at level 1:	Element weights			
Accommodation	0.20	0.35	0.05	0.05
Environment	0.65	0.25	0.05	0.05
Low costs	0.05	0.05	0.75	0.25
Performance	0.10	0.35	0.15	0.65
	Partial relevance numbers			
Accommodation	0.0200	0.1225	0.0200	0.0075
Environment	0.0650	0.0875	0.0200	0.0075
Low costs	0.0050	0.0175	0.3000	0.0375
Performance	0.0100	0.1225	0.0600	0.0975

Table 16.7   Calculating local relevance numbers

Level 1	Partial relevance numbers				LRN
Accommodation	0.0200	0.1225	0.0200	0.0075	0.17
Environment	0.0650	0.0875	0.0200	0.0075	0.18
Low cost	0.0050	0.0175	0.3000	0.0375	0.36
Performance	0.0100	0.1225	0.0600	0.0975	0.29

In thinking about implementing relevance trees it is important to remember that the technique is normative. Given an objective it indicates what must be done to achieve it. It also indicates the relative importance or priorities of the tasks ahead. In doing so it suffers from two major disadvantages. The first is the requirement to draw a relevance tree correctly, comprehensively structuring the road ahead; the second is the subjective assessment of element and criterion weights. If either of these tasks is not done well, then the result will be nonsense. It is perhaps advisable to look at the relevance trees as much for the process of using the technique as for the final result. The activity of considering the options and their relevance would probably carry substantial benefits in terms of a better understanding of future needs, even if numerical values were never to be used.

CONCLUSION

The one characteristic which clearly distinguishes qualitative from quantitative forecasting is that the underlying information on which it is based consists of judgements rather than numbers. But the distinction goes beyond that. Qualitative forecasting is usually concerned with determining the boundaries within which the long-term future might lie; quantitative forecasting tends to provide specific point forecasts and ranges for variables in the not so distant future. Qualitative forecasting offers techniques that are very different in type, from the straightforward, exploratory Delphi method to the normative relevance trees. Also, qualitative forecasting is at an early stage of development and many of its techniques are largely unproven.

Whatever the styles of qualitative techniques, their aims are the same, to use judgements systematically in forecasting and planning. In using the techniques it should be borne in mind that the skills and abilities that provide the judgements are more important than the techniques. Just as it would be pointless to try a quantitative technique with 'made-up' numerical data, so it would be folly to use a qualitative technique in the absence of real knowledge of the situation in question. The difference is that it is perhaps easier to discern the lack of accurate data than the lack of genuine expertise.

On the other hand, where real expertise does exist it would be an equal folly not to make use of it. For long-term forecasting by far the greater proportion of available information about a situation is probably in the form of judgement rather than numerical data. To use these judgements without the help of a technique usually results in a plan or forecast biased by personality, group effects, self-interest etc. Qualitative techniques offer a chance to distil the real information from the surrounding noise and refine it into something useful.

In many, indeed most, forecasting problems the relevant information is both qualitative and quantitative. The most difficult task of all is to integrate these two types of infor-

Table 16.8

Question	% answering yes
1. Do you believe in the freedom of speech?	96
2. Do you believe in the freedom of speech to the extent of allowing radicals to hold meetings and express their views to the community?	22

mation into a forecast. The first stage in the task is to recognise that the problem exists and that there is a great need to use both sources of data. The second stage is to solve the problem. Although not easy, it can be done.

In spite of this enthusiasm for qualitative forecasting, this chapter must end with a warning. In essence, most qualitative techniques come down to asking questions of experts, albeit scientifically. Doubts about the value of experts are well entrenched in management folklore. But doubts about the questions can be much more serious, making all else pale into insignificance.

Hauser[2] reports the following extract from a survey of opinion (Table 16.8).

The lesson must be that the sophistication of the techniques will only be worthwhile if the forecaster gets the basics right first. This is especially true in qualitative forecasting.

CASE STUDY

A company is trying to forecast its next two years' revenue for a new venture in Eastern Europe. Because of all the recent political, social and economic changes in the area, it has been decided to use the Delphi technique. Eight executives have been selected to take part.

1. Should all the executives be at the same level of seniority?

2. Should the executives be allowed to discuss their forecasts?

3. Should the executives adjust their forecasts towards the mean at each iteration?

4. Should the executives continue making forecasts until a consensus is reached?

Solutions

1. *Should all the executives be at the same level of seniority?*
One of the purposes of Delphi is that people at different levels of seniority can take part.

2. *Should the executives be allowed to discuss their forecasts?*
The Delphi process requires that the participators communicate only through the chairperson to avoid factors such as rank and personality playing a part. Therefore not talking to one another about their forecasts is essential.

[2] P. M. Hauser, *Social Statistic in Use*, Russell Sage, 1975.

3. *Should the executives adjust their forecasts towards the mean at each iteration?* Participants are under no requirement to adjust their predictions at each iteration in any direction, or to adjust them at all.

4. *Should the executives continue making forecasts until a consensus is reached?* Because of the previous point, a consensus may not necessarily be reached and the final forecast can then be calculated as the average of participants' final forecasts.

QUESTIONS

1. Which technique should a confectionery company use to forecast quarterly ice-cream sales for the year ahead based on a 10-year data record?

2. A newly formed software company specialising in state-of-the-art multimedia products is trying to forecast its next year's revenue. Given that there is no financial or sales track record, which technique might be suitable?

3. Apply the technique of relevance trees to the design of a new model of medium range hi-fi system.

ANSWERS TO QUESTIONS

1. Holt–Winters method.

2. Delphi.

CHAPTER SEVENTEEN

Experience of using the Delphi forecasting process

Delphi is a judgemental forecasting method which surveys have shown can be highly accurate in practice. This chapter describes the use of this technique in Zeneca Pharmaceuticals. The author is Jerry P. Raine, International Marketing Manager in the Product Strategy Department of Zeneca.

INTRODUCTION TO ZENECA

Zeneca is a major force in the world of bioscience, employing over 33 000 people, with sales of almost £4 billion in 1992. It is research intensive, with an R&D expenditure of £457 million (1992). The group aims to optimise the commercial benefits arising from the complementary nature of its capabilities in bioscience and organic chemistry. It is committed to the development of new products that satisfy customer needs and offer clear competitive advantages. Zeneca has a worldwide marketing and customer service network. The three component businesses are Pharmaceuticals, Agrochemicals and Specialties.

Pharmaceuticals is the largest member of the group and the eighteenth largest ethical pharmaceutical company in the world, with annual global sales exceeding £1.8 billion. In 1992, Pharmaceuticals provided 40 per cent of group sales and 83 per cent of trading profit.

In January 1993, Zeneca Ltd was created by separating ICI's bioscience activities from its other chemical operations. Bioscience interests had expanded over recent years and had become increasingly distinct from the traditional chemical operations of ICI. It was felt that as two independent companies the two business groups would be better able to exploit their respective opportunities.

In June 1993, the ICI Group was divided into two independent companies by means of a demerger, resulting in the formation of a streamlined chemicals business (ICI) and a separate, integrated bioscience group (Zeneca).

WHY USE DELPHI?

Forecasting is an important part of the job for any marketer. The primary need is for:

- Business planning
  - resource allocation

Figure 17.1   Zeneca pharmaceuticals headquarters, Macclesfield

- Production planning
  - efficient continuity of supply
  - capacity planning

In addition there are further uses, such as target setting and opportunity analysis, e.g. product developments.

In Zeneca each product team would be responsible for generating their own forecasts and how this was achieved was down to the personal views and experiences of each team leader. In the past the main forecasting technique used by our product team was a patient-based model which uses demography to predict the market size, then estimates of market share are made to calculate a product's unit sales and values. Diary studies, where available, had been used to form the basis of some of the market share data. However, the forecasters had to make some critical assumptions around expected market penetration. Clearly, a small difference at this stage would have a large impact on the final outputs.

In light of the importance of the decisions that were being made as a result of the team's forecasts it was clear that there are high risks associated with using just one forecasting technique. Forecasting is not an exact science, but our ability to improve the quality of our forecasting on a continuing basis is vital. Hence the need to utilise a number of methods was identified. The key principle behind this is that the average forecast generated from a number of different methods would be more accurate than relying on the forecast from just a single method.

There are a number of categories of forecasting methods:

- *Time series*:
  identifies patterns in past data and projects them into the future
- *Causal modelling*:
  explains movements in one variable through the movements in other variables
- *Judgement*:
  brings together qualitative information such as opinions, hunches, instincts.

Although we reviewed the value to us for each category it was judgement forecasting, i.e. Delphi process, that had the greatest appeal. The main reasons for this was that we wanted to bring together qualitative information in a systematic way and independent data on our market was relatively scarce. Furthermore, within Zeneca there was a wealth of experience of the market and the Delphi process is the best forecasting method for tapping into this knowledge.

DELPHI – THE PROCESS

The key feature of Delphi is that it is a group consensus forecast based on anonymity, controlled feedback and iteration. The therapeutic area in which we were interested to use the Delphi process was the prostate cancer market. The principle behind this was for eight participants from a range of medical and marketing specialties to use their own judgement to forecast a number of variables utilising only a brief package of background information. Eight participants were chosen for two reasons – this was sufficient to give us a good balance between the specialties (technical and commercial) and it was also practical. The participants were located around the world – USA, UK, France, Italy and The Netherlands. Therefore we had taken the decision that communication would be via fax and telephone. An important point to make is that everyone remained anonymous to each other – only I (acting as the Chairman) knew details of who was participating and an individual's forecast and assumptions. The eight participants were as follows:

1. International Project Physician   (Zeneca HQ).
2. Drug Team Leader   (Zeneca HQ).
3. Product Information Manager   (Zeneca HQ).
4. Product Manager   (Zeneca USA).
5. Product Manager   (Zeneca France).
6. Clinical Research Manager   (Zeneca Italy).
7. Urologist   (USA).
8. Urologist   (The Netherlands).

The process itself ran as follows (see also Figure 17.2):

Step 1   Chairman states forecast assumptions
Each participant received a briefing package of background information which was to be used only as a guide. This package was kept deliberately short and focused only on key points. A set of numbered forecasting sheets were also provided.

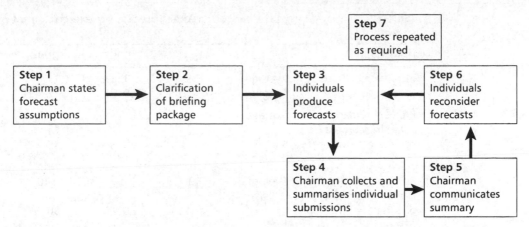

Figure 17.2   Schematic representation of the Delphi process as implemented by Zeneca

Step 2   Clarification of the briefing package
It was important to ensure that each participant understood the process and the information contained in the briefing package. Therefore the Chairman telephoned each participant a few days after the briefing package had been despatched (minimum of three days), to answer any queries on the process and the background information.

Step 3   Individuals produce forecasts in isolation using their judgement
Following the telephone conversation as stated in Step 2, the Chairman asked each participant to complete forecasting sheet No. 1 and then to fax it to him within the following two days.

Step 4   Chairman collects and summarises individual submissions: average, range and key assumptions
On receipt of each forecasting sheet No. 1 the Chairman collated the submissions and produced a summary. This summary comprised the average and range of the forecasts plus a list of the major assumptions.

Step 5   Chairman communicates summary without indication of individual responses
Within two days of receiving the forecasts, the Chairman faxed to each participant the details of the summary. At no time were participants told anything about the individual response of other participants.

Step 6   Individuals reconsider forecasts in isolation, taking account of the summary
Within a day of faxing the summary, a follow-up telephone call then took place during which the Chairman challenged the participants on their forecasts, taking into account the information presented to them in the summary.

Table 17.1   World prostate cancer market forecasting exercise: final summary

World volume		1994	1999	2004
Incidence in '000s	Average	259	313	379
(new cases)	Range	247–300	289–338	332–420
Product X market share in segment	Average	4	49	63
of prostate cancer market	Range	0–20	35–80	45–80
Product Y market share in segment	Average	39	46	40
of prostate cancer market	Range	32–45	30–60	30–55
World value		*1994*	*1999*	*2004*
Total value of prostate market	Average	464	628	757
(medical treatments) £m	Range	420–500	460–800	510–1000

Step 7   Repeat process until consensus is reached or individuals are no longer making adjustments

A participant wishing to revise their forecast was asked to fax forecast sheet No. 2 to the Chairman within the following two days. A further summary was produced by the Chairman and faxed to each participant. The participants were challenged again on their forecasts. After the second iteration all eight participants no longer wished to make adjustments to their forecasts.

The final output was an average and range of forecasts which reflected the judgement of all participants (see Table 17.1).

Some practical considerations included the following:

1. There was a need to keep the number of forecasts realistic – in total we asked for seven variables to be forecasted at three time points. This was achieved satisfactorily but if there had been many more in my view the participants would have struggled. The burden in terms of extra time and effort would have reduced their commitment and enthusiasm to partake in the process.

2. The participants need a clear indication as to how much of their time will be required during the exercise. Their commitment is essential. None of our participants had been involved in a Delphi process before (therefore thorough briefing was required) but all thoroughly enjoyed it and found it a very interesting experience.

3. The period of time for the exercise, from start to finish, should be as short as possible. We took two weeks which included two iterations. This seemed to work very well since it maintained the momentum and kept the subject fresh in the minds of the participants. It does, however, require tight scheduling. This was particularly

important because of the geographic spread of the participants and consequently of the time zone differences – some of my telephone conversations with the US participants took place at midnight (UK time !)

CONCLUSION

This was the first time that I had been involved in using Delphi as a forecasting method and so I have to be honest and say that beforehand I was slightly sceptical. After all, how can you expect people not involved in mainstream marketing to understand market characteristics, let alone forecast the performance of products?

Our experience is that the Delphi technique provided us with very valuable information enabling us to do a quality check on our own forecasts. Despite many of our participants not having any commercial acumen, they all used their judgement in such a way that produced outputs which were remarkably close to each other. As stated previously, everyone remained anonymous and only the Chairman was aware of an individual's forecast and assumptions.

Having thought about the process and the value of the outputs my assessment on the strengths and weaknesses of Delphi is:

Strengths	Weaknesses
• Eliminates peer pressure	• Requires a significant amount of commitment in time from participants
• Capitalises on the knowledge and experience of 'experts'	
	• Requires skilful/unbiased Chairman
• Can be conducted by post, fax and telephone	• There is a risk of 'game-playing' if a participant wants to prove a particular point.
• Does not require special resources	

Gaining the views and opinions of others is a valuable exercise since it can identify areas that perhaps had been overlooked. Delphi works on this principle and it certainly adds a new dimension to forecasting, which I believe should be an integral part of every forecaster's armoury. To prove this point, based on our experiences of using the Delphi process, we are planning to use this technique again in the very near future.

We will follow an identical process as described previously. However, the one key change will be in the choice of participants. Whilst the mix of technical and commercial people will remain broadly the same, as will the geographic spread, we have decided to use a number of new participants. This will mean that we can broaden our sample and call upon the experience and knowledge of even more people. We await the results with great interest.

QUESTIONS

1. Give examples of other industries or organisations where you think the Delphi technique might be particularly useful.

2. What do the author's experiences suggest are the critical success factors in using the Delphi technique in practice?

3. In many organisations and industries the use of systematic judgemental forecasting methods is limited. Based on the author's experiences, and your own, give reasons why this might be so.

APPENDIX

t-distribution table

Degrees of Freedom	Upper-Tail Area x									
	.4	.25	.1	.05	.025	.01	.005	.0025	.001	.0005
1	.0325	1.000	3.078	6.314	12.706	31.821	63.657	127.32	318.31	636.62
2	.289	0.816	1.886	2.920	4.303	6.965	9.925	14.089	22.327	31.598
3	.277	.765	1.638	2.353	3.182	4.541	5.841	7.453	10.214	12.924
4	.271	.741	1.533	2.132	2.776	3.747	4.604	5.598	7.173	8.610
5	0.267	0.727	1.476	2.015	2.571	3.365	4.032	4.773	5.893	6.869
6	.265	.718	1.440	1.943	2.447	3.143	3.707	4.317	5.208	5.959
7	.263	.711	1.415	1.895	2.365	2.998	3.499	4.029	4.785	5.408
8	.262	.706	1.397	1.860	2.306	2.896	3.355	3.833	4.501	5.041
9	.261	.703	1.383	1.833	2.262	2.821	3.250	3.690	4.297	4.781
10	0.260	0.700	1.372	1.812	2.228	2.764	3.169	3.581	4.144	4.587
11	.260	.697	1.363	1.796	2.201	2.718	3.106	3.497	4.025	4.437
12	.259	.695	1.356	1.782	2.179	2.681	3.055	3.428	3.930	4.318
13	.259	.694	1.350	1.771	2.160	2.650	3.012	3.372	3.852	4.221
14	.258	.692	1.345	1.761	2.145	2.624	2.977	3.326	3.787	4.140
15	0.258	0.691	1.341	1.753	2.131	2.602	2.947	3.286	3.733	4.073
16	.258	.690	1.337	1.746	2.120	2.583	2.921	3.252	3.686	4.015
17	.257	.689	1.333	1.740	2.110	2.567	2.898	3.222	3.646	3.965
18	.257	.688	1.330	1.734	2.101	2.552	2.878	3.197	3.610	3.922
19	.257	.688	1.328	1.729	2.093	2.539	2.861	3.174	3.579	3.883
20	0.257	0.687	1.325	1.725	2.086	2.528	2.845	3.153	3.552	3.850
21	.257	.686	1.323	1.721	2.080	2.518	2.831	3.135	3.527	3.819
22	.256	.686	1.321	1.717	2.074	2.508	2.819	3.119	3.505	3.792
23	.256	.685	1.319	1.714	2.069	2.500	2.807	3.104	3.485	9.767
24	.256	.685	1.318	1.711	2 064	2.492	2.797	3.091	3.467	7.745
25	0.256	0.684	1.316	1.708	2.060	2.485	2.787	3.078	3.450	3.725
26	.256	.684	1.315	1.706	2.056	2.479	2.779	3.067	3.435	3.707
27	.256	.684	1.314	1.703	2.052	2.473	2.771	3.057	3.421	3.690
28	.256	.683	1.313	1.701	2.048	2.467	2.763	3.047	3.408	3.674
29	.256	.683	1.311	1.699	2.045	2.462	2.756	3.038	3.396	3.659
30	0.256	0.683	1.310	1.697	2.042	2.457	2.750	3.030	3.385	3.646
40	.255	.681	1.303	1.684	2.021	2.423	2.704	2.971	3.307	3.551
60	.254	.679	1.296	1.671	2.000	2.390	2.660	2.915	3.232	3.460
120	.254	.677	1.289	1.658	1.980	2.358	2.617	2.860	3.160	3.373
∝	.253	.674	1.282	1.645	1.960	2.326	2.576	2.807	3.090	3.291

INDEX